THE SOVIET UNION BETWEEN
THE 19th AND 20th PARTY CONGRESSES
1952–1956

THE SOVIET UNION

between the

19th AND 20th PARTY CONGRESSES

1952 - 1956

by

G. D. Embree

RXTSA

THE HAGUE

MARTINUS NIJHOFF

1959

PREFACE

The years between the Nineteenth and Twentieth Party Congresses of the Communist Party of the Soviet Union comprise one of the most eventful periods in the history of the USSR. It opened with the first CPSU gathering in 13 years at a time when the Soviet Union was beset by serious domestic and foreign difficulties and was passing through a transitional period in its development. It witnessed the death of J. V. Stalin who had exercized unquestioned authority for a quarter of a century; it felt the impact of the sweeping changes undertaken by his successors as they sought to cope with the immense problems facing the new regime; and it culminated in the Twentieth Party Congress which marked the closing of one phase of the post-Stalin era and the opening of an equally challenging new one.

It would be mistaken to consider this period between October 1952 and February 1956 as an isolated unit. In fact, most of its salient features have their roots deep in the past and the full implications of the momentous changes undertaken after Stalin's death have yet to be felt. Nevertheless, it does provide a convenient – although arbitrary – demarcation of an important phase of Soviet history.

June 1959   G. D. E.

TABLE OF CONTENTS

CHAPTER I

THE NINETEENTH PARTY CONGRESS AND THE DEATH OF STALIN

On March 6, 1953, Radio Moscow announced the death of J. V. Stalin. Two days earlier a joint communiqué issued by the Central Committee of the Soviet Communist Party and the Council of Ministers had informed the world that during the night of March 1–2 he had suffered a brain hemorrhage which had incapacitated him, seriously affecting the functioning of his heart and respiratory system. Nevertheless, the news of his death was still a profound shock. With his passing an era of Soviet history came to an end and a new one began.

Stalin's heirs waited just over six hours after the announced time of his death to inform the public. In that period they thrashed out the vital questions upon which the future of the Soviet Union – as well as their own personal fortunes – so largely depended. As far as is known Stalin left no formal will bequeathing his position of dictator of the Soviet Union and leader of the Communist world. However, he left an informal legacy which was all too familiar to his associates. Part of it was the intricate web of intrigue which threaded its way through Soviet politics. Behind the Kremlin's placid façade of so-called "monolithic unity" there was the constant interaction of the rivalries, jealousies, and hatreds of power politics at its worst. These Stalin had masterfully kept in check by manipulating one rival group against another and never permitting the ultimate coordination of Soviet policy to be resolved short of his personal authority. His death destroyed this delicate balance and forced the forging of a new power relationship that was based largely upon the amount of pressure each faction was able to exert at this critical moment.

THE BACKGROUND TO 1952

Although somewhat removed in time, the crucial years of 1948 and 1949 repeatedly re-occure in any critical analysis of the events preceeding Stalin's fatal stroke because the policies adopted at that time were largely responsible for determining the power relationship when he died. It was in that period that Soviet foreign policy in Europe had met its first serious setbacks. The Berlin blockade had been broken by the Western airlift, the Truman Doctrine had stabilized Greece and Turkey, and Stalin's personal quarrel with Yugoslavia's Marshal Tito had erupted into an open breach, ending with the latter's expulsion from the Cominform. As a direct consequence, Moscow tightened its hold on the remaining Satellites. Collectivization along the Soviet pattern was pushed and the pace of industrialization was stepped up. In Asia Mao Tse-tung's conquest of China, uncontrolled from Moscow, was gathering momentum.

Important changes also had taken place inside the Soviet Union itself. The Politburo rivalry between A. A. Zhdanov and G. M. Malenkov, which had been the most significant feature of Soviet postwar domestic politics, had come to an abrupt and decisive end with Zhdanov's sudden death on August 31, 1948. Soon thereafter those who had been most closely associated with him began either to slip in the rank-conscious hierarchy or disappeared completely from the political scene. Among the first to go was A. A. Kuznetsov, one of the five members of the all-important Central Committee Secretariat, who lost his post sometime before January 1949. G. M. Popov, another member of the Secretariat and also a Secretary of the Moscow Party organization, was ousted a year later when he was transferred in January 1950 to head the Ministry of Municipal Construction. This coincided with the return of N. S. Khrushchev from the Ukraine to the Moscow apparatus and the inner-circle of the regime's elite. To fill the vacancies left by Zhdanov's death and the removal of his associates P. K. Ponomarenko, Khrushchev, and M. A. Suslov were elevated to the Secretariat where they joined Stalin and Malenkov. [1]

Of the other officials who also fell by the wayside the most important was N. A. Voznesensky, the director of the State Planning Commission, a Deputy Primer, and a member of the Politburo. He had been the Soviet Union's most promising young economist. In 1938 at the age of 35 he had been swept into his

---

[1] Brzezinski, *The Permanent Purge*, p. 153.

post at the State Planning Commission in the wake of the Great Purges. Nine years later he had been elevated to full membership in the Politburo. That year, 1947, he also published a major economic work entitled *The War Economy of the USSR in the Period of the Patriotic War*, which had been widely hailed as an important contribution to the literature of his field. Then, overnight, in the spring of 1949 his name had vanished from the Soviet press without explanation. [1]

These purges of Zhdanov's high ranking associates provided the basis of what was to be later referred to as the "Leningrad affair." However, they were not confined to merely the top echelon or to any specific region of the USSR. Between 1949 and 1952 when the Nineteenth Party Congress was convened there were extensive changes in the apparatus of every Republic. [2] In the months just prior to the Party gathering the purge was beginning to be felt on the *oblast* level. [3]

Of particular interests were those conducted in the Georgian SSR and the other Caucasian Republics during April 1952. Since it was the Politburo's custom to designate responsibility for certain areas to specific individuals, these had generally been considered to be L. P. Beria's "private domain." Therefore, it provided a curious insight into the inner-workings of the Soviet regime when he was sent by Stalin to preside over the liquidation of the men who had been his faithful, personally selected, followers since the late 1930's. While their replacements were quick to heap lavish praise upon Beria, they were all staunch Party stalwarts whose previous experience had been in Republics outside of the Caucasus under different men. At the same time there was an apparent effort made to weaken the ranks of the local Georgian police organization by placing "experienced Party workers" in its ranks. [4]

In the absence of reliable information it is difficult to intelli-

---

[1] Fainsod, *How Russia Is Ruled*, p. 272. At the Twentieth Party Congress Khrushchev implied that Stalin's execution of Voznesensky and Kuznetsov had taken place so suddenly in 1949 that it had been impossible for the other Politburo members to intervene. (Secret Speech, Gruliow [Ed.], *Current Soviet Policies*, II, p. 183.) However, Vol. LI of the *Bolshaya Sovetskaya Entsiklopediya* published in September 1958 listed 1950 as the date of Voznesensky's death. *New York Times* (*Int. Ed.*), Sept. 15, 1958, p. 2, Harrison Salisbury.

[2] Brzezinski, *op. cit.*, p. 153.

[3] Dinerstein, *The Soviet Purge: 1953 Version*, p. 3.

[4] *Zarya Vostoka*, Sept. 24, 1952, as quoted by Brzezinski, *op. cit.*, p. 154.

gently evaluate the forces motivating the general wave of purges between 1948 and 1952. Malenkov's position was such in the Secretariat after Zhdanov's death that he most likely ordered them. In fact, a remarkable number of his protégés appeared in posts formerly held by Zhdanov's associates. However, Stalin himself may have had a sizeable hand in them also. At the very least, they were carried out with his tacit approval. The Georgian purges appeared to have had more significance than merely the reshuffling of local officials and strongly suggested that some faction within the Politburo was seeking to undermine Beria's position.

THE NINETEENTH PARTY CONGRESS

It was within this framework of intrigue that the central press announced on August 20, 1952, that the long-expected Nineteenth Party Congress would meet the following October 5. [1] Despite the fact that since 1949 there had been repeated hints that a Party gathering might be held, it had never materialized. [2] The announcement immediately raised the question of why Stalin had selected that precise moment to convene the first Party Congress in 13 years. [3] No completely satisfactory answer has ever been given. Quite clearly it was part of a much larger sequence of events which was abruptly terminated by his death in March 1953. However, at the time it was felt that the agenda gave some hint of what lay behind his decision. The delegates were to be asked to approve the directives of the Fifth Five Year Plan, which had already been in operation for nearly two years, and to pass on the revision of the Communist Party Statutes, which merely brought them into conformity with established practice. While superficially important, neither of these items justified the special convocation of the Party's representatives since their ratification was a foregone conclusion. [4] Therefore,

[1] *Pravda* and *Izvestia*, Aug. 20, 1952, p. 1, Gruliow (Ed.), *Current Soviet Policies*, (I), p. 20.

[2] Salisbury, *Stalin's Russia and After*, p. 146.

[3] As the figures on Party membership presented by Malenkov to the Nineteenth Party Congress indicated, the Communist Party which existed in 1939 had been largely decimated by World War II, and the one in session in 1952 was worlds apart from its predecessor. *Pravda*, Oct. 6, 1952, pp. 2–9, Gruliow, *op. cit.*, p. 117.

[4] The texts of both were simultaniously published with the agenda. *Pravda*, Aug. 20, 1952, pp. 1–3, *ibid.*, pp. 20–33.

the first item on the agenda – the Central Committee's report
by Malenkov – attracted considerable attention. Invariably
Stalin had always retained this choice morsel for himself as a
symbol of his authority.

This more than anything else gave rise to the belief that the
Congress would settle the thorny question of the succession.
Some held that Malenkov had pressured Stalin into publicly
recognizing the power it was felt he exerted behind the scenes.
However, a more generally held theory was that the aging
dictator, realizing his advancing years (but not necessarily fore-
seeing death in the near future) had selected Malenkov as his
heir-apparent and had called the Party into session to formally
transfer at least part of his mantle of authority.

Immediately after Stalin's announcement the Soviet press was
filled with accounts of the several thousand mass meetings which
were held to discuss the two draft proposals. To guide this mass
agitation along the desired lines *Pravda* published a commentary
by Khrushchev on the changes in the Party Statutes. But it
failed to give more than slight clarification to the passing reference about the reorganisation of the Politburo and the Secretariat. [1] At the same time the Party organizations in the various
Republics met in preparation for the national gathering. Their
major reports anticipated much of the criticism which was to
come in Malenkov's address. Lackness of discipline, failure and
corruption in the field of agriculture, and the existence of
"bourgeois nationalism" were all dealt with rather severely.

This routine preparation was suddenly shoved violently into
the background by the completely unexpected publication of
Stalin's *Economic Problems of Socialism in the USSR* in *Bolshevik*,
the Party's principal theoretical journal, on October 2. At once
every available means at the regime's disposal was utilized to
spot-light this article. *Bolshevik* printed an additional 300,000
copies above its normal press run of 500,000. On October 3 and 4
it was serialized in full by *Pravda* and a special pamphlet edition
of 1,500,000 copies was also issued. [2] In Moscow alone 200,000
trained agitators read and discussed the article in factories,
schools, and offices during the month of October.

[1] *Pravda,* Aug. 26, 1952, p. 2, *ibid.,* pp. 33–35.
[2] By January 1, 1953, 20,000,000 copies of the pamphlet edition had been published. *Ibid.,* p. iii.

As a result of this timing and the prominence it received the entire character of the Congress was changed overnight. Stalin succeeded in eclipsing not only Malenkov's pre-eminent position but the entire Congress as well. In one deft stroke he had reduced it in stature from an important Party gathering to a mere backdrop for what he intended to be his last major contribution to the Communist ideology. Coming as it did only three days before the Nineteenth Congress was scheduled to open, it threw a completely new light on the reasons why he had called it into session.

In format, at least, *Economic Problems of Socialism in the USSR* was presented as his criticism of a proposed economic textbook. [1] However, there was little doubt that its significance went much deeper and that it actually represented Stalin speaking *ex cathedra* on a wide range of questions. Subsequent events in late December 1952 and early January 1953 suggested that its publication was the final shot in a great economic debate which had raged for several years within the confines of the Kremlin and was directly linked with Voznesensky's disappearance. Stalin's refutation of the price-cost relationship which Voznesensky was believed to have advocated implied that the fundamental questions of the rate of economic growth and the role of planning in a Communist country had been part of it. [2] But this was only one of the topics Stalin touched on in his discussion of the transition of a socialist economy to full Communism. He sought to put to rest those aspects of Marxist-Leninist theory which were no longer tenable in the light of the widening gap between theory and practice. To do this he rewrote – and where necessary completely rejected – those principles, including some of his own, which he said were no longer suitable

amid the new state of affairs in our socialist country.[3]

Among the more troublesome contradictions with which he dealt were the Bolshevik seizure of power in a backward country; his own theory on the stabilization of capital; Marx's beliefs that man determines his own history and the theory that social laws operate independently of man's will; Engels' statement that in a

---

[1] Cf. *Bolshevik*, 18, Sept. 1952, pp. 1–50, *ibid.*, pp. 1–20.
[2] *New York Times*, Jan. 11, 1953, p. 17, Harry Schwartz.
[3] *Bolshevik*, 18, Sept. 1952, pp. 1–50, Gruliow, *op. cit.*, p. 4.

socialist economy commodity production would end; and the need to reassure the Soviet people that within the framework of the inevitable conflict between capitalism and Communism there was the possibility of a relatively peaceful future. Despite past achievements Stalin warned there would be no lessening of the "struggle" if complete communism were to be achieved, and his emphasis on a belt-tightening economic program left little question about the supremacy of heavy industrial development. [1]

All in all, the watchwords of his article seemed to be consolidation and entrenchment of Communism in the USSR and in its Satellites rather than its aggressive expansion to other parts of the world. [2] This led some observers to believe that during the crucial postwar period of 1947–1948, after the initial recovery from the war had been achieved, the Soviet leadership had been sharply divided between policies of aggressive expansionism and conservative retrenchment. With the setbacks in Berlin and Yugoslavia and the death of Zhdanov, known to have been one of the chief advocates of expansionism, the issue apparently had been decided in favor of the conservatives. [3]

Stalin's treatment of foreign policy gave added support to this belief. He postulated the theory that the world was divided into two camps in which the Communist countries had the distinct advantage of living in complete harmony while the capitalist nations were in fierce economic competition with each other. In fact, he predicted that the pressure of finding new international markets would drive the latter to war with each other rather than permitting them to unite and make war against the Communist world. However, he still maintained that eventual conflict between the two camps remained inevitable. [4]

As a result of the publicity given Stalin's article the formal opening of the Party Congress was anti-climactic. Malenkov's major address covering Party developments since 1939 remained the most important item on the agenda, but it lost most of its anticipated luster. While Malenkov most likely retained an edge

---

[1] *Ibid.*, p. iii.

[2] *The Observer*, Jan. 11, 1953, p. 5, Edward Crankshaw.

[3] The most glaring contradiction was the Korean War. However, a strong case can be made for the argument that Moscow stumbled into a war it had not intended North Korea and China to fight. *Ibid.*, Jan. 18, 1953, p. 6, Richard Löwenthal.

[4] Gruliow, *op. cit.*, p. iii.

over his associates, the gulf between Stalin and his subordinates was considerable. Despite the fact that he, himself, did not take the rostrum except for the closing address, the Congress was never permitted to lose sight of the fact that it was Stalin's hand which moved imperceptively behind the scenes manipulating the proceedings. Malenkov's general thesis throughout his long speech was one of praise tempered with warnings and occasionally sharp criticism. He repeatedly cited Stalin's *Economic Problems of Socialism in the USSR* as his authority. Elaborating at some length on his concept of the existing state of international affairs, he used language typical of the Cold War, picturing the United States as the greatest threat to the world's security because of its allegedly aggressive designs. When Malenkov sketched in detail the industrial growth of the Soviet Union during the 13 years since the last Congress he stressed the importance of developments in heavy industry but included some criticism of those segments of industry which had failed to fulfill their quotas. He indicated that the regime was particularly disturbed about the under-employment of existing facilities but was also concerned about bureaucratic red tape, poor planning, mismanagement, and inferior standards, especially in light industry, as well as low labor productivity. [1]

In regard to agriculture Malenkov confidently announced that

the grain problem, formerly considered the most acute and serious problem ... [had] been solved, solved definitely and finally.

He based this assertion upon the claim that in 1952 the Soviet Union had produced a 131,040,000 metric ton "biological" grain yield. [2] However, he also presented the other side with a few of its previously acknowledged failures such as insufficient fodder production, the lagging animal husbandry industry, low yields in general, and the absence of more rapid improvement of labor productivity. But in general his appraisal was optimistic and found Soviet agriculture on the "upward swing" toward providing the country with

---

[1] *Pravda*, Oct. 6, 1952, pp. 2–9, *ibid.*, pp. 106–109.

[2] *Ibid.*, p. 109. "Biological" yields were an ambiguous method of calculating harvests in terms of the size of the crop in the field rather than the amount actually gathered in. As later figures indicated, Malenkov's assertions bore no relationship to reality.

a plentiful supply of food for the people and of raw materials for [the] rapidly growing light industry.[1]

When it came to analyzing the changes which had taken place in the Party since 1939 Malenkov's criticism indicated that the regime was concerned about the growing independence acquired by individual members and local units as a result of the Party's rapid growth. [2] The program he outlined advocated a policy of tightened control over the lower branches by its central authorities. He condemned corruption, nepotism, bureaucratic inefficiency, lack of discipline and the absence of ideological work which had infected large segments of local Party units and indicated that these would be no longer tolerated. [3]

M. Z. Saburov, the head of the State Planning Committee, presented Stalin's basic economic outline for the 1950–1955 period. In the Fifth Five Year Plan the level of industrial production was to rise ten per cent, despite a slackened rate of economic growth. As in previous plans the development of an industrial-military base was the primary goal with considerable increase planned in the production of such basic items as sheet-steel, copper, aluminium, lead, zinc, stainless steel, and the enlargement of the petroleum and hydro-electric power industries. The promised rise in the output of consumers' goods – while large percentage-wise – was highly inadequate in the light of the growing population and the needs of the people. Rather than depending entirely upon the construction of new production capacity, between one fourth and one third of the planned industrial increase was to come from more efficient utilization of existing facilities. (This pointed up Malenkov's criticism of industrial waste and gave some indication of how serious the problem was.). The remainder was to come from increased labor productivity and new construction. This latter was undoubtedly undertaken as a hedge both against a worsening of the international situation and the inability of substantially expanding the output of existing plants or raising productivity. [4]

[1] *Ibid.*, p. 112.
[2] In 1956 Soviet officials stated that one of the reasons for Voznesensky's liquidation was his collaboration with Kuznestov's attempt to establish a seperate Communist Party organization for the RSFSR with its headquarters in Leningrad rather than Moscow. Sulzberger, *The Big Thaw*, pp. 47–48.
[3] *Pravda*, Oct. 6, 1952, pp. 2–9, Gruliow, *op. cit.*, pp. 116–121.
[4] "Under-employment of industrial capacities and low productivity of labor

In agriculture an even greater percentage of the new yields demanded by the Plan were to come from better utilization of land already under construction. Saburov estimated that

approximately 90 per cent of the over-all grain crop increase, 50 per cent of the raw cotton increase, and more than 60 per cent of the sugar beet increase ... [were to] be obtained through heightened yields.[1]

This meant that with practically no increase in the area under cultivation the regime expected to raise the "biological" yield to about 181,600,000 metric tons in 1955. [2] (In the 25 years between 1913 and 1938 Russian grain production was able to increase by only 41,000,000 metric tons with only a five per cent increase in the area under cultivation.) [3] To achieve this new goal the regime would have to increase grain output by 12 per cent a year between 1952 and 1955. There was no precedent in Soviet history (or for that matter in any other country) to suggest that the USSR could realisticly expect to reach the projected target. [4] Equally optimistic were the demands set for the production of animal products such as milk, eggs and wool. For example, milk production was to be increased by 50 per cent with only an 18 to 20 per cent increase in the number of cattle. [5]

In short, while the Fifth Five Year Plan took cognizance of the problems facing the Soviet economy it showed no marked evidence of deviating from its predecessors to realisticly remedy them.

When Khrushchev presented his report on the revision of the Party Statutes he added little to what he already had said in his August "theses." The changes he proposed merely reflected existing practice rather than innovations. [6] Khrushchev also adopted Malenkov's policy of praising the developments which

appears to be the structural phenomena of the Soviet type of industrial control and can ... not be eliminated at will." Ronimois, "Soviet Economic Planning and the Balance of Power," pp. 35–36.

[1] *Pravda*, Oct. 10, 1952, pp. 2–4, Gruliow, *op. cit.*, p. 129.

[2] United Nations, *Economic Survey of Europe Since the War*, p. 45, and United Nations, *Economic Survey of Europe in 1955*, p. 192. (Hereafter this series is referred to by title only.)

[3] Ronimois, *op. cit.*, pp. 36–37.

[4] *Economic Survey of Europe Since the War*, p. 46. Cf. below p. 117 for a more realistic official appraisal of the grain situation.

[5] Ronimois, *op. cit.*, pp. 36–37.

[6] Mosely, "The Nineteenth Party Congress," p. 239. For a comparison of the texts of the 1939 and 1952 Party statutes cf. Meissner, *The Communist Party of the Soviet Union*, pp. 19–40.

had taken place since 1939 but reserved the major share of his speech for stern criticism of what he termed the "scandalous practices" which he said had crept into Party operation over the years. He left no question in the minds of his audience that Party officials were disturbed by the general lackness in the lower organizations and intended to curb it through more stringent control from above. Singled out for special criticism were lack of discipline, loss of revolutionary fervor, [1] the acceptance of a double standard of Party rules by some officials, nepotism, efforts to suppress criticism, the absence of self-criticism, and bureaucratic injustices carried out in the name of the Party for personal advancement. The most important revisions made in the Party's structure were the transformation of the Politburo into the Presidium, the enlargement of the Central Committee, and the amalgamation of the Orgburo with the Secretariat; yet Khrushchev barely mentioned these, and his explanation gave no real clarification of the reasons behind them. [2]

The former compact Politburo of 11 members and one candidate was enlarged to the unwieldy size of 25 members with 11 candidates. With the exception of A. A. Andreyev, who had been made the scapegoat for the agricultural failures several years before and had been replaced by Khrushchev, and A. N. Kosygin, who was demoted to candidate status, all the previous members retained their positions. N. M. Shvernik, the one previous candidate, was promoted to full membership. Added to this group were 14 new members and ten new candidates, representing a wide cross-section of the Party and the bureaucracy. [3] An

---

[1] Significantly, the Congress felt compelled to recognize this to the extent of substituting the word "Communist" for "Bolshevik" in both the Party's official name and in the title of its ideological journal. A similar tendency was noticeable in the Party's new definition. *Pravda*, Oct. 13, 1952, pp. 1–3, Gruliow, *op. cit.*, pp. 133–134.

[2] According to Khrushchev, the change was
"expedient because the title 'Presidium' better accords with the functions which the Politburo actually performs at the present time.

"It is expedient ... to concentrate the current organizational work of the Central Committee in one body, the Secretariat, in which connection the Organizational Bureau ... is to be eliminated in the future."
Ibid., p. 137.

[3] They were as follows: J. V. Stalin, V. M. Andrianov, A. B. Aristov, L. P. Beria, N. A. Bulganin, K. Ye. Voroshilov, S. D. Ignatyev, L. M. Kaganovich, D. S. Korotchenko, V. V. Kuznetsov, O. V. Kuusinen, G. M. Malenkov, V. A. Malyshev, L. G. Melnikov, A. I. Mikoyan, N. A. Mikhailov, V. M. Molotov, M. G. Pervukhin, P. K. Ponomarenko, M. Z. Saburov, M. A. Suslov, N. S. Khrushchev, D. I. Chesnokov, N. M. Shvernik, and M. F. Shkiryatov as members; and L. I. Brezhnev, A. Ya.

analysis of the new Presidium indicated a great broadening of the regime's ruling echelon. It included all ten members of the Central Committee's enlarged Secretariat and all 13 Deputy Chairmen of the USSR Council of Ministers, completely merging Party and state administration. Others were

the head of the trade unions and the former First Secretary of the Komsomols, two representatives from the Ukraine, the First Secretary of the Belorussian Party, a sprinkling of regional Party leaders, two high-ranking Party ideologists, an old Comintern specialist, and some of the Soviet Union's outstanding economic administrators.[1]

With the exception of S. D. Ignatyev, Minister of State Security, no representatives of the armed forces or the police ministries were added.

The revision elevated a new generation to the Party's high command. Only two of the new members – O. V. Kuusinen and M. F. Shkiryatov – were Old Bolsheviks, having entered the Party in 1905 and 1906, respectively. D. S. Korotchenko, M. G. Pervukhin, M. A. Suslov, A. Ya. Vyshinski, and A. G. Zverev dated their membership back to the Civil War period, but the remaining 18 had joined only in 1924 or later. In 1939 eight were so obscure that they did not participate in the Eighteenth Party Congress. [2] In fact, most of them had come to their Republic or regional Party offices during the postwar reshuffles. [3]

At the same time the Secretariat also underwent changes. It officially took over the work of the Orgburo which was merely a recognition of existing practice. Its membership was doubled, retaining the five existing Secretaries – Stalin, Malenkov, Khrushchev, Suslov, and Ponomarenko – and adding A. B. Aristov, N. A. Mikhailov, N. G. Ignatov, L. I. Brezhnev, and N. M. Pegov. [4] Here again a younger generation had made its appearance, and numerically, at least, dominated the Secretariat. [5] The rise of these new men to one of the Party's most important bodies had been so rapid and their previous positions

Vyshinsky, A. G. Zverev, N. G. Ignatov, I. G. Kabanov, A. N. Kosygin, N. S. Patolichev, N. M. Pegov, A. M. Puzanov, I. F. Tevosyan, and P. F. Yudin as candidates. *Pravda*, Oct. 17, 1952, p. 1, *ibid.*, p. 242.

[1] Fainsod, *op. cit.*, p. 278.
[2] *Ibid.*, p. 279.
[3] Brzezinski, *op. cit.*, pp. 155–156.
[4] *Pravda*, Oct. 17, 1952, p. 1, Gruliow, *op. cit.*, p. 242.
[5] Brzezinski, *op. cit.*, p. 155.

so obscure that at least one qualified observer in Moscow had difficulty identifying them. [1]

When these changes were published *Pravda* departed from the time-honored custom of listing them in order of importance. With the exception of Stalin's name, which naturally headed the lists, the others appeared in Cyrillic alphabetical order. [2] In effect, the old Party stalwarts such as Malenkov, Khrushchev, Molotov, and Beria suddenly found themselves submerged among relatively unknowns from the provinces. In the prestige-conscious Soviet regime this was a significant development.

THE EMERGING PATTERN

Contrary to the earlier expectations, the Nineteenth Party Congress did not settle the question of succession. In fact, if anything, it made it more uncertain than ever before. While it was possible to argue that the presence of a much younger generation of the Party's apparatus in the inner-circle was an important advancement of Malenkov's fortunes, [3] there was no concrete evidence to indicate that this was actually the case. For the first time some observers seriously began to question the basic assumption that the Congress had been called to clarify the succession issue. The timing of Stalin's article, his seeming disdain and indifference toward the Party gathering, the Byzantine ritual of praise heaped upon him (and no one else) by every speaker, and finally the complete reshuffling of the principal ruling bodies together with the emergence of a younger generation of virtual unknowns led to the belief that Stalin's purpose was to deliberately confuse the picture. [4]

However, the Congress did bring together a number of divergent – and in some cases seemingly contradictory – threads of an intricately woven pattern that emerged during the ensuing five months. The most dominant of these was a wide-spread drive against crime, corruption, and graft, which began in the lower levels of the bureaucracy and Party merely as a clean-up campaign but soon developed into a full-blown purge that eventually

---

[1] Salisbury, *op. cit.*, p. 149.
[2] *Pravda*, Oct. 17, 1952, p. 1, Gruliow, *op. cit.*, p. 242.
[3] Fainsod, *op. cit.*, p. 188.
[4] Salisbury, *op. cit.*, p. 149.

reached into every segment of society. Hand in hand with this came an intensification of the regime's Russification policy which was openly anti-Semitic and, ironically, found its fullest expression in the glorification of Stalin. These were accompanied by cries of "vigilance" against sabotage and subversion which were alleged to be the work of "Zionists" and foreign agents. But while this theme and the "Hate America" campaign reached a fever pitch, Stalin himself unexpectedly launched a major "peace offensive."

While it was not difficult to pick out the individual threads, their relationship to one another, or their ultimate purpose, the motivating forces behind them remained obscure because Stalin's sudden death put an end to them before the pattern had been completed. Prior to the Nineteenth Party Congress the Soviet press had been carrying on a campaign to expose and unmask corruption, crime, and graft among petty bureaucrats and minor Party officials. In these press accounts a high percentage of Jewish names – particularly in stories from the Ukraine – had appeared. Anti-Semitism, while officially frowned upon by Communist doctrine, had been utilized by the regime before. Beginning in 1948 an intensified campaign designed to silence the Soviet Jewish community was begun. Intellectuals disappeared, writers were purged, and newspapers and cultural organizations were closed. [1] Faced with the pressure to clean up what appeared to be wide-spread corruption, the Jews again became a handy scapegoat. [2] While anti-Semitism as such was not openly preached at the Congress, the vigor with which Russification was extolled by Beria and others left little question

---

[1] *Soviet Survey*, "A Minority Under Pressure," p. 2. In February 1954 when N. Khokhlov, a high-ranking MVD officer, defected to the West it was learned that certain factions within the regime had begun discussing the desirability of intensifying the anti-Semitic campaign as early as 1951. The Jews in the secret police, which soon came under the direction of S. D. Ignatyev whom Khokhlov identified as a leader of the anti-Semitic group, were among the first to feel its effects. Police General L. A. Eitingen, one of the purge's earliest victims, was demoted and arrested. But this action was reversed when Beria took control of the police following Stalin's death. However, after Beria's arrest Eitingen was re-arrested and this time executed. (Meyer, "Has Soviet Anti-Semitism Halted?", p. 8). Only in 1956 was it established that on August 12, 1952, 24 of the 400 leading Jewish writers, artists, and musicians then under arrest had been executed. Institute for the Study of the USSR, *Genocide in the USSR*, p. 96.

[2] Gruliow, *op. cit.*, iii.

as to where the Jews and other minorities stood. [1] (It was even more pronounced at the Republic Congresses held in September where writers, educators, and other intellectuals were publicly castigated for failing to toe the mark set by the Kremlin.) [2] In his report on behalf of the Central Committee Malenkov had stated that

remnants of the bourgeois ideology, survivals of private-property mentality and morality are still with us. These survivals do not wither away by themselves. They are most tenacious. They can grow and a vigorous struggle must be waged against them. Nor are we guaranteed against the infiltration of alien views, ideals and sentiments from the outside, from the capitalist states, and from inside, from the remnants of groups hostile to the Soviet regime and not yet completely destroyed by the Party.
. . . .
Alien elements, all manners of elements from the remnants of anti-Leninist groups routed by the Party, try to take over those sectors of ideological work ... wherever Party leadership and influence are relaxed, and to use them for ... dissemination of all sorts of un-Marxist viewpoints and conceptions. [3]

When the anti-Semitic press campaign began in earnest this was the language (although unattributed) it used. [4]

In a similar way, the "Hate America" campaign – a familiar part of the Soviet press's Cold War – received a marked boost at the Congress. Malenkov, Khrushchev, Beria, and Bulganin bitterly denounced the United States in venomous invectives, while praising the "peace-loving" nature of the Soviet bloc and boasting of its ability to destroy any potential aggressor. They warned the people to be on guard against subversion, and "vigilance" became the watchword. But while Malenkov and others raved about the "war-mongering" West, Stalin's *Economic Problems of Socialism in the USSR* was surprisingly mild in its criticism of the capitalist world.

The next major event in this strange drama unfolded in Czechoslovakia during November 1952 where 14 former top-ranking Party and government leaders were put on trial in the biggest show-trial staged in a Soviet Satellite. The list of the accused, which included Slansky, former Secretary General of the

[1] *Pravda*, Oct. 9, 1952, pp. 2–3, *ibid.*, pp. 161–166.
[2] Cf. *ibid.*, pp. 53–92.
[3] *Pravda*, Oct. 6, 1952, pp. 2–9, *ibid.*, p. 120.
[4] *New York Times*, Feb. 21, 1953, p. 4, Harry Schwartz, and cf. Lesny, "Der Slansky-Prozess," pp. 1–12 for a discussion of the background of the Slansky trial.

Czech Communist Party, and Clementis, former Czech Foreign Minister, read like a "Who's Who" of former government and Party officials. In addition there were seven former Deputy Ministers of Foreign Affairs, Foreign Trade, Defense, Security, and Finance, one chief of the economic section of the President's office, and three top-ranking Communist Party officials among the accused. With the exception of Clementis, all were identified as Jewish. [1]

There were a number of curious features about the Prague trials. First of all, most of the accused had been under arrest for a considerable period of time and there was no apparent reason why they should have been brought to court at that precise moment. Also they were charged with "Titoism," yet as a group they represented the staunchest advocates of complete submission to Moscow. In short, they were accused of the direct opposite of what they had advocated while in power. This led some to believe that in reality Moscow was purging the Satellite supporters of Zhdanov. [2] A third unusual factor was the way in which blatant anti-Semitism underlay the whole trial. In fact, it represented the high point of the public fostering and exploitation of anti-Semitism by the Communist world. [3] Ingenuously it was linked to "Titoism" by Slansky's confession of guilt to high treason, espionage, and betrayal of military secrets through his alleged association with Jews and "Zionists," among whom he included M. Pijade, the Yugoslav theorist, and A. Pauker, the former Communist Foreign Minister of Rumania who had been purged earlier in the year. [4]

The Soviet press covered the proceedings in great detail, but, except for one major *Pravda* editorial which cited the testimony as additional evidence that the United States was formenting espionage and subversion in Eastern Europe, there was a minimum of comment. [5] In fact, the execution of the condemned Czechs was buried in a one paragraph announcement on the fourth (and last) pages of both *Pravda* and *Izvestia*. [6]

[1] Cf. *New York Times*, Nov. 21, 1952, p. 1, John Mac Cormac.
[2] *The Observer*, Nov. 23, 1952, p. 7.
[3] *New York Times*, Nov. 22, 1952, p. 6, Harry Schwartz.
[4] *Ibid.*, Nov. 21, 1952, p. 6 and p. 1, John Mac Cormac.
[5] *Ibid.*, Dec. 23, 1952, p. 7, Harrison Salisbury.
[6] *Ibid.*, Dec. 10, 1952, p. 8.

The exact relationship of these trials to the anti-Semitic campaign in the Soviet Union is difficult to establish. They may have been ordered by Moscow as a prelude to the intensification of the persecution in the USSR or they may have been an unrelated incident. The weight of subsequent evidence seems to point to their being an intrical part of a massive convulsion which swept the Soviet empire in the following weeks. From Berlin to Bucharest, from Prague to Moscow the purges mounted and with them went anti-Semitism and charges of "Titoism." The wave of trials appeared to move from the perifery of the Communist orbit toward its center. [1]

On November 29, 1952, the press campaign in the Soviet Union against corruption took on a much stronger anti-Semitic flavor when an announcement – simply headed "Chronicle" – told of the trial and conviction by a military tribunal of a group of speculators operating a Kiev retail warehouse. Three, all having names of Jewish extraction – Khain, Yaroshetsky, and Gerzon – had been executed for

counter-revolutionary wrecking in the sphere of trade and commodity circulation [2]

while the others were given long prison sentences. Like the Prague trials the case had a number of peculiar aspects:

(1) the harshness of the sentences and the apparent attempt to twist black marketing, speculation, embezzlement, and similar crimes into treason;

(2) Russian law made no provision for trial of these crimes by a military tribunal nor the death penalty for those found guilty; [3] and

(3) the Soviet press immediately picked up the cry "Down with the Khains and Yaroshetskys!" in a greatly expanded wave of prosecutions of those accused of graft and speculation. [4]

A little less than a month later the December 22 issue of the *Bloknot Agitatora* intensified the persecution by officially defining Zionism as a

reactionary nationalist trend of the Jewish bourgeois,

[1] *The Observer*, Jan. 18, 1953, p. 6, Richard Löwenthal.
[2] Gruliow, *op. cit.*, p. vi.
[3] Salisbury, *op. cit.*, p. 152.
[4] Gruliow, *op. cit.*, p. vi.

which it called

a faithful agency of American imperialism

engaged in

carrying out espionage and subversive activities for the benefit of the United States.

It was the first time the two had been officially linked. [1]

Three days later, in a shrewd bit of timing, Stalin personally launched a major "peace offensive" calculated to reach the world on Christmas Day. He told the *New York Times*

that war between the United States of America and the Soviet Union cannot be considered inevitable and that our countries can continue to live in peace.

He also indicated that he favored diplomatic maneuvers directed toward ending the Korean War as well as negotiations exploring the possibility of conferring with the then President-elect D. Eisenhower on easing world tension. [2] Radio Moscow immediately gave his answers the full attention reserved for major events, carrying them in full on all of its English language broadcasts. Prague, Sofia, and Warsaw Radios also gave them prominence in their domestic services, but an analysis of the Soviet press and Radio Moscow's domestic service indicated that during the preceding weeks the "Hate America" campaign had reached new heights in its fury. [3]

At the same time the Soviet press added another curious piece to the already confused picture. On December 24 Suslov, who had only recently been elevated to both the Presidium and the Secretariat, criticized P. Fedoseyev in a *Pravda* article for not mentioning in his current *Izvestia* commentaries on Stalin's latest economic work that he had been removed from the editorial board of *Bolshevik* – along with two others – in 1949 for having praised Voznesensky's book *War Economy of the USSR in the Period of the Patriotic War* when it first appeared in 1947. (This was the first mention of Voznesensky's name since his mysterious disappearance nearly three years before.) Suslov made public a

---

[1] *Bloknot Agitatora*, Dec. 22, 1952, as quoted by the *New York Times*, Dec. 23, 1952, p. 7, Harrison Salisbury. The importance of anti-Semitism in Soviet foreign policy should not be overlooked. It was a means of appealing to former pro-Nazi elements in Eastern Europe as well as the Arab Middle East.

[2] *Ibid.*, Dec. 25, 1952, p. 1, James Reston.

[3] *Ibid.*, Dec. 26, 1952, pp. 1 and 9, Harry Schwartz.

previously secret Central Committee decree of July 13, 1949, which had dismissed the three editors as well as other staff members and sharply chastized D. M. Shepilov, who had been chief of the Party's propaganda and agitation section but was currently editor of *Pravda*. [1] Interestingly, Suslov's criticism was not of Fedoseyev's interpretation of Stalin's economic work but was centered around a seemingly unrelated incident which had occurred nearly five years before. [2] The article was the signal for a mass recanting by all who had been unfortunate enough to have praised the heretical book. (Until Voznesensky disappeared in 1949 it had been widely acclaimed and often quoted in the Soviet press.) In early January nearly one thousand Soviet scientists and economists met to publicly retract their former praise and to admit their "errors." [3]

THE "DOCTORS' PLOT"

But despite the publicity given this Florentine display, it was abruptly pushed into the background by *Pravda's* announcement of the so-called "Doctors' Plot" on January 13, 1953. The ten-paragraph news item – again simply headed "Chronicle" – announced the arrest of nine leading physicians – six of whom were subsequently identified as Jewish – for plotting to kill important Soviet leaders, primarily ranking military officers, on behalf of the American and British intelligence services. They were also accused of having killed A. S. Shcherbakov (in 1945) and Zhdanov (in 1948) (both of whom held military ranks while they lived) through deliberately incorrect diagnosis and treatment. *Pravda*, which was re-echoed throughout the entire Soviet press, stressed that the doctors' alleged conspiracy was primarily directed toward weakening and destroying the country's military defenses and listed Marshal A. M. Vasilevsky, Minister of War; Marshal L. A. Govorov, commander of Soviet Forces in Finland during World War II; Marshal I. S. Konev, Commander of Soviet

---

[1] *Ibid.*, Dec. 25, 1952, p. 11, Harrison Salisbury. Cf. *Osteuropa*, "Neues Licht auf den Fall Wosnessenskij," pp. 96–98 for the text of the Central Committee decree.

[2] Commenting on Voznesensky's book, Suslov referred to it as "anti-Marxist" and denounced it for setting forth "false and subjective views of the political economy of socialism." *Pravda*, Dec. 24, 1952, as quoted by Fainsod, *op. cit.*, p. 272.

[3] *New York Times*, Jan. 9, 1953, p. 5.

Ground Forces; General of the Army S. M. Shtemenko, Soviet Chief of Staff; and Admiral G. I. Levchenko, Deputy Minister of the Navy as having been marked for death. Although "other high officials" were also said to have been among the intended victims, none was mentioned by name. Five of the physicians were directly linked by the Tass story to

the international Jewish bourgeois nationalist organization 'Joint' [American Joint Distribution Committee, a Jewish relief organization] established by American intelligence.

Three others were accused of being "old agents" of British Intelligence. All the arrested doctors were closely associated with the highest echelons of Soviet civilian and military medical administration. The most important of those implicated was Prof. P. I. Yegorov, who had headed the Kremlin's Medical and Sanitary Service since 1947. He was, in effect, "court physician" to the inner-circle of the Soviet high command. [1]

Serious charges of carelessness and negligence were immediately leveled by the press at both the secret police and the Ministry of Health for their failure in not uncovering the plot earlier. But these accusations were so worded that they contained the basis for a massive purge of the Russian people in general. [2] At the same time they left little doubt about the anti-Semitic nature of the purge.

The circumstances behind the "Doctors' Plot" still remain shrouded in mystery. There is no authoritative information on its ultimate purpose, the scope of its intended victims, the part the military was to play, or Stalin's exact role. Only two points

[1] The others were Profs. M. S. Vovsi, V. M. Vinogradov, M. B. Kogan, B. B. Kogan, G. I. Maiorov, Ya. G. Etinger (all therapeutists); A. I. Feldman, otolaryngologist; and A. M. Grinshtein, neuropathologist. (*Pravda*, Jan. 13, 1953, p. 4, Gruliow, *op. cit.*, p. 244). Soon after the "Doctors' Plot" had been announced in Moscow L. Stoeckler, the leader of the Hungarian Jewish community, was also arrested for being in contact with "Joint." Until the "plot" was announced "Joint" had been distributing $ 200,000 monthly in relief payments through his office. This was the only instance in which it was still operating in Eastern Europe. *The Economist*, Jan. 24, 1953, p. 194, and *The Observer*, Feb. 22, 1953, p. 7, Richard Löwenthal.

[2] "The agencies of state security did not discover the doctors' wrecking, terrorist organization in time. Yet these agencies [the Ministry of Health and the Ministry of State Security] should have been particularly vigilant, since history already records instances of foul murders and traitors to the motherland in the guise of doctors ... besides these enemies we still have one more enemy – the carelessness of our people. One cannot doubt that as long as we have carelessness there will continue to be sabotage. Consequently: to end the sabotage it is necessary to put an end to carelessness in our ranks." *Pravda*, Jan. 13, 1953, p. 1 as quoted by Brzezinski, *op. cit.*, p. 157.

were immediately obvious: firstly, a major purge equalling, if not surpassing, the 1930's was under way; and secondly, for the first time anti-Semitic persecution was openly given the official stamp of approval. Beyond this there were a number of well-founded, but difficult to prove, conjectures. The most important was that it seemed to be another move to further discredit Beria. Initially, at least, the military appeared to have been singled out by someone to fill the role of living martyrs at the expense of its deadly rivals, the secret police.

There had been earlier evidence to support this theory. While the secret police organization in Georgia was coming under fire the Nineteenth Party Congress failed to re-elect Abakumov, but had made Marshals G. K. Zhukov and K. A. Vershinin as well as Admiral I. S. Yumashev all new candidate members. The three had previously been under a cloud. [1] Then, on November 7, 1952, the anniversary of the October Revolution, when the traditional political portraits were hung in Red Square Beria's had been preceded for the first time by both Marshals Voroshilov and Bulganin. Neither of these men were professional soldiers, but symbolicly, at least, the military had surpassed the police in an important public display. At the same time *Pravda* failed to list him as one of the "closest comrades in arms of J. V. Stalin." Also it was a military tribunal rather than the police that had tried the Ukrainian corruption cases which touched off the most recent wave of purges. [2]

During the following weeks three facts probably having an important bearing on the physicians' alleged conspiracy came to light. When it was first announced, it was assumed by the outside world that Beria still controlled the Ministry of State Security (MGB) through the man usually considered his protégé, Abakumov. [3] However, a routine *Pravda* story named Ignatyev as the nominee of the Ministry of State Security for Deputy of the

---

[1] Both Marshal Vershinin, who had been Commander-in-Chief of the Air Force, and Admiral Yumashev, wartime Commander-in-Chief of the Navy and a former Minister of the Navy, had been replaced by much junior officers. Dinerstein, *op. cit.*, p. 8.

[2] Salisbury, *op. cit.*, pp. 150–153, and *Pravda* as quoted by the *New York Times*, Jan. 3, 1953, p. 3, Harry Schwartz.

[3] Abakumov may have been Stalin's protégé rather than Beria's. This is suggested by the fact that he apparently remained in prison after he was arrested in 1952 until his execution was announced in December 1954. *The Observer*, Dec. 26, 1954, p. 1.

Moscow City Soviet. This was the first hint that he, rather than Abakumov, headed the MGB. This meant that Beria had suffered another major setback and that control of the secret police had been wrested from him. Exactly when this took place is not known. Abakumov had not been mentioned by the Soviet press for over a year. [1] However, Ignatyev, on the other hand, had been made a full member of Stalin's enlarged Presidium. While this was a significant change in a vital sector of the Soviet hierarchy, so little was known about Ignatyev's relationships within the regime's inner-circle that it was impossible to accurately identify him with a particular faction. [2]

Another change which was just as baffling concerns the military. In late February military attachés stationed in Moscow noticed that Marshal D. Sokolovsky, who captured Berlin in 1945, had replaced General Shtemenkov – one of the five intended "victims" – as Chief of Staff of the Soviet Army. Contrary to Soviet practice this rather significant change was not formally announced. It only came to light when Marshal Sokolovsky's signature appeared on the invitations to the annual Soviet Army reception. When this change occured was never revealed. General Shtemenkov's name did not appear on a January 1, 1953, obituary with those of other high-ranking officers when it should have. However, it is very unlikely he would have been included among the "victims" of the so-called plot if he had fallen completely from favor. Except for a minor item in *Krasnaya Zvezda*, the Soviet Army newspaper, stating that he had attended the anniversary reception in Berlin, he disappeared completely until early 1957. [3]

[1] *New York Times*, April 4, 1953, p. 1, Harrison Salisbury.

[2] A number of interpretations have been given Ignatyev's career. In 1953 it was generally believed that he was Malenkov's protégé. However, another theory held that he owed his loyalty directly to Stalin through A. N. Poskrebyshev, who headed his personal secretariat and was responsible for directing the liquidation of top-ranking officials in the 1930's. It was argued that Ignatyev's career advanced primarily when Malenkov's fortunes were in eclipse. (*Ibid.*, April 17, 1953, p. 24, Boris Nicolaevsky.) However, this left unexplained how he was able to survive both Stalin's death (when Poskrebyshev was apparently shot) and the repudiation of the "Doctors' Plot" (when M. D. Ryumin, his deputy in the MGB was arrested and later shot). In fact, on February 16, 1954, he was identified as First Secretary of the Bashkir Autonomous Republic, suggesting that Khrushchev, who was then apparently conducting a purge of lower-level Party organization, had been his benefactor. (*Ibid.*, Feb. 18, 1954, p. 1 Harry Schwartz.) This was further substantiated by his continued rise after the Twentieth Party Congress.

[3] There were unconfirmed rumors that he held a Siberian command. Salisbury,

The significant aspect of this incident is that his career was unlike that of the other officers named in the conspiracy. His World War II record was not outstanding. He had served on the General Staff and received the Order of Suvarov, First Class. Like many others his picture had appeared in *Pravda*, but then he was not heard of again until 1948 when he was named Chief of Staff in a general shake-up. The other military figures associated with the plot were all experienced veterans and very senior officials. In short, General Shtemenkov just did not fit into the pattern. Interestingly, he alone lost his command. All the others retained their posts following Stalin's death. Also this change – whether by design or accident – brought the man most closely associated with Marshal Zhukov to the post of Chief of Staff just prior to his reappearance on the center of the Soviet political scene. [1]

The fate of still a third key official poses an unanswered question. On February 17, 1953, *Izvestia* printed the following terse paragraph on its back page:

The administration of the Commandant of the Moscow Kremlin announces with deep grief the untimely death of Major General Kosynkin.

He was believed to have been the commander of the Kremlin guard at that time. [2]

While many events connected with the "Doctors' Plot" remained unexplained, there could be little doubt that it was the signal for a rash of similar charges throughout the Soviet Union. Although the earliest stories came from the Ukraine, the terror quickly spread and the press accounts in the local newspapers were similar enough in style and structure to indicate that they bore the stamp of the same central source. The old indictments against "Zionist" movements were rehashed and allegedly new cases of American subversion and espionage were uncovered. The cry of "vigilance" was raised against these former enemies and then skillfully turned against the Russian people themselves. [3] Many – but certainly not all – of the "villains" had Jewish

op. cit., p. 185; the *New York Times* (*Int. Ed.*), Oct. 30, 1957, p. 3, Harrison Salisbury; and Meissner "Verwaltungsumbau," p. 289.

[1] Salisbury, *op. cit.*, pp. 184–186.

[2] *Izvestia*, Feb. 17, 1953, p. 4 as quoted by Avtorkhanov, "The Political Outlook after the Twentieth Party Congress," p. 12.

[3] Cf. *Bloknot Agitatora*, 3, Jan. 1953, Gruliow, *op. cit.*, pp. 244–246.

names. Other elements were soon added. A drive against any sign of bourgeois "idealism" and "cosmopolitanism" was launched among Soviet intellectuals. The Society for the Dissemination of Political and Scientific Knowledge met to recant. [1] *Izvestia* attacked the legal profession for being influenced by Western thought. [2] *Krasnaya Zvezda* boasted about Soviet economic strength and the ease with which it could be converted to war production, [3] and the USSR broke off diplomatic relations with Israel over the pretext of the bombing of its Legation in Tel Aviv. [4]

As the terror deepened, Stalin's associates were drawn more and more into its web. The Ukraine, Khrushchev's former domain, was the scene of the largest number of cases, and his protégés came under increasing attack. The scandals in the trade organizations implicated A. I. Mikoyan. Beria had been indirectly condemned by the original charges of lackness, and, as the terror raged unabated, even Malenkov saw members of his personal apparatus in city after city engulfed by the flood. L. M. Kaganovich was a Jew. K. Ya. Voroshilov had already been "excommunicated" from the Politburo for several years. One after another of V. M. Molotov's subordinates in the Foreign Ministry were arrested, and his wife, a Jewess, was deported to Siberia. There was not one name in the Soviet hierarchy which could not be brought to account on the same charges being levelled at lesser individuals by the Soviet press. When the purge reached into the lower ranks of the officer corps not even the military leaders were immune. [5]

THE DEATH OF STALIN

With the terror at an ever-increasing tempo but just short of a climax, it was suddenly announced on March 4, 1953, that during the night of March 1–2 Stalin had suffered a brain hemorrhage. [6]

[1] *New York Times*, Jan. 16, 1953, p. 4, Harrison Salisbury.
[2] *Ibid.*, Jan. 24, 1953, p. 3.
[3] *Ibid.*, Jan. 18, 1953, p. 19, Harrison Salisbury.
[4] *Ibid.*, Feb. 12, 1953, p. 1.
[5] Salisbury, *op. cit.*, pp. 153–157. At the Twentieth Party Congress Khrushchev revealed that both Mikoyan and Molotov had been attacked by Stalin at the first Central Committee meeting after the Nineteenth Party Congress. Secret Speech, Gruliow (Ed.), *Current Soviet Policies*, II, p. 187.
[6] The announcement indicated that a completely new group of doctors was treating

Few concrete facts other than those supplied by the official medical bulletins are known about Stalin's illness and death. The possibility that it was other than natural cannot be ruled out. [1]

Various interpretations have been put forth to explain the intricate pattern of events which was arrested with Stalin's death. Few answer all the questions or stand the test of close examination in the light of subsequent events. However, a number of generalizations can be made on the basis of the available facts. When Stalin died the regime was in the throes of a political and economic crisis which would have demanded major alterations in Soviet policy had he lived. His lieutenants were engaged in a deadly struggle of their own over the question of succession while someone, most likely Stalin himself, had ordered a massive purge which showed every sign of being a reign of terror that apparently was designed to eventually liquidate the existing leadership and establish a new one in power. In all of this, the military played a much greater role behind the scenes than was generally realized.

The most striking feature of the year that preceded Stalin's death was the consistent manner in which he seemed to have manipulated events from behind the scenes. The purging of the Georgian Party organization, the Nineteenth Congress, the publication of his last economic doctrine, the Florentine display of mass recanting by those who had disagreed with him, and the purges which touched off the "Doctors' Plot," all bear Stalin's imprinture. But what were his motives? A particularly irreverent American in Moscow when the "Doctors' Plot" broke who sarcastically warned that

the old man has reached for that bottle again [2]

him. *Pravda* and *Izveslia*, March 4, 1953, p. 1, Gruliow (Ed.), *Current Soviet Policies*, (I), p. 246.

[1] According to a version attributed to Ponomarenko in 1957, Stalin suffered his fatal stroke at a Presidium meeting in late February 1953 after Voroshilov had violently opposed his plan to deport all Soviet Jews to Birobidzhan, the autonomous Jewish area in Siberia. Until his death in March Stalin was reported to have remained virtually unconscious. (*France-Soir*, June 7, 1957, as quoted by the *New York Times* (*Int. Ed.*), June 8, 1957, p. 2). As early as February 27, 1953, all home leave for Soviet troops in East Germany was reported to have been canceled and they were ordered on an "alert" status. On March 2 similar "alert" orders were issued to East German troops. They were told to give special attention to the Czech border and their own installations. *The Observer*, March 15, 1953, p. 1.

[2] Salisbury, *op. cit.*, p. 155.

may have been more correct than he imagined. It is not beyond the realm of possibility that the web of intrigue which engulfed the Soviet Union in the last years of Stalin's life had been diabolically and cunningly spun by a despotic tyrant who had grown old and was in failing health, a ruthless individual who once before had plunged the country into a blood-bath simply because he was Stalin, ruler of Russia.

Khrushchev partially substantiated this theory at the Twentieth Party Congress in 1956 when he pictured Stalin as a sick man who had repeatedly threatened to do away with his subordinates. According to Khrushchev, Stalin's

proposals after the Nineteenth Congress concerning the selection of 25 persons to the Central Committee Presidium was aimed at removing the old Political Bureau members and bringing in less experienced persons, so that these would extol him in all sorts of ways.[1]

Khrushchev also revealed how the "Doctors' Plot" had come about:

Actually, there was no 'affair' outside of the declaration of the woman doctor Timashuk,[2] who was probably influenced or ordered by someone ... to write to Stalin a letter in which she declared that doctors were applying supposedly improper methods of medical treatment.

Such a letter was sufficient for Stalin to reach an immediate conclusion that there ... [were] doctor plotters in the Soviet Union. He issued orders to arrest a group of eminent Soviet medical specialists. He personally issued advice on the conduct of the investigation and the methods of interrogation.[3]

Unfortunately, Khrushchev's explanations do not completely satisfy all of the unanswered questions, and there is the distinct possibility that he deliberately distorted the facts to protect himself. What must be recognized is that while Stalin was manipulating his various plots, each of his lieutenants was likewise fashioning his own intrigues which he hoped would become a ladder to the throne. As long as these did not interfere with his plans Stalin permitted them to continue and encouraged them since they solidified his own position and divided his opposition. In this secondary struggle Malenkov was most likely

[1] Secret Speech, Gruliow (Ed.), *Current Soviet Policies*, II, p. 187.
[2] On January 21, 1953, the central press announced that Dr. L. F. Timashuk had been awarded the Order of Lenin for uncovering the "plot." Refugees arriving in West Berlin later confirmed circumstantial evidence that she was the wife of M. B. Kogan, one of the accused. Gruliow (Ed.), *Current Soviet Policies*, (I), p. vi.
[3] Secret Speech, Gruliow (Ed.), *Current Soviet Policies*, II, p. 183.

in the strongest position because he controlled the daily operations of the Party apparatus. Beria appeared to be seriously
slipping. Interestingly, Khrushchev was beginning to attract
more and more attention in the months immediately before
Stalin's death. [1]

Then there was also the unexplained role of the military,
which is the most obscure phase of the entire drama. Immediately
after World War II Stalin went to great pains to cut it down to
size by "exiling" men such as Marshal Zhukov to remote commands hardly commensurate with their role in the destruction
of Germany and to assume for himself and the Party the lion's
share of the credit that rightly belonged to the professional
soldiers. After 1950 a change seemed to have taken place in the
Kremlin's attitude, apparently as a result of the Korean War.
In 1951 a secret decree weakened the authority of political
officers in the armed forces and re-emphasized the principle of an
unified command. [2] During the latter part of the following year
Marshal Zhukov was reported to have been reassigned to the
Ministry of War as Commander-in-Chief of Soviet Ground
Forces, the position which he had held when Stalin "exiled" him
in 1946. Likewise, in 1952 Vice Admiral N. G. Kuznetsov, wartime Admiral of the Fleet and Commander-in-Chief of the Navy
who had been demoted and relieved of his command in 1947, was
made Minister of the Navy. [3] Obviously, the prestige of the
military was on the increase.

However, despite his apparent return to grace Zhukov's name
was absent from an important obituary signed by other high-
ranking military leaders on January 1, 1953, in *Krasnaya
Zvezda*. [4] Nor was he included among the "victims" of the

---

[1] *New York Times*, Jan. 3, 1953, p. 3, Harry Schwartz.

[2] Garthoff, "The Military in Soviet Politics," p. 47.

[3] Garthoff, *Soviet Strategy in the Nuclear Age*, p. 20, In August 1952 Marshals
Zhukov, Bulganin, and Vasilevsky, as well as Communist China's General Yun Ti,
were reported to have participated in a conference at Prague which discussed the
reorganization of all Satellite armies along the Soviet pattern. (*New York Times*,
Aug. 10, 1952, p. 3). Assessing the position of the military in postwar Soviet politics is
difficult. Between June 1949 and October 1952 110 generals and marshals were
reported by the Soviet press to have died of natural causes although most of them
were in the prime of life. (The total number of generals and marshals at the time was
6,200.) These deaths may have been entirely natural or the result of a purge. *Ibid.*,
March 1, 1953, Part 4, p. 3, C. L. Sulzberger.

[4] *New York Times*, Feb. 23, 1953, p. 5, Harry Schwartz.

"Doctors' Plot" a few days later. In fact, neither were Marshal Sokolovsky nor Admiral Kuznetsov, who could logically have been expected to have been included. This may be the key to the strange "conspiracy." If it was, indeed, engineered by Stalin he probably had decided to ensure the loyalty of the military during the growing reign of terror by casting them as "victims" but at the same time sought to forestall their emergence as the only cohesive force by capitalizing on existing rivalries. [1]

However, before events had been permitted to run their course General Shtemenko's disappearance brought Marshal Sokolovsky, Zhukov's wartime associate, to the key post of Chief of Staff only a matter of weeks before Stalin died and Zhukov emerged as a major force on the domestic political scene. Summing up these events one observer in Moscow at the time felt forced to comment that

the few tangible pieces of evidence which tend to support the thesis that there was some premeditation in Stalin's death seem to point toward the Army.[2]

[1] Garthoff, *op. cit.*, pp. 20–21.
[2] Salisbury, *op. cit.*, 184.

CHAPTER II

THE POST-STALIN INTERREGNUM

THE INITIAL CRISIS AND THE STRUGGLE FOR POWER

Stalin's stroke plunged the Soviet regime into a crisis which shook it to its very foundations. As the original announcement (withheld for two days) pointed out

Comrade Stalin's grave illness ... [involved] his more or less prolonged non-participation in leading activity.[1]

What went unsaid was that the question of ruling Russia without Stalin had been catapulted from the realm of an eventual necessity to an immediate reality. With it came a hydra of deadly problems which could easily destroy those who sought to fill his shoes.

As the subsequent medical bulletins documented the treatment given Stalin in his last hours, his lieutenants hammered out a program to meet the deepening crisis. The first basic problem they faced was the succession. Next came the orderly transfer of power, the determination of the new regime's direction, and the stabilization of its authority. These were the most urgent because its survival depended upon the correct solutions being found in the first few hours. At the same time, the change in leadership spotlighted the chronic political and economic crisis which had gripped the country even before Stalin died. At issue were such questions as the continued emphasis upon the Russification of the national minorities, investment priorities, and the catastrophic failure of Soviet agriculture. All of these had to be solved within the framework of the deadly internal struggle which Stalin had masterfully kept in check. Such power as his lieutenants had enjoyed while he lived had been derived directly from his personal will. [2]

---

[1] *Pravda* and *Izvestia*, March 4, 1953, p. 1, Gruliow (Ed.), *Current Soviet Policies*, (I), p. 246; Heni, "Ärztliche Stellungnahme zur Krankheit und zum Tode Stalins," pp. 137–138; and *Osteuropa*, "Chronik 2.–15. März 1953," pp. 139–144.
[2] Fainsod, "The Soviet Union since Stalin," p. 1.

The regime's anxiety to the reaction of the Russian people when Stalin's illness and death were announced was a major factor in its calculation of the future. Even in the initial communiqué there was a marked undercurrent of fear and uncertainty beneath the assurance that the people would

display the greatest unity and cohesion ... redouble their energies in building Communism ... rally closer around the Central Committee of the Communist Party and the government of the Soviet Union.[1]

During the next few days this theme was repeatedly drummed home in the domestic propaganda. The joint signature of the communiqué by the Party's Central Committee and the Council of Ministers immediately indicated that no individual was strong enough to assert himself and assume Stalin's key role. The initial succession was a decidedly collective effort which sought to attract all segments of the population by appealing to them in the name of both the Party and the government. In subsequent communiqués the signature of the Presidium of the Supreme Soviet was also added to give an even more universal appeal since every citizen could identify himself with the Supreme Soviet.

Despite the fact that the news of his death was delayed at least six hours, the thorny problem of the succession had not been resolved sufficiently to permit a public statement of the new regime's composition to accompany Stalin's obituary published on March 6, 1953. (In fact, it did not appear for another full 24 hours.) Although it did not contain any hint of the sweeping changes which were being hammered out, his obituary was the regime's first policy statement. After only a few paragraphs of dutiful hommage to Stalin, its tone suddenly switched to an appeal for popular support for the Communist Party and its program. This is described as

the maximum satisfaction of the constantly growing material and cultural needs of all of society;

the strengthening of the armed forces to repell aggression; the striving for peace with emphasis upon international cooperation; the prevention of another war; and the strengthening of ties within the Communist world – particularly with China – and with the working classes of all countries. [2]

---

[1] *Pravda* and *Izvestia*, March 4, 1953, p. 1, Gruliow, *op. cit.*, p. 246.
[2] *Pravda* and *Izvestia*, March 6, 1953, p. 1, *ibid.*, pp. 246–247.

The next day sweeping changes in the composition of both the Party and the government were published. What bargains were struck and what compromises fashioned before the communiqué was finally released must remain a matter of conjecture, but the drastic nature of the changes indicated that the regime felt compelled to act with speed and determination in presenting a façade of unity. [1] Latter events indicated that the original compromises were not wholly acceptable to all of those involved and underlined the role fear had played in the early deliberations.

The most striking changes took place in the membership of the Presidium and Secretariat, which had both been enlarged only five months before, and in the number of ministries, which was sharply curtailed. The net effect was to concentrate the control of both the Party and the government in the hands of a small elite, by and large composed of the men who had been Politburo members before the October 1952 re-organization. By cutting down the number of those who were in a position to exert authority, the inner-circle sought to forestall as much as possible the "disorder and panic" which it anticipated. The Party's Presidium was reduced to ten members and four candidates (in order of listing): Malenkov, Beria, Molotov, Voroshilov, Khrushchev, Bulganin, Kaganovich, Mikoyan, Saburov, and Pervukhin (as members) and Shvernik, Ponomarenko, L. G. Melnikov, and M. D. Bagirov (as candidates). At the same time the composition of the Secretariat was altered. Ignatyev, P. N. Pospelov, and N. N. Shatalin were elected, and Ponomarenko, Pegov, Ignatov, and Brezhnev were relieved in connection with their transfer to other duties. This brought the membership to nine, including Malenkov. Simultaneously Khrushchev was relieved of his duties as head of the Moscow Party organization so that he could "concentrate on work in the Central Committee." [2]

---

[1] *Pravda* and *Izvestia*, March 7, 1953, p. 1, *ibid.*, pp. 247–248. In at least two instances – the dismissal of Shvernik and the unilateral reorganization of the government – the regime violated the lip service Stalin had traditionally given to democratic procedures. Ebon, "Malenkov's Power Balance," p. 8.

[2] Pegov was made Secretary of the Council of Ministers' Presidium, replacing A. F. Gorkin, who became his assistant. Ponomarenko and Ignatov were relieved in connection with their duties in the Council of Ministers. Breshnev was made head of the Political Department of the Navy Ministry. The composition of the Secretariat was as follows: Malenkov, Khrushchev, Suslov, Aristov, Mikhailov, Ignatyev, Pospelov, and Shatalin. *Pravda* and *Izvestia*, March 7, 1953, p. 1, Gruliow, *op. cit.*, pp. 247–248.

In the government there were three major areas of reorganization. At the highest level Voroshilov took over Shvernik's duties as Chairman of the Presidium of the USSR, the nominal head of the Soviet state. Malenkov assumed the position of the Chairman of the Council of Ministers, while Beria, Molotov, Bulganin, and Kaganovich were all made "First Deputy Chairmen." Also the Council of Ministers' Presidium was merged with the Bureau into one body (known as the Presidium) forming a type of inner-cabinet which was equivalent in size to the wartime Defense Council and staffed by the newly created First Deputy Chairmen. [1] The number of ministries was cut in half (from 51 to 25) [2] through a process of amalgamation which put important Presidium members in charge of the key ministries. Beria headed the newly created Ministry of Internal Security which included both the former Ministry of State Security and the Ministry of Internal Security; Molotov was placed in charge of the Ministry of Foreign Affairs; [3] Bulganin commanded the Ministry of War with Marshals Vasilevsky and Zhukov as his First Deputy Ministers; and Pervukhin took over the newly created Ministry of Electrical Power Stations and Electrical Industry. One other change attracted considerable attention. G. P. Kosyachenko, one of Voznesensky's followers, was appointed to head the State Planning Commission, and Saburov, who had held the post before, was transferred to the Ministry of Machine Building. Interestingly, Kosyachenko was so obscure in the Soviet hierarchy that he was not even a member of the Central Committee. He had also been one of the last officials to have been forced to repudiate his "error" in supporting Voznesensky. His public apology was published only in the February issue of *Planovoye Khozyaystvo*. [4]

The sum total of these lightening changes was that the ten Presidium members and the four candidates controlled the Party, the legal head of the government, the key ministries, and the trade unions. At the same time key secondary figures who might have attempted to seize power – namely Marshal Vasilevsky

---

[1] *Ibid.*

[2] Hazard, "Governmental Developments in the USSR since Stalin," p. 11.

[3] Vyshinski and Malik were made First Deputy Ministers and Kuznetsov a Deputy Minister. *Pravda* and *Izvestia*, March 7, 1953, p. 1, Gruliow, *op. cit.*, pp. 247–248.

[4] *Ibid.*, and *The Economist*, March 14, and 28, 1953, pp. 741 and 880.

and S. N. Kruglov head of the MVD – were displaced. To sooth ruffled feelings new jobs were created for those who had been ousted by the new ruling junta or snubbed during Stalin's life. [1] In the reshuffling Malenkov came out on top. Although he assumed the dual titles of

Chairman of the Council of Ministers of the USSR and Secretary of the Central Committee of the CPSU,[2]

his position did not approach Stalin's absolute authority. His strength came primarily from the day-to-day control he had exercised over the Party rank and file during the last years of Stalin's life. But it was not sufficient for him to assume independent direction of the Soviet regime.

Malenkov's rise left a number of questions unanswered. One of these was the replacement of Shvernik by Voroshilov as the titular head of the USSR and the former's public demotion in the Soviet hierarchy at Stalin's funeral before his removal had been legally sanctioned. Shvernik's office normally was of little importance aside from its decorative character. However, in an interregnum it assumed unprecedented powers. As Chairman of the Presidium of the USSR, he and Gorkin, who was Secretary of the Presidium, should have signed the decree which authorized Malenkov's promotion and the other governmental changes. However, it was issued under the collective signature of the Presidium and both men were demoted. [3] Had Shvernik objected to the regime's summary action, or had Voroshilov been kept from demanding a greater voice by "promoting" him to this honorific position? No satisfactory explanation was ever given.

In the horse-trading that took place behind the scenes Beria emerged a strong second. This represented a major victory; prior to Stalin's death he had been under a cloud and apparently the central target of the physicians' "conspiracy." Beria's power was concentrated in his control of the MVD with its own private army

---

[1] *New York Times*, March 7, 1953, p. 4, Harry Schwartz.

[2] Wolfe, "The Struggle for Succession," p. 558. Significantly, Malenkov did not feel strong enough to assume Stalin's traditional title of "General Secretary." In fact, from the moment that he died it virtually disappeared from the periodical press and was apparently the subject of considerable attention in subsequent phases of the internal struggle for power. Rush, *The Rise of Khrushchev*, pp. 34–35.

[3] Shvernik had been Chairman of the Presidium of the USSR since 1946. He was subsequently reappointed head of the Soviet trade unions. Cf. Deutscher, *Russia after Stalin*, pp. 165–167.

which included mechanized units and a small air force. For 75 hours following the announcement of Stalin's death his hand-picked MVD troops completely sealed off Moscow from the outside world. Ostensibly these maneuvers were part of the regime's precautions to prevent "violence and disorder," but at the same time they may have served as Beria's chief bargaining point since he literally held the Kremlin in the palm of his hand. Possibly because he was still uncertain of his strength at that critical moment he failed to take decisive action and thereby may have sealed his eventual fate since

> no military man could watch that demonstration and ever draw a quiet breath again .... It was too apparent that by giving a single order Beria, between two and seven o'clock of any morning, could take the Kremlin, take Moscow, and ... make himself, in all likelihood, the master of Russia.[1]

This was important because the military had been given – or had demanded – a major role in the new regime. The marshals suddenly began to exercise the influence they had been denied by Stalin since World War II. *Pravda* forcefully emphasized the change by publishing as its first picture after Stalin's death 12 Soviet leaders at his bier – six in uniform and six in civilian clothes. [2] Not since the war had the marshals enjoyed such front page coverage. The new regime appeared to be counting heavily on the Army's genuine popularity to win the support of the people, thus eliminating a potential rallying point for dissatisfaction.

Although Molotov lost out in the race for the number one spot and had been by-passed by Beria, his position was considerably stronger than it had been before. While Stalin lived Molotov had had only superficial control of the Foreign Ministry. Now he was in a position to exert major influence in the formation of foreign policy.

While the members of the Presidium represented the old stalwarts of Stalin's pre-October Politburo, the candidate members (with the exception of Shvernik) symbolized the continued struggle for power within the regime. They were the

---

[1] Salisbury, *op. cit.*, pp. 174–175.

[2] Those in uniform were Zhukov, Sokolovsky, Voroshilov, Konev, Govorov, and Bulganin. The civilians were Molotov, Khrushchev, Kaganovich, Mikoyan, Beria, and Malenkov. *Ibid.*, pp. 186–187.

younger generation of faithful lieutenants. One was Melnikov, First Secretary of the Ukrainian Party apparatus. A second was Bagirov, a former police official and then First Secretary of the Azerbaidzhan Party organization. Both these men were closely associated with the minority question, and, although they were staunch advocates of Russification, their appointment represented a superficial concession to minority pressure for greater representation. (Bagirov was the first Communist of Turkic and Moslem origin to be in the Presidium. Ponomarenko, the other candidate, was of either Ukrainian or Belorussian descent.) [1]

To give these changes the stamp of legitimacy a special session of the Supreme Soviet was called for March 14. [2] In the intervening week Stalin's funeral provided an excellent opportunity for the new regime to demonstrate the unity and solidarity which its domestic propaganda had constantly stressed since his death. The physical presence not only of the Soviet leadership, but also of ranking Communists from all over the world in Red Square did much to bolster the illusion of a harmonious transition from one regime to another. Malenkov, Beria, and Molotov utilized the opportunity to make the first detailed policy statements. [3] Their funeral orations, while ostensibly eulogies to the late dictator, actually outlined the course which had been staked out for the new government. In tones of strength and confidence they elaborated on the hints contained in the original announcement of his death. (In fact, however, while praising Stalin's contributions to the Soviet Union it was clear that the new regime did not feel bound to the past and that for the future the watchword was to be "change.") While the undercurrent of anxiety could still be detected in spots, the three speakers indicated that the regime was determined to meet the problems head-on with a positive and constructive program. The strength of Soviet military might and its ability to deal with any potential aggressor was emphasized, but they took pains to address the outside world in moderate and conciliatory terms strikingly different from the past.

All three stressed the continuity of the Party in Soviet history.

---

[1] *New York Times*, March 7, 1953, p. 1, Harry Schwartz.
[2] *Pravda* and *Izvestia*, March 7, 1953, p. 1, Gruliow, *op. cit.*, pp. 247–248.
[3] *Pravda* and *Izvestia*, March 10, 1953, pp. 1–2, *ibid.*, pp. 249–253.

To it, rather than to any individual, was given credit for the development of the Communist state. With the exception of Beria's brief reference to Malenkov as the

talented disciple of Lenin and the loyal comrade-in-arms of Stalin, [1]

no living person was singled out for special attention. Even Stalin, in whose memory the speeches were supposedly being made, was pictured as merely an outstanding member of the Party. (This sudden reduction in the size of his image was one of the most striking aspects of the funeral.) No effort was spared to identify the interests of the Party with those of the people. Everywhere they were made to appear synonymous. In this respect Malenkov, who delivered the key-note address, stated, without giving any details, that one of the Party's goals was

the future improvement in material welfare of the ... Soviet people. [2]

This was cleary a major attempt to win popular support at a critical moment and to dispel the disappointment which had resulted from the government's failure to announce the annual price cuts on March 1. In a similar vein Beria, whose speech was the most blunt and outspoken of the three, introduced another major innovation. According to him, it was the duty of the state to

solicitously and untiringly guard

the people's legal rights as set forth in the 1936 Constitution. He echoed Malenkov's economic statement but charged the state rather than the Party with the responsibility for fulfilling it. [3] In addition to being part of the regime's over-all program, these were attempts by its two most powerful members to stake out claims for themselves as champions of the people.

Another domestic issue – the nationality question – was repeatedly touched on by all three speakers, attesting to the fact that the regime understood its serious implications. However, when they failed to do more than reiterate the earlier appeals for unity and praised the benefits that allegedly were to be derived from following Stalin's policies, it was clear that the basic problem remained unresolved. It was on this point that the undercurrent of uneasiness was most clearly discernable.

[1] *Ibid.*, p. 252.
[2] *Ibid.*, pp. 249.
[3] *Ibid.*, pp. 251.

On the question of foreign policy all three emphasized that the Soviet Union's basic program was the fostering of international peace and prevention of another war. Malenkov went into the greatest detail when he said:

The Soviet Union has waged and is waging a consistent policy of preservation and strengthening of peace, a policy of struggle against the preparation and unleashing of a new war ... of international cooperation and development of business relations with all countries ... based on the Lenin-Stalin premise of the possibility of prolonged co-existence and peaceful competition of two different systems, capitalist and socialist.[1]

There is sufficient circumstantial evidence to indicate that in the week between the announcement of Stalin's death and the meeting of the Supreme Soviet on March 15 an important round in the deadly struggle for power was fought out behind the scenes. Immediately after Stalin's death Malenkov had assumed his titles and during the first few days showed every sign of attempting to transfer to himself – through a well-organized press campaign – the authority which had gone with them. From March 6 through 9 *Pravda* quoted him in its editorials, using the boldfaced type previously reserved for Stalin. On the 9th *Izvestia* carried a photo of Stalin, Malenkov, and a little girl. The following day *Pravda* published the famous retouched picture of Stalin, Mao, and Malenkov, standing alone at the signing of the 1950 Sino-Soviet Treaty. The original, which *Pravda* had published three years earlier, had included 16 other Soviet and Chinese officials, among them Mikoyan, Khrushchev, Voroshilov, Molotov, Beria, and Kaganovich. [2] Also in the same period *Pravda* carried a photograph of Malenkov addressing the Nineteenth Party Congress while Stalin looked on benevolently, [3] and Sovfoto, the official photographic news agency, released a retouched picture of Malenkov with two of his three chins missing. Then as suddenly as it had begun the boldfaced type disappeared and the number of Malenkov's quotations fell off sharply while those of Molotov and Beria began to appear with increasing frequency. Between March 13–15 *Pravda* stopped referring to Malenkov by his dual title and it shifted its emphasis to the Party's Central Committee as the ruling group. At the same

---

[1] *Ibid.*
[2] Wolfe, *op. cit.*, p. 558, and cf. Gruliow, *op. cit.*, p. 25.
[3] Fainsod, "The Communist Party since Stalin," p. 25.

time and without explanation the date for the Supreme Soviet session was postponed for one day. [1]

When it did meet on March 15 to ratify the changes in the government, the list presented by Malenkov differed significantly from the one announced immediately after Stalin's death. No explanations were made nor was the fact even mentioned. The changes were as follows: [2]

1) Mikoyan was named Deputy Chairman of the Council of Ministers of the USSR. (Previously he had been listed only as Minister of Domestic and Foreign Trade.)
2) A. I. Kozlov became Minister of Agriculture and Agricultural Procurement. (Previously Ponomarenko had been named for the post.)
3) Ponomarenko was to head the newly created Ministry of Culture.
4) P. F. Yudin was named Minister of the Building Materials Industry.
5) Andreyev was made a member of the Presidium of the Supreme Soviet.

The first and the fifth changes were of special interest, because they involved former Politburo members. Mikoyan's status as a Deputy Chairman placed him in a category by himself – below his Presidium colleagues who were First Deputy Chairmen, but above the mere ministry heads. Apparently he had been demoted in the original reorganization but in the subsequent reshuffling he succeeded in re-establishing his position. Andreyev was a similar case. Although he had fallen into disgrace over the question of agricultural policy, he had remained a member of the Politburo prior to the Nineteenth Party Congress, but had been dropped when that body was enlarged. [3] Although he had not even been mentioned in the March 7, 1953, reorganization he returned from political oblivion only a week later. In both cases at one time or another each man had found himself in opposition to Malenkov during Stalin's lifetime. [4] The implication was that Malenkov had originally overplayed his hand. However, despite these apparent "defeats," the other changes suggested that he still had significant power. Kozlov's appointment was the one Andreyev should have had on the basis of experience, although the former was himself qualified because of his previous position as head of the Central Committee's agricultural apparatus. The other two

---

[1] Wolfe, *op. cit.*, pp. 558–559. A week later it was announced that on March 14 Malenkov had resigned from the Secretariat. *Pravda*, March 21, 1953, p. 2, Gruliow, *op. cit.*, p. 258.

[2] *Pravda* and *Izvestia*, March 16, 1953, p. 1, Gruliow, *op. cit.*, pp. 256–257.

[3] Ebon, *op. cit.*, pp. 8–9, and *Pravda*, Oct. 17, 1952, p. 1, Gruliow, *op. cit.*, p. 242.

[4] Ebon, *op. cit.*, p. 9.

changes indicated that they were not based on previous experience. [1]

In presenting the regime's reorganization program Malenkov took care to explain that it was not new but had actually been worked out sometime before and that Stalin's death had merely speeded up its implementation. However, in the light of its sweeping nature and the subsequent subdivisions, in which the ministries became even more prolific than in the past, it is difficult to give Malenkov's explanation much credence. [2]

In his policy statement to the Supreme Soviet Malenkov assumed the role of a reporter, clearly indicating that he was not speaking for himself but on behalf of the Party. In sharp contrast to the personal build-up of the previous week he emphasized the collective, cohesive, and monolithic nature of the Party leadership. [3] He gave added importance to the speeches delivered at Stalin's funeral by indicating that they contained the fundamental position of the Soviet government on both domestic and foreign policy. But he was not content with this. He went on to elaborate on the regime's desire to relax international tension by making the strongest peace bid to emanate from Moscow in years:

> At the present time there is no dispute or unresolved question that cannot be settled peacefully by mutual agreement of the interested countries. This applies to our relations with all states, including the United States of America.[4]

(This was in line with the editorials published in both *Pravda* and *Izvestia* after Stalin's funeral. *Pravda* had gone so far as to describe peace as the "sacred desire of the people.") [5]

The short Supreme Soviet session (which lasted just under one hour) did nothing other than merely ratify the revisions presented to it as a *fait accompli*. In a sense, what it did not discuss was one of the most interesting features of the meeting. Two things stood out in this respect. One was the budget which was usually approved in February or March. Obviously the new government did not intend to be bound by Stalin's budget which had most likely

---

[1] *New York Times*, March 16, 1953, p. 5, Harry Schwartz.
[2] Hazard, *op. cit.*, p. 12.
[3] *Pravda* and *Izvestia*, March 16, 1953, p. 1, Gruliow, *op. cit.*, p. 257.
[4] *Ibid.*
[5] *Pravda* as quoted by the *New York Times*, March 13, 1953, p. 4.

been prepared before his death but was not yet ready to elaborate an economic policy of its own. The second was the way Stalin was all but ignored. With the exception of a relatively brief opening expression of grief his name was mentioned only twice: once by Beria in a repetition of his praise of Malenkov and when the latter once more asserted that the government revisions had been under consideration for some time. When Malenkov spoke of his earlier speech over Stalin's bier he simply referred to it as having been made "at the funeral meeting March 9." It was hardly by chance that what little eulogy Stalin did receive at the session had to be shared with K. Gottwald, the Czech President and Communist leader, who had died in Prague after returning from Stalin's funeral. The Soviet leadership seemed only too anxious to rid itself of a significant part of its heritage. [1]

On March 21, 1953, *Pravda* announced that the previous week (March 14) Malenkov had requested a plenary session of the Central Committee to release him from his position in the Secretariat. At the same session other significant alternations had also been made in its membership. In its new form the Secretariat was composed of only Khrushchev, Suslov, Pospelov, Shatalin, and Ignatyev. [2] *Pravda* gave no explanation of why this action, which supposedly took place on the day the Supreme Soviet was originally scheduled to meet, had not been announced earlier. There is some circumstantial evidence to suggest that a full plenum was never held. Between March 14 and March 21 the provincial press continued the build-up of Malenkov which had been abandoned by the central press the previous week. As late as March 21 and 22 the provincial press continued to refer to him as both the leader of the Party and the government. Then suddenly it stopped. Most of the newspapers missed a day of publication (not their usual day off) and a surprisingly large number reappeared with new editors listed on their mastheads. [3] Apparently these editors did not learn of the March 14 action until it was published in *Pravda* and *Izvestia*. This seems rather strange

---

[1] *Pravda* and *Izvestia*, March 16, 1953, p. 1, Gruliow, *op. cit.*, pp. 255–257.

[2] At the same time Shatalin was made a full member of the Central Committee. *Pravda*, March 21, 1953, p. 2, Gruliow, *op. cit.*, p. 257.

[3] In a few areas Malenkov continued to receive special treatment even through the first week of April. However, in others, particularly Georgia, Beria was advanced at his expense and was given credit by the Georgian press for deeds usually reserved for Stalin. Wolfe, *op. cit.*, pp. 558–560.

considering the size of the full Central Committee and the close liaison maintained between the Party and the press in the Soviet Union. However, it should be noted that as a rule it generally took a week or more for the provincial press to catch up with sudden shifts in regime policy first announced by *Pravda* and *Izvestia*.

Regardless of when the shake-up took place it further shattered the illusion of "monolithic unity and solidarity" that was already beginning to wear thin under the stresses and strains of daily operation. It also meant that Malenkov's initial bid to fill Stalin's shoes had been dealt its death knell. The importance of controlling the Secretariat could hardly have been lost on him since he had used it to build his own political fortunes. More than likely this new reorganization represented a clearer division of authorities and gave the titles to the people who actually controlled the power. [1]

On the whole, the situation within the ruling junta resembled a stand-off in which no individual or group had sufficient strength to overcome the others. Malenkov, despite his defeat, was the strongest. He still retained his pre-eminent position within the Presidium which was heavily weighted in favor of the bureaucracy rather than the Party, [2] and was Chairman of the Council of Ministers. Aside from this, through his protégés he controlled a large segment of the bureaucracy and the Party. However, he was the only major official who did not have direct control of a focus of power.

Beria's power lay primarily in his unified control of the police. But it would be a serious error to think of the MVD apparatus as a monolithic organization devoid of rival factions. As was the case in the Party, the bureaucracy, and the Army, each of the regime's leaders had his personal following within the secret police. When Beria assumed control immediately after Stalin's death it was the first time since 1946 that he had exercised personal authority over the police. Unquestionably, he had retained great influence in its operation during the postwar

---

[1] *New York Times*, March 21, 1953, p. 1, Harrison Salisbury.

[2] Aside from Malenkov himself there were four First Deputy Premiers, three Deputy Premiers, one minister, and the titular head of the state as against one Central Committee Secretary (Khrushchev) and two regional Party Secretaries. Löwenthal, "Party vs. State," p. 5.

period, but the removal of V.S. Abakumov (who may or may not have been his protégé) as chief of the MGB and the appointment of Ignatyev (who almost certainly owed his loyalties to someone else) clearly indicated that during the year or so preceding Stalin's death Beria's influence had greatly diminished.

Beria's strength after Stalin's death probably rested primarily upon his control of several key sections of the newly merged MVD, the passive acceptance of his leadership by the other factions within the police organization, and his ability to seize the initiative when the occasion demanded. While his new power was initially very important within the regime, it was partially offset by the increasing importance of the Army and was a decided liability among the people who, at that time, remained an unknown quantity. In short, although Beria was the second most powerful member of the triumvirate, his position was potentially vulnerable.

Although the newly created Ministry of Defense was headed by Bulganin, Marshal Zhukov probably was the most important figure there because of his standing within the Army as a professional soldier and his great popularity among the people.

With the reorganization of the Secretariat Khrushchev emerged as its most important member, assuming the responsibility of conducting the day-to-day Party business which vitally effected the lives of over 7,000,000 members. Suslov ranked second. He was a former *Pravda* editor and a leading intellectual. The other former *Pravda* editor also in the Secretariat was Pospelov, who had touched off the "Hate America" campaign in 1951. Ignatyev, of course, had headed the secret police just prior to Stalin's death but little else was known about him. Shatalin had served under Malenkov for years as head of the cadres administration.

POLICY CHANGES AT HOME AND ABROAD

The festering of political quarrels did not prevent the regime from pushing the development of its bold new programs in domestic and foreign policy. During the first few months it gave every indication of wanting to disentangle itself from the rigidity of the Stalin era, particularly in foreign policy where Stalin's uncompromising attitude had succeeded in only increasing

Western determination to checkmate every turn regardless of the cost. There were a number of compelling reasons why the regime needed a respite in which to rethink its position. Firstly, the fear of an internal upheaval made a relaxation of international tension mandatory. Secondly, regardless of what future policy it decided upon, it needed to disengage itself, at least momentarily, to obtain room to maneuver. Thirdly, its rise to power coincided with the advent of a new administration in Washington and its need to be in a receptive position for changes which might emanate from that quarter. A fourth consideration was the necessity for Moscow to shore up its position as leader of the Communist world, particularly in regard to the Chinese Peoples Republic.

It was immediately evident after Stalin's death that the regime was concerned about its relationship with Communist China. Since its emergence in 1949 Mao's government had occupied a unique position in the Communist world. Obviously too important to be relegated to satellite status it had at once been made a junior partner. Nevertheless, Stalin's tight ideological reign, China's economic dependence upon the Soviet Union, and the Korean War had prevented her from exerting the independence which is implicit in a partnership. However, in the uncertain period which immediately followed Stalin's death in March 1953 Communist China found herself in an almost unprecedented bargaining position. Mao emerged as the senior ideological spokesman of the Communist bloc; the implicit threat of independence from the Soviet empire was strong enough to provoke long-sought concessions; and the momentary weakness of Russian foreign policy provided the unequalled opportunity for Peking to claim a greater voice in deciding its role in international diplomacy.

In the communiqués which followed Stalin's death China was the only member of the Communist bloc which was repeatedly singled out for special mention. Nor was it hardly by chance that the retouched *Pravda* photograph selected for Malenkov's build-up included Mao as well as Stalin. The implication of continuity and equality of the Chinese leader with his Soviet counterparts was inescapable. Chou En-lai, who led Peking's delegation to Stalin's funeral, was reported to have been given precedence over all of the other foreign Communist leaders and to have been placed on an equal footing with the most senior Soviet officials. [1] Interestingly, Mao was the only top Communist leader of the Soviet orbit who did not journey to Moscow. This fact could hardly have been lost upon the prestige-conscious Soviet leadership.

Aside from these rather minor incidents both the Communist Chinese and the Soviets took concrete steps to reinforce their respective positions. On March 10, only three days after he had been named Deputy Foreign Minister, V. V. Kuznetsov was appointed Ambassador to Peking despite the fact that his predecessor, A. S. Panyushkin, had served less than three months in the Chinese capital. [2] The appointment of such a senior official within so short a time after Stalin's death indicated that the regime desired a much closer liaison between the two capitals.

However, it was in Moscow that the most important bargaining took place. Chou remained in the capital until March 23, presumably to take part in important economic and political negotiations. Two days after he left the Soviets announced that "recently" the two countries had signed (1) a trade protocol for 1953, (2) a protocol to the original agreements of February 1950 on credits for China, and (3) an agreement whereby the Soviet Union was to assist China in the construction and expansion of new power stations. The trade agreement specified that the USSR was to supply industrial and transportation equipment, agricultural machinery as well as pedigree cattle and seed in exchange for raw materials. [3]

While the Soviets attempted to picture these agreements as merely the expression of "fraternal" cooperation, they were actually the result of considerable Chinese pressure. In September 1952 Communist China had signed a vague economic pact with the Russians and a delegation had remained in the Soviet capital haggling over the details until Stalin's death brought sudden agreement. [4] China's improved bargaining position was illustrated by the presence of industrial equipment in the list of items that the Soviets promised to supply. Although such generous aid had been promised in the 1950 economic agreement

---

[1] Boorman, "Chronology of Sino-Soviet Relations," p. 17.
[2] *Ibid.*
[3] *Ibid.*
[4] Cf. Mehnert, "Die Sowjets in Asien," pp. 36–41 for a discussion of the 1952 Sino-Soviet negotiations.

there were few indications before 1953 that it ever actually materialized. In fact, even Soviet propaganda had stressed that Russian technicians and experts were training their Chinese counterparts to make their own industrial equipment. [1]

Four days after Chou returned to Peking he announced that the prisoner-of-war question was the only one that prevented a Korean armistice and outlined a program which was, in effect, the Indian plan for prisoner exchange that Communist China had rejected only the previous December. [2] It is impossible to say with any accuracy whether this proposal to break the Korean deadlock originated in Moscow or Peking. Information reaching London in the spring of 1953 seemed to indicate that Mao had utilized his improved bargaining position following Stalin's death to put an end to the costly Korean venture. [3]

In its dealings with the West the Soviet regime obtained its desired "breathing space" by means of a number of small, basicly insignificant, gestures which in any other country would have been meaningless but in Russia reflected a remarkable change of attitude. While paying substantial dividends they cost virtually nothing. By the first week of April 1953 there could be no doubt that a major "peace offensive" was taking shape. One indication was the decided shift away from the previously harsh tone of the central press. An analysis of the February 19–23 and March 19–23 periods indicated a 75 to 80 per cent reduction in material critical of the West. [4] *Pravda* and *Izvestia* even showed a tendency toward more objective reporting, [5] and by late March the provincial press began falling into line with the new pattern. [6] There were numerous other examples. Radio Moscow, for instance, admitted for the first time in years that Germany's defeat in the Second World War resulted from allied cooperation. [7] The "tough" policy toward foreigners in Moscow was relaxed sufficiently to allow Soviet women married to Westerners to leave the country; the British and American Embassies had their eviction notices canceled; Soviet officials became surprisingly

1 *The Economist*, April 4, 1953, p. 15.
2 Boorman, *op. cit.*, p. 17.
3 *The Economist*, April 18, 1953, p. 132.
4 *New York Times*, April 12, 1953, Part 4, p. 5, Harrison Salisbury.
5 *Ibid.*, April 3, 1953, p. 6, Harry Schwartz.
6 *Ibid.*, April 12, 1953, Part 4, p. 5, Harrison Salisbury.
7 *Ibid.*, March 22, 1953, p. 1.

accessable; and seven touring American newspaper editors were granted Soviet visas.

But the road was not entirely a smooth one. Between March 10 and March 14 there were four separate air incidents on the fringes of the Iron Curtain. [1] However, even these provided opportunities for the Soviets to demonstrate their new mood. General V. I. Chuikov, Chairman of the Soviet Control Commission in Berlin, was surprisingly conciliatory in his reply to British protests. He, in fact, offered to confer with them to prevent future "misunderstandings," and these discussions were soon expanded to include American and French representatives. [2]

In another diplomatic move General Chuikov addressed a letter to Dr. J. Wirth, a former pre-Hitler German Chancellor who had supported Communists bids to unite the country, stating that a Four Power conference designed to secure a peace treaty and unify Germany

would be in line with Soviet desires.[3]

Other almost simultaneous Soviet actions were the compromise election of D. Hammarskjöld as the new United Nations Secretary General; Molotov's willingness to intercede on behalf of nine British diplomats and missionaries held by North Korea; and his support of Communist China's offer to exchange prisoners of war. [4]

Almost immediately these had their desired effect upon the West. They brought to a head the problems of forming a coordinated Asian policy; of maintaining and fostering the North Atlantic alliance; and of resisting increasing demands for a slow-down in rearmament. Western diplomats regarded the Soviet shift in foreign policy as a shrewd tactical maneuver,

---

[1] On March 10 two MIG-15's (believed to have been Czech) attacked two American F-84's 15 miles inside West Germany, shooting one down. Two days later a Soviet MIG-15 shot down a British Lincoln bomber in the Berlin air corridor, killing five of the seven crewmen aboard. The same day a British Overseas Airways plane was warned by another MIG-15 that it had strayed from the same corridor. On March 14 a US recognisance RB-50 traded fire with a Soviet MIG-15, according to American officials, 25 miles to the seaward of the Kamchatka Peninsula. (*Facts on File*, XIII, 645, pp. 75 and 81.) It is possible that these resulted from the "alert" orders issued on Stalin's death. *The Observer*, March 15, 1953, p. 1.

[2] *Facts on File*, XIII, 646, p. 81.

[3] *Ibid.*, 648, p. 87.

[4] *Ibid.*, 647, p. 89.

well-timed to split the West while Russia wrestled with her own domestic problems. [1]

The changes initiated by the regime at home were no less dramatic than those introduced abroad. On March 28, 1953, both *Pravda* and *Izvestia* announced a sweeping general amnesty which was to be the first step in a radical transformation of the Soviet legal system. Its provisions freed all short-term prisoners serving five years or less and generally lightened the sentences of all others with the exception of those under detention for counter-revolutionary activities, major crimes against the state, banditry, and premeditated murder. Women with children under ten, expectant mothers, juvenile delinquents up to 18, men over 55 and women over 50, persons suffering from incurable disease, those sentenced for offences committed while they were in an official capacity, and persons charged with specific military offences were all to be freed regardless of the length of their sentences as long as they did not come under the exceptions. All others were to have their sentences reduced by one half and legal proceedings in progress were to be dropped unless a verdict of guilty would mean a sentence of five years or more, in which case it was to be halved. Also the cases of those who had died in prison or had completed their sentences were to be reopened and rehabilitated wherever the evidence indicated a miscarriage of justice. In addition, the amnesty instructed the USSR Ministry of Justice to present to the Council of Ministers within one month appropriate proposals for revision of the basic criminal code and similar reviews were also ordered for the various Republics. [2]

The regime had good reason to issue an amnesty. Its slave labor system was one of the most feared and hated aspects of the Stalin era. (Western estimates of the number under detention as of 1953 ranged from 2 or 3,000,000 to over 20,000,000 while Russian figures implied approximately 3,000,000.) [3] If there was

---

[1] *New York Times*, April 1, 1953, p. 1, Harrison Salisbury.

[2] *Pravda* and *Izvestia*, March 28, 1953, p. 1, Gruliow, *op. cit.*, pp. 258–259. It was not promulgated until December 25, 1958. *Soviet News*, 3976, Dec. 29, 1958, p. 262. Cf. Maurach, "Das Sowjetische Amnestiegesetz," pp. 161–170 for a discussion of the amnesty.

[3] *Report of the Ad Hoc Committee on Forced Labor*, p. 440. This corresponds to the 90,141 men and women in all Russian prisons as of January 1, 1900, and the 298,577 in exile in Siberia in 1897. Berman, *op. cit.*, pp. 1194 and 1197.

to be "disorder and panic" among the people the regime knew that it was most likely to be in protest of the oppressive police measures which had been an everyday feature of Soviet life for so many years. In fact, it was in the slave labor camps themselves that rebellions did actually break out. On May 7, two months after Stalin's death had been announced, uprisings began in the complex of camps located around Norilsk within the Arctic Circle in Siberia. Although they were put down once in May, they broke out again and did not finally subside until August 11, 1953, and only then in the wake of a general massacre. But before this took place similar strikes and rioting developed in Vorkuta during July. [1]

While the amnesty did not put an end to the slave labor system it did modify some of its worst abuses. However, its exact implications were not immediately clear because in the context of the Stalinist tradition it contained a number of important ambiguities. [2] But, if later Soviet official figures are to be given credence, 52 per cent of the implied 3,000,000 under detention when Stalin died were freed as a direct result of its provisions and the remainder had their cases reviewed. [3]

Significantly, the amnesty was issued under the signature of Voroshilov in his recently acquired capacity of Chairman of the Presidium of the USSR Supreme Soviet. It is inconceivable that either Beria or Malenkov would have failed to associate himself with such a widely popular act, had it been possible. The implication, therefore, was that, following the reshuffling of the Secretariat and the unexplained changes presented to the Supreme Soviet, the rival factions were at loggerheads. While there was general agreement that the amnesty should be issued, no individual was strong enough to claim the credit for himself. Thus, in a compromise, dictated by necessity, the announcement was made by the politically impotent Voroshilov.

The next significant development centered around the other prong of the domestic program – the improvement of the population's material well-being. Effective April 1, 1953, the prices of 125 categories of retail products were slashed. These

---

[1] Sulzberger, op. cit., pp. 17–18.
[2] Cf. Gsovski, "New Trend in Soviet Justice?", pp. 25–30.
[3] Berman, op. cit., p. 1195.

ranged in importance from an average ten per cent cut on major food items to between five to 15 per cent reductions on principal clothing items. It was the sixth of its kind since 1947, and more closely resembled the 1950 reduction, which slashed the prices of items in 234 categories from 15 to 30 per cent, than it did the previous year's cut which had included only 48 categories (almost exclusively limited to food). The 1953 reduction covered 40 items of food and liquors; 27 items of textiles and clothing; and 58 other miscellaneous categories which included household utilities, rugs, furniture, sewing machines, building materials, medicines, sporting goods, kerosene, gasoline, and bicycles. [1] Analysis of these price changes indicated that they amounted to roughly an eight per cent reduction in the over-all cost of living. However, the prices of necessities such as food and clothing still remained relatively high in terms of Soviet wages. [2] Also it must be kept in mind that the supply of many of the items affected by the reductions – particularly those in the "miscellaneous categories" – was negligible. In fact, the price cuts drove such basic commodities as potatoes and other vegetables off the market, highlighting the regime's economic difficulties and causing wide discontent.

On the heels of this news came an even more startling development. On April 4 a communiqué, issued in both the major newspapers by the Ministry of Internal Affairs, announced that its investigation of the so-called "Doctors' Plot" had revealed that the accused had been

arrested by the former USSR Ministry of State Security incorrectly, without any lawful basis

and that the

accusations ... [were] false and the documentary sources on which the investigating officials had based ... [them were] without foundation.

It went on to charge that the investigating department of the former MGB had obtained confessions from the arrested doctors

through the use of impermissible means of investigation which are strictly forbidden under Soviet law.

The announcement concluded by declaring that the accused physicians had been exonerated and freed while

[1] *New York Times*, April 1, 1953, p. 1, Harrison Salisbury.
[2] *Ibid.*, April 1, 1953, p. 1, Harry Schwartz.

the persons accused of incorrect conduct of the investigation have been arrested and brought to criminal responsibility,[1]

although the latters' names were not mentioned.

At the same time the Supreme Soviet, in a special action, revoked the Order of Lenin which had been conferred on Dr. L. F. Timashuk for her part in bringing the "plot" to light. [2]

Two days later *Pravda* carried a front page editorial which restated the communiqué and placed the blame squarely at the feet of Ignatyev, the former Minister of State Security, whose appointment to the Secretariat had been announced slightly more than a week before. He was accused of having

displayed political blindness and headlessness

and having become detached

from the people and the Party

so that it was possible for him to have been led astray by M. D. Ryumin, his former Deputy Minister who had headed the investigation section. *Pravda* also sought to saddle the latter with the blame for stirring up "national antagonism," by which it implied it meant the anti-Semitic features of the purges that had been so closely intertwined with the "Doctors' Plot." (However, anti-Semitism was not explicitly repudiated.) [3] The editorial did its best to convince its readers that his actions were counter to the regime's official policy and that injustices were being corrected. He, as well as other MGB officials involved (but not Ignatyev), were reported to have been arrested.

Pravda went on to decry the fact that Ryumin and his associates had

[1] The communiqué listed the names of six other physicians, in addition to the nine originally accused, who had been arrested. They were Profs. V. K. Vasilenko, V. F. Zelenin, B. S. Preobrazhensky, N. A. Popova, V. V. Zakusov, and N. A. Shereshevsky. Although all 15 doctors were cleared, the announcement failed to mention either M. B. Kogan or Ya. G. Etinger by name. This raises the possibility that these two died during the interrogation. *Pravda* and *Izvestia*, April 4, 1953, p. 2, Gruliow, *op. cit.*, p. 259.

[2] *New York Times*, April 4, 1953, p. 1, Harrison Salisbury.

[3] *Pravda*, April 6, 1953, p. 1, Gruliow, *op. cit.*, p. 259. Immediately after the "plot" was repudiated in Moscow, the harsh anti-Semitic persecution in the Satellites was relaxed. Leaders of the various Jewish communities were released and the offices of Jewish groups in Budapest were reopened. (*The Observer*, April 5, 1955, p. 1.) However, it was not completely abandoned as was illustrated by Radio Bratislava's anti-Zionist broadcast on May 15, 1953; Matern's speech in East Germany, May 19, 1953; and the second Slansky trial the same month. Brzezinski, *op. cit.*, p. 243. Cf. Meyer, *op. cit.*, pp. 1–9 for details of continued anti-Semitism in 1953 and 1954.

embarked on gross violation of Soviet law, including outright fabrication of evidence, and dared to mock inviolable rights of Soviet citizens which ... [were] inscribed in ... [the 1936] Constitution,[1]

repeatedly picturing the newly reorganized MVD as the guardian of the individual liberties and freedoms which its MGB predecessor had headlessly trampled underfoot. Obviously, this was more than merely an isolated incident because the editorial went so far as to tell its readers:

The great rights of citizens of the Soviet socialist state are inscribed in the USSR Constitution .... [It] guarantees USSR citizens inviolability of person. Nobody may be arrested without the decision of a court or a state prosecutor .... Nobody will be permitted to violate Soviet law.

[Everyone] ... can work peacefully and confidently, knowing that his civil rights are reliably guarded by Soviet socialist law. The citizen ... may be confident that his rights ... will be solemnly observed and defended by the Soviet government.[2]

The next day the central press carried an one paragraph announcement stating that a plenary session of the Party's Central Committee had removed Ignatyev from the Secretariat but gave no hint of his fate. [3]

BERIA'S BID FOR POWER

All available evidence supports the thesis that this was a major gambit by Beria to strengthen his position and strike down those who had usurped his authority over the secret police and destroyed his control of Georgia and the Caucasus. That he dared to strike directly at Ignatyev in the heart of the Secretariat was in itself a measure of his power since the former secret police minister obviously had strong supporters within the most inner-circles of the regime. In any case, Beria's action seriously threatened the delicate balance which existed in the Presidium since he could only improve his position at the expense of others.

Unaccustomed as Beria must have been in the role of public defender, it was apparently not a reversal of his basic philosophy. He was bent upon repairing his fortunes and probably ultimately seeking to establish himself as the dominant force on the Soviet political scene. (However, it is rather doubtful that he expected

---

[1] *Pravda*, April 6, 1953, p. 1, Gruliow, *op. cit.*, p. 260.
[2] *Ibid.*
[3] *Pravda* and *Izvestia*, April 7, 1953, p. 2, *ibid.*

to be able to rule personally. He was too shrewd a politician not to realize that the Russian people were unlikely to accept two Georgian dictators in a row. More likely he sought to be king-maker for anyone who was amenable to his dictates.) [1] To achieve this he selected the expedient vehicle of defending civil liberties and posing as the champion of the minorities at a time when there probably was general agreement within the regime that some changes were necessary but indecision as to what they should be. As a result, Beria could attack his rivals and establish his protégés in power without too much fear of initial reprisals, because the policies he enunciated struck a responsive cord among the people. In this way he forced his rivals on to the defensive on vital issues with which they were not prepared to cope. [2]

The events in this struggle, which culminated in Beria's arrest in late June 1953, are by no means clear. The pattern was one of purge and counter-purge, but it was impossible to identify with any degree of accuracy the forces behind specific changes. Nevertheless, certain general trends were quite clear. During March and April the governments of the various Republics were reorganized along the lines adopted by the central administration immediately following Stalin's death. In the course of this re-organization the police ministries (the Ministries of State Security and of Internal Affairs) were merged and made directly responsible to the MVD in Moscow. [3] In all but two of the non-Russian Republics the former MGB officials assumed control of the newly merged ministries. The exceptions were Georgia and the Ukraine where men from the central MVD apparatus were established in office. [4] Beginning in April and reaching a cre-scendo at the time of Beria's arrest, officials in at least four Republics – the Ukraine, Georgia, Lithuania, and Latvia – were severely reprimanded for their over-zealous Russification policy and changes strongly favoring the expression of national cultures were instigated. Throughout this period the central press concentrated on the theme of collective leadership and no single individual was given prominence. Presidium members were

[1] Salisbury, *op. cit.*, pp. 176–177.
[2] Brzezinski, *op. cit.*, pp. 158–159.
[3] *New York Times*, April 22, 1953, p. 14.
[4] Tepfers, "The Soviet Political Police Today," p. 44.

mentioned by name only when the news required it, which meant that many issues of *Izvestia*, *Pravda*, and *Trud* did not include Malenkov's name. (Over a period of several weeks Molotov and Mikoyan, because of their dealings with foreign envoys, and Voroshilov, because of the honors bestowed on him as head of the Soviet state, received the greatest publicity.) The most striking example of this new emphasis upon collective leadership was *Pravda's* mid-April editorial, precisely six weeks to the day after Stalin's death. It said in part:

One of the fundamental principles of Party leadership is collectivity in deciding all important problems of Party work.

The principle of collectivity in work means, above all, that decisions adopted by Party committees on all cardinal questions are the fruits of collective discussions. No matter how experienced leaders may be, no matter what their knowledge and ability, they do not possess and they cannot replace the initiative of a whole collective. In any collegium, in any directing collective, there are people who possess diverse experience without relying upon which the leaders cannot make correct decisions and exercise qualified leadership.

Leaders cannot consider criticism of themselves a personal affront. They must be able to accept criticism courageously and show readiness to bend their will to the will of the collective. Without such courage, without the ability to overcome one's vanity and to bend one's will to the will of the collective, there can be no collective leadership.[1]

Following the revelations about the "Doctors' Plot" Beria waited only one week to make his next move – the purging of the Georgian Republic and the restoration of his followers. Before it subsided the top leadership – as well as an unknown number of minor followers – of the Georgian Party and government had been emptied and refilled by men jailed during 1952. [2] The pattern of the purge was highly reminiscent of its week-old predecessor in Moscow. [3] Local Georgian newspapers abruptly ended their praise of Malenkov and switched to a glorification of Beria, whom Radio Tiflis referred to as the "best son of Georgia." [4]

---

[1] *Pravda*, April 16, 1953, as quoted by *News from Behind the Iron Curtain*, "Collective Leadership," p. 23.

[2] Brzezinski, *op. cit.*, p. 159.

[3] The official organ of the Georgian Communist Party, *Zarya Vostoka*, linked the two as part of the same conspiracy. General N. Rukhadze, the Georgian security chief, was accused of having fabricated charges against Beria's followers and with having tried to "inflame the feeling of national enmity [as well as creating] ... provocative affairs about non-existent nationalism."
Zarya Vostoka, April 28, 1953, as quoted by *Ibid*.

[4] Quoted by the *New York Times*, April 17, 1953, p. 10, Harry Schwartz. The

Other Republics, particularly those adjoining Georgia, went through similar convulsions as the Moscow factions vied with each other for control. This resulted in a bewildering rapid turnover of personnel. In Belorussia, for example, five Justice Ministers were named between March and June 1953. [1] The success of Beria's campaign can be gauged by the fact that in at least seven Republics his MVD appointees were removed within three months of his arrest. However, in some Republics, for example Estonia and Latvia, his efforts were apparently checkmated and even reversed. [2] But generally his tide was rising and in Eastern Europe there was speculation among usually well informed Communist officials about a Beria dictatorship. [3]

Along with the purges went an editorial campaign stressing the inviolability of Soviet law. No less a figure than the Soviet Justice Minister P. Gorshenin wrote a special *Pravda* article condemning those who preached racial hatred and promising that they would be properly dealt with under the law. Adding a somewhat ominous note, he promised that his ministry would punish anyone who violated Soviet civil liberties regardless of his post in the state apparatus. [4]

It is difficult to specify at what moment Beria's fortunes reached their pinnacle and reversed themselves. The series of events leading to his downfall were long and complicated, but the evidence suggests that his fate was closely tied to the spread of the purges to the Ukraine, long the domain of Khrushchev, and the active intervention of the Army. In mid-May *Pravda* announced that the Red Banner of Labor, one of the highest Soviet awards, had been given to G. I. Petrovsky, a former head of the Ukrainian government, candidate member of the Politburo, and an Old Bolshevik who had disappeared in June 1938 after having been denounced for "bourgeois nationalism." As is the Soviet custom, the award was made in recognition of his 75th birthday. However, he was actually 76 at the time, indicating that someone in the regime was anxious to make public his

---

extent of this shift was illustrated by the fact that in covering Stalin's funeral *Zarya Vostoka*, only reported Malenkov's speech. Brzezinski, *op. cit.*, p. 243.

[1] *Ibid.*
[2] *Ibid.*, p. 160.
[3] *Ibid.*
[4] *New York Times*, April 17, 1953, p. 3.

rehabilitation despite (or because of) the previous accusations. Diplomatic observers at the time felt it was another important conciliatory move which might be added to the list that could be directly or indirectly attributed to Beria. An interesting feature of Petrovsky's case was that he originally had been purged soon after Khrushchev took control of the Ukrainian Communist Party. [1]

At the same time a strange, and seemingly unrelated, vacillation took place in Soviet policy toward East Germany, which, in effect, canceled itself out. It was related to Beria because his security forces were responsible for its administration. On May 21 P. F. Yudin, editor of the Cominform journal, *For A Lasting Peace, For A People's Democracy*, was appointed Political Adviser to General Chuikov, replacing V. S. Semyonov who returned to Moscow. [2] (Western observers believed that he was a high ranking police official.) [3] On May 28 Semyonov suddenly returned to Berlin at the direction of the Soviet Council of Ministers in the new post of Supreme Commander of the USSR in Germany. Nevertheless, Yudin retained his job. [4] The confusion was multiplied when Army General Chuikov, who had commanded the 62nd Army at Stalingrad and had been Commander-in-Chief, Germany, for five years, was suddenly

transferred to responsible work in the Ministry of Defense. [5]

However, there was obviously more to it than this because as many as 200 leading Soviet officials serving under him were also recalled shortly after he left. On June 13 – still three days before the riots began – *Tägliche Rundschau*, one of the official organs of the East German regime, put part of the blame for the mounting tension on his shoulders when it declared that

the former Soviet Control Commission ... [was] responsible up to a point for mistakes [that had already been] committed.[6]

---

[1] *Ibid.*, May 15, 1953, p. 9, Harry Schwartz. Since his name was not removed from the 1945 edition of the *History of the VKB(b)* (*Short Course*) he apparently was never charged with treason. His biography which appeared in 1955 in the *Bolshaya Sovetskaya Entsiklopediya* claimed that since 1939 he had been Deputy Director of the Museum of the USSR Revolution. Rush, *op. cit.*, p. 100.

[2] *News from Behind the Iron Curtain*, "Chronology For 1953," p. 13.

[3] *New York Times*, June 22, 1953, p. 6, Harry Schwartz.

[4] *News from Behind the Iron Curtain*, *op. cit.*, p. 13.

[5] Quoted by Salisbury, *op. cit.*, p. 189.

[6] *Tägliche Rundschau*, June 13, 1953, as quoted by *The Observer*, June 14, 1953, Richard Löwenthal.

Chuikov's replacement was Colonel General A. A. Grechko, a young Ukrainian who had held the important Kiev command under the guidance of General Konev.

A number of the details of this change in command were especially interesting. Both Konev and Grechko were members of the Ukrainian Communist Party and, despite their positions in the Army, were thought to be Khrushchev's protégés. This marked the first visible occasion when Khrushchev's Party organization had joined hands with the Army to strike down an opponent. Despite the multitude of changes which took place in the spring of 1953 this was the first major one to affect the military, and, interestingly, it was also the second time within less than six months that a change in command had foreshadowed an important political change. [1]

On June 12, in what may have been a reprisal for the removal of General Chuikov, Beria apparently struck deeply into Khrushchev's "private domain" by purging Melnikov from his post as First Secretary of the Ukrainian Communist Party. [2] He was formally charged with having violated the "Leninist-Stalinist nationality policy," particularly in the Western Ukraine (the area acquired from Poland in 1939) where he had placed officials from the Eastern Ukraine in important positions and emphasized the use of Russian in the higher schools. In other words, what had been standard practice under Stalin's Russification program was suddenly a crime. Melnikov was also made the scapegoat for agricultural failures stemming from mismanagement of the collectivized farms. Not only did he loose his post as Secretary but he was removed from the Ukrainian Politburo as well. As if to rub salt into the wound, A. Ye. Korneichuk, a famous Ukrainian poet and playwright, formerly condemned for "bourgeois nationalist" tendencies and other deviations, was elevated to fill the vacancy. Only a short time before he had been named First Deputy Chairman of the Ukrainian Council of Ministers. [3]

[1] Salisbury, op. cit., p. 189.

[2] Melnikov was replaced by A. I. Kirichenko, a native Ukrainian. The Economist, June 20, 1953, p. 825.

[3] New York Times, June 13, 1953, p. 1, Harrison Salisbury, and June 15, 1953, p. 8, Harry Schwartz. Korneichuk had not been completely out of favor before Stalin died. He had been elected to the Central Committee at the Nineteenth Congress and had told the Party gathering of the "debt" the Ukrainians owed Stalin and the Great Russians. (Pravda, Oct. 11, 1952, p. 2, Gruliow, op. cit., p. 175.) Shortly after

As these changes reached a climax, the Berlin riots exploded. No completely satisfactory explanation of their cause has ever been given. Although there can be little doubt that the events which began on June 16, 1953, in Berlin were connected with Beria's arrest only ten days later the precise connection between the two cannot be documented. A number of circumstances surrounding the riots were peculiar. Observers on the scene reported that the first demonstrations had a well-organized appearance. Within three hours after they started, the Politburo of the East German Socialist Unity (Communist) Party issued a long and detailed communiqué granting the demanded repeal of the ten per cent increase in work norms. It appeared so soon and was so carefully worded that it caused one observer to speculate that the government had gotten wind of the demonstrations before they materialized. [1] At the same time the official organ of the East German Communists inflamed the demonstrators by saying that the Party would not grant the concessions. [2] *Pravda's* reaction was also unusual. For the first two days it gave more or less factual accounts of the riots, placing the blame squarely on East German authorities and the Communist Party. It was only on the 18th that it interjected the usual bias, attributing everything to Western "agents." [3]

BERIA'S ARREST AND ITS REPERCUSSIONS

Although Beria's arrest was not publicly announced until July 10, circumstantial evidence indicates that it took place earlier, [4] and June 26 was later officially suggested as the date. [5] However, the momentum of the new nationality program was so

Melnikov's removal V. Bondarchuk was dismissed as the Ukrainian Deputy Premier *New York Times*, June 14, 1953, p. 4.

[1] *New York Times*, June 17, 1953, p. 1, Walter Sulivan.

[2] *Ibid.*, June 23, 1953, p. 8, Harry Schwartz.

[3] *Pravda*, June 18, 1953, as quoted by *Ibid.*, June 18, 1953, p. 8, and Salisbury, *op. cit.*, p. 190. Cf. Contius, "Der 17. Juni in der Sowjetpresse," pp. 269–274 for samples of the Communist press during this period and *Osteuropa*, "Staat und Revolution," pp. 306 for the text of orders issued by the Soviet Commandant in Berlin during the uprising.

[4] *Pravda*, July 10, 1953, p. 1, *Current Digest of the Soviet Press*, V, 24, p. 9. (Hereafter cited as the *Current Digest*.) On June 28 *Pravda* published a list of Soviet officials who had attended the opera, *The Decembrists*, the previous evening. Beria's name was not included. *New York Times*, June 29, 1953, p. 2.

[5] Brzezinski, *op. cit.*, p. 161.

great that between the Berlin riots and Beria's arrest two more
Republics – Lithuania and Latvia – were castigated for failing
to correctly interpret the new emphasis upon national differences. [1] At the same time *Kommunist*, the Party's leading
ideological publication, printed an article by Fedosev attacking
those who sought to hide chauvinism and nationalism under the
banner of patriotism. This was a serious attack upon the predominance of the Great Russians and Great Russian chauvinism
which had suddenly replaced "bourgeois nationalism" as the
enemy that was to be hunted down and destroyed. This important – and previously heretical – position was authoratively
set forth by the same man who only six months before had been
severely criticized for his economic deviations as a former
Bolshevik editor. In a sense, then, the article was also a veiled
attack on Suslov, who had dealt the earlier public castigation and
was currently the second ranking member of the Secretariat. [2]

In the interval between Beria's disappearance from the public
eye and the announcement of his arrest the central press clearly
foreshadowed his fate. On July 4 *Pravda* carried a special editorial
on unity and the combatting of Party careerists. [3] An ominous
Izvestia editorial declared that the Party had

crushed all its enemies who have tried to sow in Party ranks a lack of
confidence in the victory of socialism and subvert the unity of the Party
and by this token to frustrate the building of a socialist society.[4]

When Beria's arrest was officially announced, he was charged
with a host of crimes covering a multitude of the regime's sins.
They included trying to place the MVD in control of both the
government and the Party; using it as a vehicle to personal
power; turning minority groups against each other and encouraging "bourgeois nationalism"; and sabotaging government
efforts to protect civil liberties. He also was made the scapegoat
for the regime's agricultural failures and for good measure he
was said to have been working against the state

and in the interests of foreign capitals

along lines which would have restored capitalism to the USSR.
Pravda went to some lengths to emphasize that the "plotting"

[1] *New York Times*, June 18, 1953, p. 8, and June 28, 1953, p. 16.
[2] *Ibid.*, June 26, 1953, p. 1, Harrison Salisbury, and p. 4, Harry Schwartz.
[3] *Ibid.*, July 11, 1953, p. 5.
[4] *Izvestia* as quoted by the *New York Times*, July 7, 1953, p. 8.

had been nipped in the bud by the remaining Soviet leadership working as a unit. [1] Of these charges, the only one which rang true was that dealing with his personal ambitions.

In the aftermath of the arrest the Party quickly pressed its organization into operation and agitators repeatedly harangued mass meetings on the unity of the Party and government. These were especially numerous in the Republics where Beria's purges had been particularly active. It also reversed the new nationality doctrine which he had introduced. The rapidity with which the regime acted on this point – especially in the Ukraine where the volume of denunciations was heavy – indicates that he had struck a sensitive nerve. For example, the Western Ukranians, who only a month before had been told of the evils of Great Russian chauvinism, were now called upon to once again publicly recognize the "debt" they owed it for their freedom, happiness, and way of life. The Party also felt it necessary to promise a short range improvement in living standards in the Ukraine similar to the program already instigated in the RSFSR among the Great Russians. [2]

Pravda did not stress the international implications of the accusations but laid its heaviest emphasis upon the threat Beria posed to the security of the government. Emphasizing collective leadership, the press called the people to rally around the Party and the government to show that they had not been weakened or divided and also to rid the country of the harmful aspects of Beria's activities. [3] *Pravda's* editorials indicated that the regime's new policy was to follow these general lines:

1) increased anti-capitalist propaganda at home;
2) continued "peace offensive" abroad;
3) purge of Beria's followers;
4) more severe policy toward non-Russian minorities at home; and
5) continued reliance upon the current Five Year plan and the predominance of heavy industry.[4]

[1] *Pravda*, July 10, 1953, p. 1, *Current Digest*, V, 24, p. 9. Interestingly, the regime felt it necessary to repeat these obviously absurd changes in the secret explanation circulated to the Cominform. It also included the additional charges that he had gained control of the Kremlin guard; that he had placed Presidium members under surveillance; that he was a moral degenerate; and that he had fabricated evidence in the "Leningrad affair." (However, there was no explanation as to what this latter was.) Bialer, "I Chose Truth," p. 6.

[2] *New York Times*, July 13, 1953, p. 1, Harrison Salisbury.

[3] *Ibid.*, July 12, 1953, p. 6.

[4] *Pravda*, July 10, 1953, p. 1, *Current Digest*, V, 24, p. 9, and the *New York Times*, July 11, 1953, p. 4, Harry Schwartz.

Interestingly, the press did not use Beria's arrest as an opportunity to enhance the prestige of any particular individual. It merely noted that Malenkov was the one who presented the case to the Central Committee in whose name the official action was taken. However, it did not elaborate on his role. [1]

Beria was apparently brought down by a coalition consisting of the Khrushchev-Malenkov Party organization, the old guard, and the Army. There was no force outside of the Army which could have successfully challenged Beria's MVD organization. [2] More important than the physical participation of the troops (which from all indications was negligible) was the decisive role that the marshals played in the policy-making circles. The fact that they could muster sufficient strength to break their hated enemy, the police, illustrated the growing importance they exerted in the delicate internal balance of power.

The official details of Beria's arrest remain unknown, but the absence of military concentrations or increased security measures in Moscow at the time suggest that it was accomplished quietly and without difficulty. [3] Khrushchev is reported to have told French Senator P. Commin in 1956 that a special session of the Presidium was convened at which Beria was cross-examined and accused of plotting to seize power. After four hours of questioning it was decided that he had to be executed and he was shot on the spot. [4] If this version is correct, then it clarifies one aspect of the Beria case which puzzled Western observers. Once the original wave of denunciations had subsided after his arrest, his name almost totally disappeared from the Soviet press. [5] The appointment of

[1] *New York Times*, July 12, 1953, p. 6.

[2] Western estimates of Beria's strength were vague. They placed the total number of men under his command (counting intelligence and counter-intelligence personnel, frontier guards, uniformed civil police, labor camp guards, and internal security troops) at anywhere from 400,000 to 750,000. The last category included an estimated 14 well-equiped divisions (some mechanized and motorized) as well as a small police air force. *Ibid.*, July 14, 1953, p. 5, Hanson Baldwin.

[3] However, it was later learned that Army units from *outside* the Moscow Military District had been alerted and secretly transported to the capital the night of his arrest. This had been felt necessary because the commander of the Moscow Military District and the Commandants of the Moscow Garrison and the Kremlin Guard were thought to have been in league with Beria. Garthoff, *op. cit.*, p. 22.

[4] *Sotsialisticheskii Vestnik*, XXXVI, 7–8, 1956, p. 146 as quoted by Wolfe, *Khrushchev and Stalin's Ghost*, pp. 316–17.

[5] The appearance of his name in *Sovetskoye Gosudarstvo i Pravo* in early October was the first time it had been used in the press for several weeks. *New York Times*, Oct. 3, 1953, p. 3.

Kruglov, [1] Beria's subordinate, as his successor raises the possibility that Beria's rivals were successful in turning elements of his own police against him. (Kruglov, who had been chief of the MVD since 1946, had been demoted to Deputy Minister in March 1953 when Beria merged both police ministries under his personal direction.)

It makes little difference how Beria actually met his end, since the general pattern of events which developed in the wake of his arrest was not affected. It was as follows: (1) the immediate reversal of his policies, the purging of his followers, and where possible the rehabilitation of his victims; (2) recognition of the increased position of the Army within the Soviet hierarchy; (3) the emasculation of the secret police; and (4) increased emphasis upon collective leadership within the framework of the supremacy of the Party.

The hand of the Soviet Army was clearly visible behind every phase of Beria's destruction and the weakening of his police apparatus. The same Central Committee session which ordered Beria's arrest elevated Marshal Zhukov from candidate status to full membership. [2] At the mass meetings which were held in every military district Zhukov joined with other marshals such as Bulganin, Sokolovsky, Govorov, and S. M. Budyonny, in publicly denouncing Beria and pledging the support of the military to the new government. [3] Significantly, the first of these quoted by the press was one in Tiflis addressed by Army General I. Antonov, the Great Russian Commander of the Trans-Caucasian district who had held his post throughout the turbulence which racked Georgia and the adjoining Republics. [4] However, the Army's influence was not limited merely to making speeches. In Georgia, where Beria's associates were rapidly removed, Army men assumed direct control. Besides General Antonov, a close friend of Marshal Zhukov who retained military command of the area, V. P. Mzhavanadze was made the new Party First Secretary. He had a long service record as both a regular Army man and more recently as chief of its Political Administration in the Ukraine. As a Khrushchev protégé he

---

[1] *Pravda*, Aug. 9, 1953, p. 4, *Current Digest*, V, 35, p. 7.
[2] Salisbury, *op. cit.*, p. 193.
[3] *New York Times*, July 17, 1953, p. 1, Harrison Salisbury.
[4] *Ibid.*, July 16, 1953, p. 8, Harry Schwartz.

personified the new link between the Party and the Army. General A. N. Inauri, a Georgian who had served largely outside the Republic, became the local Minister of the Interior. [1]

The post-Beria wave of purges resulted in a thorough reshuffling of the Party and state apparatus throughout the Soviet Union. Their intensity usually was in direct proportion to Beria's original success. Consequently, the Caucasian Republics, where a bewildering number of changes took place in the successive waves which did not subside until late in the year, were the hardest hit. One of the most important of those to fall by the wayside was Bagirov, Premier of the Azerbaidzhan Republic and a candidate member of the CPSU Presidium. Although at the time of his removal he was not directly linked to Beria's downfall and the newspapers in his Republic had been actively praising Malenkov, his police career had long marked him as the former's close protégé. [2] At the same time some former deposed officials were rehabilitated. For example, Melnikov was made Soviet Ambassador to Rumania. Apparently, his benefactors in the Presidium were not in a position to return him to the Ukraine. Another interesting sidelight to this appointment was the fact that relations between Rumania and the Ukraine had not always been the best – particularly during World War II. [3]

The purges of the MVD itself effectively denuded the Beria apparatus of its leadership. Reported executed with Beria were six of his closest associates: V. M. Merkulov, former Minister of State Control whose arrest was not made public until just before the December trial that officially set Beria's fate; V. G. Dekanozov, formerly MVD Minister for Georgia; B. Z. Kublov, former Deputy Minister of International Affairs for the Soviet Union; S. A. Goglidze, reputedly the MVD "Czar" of Siberia; P. Y. Meshnik, Ukrainian MVD Chief, and L. E. Vlodzimirsky, who headed the investigation department of the central MVD apparatus. (This was the department responsible for such special

---

[1] Salisbury, *op. cit.*, p. 194.

[2] *Ibid.*, July 19, 1953, p. 12, Harrison Salisbury. Not until Bagirov's trial and execution were announced in May 1956 was he officially linked to Beria. (*Bakinsky Rabochy*, May 7, 1955, p. 2, Gruliow (Ed.), *Current Soviet Policies*, II, pp. 216–217.) However, the real reason for his removal may have been the regime's fear of his influence and personal ambitions among Soviet Moslems.

[3] *New York Times*, July 27, 1953, p. 2; July 28, 1953, p. 6; and July 29, 1953, p. 4.

matters as the "Doctors' Plot.") [1] Consequently, those executed included almost every high-ranking Internal Affairs officer in the Soviet Union.[2]

But not only the important officials were affected. The entire organization eventually felt the wrath of the purge, causing a number of important defections among MVD officers in the intelligence service.

Merely the purging of the secret police was not sufficient to satisfy the coalition which brought Beria down. In a series of actions difficult to document the secret police was largely stripped of its power and reduced to a subservient position from which it no longer posed a threat. This was partially accomplished by destroying some of the mystery which surrounded the police. In unprecedented action the MVD was publicly criticized by a few party meetings in Azerbaidzhan, Moldavia, and Leningrad. The speakers demanded that it be brought to heel by responsible Party officials and that the courts strictly observe Soviet law, but such criticism was restricted to the lower police functionaries. [3]

The first part of the MVD's "empire" to be shorn away was the Soviet atomic energy program. Within a few days of Beria's arrest the Ministry of Medium Machine Construction was created apparently to assume this function, and V. A. Malyshev, one of the Soviet Union's top engineers, was placed in charge. [4] During September the "chief legal instrument of terror," the Special Board of the MVD, was abolished by a secret edict. It had been created on November 5, 1934, by a special decree which authorized the secret police (then the NKVD) to sentence persons considered to be "socially dangerous" to labor camps through a secret administrative procedure in which there was no counsel, no right of appeal, and immediate sentencing. [5] After Beria's arrest special military tribunals and civil courts reviewed thousands of cases tried by the MVD and rehabilitated (in many cases posthumously) those who had been unjustly convicted. In the latter half of 1953 the administration of the concentration camps was

---

[1] *Ibid.*, Dec. 24, 1953, p. 4.
[2] *Ibid.*, Dec. 18, 1953, p. 12.
[3] Cf. *Current Digest*, V, 30, p. 16.
[4] *New York Times*, July 17, 1953, p. 1, Harrison Salisbury.
[5] Berman, *op. cit.*, p. 1192.

taken out of the hands of the MVD and given to the Ministry of Justice which instigated important changes designed to alleviate some of their worst features. [1]

Various communiqués from the state administration seemed to indicate that in other changes regular Army troops replaced MVD forces guarding ammunition dumps, arms factories, railroads, and airports. Marshal Bulganin's order-of-the-day on September 5 addressed to the Frontier and Internal Security troops (formerly under MVD control) suggested that they also had been transferred to the jurisdiction of the Ministry of Defense. [2]

By the end of 1953 Western intelligence officials believed that the MVD's "economic section" had been disbanded and its major construction and economic projects carried out by slave labor had either been abandoned or transferred to other ministries. [3] This coincided with the reappearance of Aristov, a former Party Secretary and Presidium member in the short-lived 1952 reorganization, in an important government post in the Khabarovsk region, which had been virtually the private domain of the MVD because of its concentration camps and economic enterprises. It was generally assumed that his presence as well as the reorganization of the important Kolyma gold producing area into the separate Magadan *Oblast* amounted to a reassertion of government control in vital areas formerly under police jurisdiction. [4] (Despite these changes at the top there was still little visible evidence in the remote parts of Siberia during the fall of 1953 that MVD control had diminished in the slightest since Stalin's death. In fact, unlike the Moscow area where it had ceased to operate as openly as in the past, in the hinterland it made no pretence of hiding its activities.) [5]

The Party attacked the position of the police in still another way. In September 1953 as a part of an accelerated agricultural program it radically revamped the Machine-Tractor Stations and thousands of Party officials were ordered into the countryside to improve the regime's hold on the peasants. Prior to this re-

---

[1] *Ibid.*, pp. 1192 and 1198.
[2] Fainsod, "The Soviet Union since Stalin," p. 3.
[3] *New York Times*, Jan. 11, 1954, p. 3, C. L. Sulzberger.
[4] *Ibid.*, Dec. 20, 1953, p. 19, William Ryan.
[5] Salisbury, *op. cit.*, pp. 198–217.

THE POST-STALIN INTERREGNUM 65

organization the MTS had been the hub of police authority in the country, but under the new program MVD officials were replaced by Party cadres as the chief instrument of control. [1]

But the importance of the destruction of the MVD was not limited to the Soviet Union. It had highly significant implications in the Satellites where Communism maintained its tight reign on reluctant peoples through a police network which was ultimately directed from Moscow. Beria's liquidation and the curtailment of police powers in the USSR lead to widespread demoralization of police officials throughout Eastern Europe. As a result a primary instrument of control in the Satellites was seriously undermined. [2]

It also forced the Soviet regime to completely revamp its day-to-day relationships with its Eastern European counterparts. At the height of police power Moscow's decisions and directives were communicated through the hoard of Soviet "advisers" attached to the Satellite police ministries rather than through diplomatic or Party channels. A high percentage of these "advisers" were recalled to Moscow after Beria's arrest and liquidated in the general "cleansing" of the police apparatus. Consequently, the regime's contacts with the Satellites were shifted more and more to the level of official relations with the local leaders through normal diplomatic and Party channels. As a result Eastern European leaders gained a trifle more elbow room in which to implement the "general line" in the light of their own judgement and local conditions. [3]

As the fortunes of the secret police declined, those of the Army rose. After Beria's demise it replaced police officials in at least two key areas: (1) the Republic of Georgia and (2) the all-important Kremlin guard. [4] In this latter instance Major General A. I. Vedenin replaced Lieutenant General N. K. Spiridonov. About the same time important Army commanders in the Moscow area thought to have been in league with Beria were also deposed. Major General I. S. Kolesnikov replaced Lieutenant General K. R. Sinilov as commander of the Moscow City garrison.

---

[1] *New York Times*, Dec. 20, 1953, p. 19, William Ryan.
[2] Brzezinski, "Ideology and Power: Crisis in the Soviet Bloc," p. 12.
[3] *The Observer*, Jan. 16, 1955, p. 5, Richard Löwenthal.
[4] Traditionally, Stalin had kept the police and the Army in check by dividing responsibility for controlling the important Moscow garrison. Dinerstein, *op. cit.*, p. 5.

Colonel General P. A. Artemev, Commandant of the Moscow Military District disappeared and Colonel General Moskalenko replaced him. [1] Also during the six months between Beria's arrest and the announcement of his execution important promotions were made among ranking officers in the Navy, Air Force, artillery, tank corps, and the office of the Deputy Chief of Staff. [2]

By the end of 1953 Kruglov's name began to appear farther and farther down the official lists which indicated the relative position of the various members of the Soviet hierarchy. Western officials who knew him described him as a "typical 'flatfoot' " with little interest in politics. [3]

The final step in this process came on March 13, 1954, when, in a general subdivision of ministries, the police powers were once again divided along traditional lines. However, this time there was an important difference. The Ministry of Internal Affairs (MVD) retained its ministerial status, but the other half was formed into the Committee of State Security (KGB). Although its head, Colonel General I. A. Serov, a highly experienced police official who was believed to be Khrushchev's protégé, enjoyed a position of cabinet rank his organization was made responsible to the Council of Ministers. [4]

In considering these actions taken by the police after Beria's arrest it must be remembered that they did not destroy its effectiveness as an instrument for controlling the Russian people. Rather they appeared to be designed primarily

to forestall any individual leader from gaining personal control of the police . . . and to deter the police agencies themselves from exercising unchecked power.[1]

---

[1] *New York Times*, Nov. 16, 1953, p. 3, Harry Schwartz. Interestingly, Moskalenko was virtually unknown in 1952, but he was promoted in 1953 and 1955 and the following year made a member of the Central Committee. He was considered to be a Khrushchev supporter. Garthoff, "The Military in Soviet Politics," p. 47.

[2] Colonel General P. F. Zhigarev, head of the Air Force, promoted to full marshal; General M. I. Nedelin was made Marshal of Artillery; Colonel General M. S. Malinin, Deputy Chief of Staff, promoted to full general; and Admiral V. A. Fokin replaced Admiral A. G. Golovko, as Naval Chief of Staff. Also Colonel General A. I. Radzievsky replaced Marshal S. I. Bogdanov. (*New York Times*, Dec. 24, 1953, Harry Schwartz.) In all, ten generals and admirals received promotions during the three months following Beria's arrest. Garthoff, *Soviet Strategy in the Nuclear Age*, p. 22.

[3] Salisbury, *op. cit.*, p. 244.

[4] In the subdivision of ministries the KGB was the only one given this special status. (*New York Times*, April 28, 1954, p. 8, Harrison Salisbury.) The following August the Republic KGB heads were made members of their respective Council of Ministers.

Beria's official end illustrated better than anything else the new relationship which existed between the Party and the Army. As the months dragged on and his name disappeared from the press, diplomatic observers became convinced that the regime would merely announce that his execution had taken place. However, in November Marshal Zhukov made his famous toast to "Justice" which was widely interpreted as a public nudge for the Party to end the "Beria Affair." [2] Six weeks later it was announced that the former secret police chief and six of his associates had been tried, convicted, and executed by a tribunal meeting in secret session which included ranking military officers. [3] Marshal Konev, one of the "victims" of the original "Doctors' Plot," served as the tribunal's chairman. During Beria's greatest period of success his name did not appear in the Soviet press which suggested that he was out of favor. [4] (His reappearance in October coincides with Khrushchev's public emergence as a leading figure. Konev was known to have been one of his protégés.)

That this announcement came at the moment it did was an indication of the military's strength. The regime's foreign policy was directed towards enlarging the existing differences among the Western powers so that they could not present a united front at the January Four Power Foreign Ministers' Conference. News of Beria's execution undid much of this, driving the Western Big Three into each others arms on the eve of the conference. Apparently, in this instance the Party was forced to bow to the will of the Army at the expense of its foreign policy.

A few days later another symbolic gesture to the Army was the unveiling of a bronze bust of Marshal Zhukov in his home village as the first public tribute of its kind since he had been "exiled" by

[1] "The Soviet Police System," *Notes – Soviet Affairs*, 172, May 13, 1955, p. 1. (Hereafter referred to by number.)

[2] Salisbury, *op. cit.*, p. 195.

[3] His judges were Marshal Konev, chairman; Lieutenant General E. I. Zeidin, deputy chairman; Colonel General Moskalenko; N. A. Mikhailov, Secretary of the Moscow Oblast; M. I. Kushava, Chairman of the Georgian Council of Trade Unions; Shvernik, head of the Soviet Trade Unions; L. A. Gromov, Chairman of the Moscow City Court; and K. F. Lunev, First Deputy Minister of Internal Affairs. Beria's conviction was illegal because he was tried in secret by a bench of judges which violated the provisions of Soviet law. *New York Times*, Dec. 24, 1953, p. 1, and Dec. 25, 1954, p. 3, Harrison Salisbury; and Gsovski, *op. cit.*, p. 16.

[4] *New York Times*, Dec. 24, 1953, p. 1, Harry Schwartz.

Stalin after World War II. [1] Also when the 1954 Supreme Soviet was elected it contained two more military delegates than before. [2] For the most part the Army was content to exert its influence behind the scenes and not demand a public role except on those rare occasions, such as Zhukov's November toast, when differences could not be resolved. Within the Ministry of Defense a triumvirate of marshals – Zhukov, Sokolovsky, and Vasilensky – put forth the Army's case. The prominence of Fleet Admiral Kuznetsov, a firm believer in a strong Navy, after the unification of the service ministries indicated that apparently the Navy's position had been strengthened rather than weakened. [3] Despite Bulganin's presence as Minister of Defense the real power seemed to rest more and more with Marshal Zhukov.

In employing this new-found power it was believed that the conservative and moderate points of view dominated the thinking of Soviet marshals and that they exercized a restraining influence which stressed the adoption of a realistic approach toward the West, particularly in regard to its tremendous industrial advantage and the acute Russian agricultural crisis. They were, therefore, believed to have advised the regime to reduce the number of areas of friction between East and West which might touch off a major war until this imbalance had been corrected. They recognized that the revolutionary potential in Europe no longer existed and that the concentrated Western build-up made direct aggression unfeasible. In regard to other Communist countries they were thought to have desired the retention of tight control over the Eastern European Satellites which guarded the traditional invasion route and to have pressed for the consolidation of the Sino-Soviet alliance, particularly in regard to the coordination of the two countries' military forces. This view of foreign policy – which was attributed personally to Marshal Zhukov – had a number of significant domestic implications. It was felt that the professional Soviet military men had made the

[1] Salisbury, op. cit., p. 196.

[2] While this could legally be explained as representation of Soviet troops stationed abroad – as provided by the 1945 decree – there were already 60 military men in the Supreme Soviet representing civilian constituencies. ("The Army in the New Soviet 'Parliament', " BBC, March 23, 1954.) Interestingly, Shtemenko, the former Chief of Staff, was the only commander of a military district not re-elected in 1954. Cf. Meissner, op. cit., pp. 287–289 for the names of the 74 military men elected in 1954.

[3] New York Times, July 26, 1953, p. 10, Hanson Baldwin.

rapid development of heavy industry, the improvement of transportation and communication facilities, the training of thousands of skilled technicians, and the solution of the agricultural crisis the minimum conditions to be satisfied before the USSR could realistically think of becoming involved in a major conflict with the West. [1]

With the liquidation of Beria (for all practical purposes in late June) a new period in the post-Stalin era began. The power of the secret police had been broken by a coalition which ruled through a truly collective but uneasy leadership held together by mutual fear and the desire for survival. Since none of the rival factions held a dominating edge the leadership was plagued by inherent instability. Momentarily, Malenkov gave the impression of being the strongest of the surviving rivals since the Army showed no signs of Bonapartism. However, Khrushchev was rising rapidly as his principal rival. In retrospect, Beria's destruction probably injured Malenkov more than helping him because it more sharply exposed his fundamental weakness of having no direct control over a power bloc. [2] Although technically the police were made subordinate to the bureaucracy, their curbing was really a major victory for Khrushchev because it reasserted the position of the Party as the ultimate authority. By bringing the police to heel and controlling the Army through the Political Administration it held in check the two elements which could produce a potential *coup*.

[1] *Ibid.*, Nov. 21, 1953, p. 1, Drew Middleton.
[2] For the view that the creation of the KGB improved Malenkov's position *vis-à-vis* Khrushchev cf. Meissner, *op. cit.*, pp. 284–285.

CHAPTER III

THE NEW FOREIGN AND DOMESTIC POLICIES

THE END OF THE INTERREGNUM

Beria's removal in June 1953 brought to an end the post-Stalin interregnum and paved the way for the introduction of the new regime's own policies. Although the first five months following the dictator's demise had witnessed important changes both at home and abroad, these were essentially stop-gap measures intended only to give the regime a breathing-space. With the exception of the initial review immediately following Stalin's death, signs of a comprehensive policy re-evaluation did not appear until the late spring and early summer. (Interestingly, they coincided with the concerted effort to move against Beria.)

The concrete program which then emerged was made public in a series of speeches, decrees, and documents during the summer and fall of 1953. The rationale for the regime's authority as well as the fundamental direction of both its domestic and foreign programs was set forth on the Communist Party's 50th anniversary in late July by the publication of a new version of the Party's history. A few days later, speaking before the August session of the Supreme Soviet, Malenkov delivered a remarkably candid survey of the regime's economic weaknesses and sketched the general outline of how they were to be rectified. A month later Khrushchev added more details of the extent of the agricultural crisis in a major report to the Party's Central Committee. This was followed by important policy statements by Mikoyan as Minister of Trade; Kosygin, the Minister of Manufactured Consumers' Goods Industry; and V. P. Zotov, Minister of Food Industry. The recommendations that these officials made were translated into seven basic government decrees during September and October. [1] This comprehensive reappraisal sought to deal realisticly with three major areas: (1) the development of a

[1] Cf. Volin, "The Malenkov-Khrushchev New Economic Policy," p. 188.

flexible foreign policy having the same goals but employing more imaginative techniques; (2) the maintenance of popular support through improved living standards, especially for the middle and upper classes; and (3) the solution of a nearly catastrophic agricultural crisis within the framework of collectivization.

This did not mean that the regime was striking out in a completely new direction, rather that the policies of the previous five months were being coordinated into an over-all blueprint at a time when stop-gap measures no longer satisfied either the immediate or long-term need. This can be seen by glancing at a few of the things which had transpired while Beria's bid for power held the greater share of attention.

During the spring of 1953 when the rigid economic policies in the Satellites were being relaxed under pressure from the discontented workers, the Soviet regime increased the amount of consumers' goods available to its own people. [1] There were two reasons for this action. Besides desiring to increase the already meager supply, it had to replace the stocks which were depleted by a buying scare which swept the Soviet Union in late June with rumors that the ruble was to be devaluated. (In December 1947 devaluation had seriously hurt most of the population because only bank deposits were exchanged at par while currency – the traditional form of savings – was reissued at the rate of ten to one.) To prevent panic Zverev, Soviet Finance Minister, took the previously unheard of step of reassuring the people that their money was sound. [2] Also in June the regime reduced the annual forced "loan" by half. This reduced the workers' contribution from one month's salary to roughly two weeks' pay. [3]

Soviet diplomatic maneuvers also reopened a number of questions which had been effectively shelved by Stalin's insistence upon a rigid foreign policy. Nations along the entire perimeter of the Soviet empire were affected in one way or another by the unfreezing of the Russian Foreign Ministry. The

---

[1] Symbolically, Moscow's new major department store, *Glavny's Universalni Magazine (GUM)*, was opened the day Beria's arrest was announced. *New York Times (Int. Ed.)*, Jan. 28, 1956, p. 4, C. L. Sulzberger.

[2] *Ibid.*, July 22, 1953, p. 7, Eddie Gilmore.

[3] *Ibid.*, June 22, 1953, p. 5.

ideological basis for this new course was set out in *Kommunist* when it said that

for the quick and multilateral development of the Soviet state, peace is necessary, because only in a condition of peace is it possible with the rapidity that is desirable ... to go forward with the cause of the construction of Communism in the USSR.

But it emphasized that this policy in no way meant an abandonment of the

moral and political support to the liberation movement in colonial countries.

nor did it alter the belief that capitalism would die of its own accord. [1]

President Eisenhower's speech in April calling upon the USSR for deeds rather than words provided the regime with one of its earliest opportunities to illustrate its mood. Originally the central press gave it wide coverage, including a liberal number of quotations, but nine days later both *Pravda* and *Izvestia* surprised the world by printing the full text. The translation was accurate and retained all his critical remarks about the USSR. In addition, both newspapers published a long editorial, setting forth Soviet reaction. [2] Although the reply, which covered *Pravda's* entire front page, was critical of American policy and personally attacked Secretary of State J. F. Dulles, its general tone was considerably more moderate than in the past and it lacked the venomous clichés which normally punctuated its editorial comment on the United States. It chided Eisenhower for not heeding his own advice about words and deeds and deplored the fact that he had established a number of conditions. However, it concluded by saying that the Soviet government was ready

for a serious business-like discussion of the respective problems, both by way of direct talks and also, whenever appropriate, within the framework of the United Nations.

To indicate that this was to be taken seriously it also added that

the Soviet leaders ... did not tie up their appeals for the peaceful settlement of international problems with any preliminary demands.[3]

This general line was followed up in a number of ways: the

---

[1] *Kommunist* as quoted by *ibid.*, May 7, 1953, p. 14, Harrison Salisbury.
[2] *Ibid.*, April 25 and 26, 1953, p. 1, Harrison Salisbury.
[3] *Pravda*, April 25, 1953, *Soviet News*, 2786, May 2, 1953, p. 4.

May Day celebration emphasized strength but refrained from name-calling; [1] Molotov told a Soviet Peace Congress that the time was right for a Five Power peace pact; [2] and *Pravda* said that if a truce in Korea was possible then one in the Cold War was also possible. [3] But at the same time there were dissident notes. Poland and Czechoslovakia increased their military budgets; Hungary enlarged its army; and Rumania talked of the dangers of war. The most contradictory event was the Communist inspired and equiped invasion of Laos (which soon was either called off or brought to an end by the monsoons.) [4] On such crucial issues as the unification of Germany and an Austrian State Treaty Moscow remained as firm as ever. Although it welcomed Churchill's proposals for a high-level Four Power conference and agreed that the German question was the crucial issue, it rejected the Western idea of demonstrating its good faith. [5] However, the transfer of Soviet control in both Germany and Austria from military to civil authorities indicated that the door was not entirely closed. [6]

Also during the late spring and early summer of 1953 Soviet diplomacy became active in the Balkans and the Middle East where it re-established diplomatic relations with Greece, Yugoslavia, [7] and Israel and renounced all its territorial claims to Kars, Ardahara, and Artvin in Eastern Turkey which it had maintained since the end of World War II. The USSR also dropped its demands for Soviet bases in Turkey and offered to negotiate revision of the vital Montreux Convention governing use of the Dardanelles. These latter concessions were claims which could never have been obtained except at the price of war. [8]

The Soviets likewise began to utilize economic diplomacy on a

---

[1] *New York Times*, May 2, 1953, p. 1, Harrison Salisbury.

[2] *Ibid.*, April 28, 1953, p. 1.

[3] *Pravda*, May 1, 1953, as quoted by *ibid.*, May 1, 1953, p. 3.

[4] *Ibid.*, May 3, 1953, Part 4, p. 3, C. L. Sulzberger.

[5] *Ibid.*, May 24 and 25, 1953, p. 1, Harrison Salisbury.

[6] *Ibid.*, June 7, 1953, p. 30.

[7] In 1957 B. Morros, an American counter-spy, reported that a plot to assassinate Marshal Tito on March 28, 1953, had been temporarily called off as a result of Stalin's death and finally canceled the following May 4 only minutes before it was to be put into operation. *Ibid. (Int. Ed.)*, Nov. 26, 1957, p. 3.

[8] *Ibid.*, June 12, 1953, p. 4, C. L. Sulzberger, and July 21, 1953, p. 1, Dana Adams Schmidt.

much wider scale. In the past they had made vague offers of economic assistance which never materialized, but during July Moscow extended extensive credits to Argentine, the first ever granted to a country outside the Communist orbit. It also offered for sale Soviet equipment and precision instruments which it and Peking were trying to buy elsewhere from the West. [1] The same month the regime made its first contribution (4,000,000 rubles) to the United Nations Technical Assistance Fund [2] and continued a concentrated trade drive which resulted in important treaties with several countries outside the Communist world. [3] Cordial negotiations replaced the usual haggling and the Soviets dropped their usual insistence upon the West abandoning its economic embargo. [4] In short, there could be no doubt in the months following Stalin's death that the USSR had rediscovered the advantages of "ruble diplomacy."

Although Malenkov's name was most often associated with the pronouncement of the regime's new program it bore the imprint of a collective effort. The Party Manifesto, coming as it did after Beria's arrest, emphatically accented this point. It provided the rationale for the principle of collective leadership, crediting the Party and not Stalin's genius with the major accomplishments of the Soviet regime. In fact, it openly condemned the "cult of the individual." In the context of the Manifesto the new regime was merely acting on behalf of the Party. (Interestingly, the Manifesto was issued under the signature of the

Department of Propaganda and Agitation of the Central Committee of the Communist Party and the Institute of Marx-Engels-Lenin-Stalin

and no living individual was mentioned in its text.) Besides stressing collective leadership the Manifesto reaffirmed in almost exactly the same words used by Malenkov at Stalin's funeral (without giving their source) the domestic program of increasing the material welfare of the people and a foreign policy based upon peaceful co-existence. [5]

[1] *The Economist*, July 11, 1953, p. 93.
[2] *New York Times*, July 16, 1953, p. 1, Michael Hoffman. The Soviet offer was soon followed by a similar one from Poland. *The Economist*, July 25, 1953, p. 249.
[3] Argentina, Egypt, France, Iran, Japan, the Netherlands, and Sweden. Similar treaties were signed with Albania, Bulgaria, Communist China, Hungary, and Poland. *New York Times*, April 26, 1953, p. 25, and June 14, 1953, Part 4, p. 3, Harry Schwartz.
[4] *Ibid.*, July 22, 1953, Michael L. Hoffman.
[5] Cf. *Fiftieth Anniversary of the Communist Party of the Soviet Union: 1903–1953*, pp. 1–39.

THE MALENKOV-KHRUSHCHEV ECONOMIC PROGRAM

These were the principles which formed the basis of Malenkov's two hour address to the August 8, 1953, session of the Supreme Soviet. In it he departed from custom and presented a surprisingly frank analysis of the short-comings of the Soviet economy, [1] not hesitating to admit that the development of heavy industry had been achieved at the expense of the nation's standard of living. The remedies he proposed appeared to be designed to attract the widest possible political support for the regime while at the same time introducing a moderate degree of economic balance which had been lacking under Stalin. One of their common characteristics was the presence of incentives for better performance. He tacitly implied that

the revolutionary impetus which had formerly been counted upon to spur unusual individual effort in the economic sphere could no longer be considered an effective stimulus and that the regime could now expect from management, labor, and the peasantry only a labor imput commensurate with the material benefits provided by the government.[2]

It would be a serious mistake to consider Malenkov's proposals a basic deviation from traditional Soviet economic policy. He carefully made this clear in almost the opening paragraph of his speech when he reaffirmed with vigor that:

We shall in every way continue to develop heavy industry ... and to develop and perfect our transportation system. We must always remember that heavy industry is the basis of our socialist economy, because without ... [its] development it is impossible to ensure the future development of light industry, the growth of the productive forces of agriculture, and the strengthening of the defensive power of our country.[3]

However, the regime astutely saw that through a slight modification of its investment policy it could introduce changes in the standard of living which, under existing conditions in the Soviet Union, would appear to be substantial while not basicly affecting the growth of heavy industry. For example, a ten per cent cut in the funds normally set aside for heavy industry could mean the doubling of capital investment in light industry. A similar 13 per cent in the reduction of military expenditures could make it

---

[1] It would be necessary to go back to the New Economic Policy of the early 1920's to find a comparable public admission of failure.
[2] Herman, "Soviet Economic Policy since stalin," p. 10.
[3] *Soviet News*, 2822, Aug. 12, 1953, p. 2.

possible to increase the pay of every employed worker by two weeks salary. Or an even smaller reduction of ten per cent could mean a 50 per cent increase in the appropriation for housing. [1]

By the time Malenkov spoke the regime had already cut prices and increased the workers' annual take-home pay by the equivalent of two weeks salary. Therefore, the most immediate problem was to supply the economy with consumers' goods to meet the greatly increased demand. Originally, the regime had dipped into its large stockpiles and undertaken programs to step up imports. However, these were stop-gap measures and could not be continued indefinitely. For this reason Malenkov's emphasis in August was upon increasing their domestic production. Within "the next two or three years" he promised his audience "a sharp advance" in the domestic production of the basic items of consumption.

Since it was possible to fulfill these promises only through the cooperation of the agricultural sector of the economy which provided a substantial portion of the necessary raw materials, Malenkov spoke with equal candor about the failure of the peasants to meet the regime's needs. He singled out the livestock industry and the producers of vegetables and potatoes for special criticism. Here too, he offered a program of increased material incentives in the form of higher government prices for forced deliveries and more effective disposal of surpluses. He also supported tax relief designed to encourage the private ownership of livestock and promised improvement of technical service offered by the Machine-Tractor Stations. However, Malenkov emphasized that all of these remedies were to be fitted into the framework of the collective farm system which was to remain basicly untouched.

Equally important were his promised reorganization and expansion of the internal trade network, which would have responsibility for the distribution of the promised increase in consumers' goods, and the allocation of a higher priority to badly needed construction. [2]

By abandoning the hypocritical position maintained during Stalin's lifetime for a frank analysis of economic realities the

[1] Herman, *op. cit.*, pp. 8–9.
[2] *Soviet News*, 2822, Aug. 12, 1953, pp. 3–4.

regime lost very little because the enumerated failures certainly came as no surprise to the average Russian. Malenkov's speech was carefully written to exploit vague hopes without setting specific goals. The major exception was the time-limit of "the next two or three years" in which the changes were to be made. He carefully cast the regime in the role of servant of the people and repeatedly spoke of the Party's "duty" and "obligations" to the nation, using such phrases as "the Soviet people are entitled to demand" in his attempt to associate the government with popular sentiment.

The second half of Malenkov's speech dealt with foreign policy and was radically different in tone. He spoke confidently, listing no failures, as he recalled the various steps the Soviets had taken after Stalin's death to reduce world tension. (Although he was probably speaking primarily for foreign consumption, he did not overlook his domestic audience.) His dominant theme was the peaceful intentions of the Soviet Union, but he made it clear – especially when he quietly announced that the USSR had broken America's monopoly in the development of hydrogen weapons – that Moscow planned to continue strengthening its military might and was prepared to thwart any aggressors. Although he chided the United States for its foreign policy his speech was not belligerent and did not contain the clichés that had been typical of the worst phases of the Cold War. In fact, his reiteration of his March declaration that there were

no outstanding issues in dispute which could not be settled in a peaceful way on the basis of mutual agreement [1]

and his insistence that co-existence and improved international business relations were the regime's goal set the tone for his remarks. Mentioning nearly every country on the USSR's perimeter – as well as others – he indicated that the new flexible Russian foreign policy had something to offer to nearly everyone. He sought to allay any remaining fears by proclaiming that:

The Soviet Union has no territorial claims against any state whatsoever, including any of its neighbors .... It is the inviolable principle of our foreign policy to respect the national freedom and sovereignty of any country, large or small. It is obvious that the difference in the social and economic system in our country and in some neighboring states cannot

[1] *Soviet News*, 2823, Aug. 13, 1953, p. 2.

serve as an obstacle to the strengthening of friendly relations among them.[1]

On fundamental issues he spelled out Soviet policy for the future. The regime approved the Korean armistice and felt that it could be the basis for a "normalization" of the relations among all countries of the Far East, except that the American rearmament of Japan provided a serious obstacle. He proposed Big Power negotiations to settle the outstanding international problems, including disarmament, but he warned that the West had to abandon its "prejudiced attitude" toward a Five Power peace pact and recognize Communist China's right to membership in the United Nations. He made it clearly evident that in Europe one of Russia's chief goals was the destruction of the proposed European Defense Community and that while the Soviets considered the settlement of the German question one of the first magnitude their price continued to be neutralization. Malenkov also hinted that the fate of an Austrian State Treaty hinged on the solution of Germany's status. [2]

The regime's 1953 budget, which was also presented to the same Supreme Soviet session, shed a little light on the extent of the anticipated economic changes. However, for the most part the Soviet practice of presenting only selected figures with a minimum of explanation left a number of questions unanswered. It re-emphasized that despite major concessions to the consumer, heavy industry would continue to receive priority. Nevertheless, the reduction of the turnover tax to less than one half of the total revenue (it had been between 60–65 per cent), approximately a 25 per cent increase in the expenditure for housing, and the radical revision of the agricultural tax favoring the peasants were all important changes from the past. (The reduction of the agricultural tax was both an incentive to increase production and a move to bring the tax structure into line with the much lower income the peasants received as a result of the radical price cuts announced the previous spring.) Despite a three per cent reduction (which could easily have been accounted for by these same price cuts) military expenditures in the new budget were still roughly 40 per cent higher than they had been before the

[1] *Ibid.*
[2] *Ibid.*, pp. 1–3.

Korean War. At the same time there were important appropriations which were not accounted for and may have also covered military or related expenditures. [1]

Although it was not until October that Mikoyan, as Minister of Trade, spelled out in precise details the extent of the planned increase in the production of consumers' goods, Khruschev dealt with the agricultural crisis in early September. His report to the Central Committee was even more candid than Malenkov's, giving the outside world one of its rare glimpses at the true state of Soviet agriculture. The fact that Khrushchev delivered this critical analysis of agricultural policy was symbolic of his rapidly increasing importance within the regime. After Stalin's death he had worked unobtrusively behind the scenes consolidating his position and by August 1953 his name began appearing third in the Soviet hierarchy, jumping over Voroshilov. [2] Soon after he had delivered his agricultural report Radio Moscow announced still another advancement, his appointment as First Secretary of the CPSU. [3] This was particularly significant because it apparently had a direct bearing upon the continuing struggle for power within the Presidium. From March until September Khrushchev had been the senior member of the Secretariat without any special title. After Stalin's death neither Malenkov nor Khrushchev had assumed his title of General Secretary which was the one traditionally held by the majority of leaders of Communist Parties throughout the world. The title of First Secretary had existed only in the lower levels of the Soviet Party organization and had never been applied to the Secretariat of the CPSU. [4] Apparently, its use in connection with Khrushchev's name was a compromise which recognized his growing prominence without transfering to him the special distinctions that were inescapable with the title General Secretary.

[1] *NewYork Times*, Aug. 6, 1953, p. 1, Harrison Salisbury, and p. 6, Harry Schwartz.
[2] *Ibid.*, Aug. 29, 1953, p. 3, Harry Schwartz.
[3] *Ibid.*, Sept. 13, 1953, p. 1.
[4] The title of First Secretary was first applied to the head of a national Communist Party on July 2, 1953, in Hungary when M. Rákosi gave his post of Chairman of the Council of Ministers to I. Nagy and exchanged the title "General Secretary of the Central Committee" for "First Secretary of the Central Committee." Comparable changes took place in Poland, East Germany, Rumania, Bulgaria, and Albania. In Czechoslovakia the senior Party Secretary, who previously had had no title, became First Secretary only a few days before Khrushchev adopted the title. Rush, *op. cit.*, pp. 10 and 99.

The facts which Khrushchev had to face in presenting a realistic report to the Central Committee were not pleasant. They amounted to an admission that the Soviet pattern of collectivization had failed miserably. However, almost in his opening sentence he reassured his audience that the regime had no intention of abandoning it. [1] While industrial production had more than doubled since 1940 there had been only a 40 per cent increase in agricultural output. [2] He even cast doubt on the statement Malenkov had made at the Nineteenth Party Congress the previous year that the grain shortage had been permanently solved when he revealed that the regime was

in general satisfying the country's need for grain crops, in the sense that our country is supplied with bread ... [but] an obvious discrepancy between the population's growing needs [for bread, meat, dairy products, vegetables, etc.] and the production level ... [had] been formed during the past years. [3]

What Khrushchev meant by the "obvious discrepancy" was fully illustrated by his statistics. The crop picture was not uniform. The acreage sown in flax and hemp in 1953 failed to equal the prewar level and even showed a downward trend after 1950. At the same time cotton, sugar beets, and wheat acreages were above the 1939 levels. The so-called "industrial crops" – especially fodder crops including the sown grasses (tame hay) – showed a gain, but the total grain acreage fell. (Because of low yields the statistics on fodder crop acreage were actually deceiving.) [4]

---

[1] "The collective farm system created under the leadership of the Communist Party has a decided advantage over any private-ownership agricultural system, whether small-or-large-scale capitalist farming."
Pravda and *Izvestia*, Sept. 15, 1953, p. 1–6, *Current Digest*, V, 39, p. 11.
[2] "Even this modest increase seem[ed] to be overoptimistic." Volin, *op. cit.*, p. 197.
[3] *Pravda* and *Izvestia*, Sept. 15, 1953, pp. 1–6, *Current Digest*, V, 39, p. 11. Khrushchev's revelations five years later belied his assurances about the bread supply. *Soviet News*, Supplement to 3992, p. ii.
[4] Volin, *op. cit.*, pp. 197–198.

Distribution of Sown Crop Area in the Soviet Union for Specified Years
(in millions of acres)

Crop	1938		1940		1952	
	Areas	Per cent of Total	Areas	Per cent of Total	Areas	Per cent of Total
Grains and legumes	253.0	74.8	272.8	73.4	265.1	68.9
Wheat [a]	(102.5)	(30.3)	(99.1)	(26.7)	(46.2)	(29.7)
Industrial crops	27.2	8.0	28.9	7.8	31.6	8.2
Potatoes and other vegetables	23.2	6.9	24.4	6.6	24.5	6.4
Fodder crops	34.9	10.3	44.5	12.0	63.5	16.5
Total sown area	338.3	100.0	371.6 [b]	100.0	384.7	100.0

[a] = In 1953 the area sown to wheat was 4,900,000 acres and total sown acres increased by 3,500,000 acres.
[b] = Includes one million acres sown to unspecified crops.

(Source: official Soviet figures as quoted by Volin, "The Malenkov-Khrushchev New Economic Policy," p. 197.)

However, the chronic weak spot in Soviet agriculture was the livestock industry.

Number of Livestock in the Soviet Union January 1 for Selected Years
(in millions)

	1916[b]	1928[b]	1938[c]	1941[c]	1951	1953	(Plan) 1955[d]
Total cattle	58.4	66.8	59.8	54.5	57.1	56.6	68.0
Cows [a]	28.8	33.2	22.7	27.8	24.3	24.3	N.A.[e]
Pigs	96.3	114.6	75.0	91.6	24.4	28.5	35.5
Sheep and goats	23.0	27.7	32.3	27.5	99.0	109.9	159.4

[a] = Included in total cattle.
[b] = Winter figures not previously given and may not be strictly comparable because of border changes.
[c] = Figures roughly comparable with postwar period.
[d] = Average of maximum and minimum goals for 1955.
[e] = Not available.

[Sources: 1916, 1928, 1938, 1941: Volin, "The Malenkov-Khrushchev New Economic Policy," p. 198 (based on official figures).
1951, 1953: *The National Economy of the USSR – A Statistical Collection*, pp. 115–116.
1955 (Plan): *Economic Survey of Europe Since the War*, p. 47.
1928 (Cows): Volin, *A Survey of Soviet Russian Agriculture*, p. 154.]

Five years later (in December 1958) Khrushchev gave a much more meaningful analysis of the seriousness of the agricultural crisis when he revealed for the first time the actual procurement figures for 1953.

Agricultural Production
(in million of metric tons)

Commodity	Average 1933–37	1947	1949	1953
Grain				29.8
Including Wheat				18.1
Sugar beets	15.9	13.5	15.3	22.8
Sugar produced	1.7	1.3	1.7	3.0
Potatoes	73.8	71.6	76.2	5.1[a]
Vegetables				2.2
Sunflower seeds	2.1	1.7	1.6[b]	1.5
Raw cotton				3.7
Flax fiber	0.6	0.2	0.3[b]	0.08
Meat (liveweight)	1.9[c]			3.3
Including Pork	0.95[d]			0.5
Milk	22.37[e]			10.4
Factory butter	0.15[f]	0.2	0.24[b]	0.35
Wool	0.06[g]			0.19
Eggs				2,499.0[h]

(All figures are for postwar boundries unless otherwise indicated.)

[a] There is no apparent explanation for such a large discrepancy
[b] 1948 rather than 1949.
[c] Carcass weights including lard and other fats. This and pork figure for this period include only prewar area.
[d] For 1934–37 (average): (carcass weight including lard and other fats).
[e] 1934–1937 average of gross milk production for prewar area.
[f] Prewar area.
[g] Prewar area. Includes wool and hair from camels, sheep, and goats.
[h] Million units rather than metric tons.

(Sources: 1933–37, 1947, and 1949 figures compiled by the United States Department of Agriculture from Soviet sources. Volin, *A Survey of Soviet Russian Agriculture*, pp. 129–131, 133, 146, 164–165. 1953 figures from *Soviet News*, Supplement to 3992, p. ii.)

(It must be kept in mind that between 1928 and 1953 the population increased from an estimated 150,000,000 to approximately 193,680,000.) [1]

[1] The 1928 figure from the *New York Times*, Sept. 14, 1953, p. 2, Harry Schwartz. The 1953 figure calculated from the official 200,200,000 of 1956 minus the average annual increase of 3, 260,000 during the Fifth Five Year Plan. *Pravda*, Feb. 15, 1956, pp. 1–11, Gruliow (Ed.), *Current Soviet Policies*, II, p. 45.

In terms of everyday consumption this meant that Soviet agricultural production was not capable of feeding the constantly expanding population on little more than a low calorie diet consisting of dark bread, cereal, and grain with only occasional additions of meat, butter, milk, vegetables, and fruit. [1] While Khrushchev admitted that the repeated postwar attempts to alleviate the crisis had failed, [2] he refused to acknowledge that the system of collective farming employed in the Soviet Union was basicly unworkable. Rather he said it was sound but that a few of its aspects had been distorted. One of these was that the regime's preoccupation with heavy industry had led to the failure to produce sufficient farm machinery. Another was the gradual squeezing out of the private holdings on the collectives. Khrushchev was also generally critical of the unsatisfactory use the MTS made of their equipment as well as their lack of ideological leadership in the Party's efforts to control the countryside. [3] (Postwar Soviet émigrés regarded the MTS as one of the most serious obstacles to the solution of the agricultural crisis, because their political functions had largely replaced their technical function of supplying machinery. Rather than being closely coordinated with actual farming operations, the MTS and the collectives were often at loggerheads over the use of equipment at the most opportune times and the size of the annual rent that was charged for it.) [4] Khrushchev also spoke out against lax labor discipline in the country and the national labor policy which siphonned-off farm laborers to higher paying jobs in the cities. [5] However, he did not mention other important reasons for the serious labor shortage. Arrests and deportations for collaboration in areas occupied by the Germans, severe losses during the war, and the existence of an agricultural bureaucracy that required at least 14 administrative officials on even the smallest collective

[1] *New York Times*, Sept. 20, 1953, p. 4, Harry Schwartz.

[2] Elaborate plans for increasing livestock numbers had been announced in 1947 and 1949. The failure of both may have been a contributing factor in Andreyev's removal as the Politburo's agricultural specialist and Khrushchev's return to Moscow in 1950 to fill his post. Khrushchev's goal was to transform the small and medium size collectives into huge *agrogorods* more closely resembling factories than farms. However, this also failed and was criticized by Malenkov at the Nineteenth Party Congress in October 1952. *Ibid.*, Sept. 14, 1953, p. 2, Harry Schwartz.

[3] *Pravda* and *Izvestia*, Sept. 15, 1953, pp. 1–6, *Current Digest*, V, 39, p. 11.

[4] *New York Times*, Jan. 7, 1954, p. 1, Drew Middleton.

[5] *Pravda* and *Izvestia*, Sept. 15, 1953, pp. 1–6, *Current Digest*, V, 29, p. 12.

all meant that much of the field work was actually being done by women and old men. [1] But he did correctly observe that the livestock industry suffered because it was unprofitable due to low purchasing prices and that in general what he termed the principle of material incentive and self-interest had been consistently violated in agriculture over the years.

The regime's remedies for these faults came in a series of decrees published during the remainder of September. They formed a pattern of considerable concessions tempered by the simultaneous tightening of its hold on the countryside. The concessions were primarily designed to stimulate production by offering the peasants increased material incentives. There were four major ones: (1) revamping of the formal tax structure; (2) reduction of the quotas governing the forced delivery of livestock and potatoes; (3) increasing of the prices paid for such compulsory deliveries; and (4) the official recognition of *kolkhosy* trade as an essential factor in the economic life of the countryside. [2]

The first of these came in August 1953 when the basic agricultural tax structure was reorganized. Among other changes it provided for the creation of a flat tax rate based on acreage rather than on a complicated sliding rate computed from the assumed profitableness of various crops under cultivation. As a result, it completely reversed the previous policy of discouraging rather than encouraging the most economic use of land. Also all tax arrears were wiped out, and special additional concessions were made to encourage the private ownership of livestock. However, the same law contained provisions to ensure that the cultivation of private plots did not get out of hand and encroach on the required work of the collectives. Severe tax penalties of 50 and 75 per cent, respectively, were to be imposed on *kolkhosy* households in which *any* able-bodied member failed to fulfill his or her required minimum amount of labor or who did not belong to a collective or had been expelled from one.

Other concessions reduced compulsory deliveries of meat and potatoes as well as cancelling all arrears prior to January 1, 1953. Peasants who did not own livestock were exempted from meat deliveries until the end of 1954. The increase in the prices for the

---

[1] *New York Times*, Jan. 7, 1954, p. 1, Drew Middleton.
[2] Volin, *op. cit.*, p. 201.

revised compulsory deliveries, which effected both the *kolkhozniki*
and the *kolkhosy*, were as follows:

1) livestock and poultry more than five and one half times;
2) milk and butter double;
3) potatoes two and one half times more; and
4) vegetables between 25–40 per cent higher.[1]

These were not as great as may first appear because of the very
small base from which they were originally calculated. Prices for
surplus deliveries, which were already higher, were further increased – on the average of 30 per cent for meat and 50 per cent
for milk. [2] The rural trade network, which had seemed to be
doomed by Stalin's "product exchange" system outlined in his
Economic Problems of Socialism in the USSR only a year before,
was given a new lease on life when it received the regime's official blessing. Spurred on by the desire to get food to the
markets, apparently regardless of how it was accomplished, its
limited expansion was even encouraged. Attacking the problem
from yet another angle the government capital investment in the
key industries producing fertilizers, machinery, and building
supplies was to be increased immediately. [3]

Set off against these concessions was the simultaneous tightening of the regime's hold on the countryside through a complete
revamping of the Party's system of controls. The police, who had
previously used the MTS as the hub of their activities among the
peasants, were replaced by greatly strengthened Party cadres as
the most important element of control. [4] In the past the Party
organization had operated primarily from its *rayon* centers from
which it had supervised the *kolkhozy*, the *sovkhozy*, and the MTS.
Under this arrangement the MTS organizations maintained the
post of assistant director for political affairs, but in the reorganization undertaken in September 1953 this was abolished
and the MTS were made the fulcrums of control. The *rayons* were
divided into zones – one for each MTS – and a *rayon* Party
Secretary was assigned directly to each with his headquarters at
the MTS. He was also given a staff of full-time Party instructors
whose responsibility was limited to the supervision of one or, at

[1] *Pravda* and *Izvestia*, Sept. 15, 1953, pp. 1–6, *Current Digest*, V, 39, p. 11.
[2] Volin, *op. cit.*, p. 203.
[3] *Ibid.*, p. 201.
[4] *New York Times*, Dec. 20, 1953, p. 19, William Ryan.

the most, two *kolkhozy* in the zone. (At the same time the Party apparatus in the *rayon* centers was reorganized.) [1] In addition to increasing their facilities for indoctrination and political control the MTS were assigned a greater control over actual farming operations than they had enjoyed in the past. [2] The thousands of new jobs – technical as well as political – were filled through an officially stimulated "voluntary" transfer of both skilled laborers and Party members from the city to the country. Khrushchev implied that in the selection of Party officials organizational experience rather than formal agricultural training was more important. [3] The astonishing feature about these herculean efforts was that they were undertaken by the regime not to obtain any new goals but merely to reach the targets set by Stalin's Fifth Five Year Plan which in some cases failed to equal Czarist production.

Although Malenkov dealt exclusively with generalities, Mikoyan outlined in considerable detail the planned increases in consumers' goods production. The program he outlined called for a nearly 50 per cent increase in volume by the end of three years. It required the conversion of several industrial ministries previously devoted exclusively to the production of heavy industrial goods or armaments as well as the reorganization and expansion of the internal trade network. For three of the most important mass consumption items (cotton and woolen goods and leather footwear) his projected figures indicated a slight rise in 1954, a sharper increase the following year, and a more gradual rise in 1956. But significantly, the 1955 figures for these items were only slightly higher than those originally anticipated by the Fifth Five Year Plan: two per cent for cotton goods; five per cent for woolen; and practically none for leather footwear. [4]

---

[1] Fainsod, "The Communist Party since Stalin," p. 32.

[2] Volin, *op. cit.*, p. 205.

[3] The magnitude of this transfer was illustrated by the *Pravda* report that by January 1954 100,000 agricultural specialists, skilled laborers, and Party leaders had been sent to the countryside. Prior to the reorganization of the agricultural sections of the *rayon* Party groups they employed approximately 11,000 full-time Party workers. By May 1955 more than 30,000 Party officials had been assigned to the MTS. This was apparently in addition to the 3,747 full-time Party Secretaries authorized in September 1953 for direct assignment to the larger collective farms. (Fainsod, *op. cit.*, p. 32.) Even so, at the Twentieth Party Congress there was evidence that the Party was disturbed by the failure of this new organization to solve the agricultural problems. "The Twentieth Congress of the Communist Party of the Soviet Union," *Notes – Soviet Affairs*, 187, April 19, 1956.

[4] Volin, *op. cit.*, p. 191.

Production and Production Goals for Specified Products in the Soviet Union for Selected Years Compared with 1940

Year	Cotton Goods		Woolen Goods		Leather Footwear	
	Million yards	Index 1940 = 100	Million yards	Index 1940 = 100	Million pairs	Index 1940 = 100
1940	4,182	100	131.6	100	205	100
1952	5,395	129	223.4	181	250	122
1953	5,665	135	243.5	198	260	127
1954*	6,068	145	264.7	215	267	130
1955*	6,854	164	296.4	241	318	155
1956*	7,093	170	366.1	297	350	171

* = Goals

(Source: Volin, "The Malenkov-Khrushchev New Economic Policy," p. 191.)

However, there were fundamental increases planned in the field of durable household goods and luxury items. In many cases the new targets were several hundred per cent higher than the previously planned goals. (These spectacular rates of increase were indicative of their extremely low production base.) [1] The reasons for this pattern were not difficult to explain. The noticeably higher percentages were confined to the metal industries where the raw materials could be diverted from existing production – most likely without seriously affecting the rapid growth of heavy industry – but the lower increases were planned for textiles and similar items dependent upon agriculture for raw materials. [2]

At least in terms of stated objectives, these economic revisions were an important step forward in overcoming the imbalance which had developed during the quarter century of Stalin's tenure in office. However, even the planned improvements did not promise to substantially raise the standard of living of the average individual. The largest increases were authorized for items financially out of reach for most people. This suggests that the regime was catering primarily to the relatively small but restless middle and upper classes who had some idea of conditions in the West. In agriculture the story was much the same. The 1953 spring price reductions had driven even the staple food items such as bread and potatoes off the markets and forced the

[1] *Ibid., op. cit.,* p. 193.
[2] *Economic Survey of Europe in 1953,* p. 50.

Production and Production Goals for Specified Consumers' Goods in the Soviet Union for Selected Years

Commodity	Unit	Production 1950	Production Goals 1954	Production Goals 1955	Production Goals 1956
Bedsteads (iron)	1,000 pieces	N.A.*	13,500	16,500	N.A.
Bicycles	1,000	650	2,510	3,445	3,800
Cameras	1,000	N.A.	915	1,200	N.A.
Clocks and watches	1,000	7,586	16,800	22,000	23,000
Phonographs	1,000	N.A.	921	1,125	N.A.
Irons (electric)	1,000	486	3,550	4,375	N.A.
Radios and television sets	1,000	1,029	3,186	4,527	5,400
Refrigerators (electric)	1,000	N.A.	207	330	N.A.
Samovars	1,000	223	675	890	N.A.
Sewing machines	1,000	503	1,335	2,615	3,000
Spoons (stainless steel)	1,000	3,440	11,700	17,200	N.A.
Stoves and burners	1,000	1,300**	2,966	3,843	N.A.
Vacuum cleaners	1,000	N.A.	243	483	500
Silk goods	M.yards	133	551	627	693
Household utensils:					
Aluminium ⎱	Metric	35,667	90,000	107,000	N.A.
Iron ⎰	tons	88,000**	265,145	395,470	N.A.

N.A.   * = Not Available.
       ** = Rough approximation.

(Source: Volin, "The Malenkov-Khrushchev New Economic Policy," p. 192. For important corrections cf. p. 538 of the same volume of *The Journal of Political Economy* in which this article appeared.)

regime to dip into its reserves. Barring unforeseen difficulties the program of incentives outlined in September could not alter the situation, at best, for several years. Even then there was serious question as to whether the available supplies would completely satisfy market demands. The government found itself in the almost untenable position of having promised increases in the marketable supply of meat and other livestock products while simultaneously seeking to greatly enlarge the size of the already badly depleted herds.

The drastic nature of these revisions was highly indicative of the seriousness of the economic and political crises that gripped the entire Soviet bloc. The Stalinization of Eastern Europe had been achieved only at the cost of economic chaos and, therefore, similar alterations were undertaken in the Satellites under the guidance and direction of Moscow which had already supervised the reorganization of their regimes in line with the post-Stalin changes adopted in the USSR.

From the very beginning the regime's program encountered seemingly insurmountable difficulties. It required the creation of new economic ministeries – the Ministries of Food, Consumers' Goods, Domestic Trade, Foreign Trade, State Farms, and Agricultural Procurement [1] – but even these were not sufficient and much of the work had to be parcelled out to those previously devoted exclusively to heavy industry or armament, thus requiring major retooling and re-education of both labor and management. The coordination of production, so vitally necessary, had been notoriously lacking in the past. There was also the problem of overcoming the bureaucratic inertia which threatened to swamp the program before it became operational, and the powerful vested positions were challenged for the first time in years. In addition, an important psychological hurtle had to be cleared. The Soviet state had worshipped at the altar of heavy industry for so many years that it had become a fetish that could not easily be replaced. The concept of satisfying consumer demands was so alien to the Soviet managerial mentality that more than Mikoyan's admonishments were needed to change it.

An added headache was the construction of new factories, stores, and transportation facilities which were needed if the program's promises were to be fulfilled. But an even more serious difficulty was the dependence of much of the consumers' goods production upon the supply of agricultural raw materials. Even under the best conditions this could not be achieved overnight. [2] By late November and early December 1953 all of these factors were making themselves felt and the program showed signs of becoming the victim of the forces which had previously sapped the vitality of other reform movements. [3]

---

[1] *New York Times*, Sept. 15, 1953, p. 1, Harrison Salisbury.

[2] Volin, *op. cit.*, pp. 193–195.

[3] Cf. *Current Digest*, V, 49, pp. 12–19, and 50, pp. 18–21 for examples of press criticism.

THE LITERARY CONTROVERSY

While the regime was grappling with the economic crisis it also was forced to come to grips with yet another domestic issue, which, in a sense, posed an even greater challenge. Allocated sufficient resources and the necessary priorities, the material improvement of living conditions was only a question of time. However, no such automatic process governed the improvement of the nation's intellectual and cultural life. Here the regime was faced with one of its basic dilemmas. The need for at least a partial relaxation of the rigid control of the past was clearly evident, but even the most gradual loosening of the intellectual fetters set into motion forces which ultimately could threaten the regime's very existence. The confusion in literary circles during the first two years after Stalin's death best illustrated the various stages through which it passed in its quest for a policy of controlled liberalism that was in conformity with the needs of Soviet totalitarianism.

Stalin's death immediately released pent-up pressure for changes. Between 1950 and 1952 a few minor concessions from the regime had resulted in a new boldness in criticism of the depths to which writing had fallen, but even this was generally directed only at editorial boards and not at authors. [1] Even despite Malenkov's emphatic declaration at the Nineteenth Party Congress five months before Stalin's death that what Russia needed were

Soviet Gogols and Shchedrins who, with the fire of their satire, would burn away everything that is undesirable, rotten, and moribund, everything that retards our progress,[2]

Soviet writers were too familiar with recent history, i.e., the postwar Zhdanov-period, when just this type of writing had brought fiery denunciation, to plunge into the water without first testing it for a considerable time with their toes. [3]

[1] Simons, "Soviet Literature: 1950–1955," p. 100.
[2] *Pravda*, Oct. 6, 1952, pp. 2–9, Gruliow (Ed.), *Current Soviet Policies*, (I), p. 114.
[3] Although Stalin's heirs never publicly identified themselves with the rival factions which fought out the literary battle in the press during 1953 and 1954, a plausible argument can be made for Malenkov's support of liberalization: 1) the slight concessions before 1952 paralleled his rise after Zhdanov's death; 2) his speech at the Nineteenth Party Congress; and 3) the course of the post-Stalin liberalization which roughly followed his political fortunes.

However, less than a month after Stalin's death the April issue of *Literaturnaya Gazeta* published O. Berggoltz's frank criticism of the faults of Soviet lyric poetry. This article, which must have been prepared some time earlier in anticipation of a shift in the regime's policy, condemned it for lacking

the most important thing ... : the human being.

She blamed this on the critics who chided authors for expressing such emotions as doubt, irresolution, grief, or even sorrow. This was striking directly at the heart of the "Zhdanov movement." A. Tvardovsky, editor of *Novy Mir*, followed suit in his own magazine in June with a long narrative poem devoted to the short-comings of Soviet literature. (The climate had not entirely changed for it drew heavy criticism.) [1] Similar opinions began to appear in other literary magazines and quickly spread to the pages of the central press where theater productions, movies, short stories, etc. were singled out for their poor quality. Even at this early stage some of the comment in *Pravda* went to lengths which only a few months before would not have been tolerated. For example, "People's Artist" N. K. Cherkasov wrote:

There is nothing more harmful to art than attempts to ... limit artistic individuality. Those artists who confuse unity with conformity do not have enough breadth of scope. We have a single artistic method – the method of socialist realism – which also determines our artists' community of views. But it does not to any extent presuppose the sameness or similarity of one work to another.

. . . . . .

The only thing needed is to keep ... [the] guidance [of the Chief Administration on Affairs of the Arts of the USSR Ministry of Culture] from becoming petty supervision and to keep formalism from entering .... Why is it that the management of the largest theater ... cannot determine for itself whether a projected work is worthy of the audience's attention or not?

Why is it that some official in the apparatus of the ... [bureaucracy] thinks he knows better than the theater group itself whether a work that has been chosen conforms to the potentials of a given theater or not? [2]

A similar *Izvestia* article sharply attacking the quality of short stories wrestled with the dilemma of improving their standards without destroying their usefulness to the regime:

---

[1] Crankshaw, *Russia without Stalin*, pp. 141–143.
[2] *Pravda*, Oct. 9, 1953, p. 3, *Current Digest*, V, 34, pp. 32–34.

Our socialist reality and the life and work of Soviet people are an inexhaustible source for the most varied subjects and for genuine stories, stories free from the crude or sketchy, stories which depict the spiritual wealth of Soviet man. These may be deeply dramatic or simply gay, 'entertaining' tales (which are also needed) but they must be artisticly genuine and reflect the truly deep poetic truth of our remarkable times.[1]

These individual voices were brought together in a rising chorus at the All-Union Congress of Young Critics during early autumn, effectively setting the scene for the official blessing of the new course in October 1953 when the Plenary Session of the Writers' Union met to discuss Soviet drama. A. A. Fadeyev, a novelist and member of the Central Committee, presided and Ponomarenko in his capacities of Minister of Culture and candidate of the Party Presidium represented the regime. Writer after writer condemned the Zhdanov era and its policies. By implication (but never directly) the Party was also brought to task. However, it is important to keep in mind that at no time did the assembled delegates deny that the Party was omnipotent in determining the country's aesthetic climate. [2]

Against this background came I. Ehrenburg's lengthy article "On the Work of a Writer" in the October issue of *Znamya* in which he surveyed Soviet literature and the system that governed it, finding both lacking:

A writer is not an apparatus mechanically recording events. A writer writes a book not because he can write or because he is a member of the Union of Soviet Writers and might be asked why he has not published anything for a long time, not because he must earn a living, but because he is compelled to tell the people something he personally feels, because he has 'begun to ache' from his book, because he has seen people and deeds and feelings which must be described. This is the way stiring books are born and even if they sometimes contain artistic shortcomings such books will invariably move the readers.

This is why I cannot understand some critics who blame an author: he did not write a novel about the Volga-Don Canal, about the textile industry, or the struggle for peace. Would it not be better to reproach another author who has written a book when he felt no spiritual need to do so and might well have gone on living tranquilly without writing it?

. . . .

Before the life of a writer was hard, and in Chekhov's letters one can find mention of newspapers and magazines ordering stories from him. But not even the most unconscionable editor would ... have dared to dictate to

---

[1] *Izvestia*, Aug. 22, 1953, p. 3, *ibid.*
[2] Crankshaw, *op. cit.*, pp. 143–144.

Chekhov the theme on which to write. Can you imagine placing an order with Tolstoi to write *Anna Karenina* or with Gorky to write *Mother*? [1]

While writing specifically about music but nevertheless stating truths which were directly applicable to the whole gammit of artistic endeavour, A. Khachaturyan bluntly stated:

> I think the time has come to revise our established system of institutional guardianship over composers. I will say more: we must resolutely reject the wrong practice of interference with the composer's creative processes by officials of music institutions. Creative problems cannot be solved by bureaucratic methods. The artist is obliged to find the correct creative answer to a problem of music in the light of the great vital tasks which our Party has set. That is what makes him a Soviet artist.

> Wise planning and concern in the guidance of the country's music should not be replaced by interference with the very process of composition or performance, by forcing on the composer the tastes of officials of music institutions, who stand aside from creative work by conceiving themselves as 'over' the work of creation .... Let the artist be trusted more fully, and he will approach with even greater responsibility and freedom the task of solving the creative problem of our times. [2]

While such articles brought a certain degree of defensive criticism the tone which they established generally prevailed through the closing days of 1953 and the first weeks of 1954. The December issue of *Novy Mir* (edited by Tvardovsky) published a lengthy and impassioned article by V. Pomerantsev, taking up Ehrenburg's position which set off a violent stream of both praise and criticism. He demanded that

the degree of frankness must be the first criterion

of any literary work. But, more important than this or his attacks on the Writers' Union, he probed more deeply than others into the need for modifying the stereotyped "positive" character which dominated Soviet literature. [3] This stirred up literary circles throughout both the Soviet Union and the Satellites, resulting in an almost immediate retaliation from the defenders of the Party's position who apparently were more disturbed about his attempt to redraw the typical character than his call for frankness. [4] With criticism of his position in both the *Literatur-*

---

[1] *Znamya*, 10, Oct. 1953, *Current Digest*, V, 52, pp. 6–7.
[2] *Sovetskyaya Muzyka*, 11, Nov. 1953, pp. 7–13, *Current Digest*, V, 46, pp. 1–5.
[3] Crankshaw, *op. cit.*, p. 150; Alexandrova, "Soviet Literature since Stalin," p. 12; and *Novy Mir*, 12, Dec. 1953, pp. 218–245, *Currrent Digest*, VI, 5, pp. 1–9, and 6, pp. 1–7.
[4] Alexandrova, *op. cit.*, p. 12.

naya Gazeta and *Novy Mir* by V. Vasilevski and L. Skorino, respectively, the first intensive counterattack against such liberalism in the arts was begun.

Vasilevski declared that the article proved that

many of Pomerantsev's correct ideas are not new but naïve and generally known, and that many of his controversial ideas are theoretically unfounded, unprovable, or simply wrong.

Commenting on the latter's insistence on the degree of sincerety as the meassure of any literary work, Vasikevski emphasized that

the first test for the Marxist has been and will continue to be evaluation of the ideological-artistic quality of the work.

He also warned in considering "sincerity" and "faithfulness" separately:

Pomerantsev completely overlooks the question of the writer's world outlook, his Party stand.[1]

In the Stalin era such official criticism would have been followed very shortly by punitive measures that would have permanently closed the discussion, but the new regime had loosened the reigns to the extent that it was no longer an automatic procedure. The next round was initiated by a letter published in *Komsomolskaya Pravda*, signed by four students (three of them postgraduates) and a teacher at Moscow State University, stating that although they disagreed with some aspects of Pomerantsev's views, they considered Vasilevski's criticism merely

introduced elements of crude shouting into a business-like discussion of literary problems.

After examining the criticism which the two authors leveled at Pomerantsev and charging that Skorino had purposefully avoided discussing the real questions raised by his controversial article, the letter posed the following question:

One is tempted to ask Skorino: Why have literary criticism at all? Should it not surrender its place to dithyrambs?[2]

While several other members of the Soviet literary world rallied to support the "liberal" position, the conservative elements struck back behind the shield of social morality. The

---

[1] *Literaturnaya Gazeta*, Jan. 30, 1954, p. 3, *Current Digest*, VI, 6, pp. 8–9.
[2] *Komsomolskaya Pravda*, March 17, 1954, p. 3, *ibid.*, VI, 7, p. 3.

same issue of *Komsomolskaya Pravda* which published this letter denounced N. Virta for using his literary position to hood-wink local officials in one village into providing him with a luxurious way of life [1], and the *Literaturnaya Gazeta* (in a story summarized by *Pravda*) in April publicly ridiculed A. A. Surov, Ts. Galsanov and A. Voloshin for drunkenness and "hooli-ganism." [2] A month later *Pravda* announced that Virta, Surov, Galsanov, and L. Korobov had been expelled from the Writers' Union for having

committed amoral and antisocial acts incompatible with the calling of Soviet writers.[3]

While there may have been some validity in the charges, there seemed to be indications that they were merely pretexts for more fundamental reasons. On May 25, 1954, A. Surkov, First Secretary of the Writers' Union, published a lengthy article in *Pravda* which indicated that these had been the opening moves in a campaign directed toward whipping the recalcitrant members of the literary circle into line for the Second All-Soviet Congress of Writers scheduled for the following September. He set the tone for the gathering by stressing the role literature had played in building the Soviet state; sharply attacked Pomerantsev; and denounced the magazines *Novy Mir, Oktyabr*, and *Znamya* for opening up their pages to the liberal point of view both in the form of criticism and literary works. [4]

This let loose a rain of criticism and reprisals from which few who had spoken out in favor of the "new course" were immune. A modified and slightly more flexible "Zhdanovism" seemed to be the regime's new position although none of its leaders personally entered the various skirmishes. Even *Kommunist* was called on to back up the Party's position. [5]

It is impossible to enumerate all of those who felt the lash of criticism in the six months that preceeded the Writers' Congress. Significantly, it had to be postponed from September to December 1954, suggesting that it took longer to subdue the rebellious

---

[1] *Ibid.*, p. 4.
[2] *Literaturnaya Gazeta*, April 6, 1954, p. 2, *ibid.*, VI, 16, pp. 10–11.
[3] *Pravda*, May 6, 1954, p. 2, *ibid.*, VI, 18, p. 30.
[4] *Pravda*, May 25, 1954, pp. 2–3, *ibid.*, VI, 19, pp. 3–5.
[5] *World Today*, "The Dilemma of Soviet Writers: Inspiration or Conformity," pp. 157–159.

writers than had been first anticipated. The plays of I. Goro-
detsky, A. Mariengof, Virta and A. Zorin were pillored less than
a year after the regime had called for better dramatic writing.
The reason was that they portrayed "bad" characters and exposed evils which were not attributed to the bourgeois past but by
implication called products of the Soviet system. [1] Zorin's play
The Guest received more than its share of scathing denunciations
because he dared to use the conflict between the two Soviet
generations as its central theme. He had pictured the younger
Kirpichev not as the survival of the past but as the inevitable
product of Soviet society, thriving on its more unsavoury aspects.
In one passage the older Kirpichev summed up the problem
with the observation:

> The country had become stronger and the people have become richer.
> But alongside the toilers and hard workers there have appeared, inper-
> ceptibly and abundantly, such people as you: white collar aristocrats,
> greedy and conceited, far from the people.

The reason for this corruption Zorin saw as the love of sheer
power. [2]

The literary magazines which had published the creative work
and criticism of the authors now out of favor came in for a
sizeable share of the castigation. Of the six important literary
reviews in the Soviet Union (all of which existed solely by the
grace of the regime) only the quasi-official *Literaturnaya Gazeta*
escaped condemnation. (In fact, it led the campaign against the
others.) The editors of *Novy Mir*, *Oktyabr*, and *Zvezda* were
dismissed for various "deviations" and only *Teatr* and *Znamya*
were let off with a public dressing down.

Superficially, at least, these developments seemed to bring the
brief career of the "new course" full circle, but, as the developments centering around Ehrenburg's novel *The Thaw*, and later
the Writers' Congress itself, showed, this was not the case. His
novel, with its symbolic title, first appeared in serial form during

---

[1] Crankshaw, *op. cit.*, p. 152, and cf. *Pravda*, June 3, 1954, pp. 4–5, *Current Digest*,
VI, 21, pp. 21–24.

[2] An admittedly incomplete list catalogued six major attacks between May 25
and June 9, 1954, on Zorin and his play. (Cf. Crankskaw, *op. cit.*, pp. 153–155.)
An amusing sidelight was the abrupt *volte-face* done by the sure-footed K. Simonov,
who found himself in the unenviable position of having praised *The Guests* as a model
of satire. By July 10 he had again sensed the direction of the wind and launched a
scathing attack against it. *World Today, op. cit.*, p. 158.

May 1954 in *Znamya* and was avidly read because it was the first truly human novel to appear in the Soviet Union for many years. Although it was criticized by *Komsomolskaya Pravda* as early as June 6, among other reasons, because it

did not present a single genuine advanced, strong, vigorous Soviet man,

the real controversy (which lasted through the December Congress) did not begin until it was scored by K. Simonov in the *Literaturnaya Gazeta* in mid-July. Ehrenburg then countered with a rebuttle of his own in the same journal. The question still continued to seethe despite the verdict against him by its editor in October and an article in *Kommunist* which

reaffirmed the hegemony of the Party and restated the principle of socialist realism.

Probably the most significant sign of change was that throughout it all *The Thaw* was not withdrawn, but, in fact, re-issued, although in a much smaller edition. [1]

Although most of what transpired at the Second All-Union Congress of Soviet Writers bore the unmistakable imprint of advanced preparation designed to ensure the continued supremacy of the Party in literary circles, there were still signs that the regime had neither completely returned to the Zhdanov era nor fully quelled the "rebellion." One of these was the vigorous three month debate in the pages of the *Literaturnaya Gazeta* which preceded the Congress and questioned the value of the Writers' Union, the very bulwark of Party control. [2] Another was the nature of some of the criticism voiced (and duly reported by *Literaturnaya Gazeta*) at the Congress. In effect, a handful of writers recapitulated (although not in an organized fashion) the essential points of the controversy. [3] More than anything else, however, the election of M. A. Sholokhov, V. Panova, Tvardovsky, and V. S. Grossman, all of whom had felt the regime's wrath, to the new Presidium of Writers' Union symbolized its new willingness to mete out less severe punishment for those who went astray but were willing to admit their errors. [4]

[1] Forty-five thousand copies were issued when 250,000 would have been more likely by Soviet standards. Crankshaw, *op. cit.*, pp. 157–158; *Komsomolskaya Pravda*, June 6, 1954, p. 2, *Current Digest*, VI, 20, pp. 5–6; and *Literaturnaya Gazeta*, Aug. 3, 1954, p. 3, *ibid.*, VI, 32, pp. 13–15.

[2] *Literaturnaya Gazeta*, Aug. 3, 1954, p. 3, *Current Digest*, VI, 32, pp. 13–15.

[3] Cf. Struve, "The Second Congress of Soviet Writers," pp. 8–9, and *World Today*, *op. cit.*, pp. 161–162.

[4] *New York Times*, Dec. 27, 1954, p. 4, Clifton Daniels.

Far from clearing the air, the Writers' Congress left a confused and befuddled climate in Soviet literary circles. Although it had repeated faithfully the importance of the doctrine of social realism and left little question that those who violated it would be punished, the regime did not provide the authors with a sharply defined yardstick of what it was. Unlike the Zhdanov period when there was little doubt as to what was forbidden, the writers had little to guide them through the maze of treacherous pitfalls confronting them in their attempt to produce acceptable literary works.

THE ANTI-RELIGIOUS PROPAGANDA CAMPAIGN

While the regime was groping its way toward a new relationship with the country's intellectuals it was fashioning a different policy for still another sector of the Soviet society. Beginning in December 1953 a well-organized internal propaganda campaign was launched against religion which reached a fever pitch the following summer only to be dramatically called off on November 10, 1954, by a special Central Committee decree. This strange pattern of events ended a period of relative *détente* which had characterized the relationship between the churches and the Communist Party since Russia's entrance into the Second World War. In essence, Stalin had toned down his atheist propaganda and permitted the churches a limited sphere of independence in return for their support of the regime's foreign and domestic policy. [1] During this *rapprochement* the regime's propaganda was largely confined to rational arguments which sought to prove that religion was incompatible with science and the progress of human knowledge. To further this end the "Society for the Dissemination of Political and Scientific Knowledge" had been founded in 1947. [2]

Suddenly and without warning the new anti-religious campaign erupted in the pages of *Komsomolskaya Pravda* on December 18, 1953, with a denunciation of "religious superstition." Rapidly

---

[1] Timasheff, "The Anti-Religious Campaign in the Soviet Union," pp. 329–330. Cf. Gurian (Ed.), *The Soviet Union: Background, Ideology, and Reality*, pp. 153–158. The churches first took part in one of Stalin's "peace offensives" in May 1952. *World Today*, "A Revival of Religious Feeling in the USSR," p. 440.

[2] Pierre, "Religion in the Soviet Land," p. 21.

gathering momentum in the following months, it exploded in all its fury in the summer when it was picked up by the central press. It discarded the rational approach of the previous decade for a highly emotional one reminiscent of early days of the Soviet regime when religious beliefs and those who practiced them were ridiculed and condemned.

All of the various propaganda media at the regime's disposal were drawn into the well-organized campaign. Although the provincial and central press were its primary agents, the domestic radio added its voice to the effort, hundreds of lecturers were sent into the countryside to preach atheism, and special books and pamphlets were distributed to drive the point home. The anti-religious museums in Moscow, Leningrad, and Kiev were reopened and mobile exhibitions were organized to tour the collective farms. The entire effort bore the unmistakable imprint of a highly centralized attempt to discredit and destroy religion in the Soviet Union. [1]

Then, as suddenly as it had begun, the entire campaign was called off on November 10, 1954, by a special Central Committee decree signed by Khrushchev which severely reprimanded the Party for its handling of the affair and restored the *détente* that had existed between church and state less than a year before. In tones obviously calculated to placate public ire Khrushchev made the astonishingly frank admission that

gross errors ... [had] been committed in [spreading] scientific-atheist propaganda among the public in many localities.

Instead of the development of systematic and painstaking work to spread knowledge of natural sciences and an ideological struggle against religion, some central and local newspapers and also the statements of lecturers and speakers ... [had] contained insulting attacks upon the clergy and believers who perform religious rites.

. . . .

Such errors in anti-religious propaganda are fundamentally at variance with the program and policy of the Communist Party toward religion and believers, and they are a violation of the Party's repeated instructions on the impermissibility of offending the feelings of believers.

But while this was a retreat from an extreme position Khrushchev

---

[1] For example, three books designed to reach all age groups were published in August. For detailed accounts of the campaign's development cf. Timasheff, *op. cit.*, pp. 329–44; *World Today, op. cit.*, pp. 439–446; and "Religion – The Janus Face of Communism," *Notes – Soviet Affairs*, 164, Aug. 23, 1954.

clearly indicated that the Party was making no fundamental change in its basic policy toward religion.

> Rectification of mistakes committed in anti-religious propaganda must not lead to a relaxation of scientific-atheist propaganda, which is an integral part of the Communist education of the working people and has as its aim the dissemination of scientific, materialist knowledge among the masses, and the liberation of believers from influence of religious beliefs.[1]

Apparently to make certain that the new relationship was fully understood, the central press reported the following month that Malenkov had received Alexei, Patriarch of Moscow and All Russia, in an official audience at which G. G. Karpov of the Council of Ministers' Council on Affairs of the Russian Orthodox Church had also been present. [2]

This strange pattern of events immediately posed two unanswered questions: (1) what reason did the regime have for suddenly destroying the existing *détente* with the churches, and (2) why was the vigorous propaganda campaign so abruptly called off only three or four months after it had reached the peak of its fury? No official explanations were ever offered. Therefore, any answers must be based largely upon speculation. However, a number of factors may shed some light on the problem.

It is significant that the Soviet press did not direct its attacks so much against the Orthodox Church, which had always been closely tied to the Russian state, as it did against the various minority sects that were more difficult to control. [3] The two groups that seemed to attract the most attention were the Baptists and the Moslems. The former represented the most important Christian minority in the Soviet Union. According to *Bratsky Vestnik*, the official organ of the All-Union Council of Evangelical Christian Baptists, the adult (baptized) membership

---

[1] *Pravda*, Nov. 11, 1954, p. 2, *Trud* and *Komsomolskaya Pravda*, Nov. 12, 1954, *Current Digest*, VI, 43, pp. 13–14. Cf. *Partiynaya Zhizn*, 15, Nov. 1954, pp. 9–15, *ibid.*, VI, 49, pp. 9–12 for examples of the "excesses" referred to by Khrushchev. Six months later Radio Moscow declared that:

"Recently the struggle against religion was relaxed owing to poor atheistic propaganda by some Party, trade union, Komsomol, and other organizations which incorrectly interpreted the Soviet constitutional provisions on religion as a renunciation of scientific-atheistic propaganda. This is contrary to Party policy."
Quoted by the *New York Times*, May 15, 1955, p. 5.

[2] *Pravda* and *Izvestia*, Dec. 12, 1954, p. 1, *Current Digest*, VI, 49, p. 9.

[3] *World Today, op. cit.*, p. 443.

numbered half a million, organized in 5,400 church communities.[1] The feature that most perturbed the regime about this and similar sects was the ease with which they were able to adapt themselves to the Soviet way of life and operate effectively with a very flexible organization rather than a rigid one similar to that of the Orthodox Church. For example, while the Baptists were officially forbidden to preach without written permission from the district *starosta* (warden) of the church, the various congregations overcame such obstacles by permitting any member to do so. Another disturbing aspect was the way the sects linked Christianity with Communist ideology to the extent of preaching that

Communism ... [was] only the logical outcome of Christianity, and the Communist Party and the Soviet regime ... [were] putting Christian ideals into practice,

and that

the Christ of the legends is the spiritual father and precursor of the Communist Party.[2]

While these quotations represent the regime's version of illicit sectarian religious doctrine, it is only necessary to turn to *Bratsky Vestnik's* official statement that the purpose of the Christian church was

to establish a Christian state in which all social contradictions would be eliminated and the exploitation of man by man would have to come to an end, where there would be no slaves or beggars, and which would be governed by labor and social justice[3]

to see why the regime could not permit this admittedly popular doctrine to continue unchecked. As long as it failed to reconcile the inherient inconsistencies of the day-to-day operation of Communism and its own ideology there existed the danger that such a religious doctrine might become the nucleus of a rival ideology.

Islam posed a problem also because of its potential number of followers, who were located in Central Asia where Russian influence and control were not as deeply rooted as in the pre-

---

[1] A few hundred of these church communities were located in areas acquired by the USSR after 1939. For example, 91 with 6,600 members were to be found in Latvia. *Bratsky Vestnik*, 2, 1954 as quoted by *Soviet Studies*, "Some Data about Religious Communities," p. 471.

[2] *Molodoi Kommunist*, 8, 1953 as quoted by *World Today*, *op. cit.*, p. 443.

[3] *Bratsky Vestnik*, 2, 1954, p. 32 as quoted by *Soviet Studies*, *op. cit.*, p. 471.

dominantly Slavic areas of the USSR. However, it would be a mistake to overestimate its strength. Nearly 40 years of repression had largely succeeded in reducing its influence to a shadow of its former self. While its organization still functioned, the number of mosques and *medresscha* (seminaries) had fallen off to a mere handful. [1] Until early 1955 when Khrushchev's foreign policy did a sudden *volte face* Soviet doctrine maintained that Islam was incompatible with Communism. [2] Also the threat of a Pan-Islam movement which had been always deeply feared by the Soviets took on even more sinister implications when the West indicated its determination to form a military alliance along the USSR's southern flank.

But in the best tradition of opportunism, the regime began an even greater use of these religious groups in its foreign policy at the height of their repression at home. Aside from its utilization of the leaders of the various sects for its "peace offensive," [3] probably the best example of Moscow's exploitation of religion for its own ends was its contrasting attitude toward Islam in its domestic and foreign propaganda. On March 22, 1954, in an Arabic language broadcast beamed to the Middle East Moscow Radio told its listeners that:

> The Soviet Constitution guarantees freedom of religion to all citizens of the USSR . . . . It never interferes in the affairs of the churches and grants full freedom for preaching religion to its citizens. Religious centers of all kinds have the right to organize their meetings, publish books and magazines, and to have their religious schools. Religious leaders enjoy the right to take part in elections equally with all other citizens. [4]

Yet in April *Kommunist Tadzhikistana* went out of its way to denounce the fast of Ramadan as an "old wives tale." However, a few weeks later Tass gave it and the subsequent feast of Uraza Bairam wide coverage. On June 2 it quoted the Moslem Board

[1] In 1943 the regime had sought to formalize its control over Islam by creating four "Spiritual Departments." (One each for Central Asia, the Trans-Caucasus, the North Caucasus, and Siberia.) In 1958 an official of one of these "guessed" that 65 per cent of the Soviet Moslem population followed the Koran. In Central Asia he said that there were only 200 mosques under the supervision of priests appointed by the Mufti of Tashkent. However, there were about a thousand village and neighborhood mosques. *The Times*, Sept. 16, 1958. Cf. Sulzberger, op. cit., pp. 202–208 for additional figures.

[2] Wheeler, "Recent Soviet Attitudes toward Islam," pp. 12–13.

[3] *New York Times*, Sept. 15, 1954, p. 9, and *News*, 12, 1954, p. 23, and 15, 1954, p. 24.

[4] Radio Moscow, (Arabic Service), March 24, 1954.

of Central Asia and Kazakhstan as saying that large numbers of Moslems had participated in these celebrations. (Ten thousand were reported to have gathered at the central mosque in Tashkent alone.) However, this was not mentioned by the domestic press or radio. In mid-June *Izvestia* gave only brief mention to the national congress of Moslem leaders, but Tass distributed the story for foreign consumption in Arabic, Persian, and Russian, emphasizing the special appeals it made to all Moslems for peace. Almost simultaneously *Kazakhstanaskaya Pravda* published a long tirade against "The Reactionnary Essence of Pan-Islamism and Pan-Turkism." [1] Yet at nearly the same time two plane loads of carefully selected Moslem pilgrims were dispatched to Mecca from the USSR. [2]

The regime had other reasons for attacking religion. Rather than being an isolated phenomenon the continued presence of religious belief after nearly 40 years of atheist propaganda was part of a much larger problem facing Moscow. In the nearly four decades following the establishment of the Bolshevik state revolutionary morale had suffered greatly. This problem had been recognized at the Nineteenth Party Congress in October 1952 when the regime had called for an intensive program to strengthen Party discipline and a moral regeneration of Soviet society along more doctrinaire lines. The easing of domestic tension and the slight relaxation of the regime's iron grip after Stalin's death only served to aggravate an already serious problem. Being preoccupied with the more immediate issues of political and economic survival, it may have been that his lieutenants were not able to focus their attention on these issues until the latter part of 1953. With the anti-religious campaign the Soviet press also whipped up similar ones against juvenile delinquence, drunkenness, and moral laxness that attracted less attention outside of the USSR but which were equally severe in their condemnation of "forbidden" practices.

A large percentage of the anti-religious propaganda was directed primarily toward the younger generation. It must have

---

[1] "Two Faces of Soviet Moslem Policy," BBC, July 16, 1954. Cf. *Zarya Vostoka*, Oct. 10, 1954, pp. 2–3, *Current Digest*, VI, 40, pp. 9–11 for an excellent example of the domestic policy toward Islam.

[2] *New York Times*, Sept. 15, 1954, p. 9. In 1953 Moscow had permitted the first Soviet pilgrims to visit Mecca since 1945. *Notes – Soviet Affairs, op. cit.*, p. 7.

been particularly galling to the regime's theorists to witness the extent to which the Soviet youth of the "new generation" had become embroiled with religious beliefs. In the older elements of the population this could be explained away as the last remaining vestiges of their "bourgeois past," but it had to be acknowledged by anyone willing to face the facts that the Soviet system had failed miserably in its attempt to completely re-educate the younger generation in Marxist ideology. Naturally enough, the Komsomol organizations came under sharp condemnation for their inability to provide a program attractive enough to hold the allegiance of the young people. [1] The churches, particularly the minority sects with their simplicity of worship and their fresh and appealing egalitarian doctrines, apparently filled the ideological and spiritual void created by dissolutionment in the Soviet system and the transformation over the years of the Komsomols from a militant elite to an almost all-inclusive club lacking motivation. [2]

Other aspects of the anti-religious campaign were directed against the older worshippers for a variety of reasons. Certainly an important one was the destruction of any group that the regime could not thoroughly dominate and which might provide the nucleus for the organization of dissatisfaction and opposition. Also there was very likely a good deal of truth in the claims that the celebration of religious festivals (particularly by the peasants during the harvest season) caused setbacks in agricultural and industrial production which the economy could ill afford. [3] Likewise the regime's incessant attack on the high degree of superstition and low spiritual level (particularly in the Orthodox Church) of Russian religious practices cannot be completely disregarded. The Soviets constantly faced the difficult task of dragging a reluctant and backward society into the twentieth century. Their problem was epitomized by the constant contradiction presented by the supposedly highly indoctrinated Party members who were taken in by the charlatans plying their trade under the guise of religion or on its outer fringes. [4]

[1] *Komsomolskaya Pravda,* Feb. 20, 1954, p. 3, *Current Digest,* VI, 7, p. 15.
[2] Two disgruntled Komsomol members interviewed by the author in 1957 stated that they belonged only because it was the key to promotion in their factories.
[3] Cf. *Current Digest,* VI, 32, pp. 1–9.
[4] Cf. Crankshaw, *op. cit.,* pp. 39–53.

Why were these efforts so abruptly terminated? Khrushchev's remonstrations to the Party on behalf of the Central Committee were an unprecedented step and immediately raised considerable speculation as to what pressures had forced the regime to back down from its extreme position. One Western argument was that the Party's efforts to curb religious practices had run into unexpectedly strong popular resistance. The major difficulty in evaluating this thesis is the absence of a reliable means of determining the extent of religious belief in the Soviet Union. Even accurate statistics on church membership are unavailable. [1] The only indirect (and admittedly very poor) gauge is the intensity of the attacks leveled at the various sects by the Soviet press. *Partiynaya Zhizn*, one of the two important theoretical journals, illustrated the failure of the Party to eliminate religious belief in nearly 40 years of atheistic propaganda when it was forced to admit that:

Recently the church and various religious sects have considerably increased their activities and are strongly disseminating religious ideology among the backward elements of the population.[2]

This tallied with non-Soviet reports that for the Easter services in 1954 there were more churches open, more priests officiating, and more people of all ages in attendance than at any other time since 1917. (Except for considerable sums being spent by the government to restore Moscow's historic churches, the cost of renovating and reconstruction fell entirely upon the peasant congregations.) But it would be a mistake to misjudge the strength of this movement. Although religion was still alive in the Soviet Union, compared to pre-Revolutionary Russia atheism had made serious inroads. [3]

---

[1] Cf. Posselt, "Das Schicksal des Ostprotestantismus," p. 49 for estimates of the size of the membership of 23 Protestant denominations in the USSR.

[2] *Partiynaya Zhizn*, Aug. 9, 1954, as quoted by the *New York Times*, Aug. 10, 1954, p. 1, Harrison Salisbury.

[3] *Ibid.*, Aug. 12, 1954, p. 22; April 25, 1954, p. 23; and May 12, 1954, p. 3. According to Soviet figures the following number of churches were open in 1956:

20,000	Orthodox
5,400	Baptist
1,500	Roman Catholic (including Old Believers) *
800	Lutheran or Reform
500	Seventh Day Adventist
500	Jewish Synagogues
100	Armenian
50	Buddhist

(No figures were given for Islamic mosques). (*Continued on p.* 106)

There is little question that the Malenkov-Khrushchev struggle for power which terminated in the February 1955 government reorganization was a factor in these events, but its precise relationship remains a mystery. The entire anti-religious propaganda campaign may have been a fundamental part of the philosophy behind the "new course" or its abrupt abandonment may simply have been one of the tactical moves which became more and more frequent as the power struggle gained momentum. Many years before Zhdanov had explained that the first period of acute religious persecution (1922–23) had coincided with the early years of the NEP because the granting of increased economic concessions entailed additional vigilance on the ideological front. At the beginning of the Second World War Stalin had demonstrated a corollary of this principle when he eased religious persecution at the moment that the loyalty of the people was most sorely needed. If these policies were continued in the post-Stalin era then the repression which began in December 1953 was a counterweight to the economic concessions announced the previous fall. With the shift in political fortunes on the domestic scene and the rapidly approaching crisis the lessening of anti-religious propaganda may have reflected the regime's desire to keep from alienating the people during such a crucial period.

However, this does not fully explain the Central Committee decree. If this were its only purpose the same thing could have been accomplished in a much different way such as letting the propaganda campaign taper off and die a natural death. Therefore, the sudden calling off of the Party wolves may have been an attempt by Khrushchev to identify himself with a popular measure at a critical moment, much as Beria and his police apparatus had suddenly emerged as the defenders of civil liberties soon after Stalin's death by repudiating the "Doctors' Plot." In this connection, it is significant that Khrushchev deliberately destroyed the principle of collectivity when it was receiving its greatest publicity by issuing the decree over his signature rather

* (*Continued from p.* 105) No explanation as to why the Old Believers, an Orthodox sect, were included with the Roman Catholic Church was given. Published in "Religion in the Soviet Union," *Notes – Soviet Affairs*, 186, March 28, 1956, p. 4. The number of Orthodox bishops had decreased by 75 per cent and the number of priests by 50 per cent between 1917 and 1956. Only 50 new candidates for the priesthood were taken annually by Orthodox seminaries. Sulzberger, *op. cit.*, pp. 50–51.

than that of the anonymous Central Committee, as was the custom. An important agricultural report stressing the over-fulfillment of the 1954 production goals of both the state and collective farms, a field Khrushchev had publicly championed since Stalin's death, was issued only two days earlier under the collective signature of both the Central Committee and the USSR Council of Ministers. Likewise, the Party greeting to the Second All-Union Congress of Soviet Writers on December 16, 1954, was a collective affair. [1]

COLLECTIVE   LEADERSHIP   AND   THE   STRUGGLE
FOR POWER

While there is no concrete evidence as to Khrushchev's motives, this incident does serve to highlight the shift that had taken place in the regime's delicate internal balance. One of the out-standing features of the August 1953–February 1955 period was the collective nature of the regime's operation. This was not merely an artificial creation of official pronouncements, but was observed by the diplomatic corps as being a real part of the Soviet high-command's day-to-day working relationship. (In fact, at the time, the idea of internal conflicts found more sup-port outside of Russia than it did among Western observers stationed in the Soviet capital.) [2] The delicate balance which existed within the regime permitted no faction or individual to act independently, and the critical domestic and foreign problems demanding attention forged a working relationship which proved harmonious as long as the clashing personalities could be chan-neled along common programs. One of the basic difficulties with this arrangement was that the balance was not static but con-tinuously readjusting itself in terms of the changing power positions of its various components. With the secret police brought to heel and the willingness of the marshals to remain in the background as long as their interests were observed, the two major rival factions were clearly the bureaucracy, in general personified by Malenkov, and the Party, headed by Khrushchev. [3]

---

[1] *Pravda*, Nov. 8, 1954, p. 1, and *Izvestia*, Nov. 10, 1954, *Current Digest*, VI, 43, pp. 7–8; and *Pravda* and *Izvestia*, Dec. 16, 1954, p. 1, *ibid.*, VI, 48, pp. 3–4.
[2] Salisbury, *op. cit.*, p. 225.
[3] It must be kept in mind that the actual division of authority was not as sharp

Each assumed responsibility for a sector of the economy, and thereby tied his political fortunes to its success or failure.

In August 1953 the internal balance had slightly favored Malenkov, but the power inherent in Khrushchev's position as First Secretary of the Party gave him an advantage which Malenkov, without direct control of a focus of power, lacked. The events of late 1953 and the first three months of the following year strongly suggested that both protagonists were busily engaged in building up their respective positions. In December five important ministers [1] were elevated to the rank of Deputy Premier. They had all held this position while Stalin lived, but lost it as a result of the earliest reorganization. (Only Mikoyan had held that rank since Stalin's death.) Thus, in effect, the administrative pattern which existed before March 1953 when a ten-member steering committee was reputed to run the bureaucracy, was recreated. Taken as a group, whose average age was only 50, these five represented the most able young executives of the Soviet Union. This move, as well as a further subdivision of ministries in the late spring, suggested that Malenkov was attempting to build the emerging generation of industrialists into a rival of the Party. [2]

During the next few months another series of purges swept through the lower levels of both the government and Party organizations. They began in November and December 1953 and did not die out until early spring after the Republic Party Congresses and the Supreme Soviet elections. Precisely what forces precipitated these is not clear, although a number of motivating factors seemed to have been present. Some – particularly those in Georgia and the other Caucasian Republics – could be linked to the continuing removal of Beria's lesser protégés. Others were the product of the Presidium rivalry, and

as implied by the official titles. Malenkov continued to excercise influence in the Party and Khrushchev did likewise in the bureaucracy.

[1] Pervukhin, Minister of Electric Power Stations and Electrical Industry; I. F. Tevosyan, Minister of Metallurgical Industries; Kosygin, Minister of Manufactured Goods; Malyshev, Minister of Medium Machine Building; and Saburov, Chairman of the State Planning Commission. (The latter had been reappointed to his old job the previous June 29.) Meissner, "Tagung des Obersten Sowjet," p. 364.

[2] The subdivision of the ministries may have had no connection with this but simply have been a return to the traditional patttern of organization once the initial crisis following Stalin's death had passed. Economic motives may also have been involved.

still others were simply the result of the first general house-cleaning of regional officials since Stalin's death.

The 1954 Party Congress in Georgia provided an interesting balance sheet of the toll taken by the successive waves of purges which had racked the unfortunate Republic since 1952. Between the Fifteenth Congress in September of that year and February 1, 1954, 3,011 Party members and 1,029 candidates had been expelled. [1] The rate of attrition was particularly high among the membership of the Party's governing bodies. Fifty out of 74 of its Central Committee members were not re-elected in 1954, and 23 of the 37 candidates suffered the same fate. Among those dropped were

(1) ten former ministers;

(2) eight leading Army dignitaries and police officials;

(3) a former President of the Georgian Supreme Soviet;

(4) the Secretary of the above organization's Presidium;

(5) editors of two important Georgian newspapers;

(6) the First and Second Secretaries of the Georgian Komsomols; and

(7) two successive First Secretaries of the Georgian Party.

The turnover was so great that

in several cases replacements could not be found on the spot and ... had to be brought in ... from other parts of the country.

Interestingly, however, Moscow seemed to feel it necessary to send officials who were of Georgian origin. Of the 139 in the new Central Committee elected in 1954 only 13 had names of Slavic derivation. With the possible exception of Armenia, this was probably fewer than in any other Republic. However, it should be remembered that the Commander of the Trans-Caucasian Military District was a Great Russian. [2]

Similar changes – although not as far reaching – took place in all of the other 14 non-Russian Republic Party organizations. Only in the Kirgiz SSR did the Secretariat remain intact.

[1] These figures apparently do not include those ousted in April 1952 nor do they contain any indication of how many were removed as a result of Beria's arrest in June 1953. *New York Times*, Feb. 22, 1954, p. 4, and Feb. 28, 1954, p. 15, Harrison Salisbury. There were 160,045 members and 13,253 candidates in the Georgian Party organization as of September 1952. *Zarya Vostoka*, Sept. 16, 1952, pp. 2-4, Gruliow, *op. cit.*, p. 68.

[2] "The Georgian Purge – A Final Balance Sheet," BBC, May 26, 1954.

Otherwise there were sweeping revisions: a complete turnover took place in Armenia, Georgia, and Kazakhstan; new First and Second Secretaries were elected in the Ukraine; Second Secretaries were replaced in Belorussia, Estonia, Latvia, Lithuania, the Karelo-Finnish SSR, and Turkmenistan; and a number of Third Secretaries were also purged. [1] The first indication of another trend was also apparent. In the Ukraine and Kazakhstan the Congresses increased the number of Secretaries from the three provided for by the Party Statutes adopted at the Nineteenth Party Congress in 1952 to four and five, respectively. During the next two years similar additions were made to the other non-Russian Republic Secretariats (apparently at Khrushchev's direction) without even the formalities of elections. The implication was that Khrushchev was "packing" the regional organization with hand-picked men. [2]

Even on the *oblast* level the number of changes was significant. New First Secretaries were appointed in, among others, Moscow, Smolensk, Tula, and Leningrad. [3] Khrushchev personally conducted the purge of the Leningrad organization which resulted in the removal of V. M. Andrianov, who had been a member of Stalin's short-lived Presidium and was the most important official to be removed since Beria's down-fall. [4]

There is the possibility that Khrushchev used these purges as a means of both settling old scores and removing opposition to his virgin lands program which was announced in February after most of them had been completed. A number of facts suggested this. In 1946 Andrianov had been directly under Andreyev, the man who preceded Khrushchev as the Politburo's agricultural authority. Also he presumably owed his post to Malenkov and,

[1] Cf. pp. 334–335.

[2] Rush, *op. cit.*, p. 24.

[3] Fainsod, *op. cit.*, p. 27. For example, in the RSFSR, the Ukrainian SSR, and Belorussian SSR (which accounted for 86 of the 125 *oblasts*, 12 of the 16 Autonomous Republics, and six of the nine Autonomous *Oblasts*) the turnover between April 1953 and April 1954 was as follows: RSFSR: 17 of 47 *oblast* Secretaries replaced and six new ones created, three of the 12 Secretaries of *oblast* organizations in the Autonomous Republics replaced, and two of the five Secretaries of the Autonomous *Oblasts* were new also; Ukrainian SSR: eight of 24 *oblast* Secretaries replaced and one new *oblast* created; and Belorussian SSR: five of seven *oblast* Secretaries replaced. Meissner, "Neuwahl des obersten 'Sowjetparlaments' und Parteisäuberungen," pp. 224–225; "Ukraine," p. 298; "Verwaltungsumbau," p. 293; and "RSFSR, Moldau, Weissrussland." p. 383.

[4] *The Economist*, Dec. 5, 1953, p. 3.

therefore, probably was somehow involved in what in later years became known as the "Leningrad affair." Interestingly, G. A. Arutinov, who had been the First Secretary of the Armenian Party since 1937 but who was purged in late 1953, had been the first Party official to publicly criticize Khrushchev's *agrogorod* program. V. I. Nedosekin of the Tula *Oblast* was replaced for his failure to implement Khrushchev's September 1953 agricultural directives calling for the transfer of technicians and specialists from the cities to the countryside. [1] In the course of these shake-ups *Izvestia* identified Ignatiev, the former MVD chief during the "Doctors' Plot," as the First Secretary of the Bashkir Autonomous Republic, a key oil producing region in the Urals. [2]

While these changes were taking place in the Party similar but not as extensive ones were in progress in the governments of Armenia, Azerbaidzhan, Kazakhstan, Lithuania, the RSFSR and the Ukraine. [3] They coincided with numerous shifts in Soviet diplomatic personnel abroad. [4]

When taken with the earlier purges of Beria's supporters, the turnover in the leadership during the year from April 1953 to April 1954 was fantastically high, hitting hardest among the non-Russian peoples. It would be necessary to go back to the Great Purges of the 1930's to find a comparable period of such turbulence among the top Soviet officials. The magnitude of this upheaval was not entirely apparent because the removal of the important officials had repercussions that were transmitted to their countless subordinates whose political fortunes were determined from above.

The purge in Kazakhstan should be singled out for special attention because the removal of Z. Shayakhmetov and I. I. Afonov from the two most important positions in the Kazhak Secretariat during February 1954 was of greater significance than merely the replacement of local leaders with two outsiders more

[1] *New York Times*, Dec. 11, 1953, p. 3, Harry Schwartz.

[2] *Izvestia*, Feb. 16, 1954, as quoted by *ibid.*, Feb. 18, 1954, p. 1, Harry Schwartz. He had held this post during World War II. Meissner, "Neuwahl des obersten 'Sowjetparlaments' und Parteisäuberungen," p. 222.

[3] Even in the USSR's Council of Ministers there was a high percentage of new faces. By April 1954 five of the 16 Deputy Premiers and eight of the remaining 16 members were new. Meissner, *op. cit.*, pp. 212–213; "Zweite Verwaltungsreform nach Stalin," pp. 458 and 463; "Ukraine," p. 297; and "RSFSR, Moldau, Weiss-russland," p. 384,

[4] *New York Times*, Feb. 8, 1954, p. 1.

closely identified with the central regime. It, in fact, heralded the advent of Khrushchev's gigantic agricultural gamble known as the virgin lands program which he presented to the Central Committee the same month. The transfer of Ponomarenko from the Ministry of Culture to the leadership of the Kazakh Party and the naming of Brezhnev as his assistant was intended to ensure the existence of firm authority in the hands of reliable personnel once the program got under way. [1]

Khrushchev's daring departure in the field of agriculture was not only a desperate bid to solve the agricultural crisis but also a measure of his success in gradually shifting the delicate balance within the Presidium. His increased prominence in the public eye during the spring and summer of 1954 could leave no doubt that he was on an equal footing with Malenkov within the regime. [2] Nothing highlighted this fact more than the attention devoted to the former's 60th birthday on April 17, 1954. Both *Pravda* and *Izvestia* printed his picture on page one along with the Central Committee's decree awarding him the title "Hero of Socialist Labor" as well as the Order of Lenin and the Hammer and Sickle gold medal. (Stalin did not receive both until his 50th birthday when he was securely in power.) [3] In the next few days both newspapers carried greetings from 12 Communist and Workers' parties (including the CPSU and the Chinese). The coverage given the event by the rest of the Soviet press was only fractionally less. [4] This was the first time since the formation of the post-Stalin government that the press had published greetings from foreign Communist Parties. When Kaganovich celebrated his 60th birthday in November 1953 he had been honored and had his picture published but received no public greetings. [5]

Less than two weeks later Khrushchev was again in the public eye when he and Malenkov simultaneously addressed different chambers of the newly elected Supreme Soviet [6] on the same

[1] *Pravda*, Feb. 22, 1954, p. 2, *Current Digest*, VI, 8, pp. 22–23. Later the same month Ye. B. Taiblkov, head of the Kazakh government, was also removed for his "shortcomings and mistakes." Quoted by the *New York Times*, Feb. 26, 1954, p. 26.

[2] Molotov, the third member of the triumvirate, exercised wide authority in the formation of foreign policy but was also believed to have considerable influence in domestic matters as well.

[3] *The Economist*, April 24, 1954, p. 292.

[4] *Current Digest*, VI, 16, pp. 22–23.

[5] *New York Times*, April 20, 1954.

[6] The official election ticket polled the largest popular vote and the highest

general subjects. This was unusual because only Malenkov's position as Chairman of the Council of Ministers entitled him to make such an address. Khrushchev's speech could have been a sign of rivalry or an effort by the regime to publicly display its collective nature and the close ties between the Party and the state. [1] This was only one of an increasing number of public appearances during the following weeks in which both Malenkov and Khrushchev took part on an equal footing. Many of these centered around the celebration of the 300th anniversary of the union of Russia and the Ukraine. [2]

As the year wore on collective leadership was stressed with increasing intensity. [3] *Pravda* repeatedly voiced the theme and on June 8, 1954, ceased to list the regime's members in order of importance. Whenever possible they were simply referred to as the leaders of the Party and the government (which apparently included the Party Presidium and Secretariat but not the government Ministries). When it was impossible to avoid listing them by name full members of the Presidium were arranged in Cyrillic alphabetical order. [4] However, there were a number of incidents to indicate that all was not as tranquil beneath the surface as the regime hoped to imply. For example, on May 30 *Pravda* quoted I. Nagy as having told the Hungarian Communist Party that sometimes the Party assumed the govern-

percentage – 99.79 – of affirmative votes ever recorded in a Soviet election. For the results of previous elections cf. Meissner, "Neuwahl des obersten 'Sowjetparlaments' und Parteisäuberungen," p. 210.

[1] The Soviet Embassy in London distributed translations of Malenkov's speech on April 28, two days after it had been delivered, but did not officially release Khrushchev's until May 5, although it published four news bulletins in the interval. It advertized reprints of Malenkov's but none of Khrushchev's. *Soviet News*, 2933, April 28, 1954, and 2938, May 5, 1954.

[2] It spotlighted the increased importance of men trained in the Ukrainian Party under Khrushchev's tutelage. Among them were Brezhnev in Kazakhstan; Z. T. Serdyuk, First Secretary of the Moldavian Party; Mzhavanadze in Georgia; R. A. Rudenko, Procurator General of the USSR; Marshal Konev; and General Grechko, Soviet Commander-in-Chief, Germany. *New York Times*, March 1, 1954, p. 6.

[3] Observers outside the USSR tended to view this as a sign of intensified internal strife while others in Moscow felt it merely reflected the existing situation. Cf. *Ibid.*, June 2, 1954, p. 30, and Salisbury, *op. cit.*, Chapter 14.

[4] Radio Moscow's English language broadcasts merely translated the Cyrillic alphabetical listings. (*New York Times*, Aug. 8, 1954, p. 13.) The candidate members of the Presidium and CPSU Secretaries continued to be ranked according to importance until November 6 and 7, 1954, when the alphabetical listing was also adopted for them. Meissner, *op. cit.*, p. 47, and "Soviet Hierarchy abandons Order of Precedence," BBC, July 7, 1954.

ment's functions and when this happened it

reduces the independence, authority, and responsibility of the organs of
state power. At the same time this makes it difficult for the Party to direct
the activities of the organs of the state.

It is an incorrect opinion, damaging to the case of strengthening the
people's democratic state, that the Party itself is directly able to solve
all tasks. It also weakens the strength of the union of the working class
and the working peasants.[1]

Despite the supposedly "faceless" character of the leadership
individual members repeatedly made specific references to their
World War II activities, and *Pravda* hinted at the shifts taking
place behind the scenes when it printed individual notices of
visits by the Communist China's Foreign Minister to Khrushchev,
Voroshilov, and Malenkov (in that order). Normal diplomatic
protocol would not have required the one to Khrushchev because
he held no official government post. [2]

Probably the most significant event in this behind-the-scenes
struggle was Khrushchev's mid-June Prague speech in which he
assumed a greatly increased belligerent attitude and warned the
West that a Third World War would ruin the capitalist world. He
recalled one of Churchill's old statements that the Bolsheviks
understood nothing but force and paraphrased Lenin to the
effect that

while capitalist encirclement exists it is very difficult and complicated
to come to terms.

But he became more bellicose when he declared:

We always knew that to live with the enemy one must be strong. We
have done everything possible. We created atomic energy; we created the
atom bomb; we outstripped the capitalists and created the hydrogen bomb
before them .... They think they can intimidate us. But nothing can
freighten us, because if they know what a bomb means, so do we.[3]

To listeners who heard him speaking over Radio Prague it
sounded as if he had departed from a prepared text and become
carried away with his own oratory. This belief was strengthened
when the promised Czech translation was delayed for 40 minutes
and contained important variations. The following day *Pravda*
printed yet a third version. The remarks about Churchill and

[1] *Pravda*, May 30, 1954, as quoted by the *New York Times*, June 1, 1954, p. 11,
Harrison Salisbury.
[2] *Ibid.*, Aug. 8, 1954, p. 13.
[3] Quoted by *The Observer*, July 4, 1954, p. 1, Edward Crankshaw.

Lenin were removed and the passage about the atomic bomb markedly softened, and *Pravda* concluded by commenting that the Soviet Union proposed banning atomic weapons,

not because we are weak but because we really carry out a peace-loving policy in the interests of the working masses.[1]

Two other possibly related events soon transpired. One was the June session of the Central Committee and the other was the announcement the following month that Ryumin, Ignatiev's Deputy in the Ministry of State Security during the "Doctors' Plot," had been brought to trial and executed. [2] The precise relationship of these to the struggle for power is difficult to establish. One interesting aspect is that despite the fact that he had launched the virgin lands program just a few months before it was the first time since Stalin's death that Khrushchev was not credited with having delivered the major agricultural report to the Central Committee. This is of special significance because the session decreed that the material incentives established for vegetables, potatoes, and meat production the previous September should be extended to grain (the principal crop of the virgin lands) to improve what was acknowledged to be a serious situation. [3] Why Khrushchev did not associate himself with what was bound to be a popular measure is difficult to explain unless his fortunes within the Presidium had been seriously impaired by his Prague speech. Likewise, there was no apparent reason for the timing of the Ryumin execution unless it was intended to be a pointed reminder to those who had "careerist and adventurist purposes."

Regardless of these considerations, which may or may not be related, there was general agreement among Western observers in Moscow that the mere fact that the Central Committee met in June 1954 was an important indication that it was assuming more than the rubber stamp authority it enjoyed under Stalin and that the much discussed collective leadership was a working reality. [4] But it was a relationship which could easily be disturbed by factors other than personal ambitions. One of these was the success or failure of the economic policies advocated by the two

[1] *Pravda* as quoted by *ibid.*
[2] *Komsomolsakaya Pravda*, July 23, 1954, p. 1, *Current Digest*, VI, 25, p. 14.
[3] *Pravda* and *Izvestia*, June 27, 1954, p. 1, *ibid.*, VI, 26, pp. 4–14. Cf. p. 116.
[4] *New York Times*, July 1, 1954, p. 5.

major protagonists. Khrushchev staked his fortunes on agricultural policy while Malenkov tied his to industrial development, particularly in those areas dealing with consumers' goods production.

THE VIRGIN LANDS PROGRAM

During the last six months of 1953 the highest degree of cooperation existed between Khrushchev and Malenkov in the field of economics. The program put forth in the late summer and early fall of that year, was carried out without any apparent internal disagreement until 1954. Then suddenly Khrushchev initiated a drastic departure in agricultural policy which completely reversed the position he had taken only six months before and launched a huge new program in an area hardly mentioned the previous September.

The report Khrushchev delivered to the February session of the Party Central Committee was again a realistic analysis of the continuing agricultural crisis, remarkably free from the dogmatic polemics which had marred Soviet utterances on the subject before Stalin's death. However, this time he dealt almost exclusively with the problems arising from the deficiencies in grain production. This was surprising because, although in September 1953 he had painted a somewhat less optimistic picture of grain yields than Malenkov's famous assertion that they had reached the stage where they were no longer a problem, Khrushchev had praised the record 119,000,000 acres then under cultivation and referred to it as an area of Soviet farming where there were

more considerable achievements than in other branches of agriculture.

He had, however, stressed the need for increasing the per acre yield production. To judge by the important decrees which implemented his recommendations, the regime appeared to feel that no grain problem, comparable with those concerning livestock, potatoes and vegetables, existed. [1]

However, in February 1954 his analysis was indeed grim:

The level of grain production so far has not met all of the requirements of the national economy. The amount of grain remaining on the collective farms after they have met their obligations to the state does not fully

[1] Volin, "The New Battle for Grain in Soviet Russia," p. 195.

meet the requirements of the communal community. A shortage of grain for the requirements of collective farm animal husbandry is particularly felt.

Yet it is precisely now, when the Party and government are organizing a major advance in the production of consumers' goods – a major factor which is a rapid advance in animal husbandry – that the shortage of feed grain is especially intolerable.[1]

As things stood there was not enough grain to properly feed the ever-growing population which, because of rapid industrialization, was demanding a better diet, to provide the non-grain growing sectors of agriculture with a dependable supply, nor to assure adequate reserves "for all contingencies," i.e., famines such as those of the late 1920's or an all-out war. [2]

But even then Khrushchev failed to fully reveal the catastrophic nature of the crisis. Only in December 1958 did he tell the Central Committee that, instead of the 145, 161, 300 metric ton "biological" yield Malenkov had claimed for 1952, there had been a "biological" harvest of only 91,935,483 metric tons. This was serious enough but what made matters worse had been the regime's failure to procure more than 33,870,983 metric tons of this for actual use. Even this amount had been obtained only because the collective and state farms had turned in part of their seed stock to the state. The following year – 1953 – the situation had been even worse since despite the comparatively low yield of 1952 it had been a record crop. When the 1953 harvest had been gathered in the regime was able to count only 30,629,032 metric tons. This did not even cover the 32,741,935 metric tons the state had been forced to distribute during the year as food, feed, and seed. The deficit was made up from the national reserves, a situation which Khrushchev told the 1958 Central Committee

could not be permitted at all.

As Khrushchev admitted, Soviet grain production between 1949 and 1953 had been roughly the same as during the 1910–1914 period. [3]

---

[1] *Pravda* and *Izvestia*, March 21, 1954, pp. 1–5, *Current Digest*, VI, 12, p. 4.

[2] *Ibid.*

[3] While these figures most likely represent a much truer picture of Soviet agriculture, they should be viewed critically since Khrushchev cited them as evidence against the "anti-Party" group in 1958.

Sown Area, Actual (Elevator) Crop, and Total Grain Returns

	Grain area (in millions of hectares)	Per hectare production (in centers)	Total grain returns (in millions of metric tons)
1910–1914 (average per year over present territory)	102.5	7.0	70.6
1949–1953 (average per year)	105.2	7.7	79.7

(Source: *Soviet News*, Supplement to 3992, Jan. 23, 1959, p. v.)

The solution which Khrushchev put forth in 1954 to remedy this crisis was a good index of its seriousness. Completely reversing the position he had taken six months before which emphasized the raising of per acre yields, he proposed the breath-taking agricultural gamble of plowing up 32,000,000 acres of virgin and idle land for grain cultivation in 1954 and 1955. [1] From this 12 per cent increase in the total grain acreage, Khrushchev expected to harvest between 18 and 20,000,000 metric tons annually, three quarters of it marketable. In fact, in the immediate future he planned to be able to raise the level of state grain procurements and purchases by 35 to 40 per cent of the 1953 quota.

The development of this gigantic undertaking was to take place primarily in the Urals, Siberia, and Kazakhstan (this one Republic was to supply almost half of the original acreage) and to a lesser extent in the Volga region and North Caucasus as well as the Far Eastern regions. [2] As Khrushchev himself stressed, only through complete mechanization could the program succeed. Therefore, the Central Committee originally ordered 120,000 15 horsepower tractors and 10,000 combines as well as equal numbers of tractor plows, seeders, and various other machinery to be shipped to the virgin lands. But since these sparsely populated areas could hardly be expected to provide sufficient labor –let alone trained technicians and agricultural specialists – for this

[1] "Virgin land" was defined as that which had not been cultivated within the past 25 years and "idle land" as that which had not been cultivated for two years. In fact, the vast majority of the land eventually utilized by this campaign was brought under the plow for the first time. *Economic Survey of Europe in 1954*, p. 74.

[2] Volin, *op. cit.*, 195. For a discussion of the productive capacity of Soviet Asia cf. Barth, "Wieviel Menschen kann Russisch-Asien ernähren?", pp. 95–103.

daring venture special provisions for recruiting personnel were required. The Komsomols were initially told to provide 100,000 skilled volunteers and enterprises throughout the Soviet Union were instructed to be prepared to send their most qualified workers. The incentives included three months' pay from their previous job, transportation expenses, and bonuses of 15 per cent for the first two years and for overfulfilment of the quota. [1]

But these were only initial figures. Despite early reports of mismanagement, enormous waste, chaos, and confusion caused by the tremendous magnitude of the program and the speed with which it was begun, the Central Committee announced on August 17, 1954, an increase which raised the original goal for 1955 to 37,000,000 acres and that of 1956 to between 69 and 74,000,000 acres. [2] Initially all of this was to be devoted almost exclusively to grain (primarily wheat) but in subsequent years crop rotation, based upon local needs, was to be practised. [3] In effect, within three years the Soviet Union intended to place under cultivation an area nearly equal to the record 76,000,000 acres of wheat planted in the United States during 1949. In terms of the Soviet Union, it meant that within three years the total cultivated area was to be increased by one sixth. [4]

This increase in the projected goal indicated that in the minds of its planners the program had been successful beyond expectations. A number of factors probably contributed to this optimism. One was that the anticipated 1954 yield from the less than 9,000,000 acres plowed and seeded in the first month of the program was enough to off-set the poor harvest in the Ukraine and other southern regions and even increase government acquisitions above those of the previous year. Another was that plowing for the coming year was considerably ahead of schedule. Also the sheer momentum generated by such a gigantic program was an important factor in its continued expansion. However,

---

[1] *Pravda* and *Izvestia*, March 6, 1954, p. 1, *Current Digest*, VI, 9, pp. 5–6.

[2] Volin, "Khrushchev's Economic Neo-Stalinism," p. 459.

[3] *New York Times*, Aug. 17, 1954, p. 5, and the *Economic Survey of Europe in 1954*, p. 74.

[4] By 1954 the American wheat acreage had been reduced to 54,000,000 acres because of over production. (Volin, "The New Battle for Grain in Soviet Russia," p. 195.) During 1954 the USSR also increased the cotton acreage in Uzbekistan, Turkmenia, Tadzhikistan, and Azerbaidzhan in an attempt to meet the goals of the current Five Year Plan. *Economic Survey of Europe in 1954*, pp. 74 and 76–77.

there was yet another side to the story. While there were great successes there were also great failures. It was officially admitted that much of the harvest was lost because of the complete lack of facilities to gather it in, store it, or transport it from the remote virgin lands to the market. [1] Thousands of trucks from the urban centers were mobilized and farm machinery from other areas of the Soviet Union, primarily the Ukraine, where the harvest was completed earlier, were transported to the new development project.

Also there was scanty provision made for the thousands of people who were transported from the older areas of the Soviet Union to the new lands. By mid-1954 150,000 trained specialists had been brought in. By the end of the year the total influx of workers, including collective farmers and working members of their families, was about 200,000. Among these during the second half of 1954 were large numbers of demobilized soldiers who were settled as units, often under their former commanding officers. The Komsomols supplied their quota and announced that there were an additional 500,000 "volunteers" waiting to go. [2]

Precisely how "voluntary" some of these transfers were is open to question. Almost as soon as the program was announced there were persistent rumors that it was being used to conceal vast, mass deportations from the Western boarder lands and the re-settlement of Slavs. Reports from Bucharest put the number of Rumanians deported from Bessarabia during the first year and a half at between 500,000 to 750,000 – in other words, half of its Rumanian population. These were partially substantiated by *Sovetskaya Moldavia* and *Izvestia* of the Moldavian SSR in March 1955 when they announced a "planned emigration" from 22 Moldavian districts to Kazakhstan. To begin with, there was no economic justification for such a population transfer. During World War II Bessarabia lost one sixth of its population of over 3,000,000 and in 1952 Stalin began a resettlement program directed at replacing the German population he had removed during the war. What seemed to indicate that his lieutenants were following the Czarist policy of removing Rumanians from Bessarabia was that all of the 22 districts effected by the "planned

---

[1] Volin, "Khrushchev's Economic Neo-Stalinism," p. 460.
[2] *Economic Survey of Europe in 1954*, pp. 74–75.

emigration" were west of the Dniester River. For example, in the northern-most Moldavian department of Hotin only two of the four districts had a majority of Rumanians, and it was precisely these two that were selected. [1]

Whereas the original emphasis had been upon single men, by the fall of 1954 it had shifted to transfering family groups and whole collective farms as permanent settlers. [2] Housing, schools, adequate medical care and even such basic necessities as water were lacking. (During the summer tents were issued for 100,000 people.) [3] The first winter took a terrible toll in lives and suffering.

The inducements offered to those who would go to the virgin lands were many. Beside paying for transportation, loans of 10–20,000 rubles for housing, special tax concessions, and outright financial grants were made available during the late summer of 1954. [4] Earlier in the year economic incentives similar to those formerly restricted to livestock, vegetables, and potatoes, were offered for grain. Compulsory delivery quotas were lowered (entirely abolished for small peasant holdings) and the price paid for grain above these was also raised. [5]

The tremendous size of this program alone made it a considerable gamble. There was always the question of whether the substantial investment involved would not be used more profitably if applied to improving existing agricultural areas. However, there was an even greater element of risk in this particular venture because climatic and soil conditions of the regions involved did not lend themselves to the continued successful cultivation of grains. A Soviet survey of Siberia warned that while there were many areas of rich soil where several year's crops could be grown without expending fertilizers these were interlaced with tracts of poor soil and therefore should be brought into production gradually after reclamation.[6]

[1] *The Economist*, July 23, 1955, p. 322.
[2] *New York Times*, Sept. 13, 1954, p. 4, Clifton Daniel.
[3] *Economic Survey of Europe in 1954*, p. 75.
[4] The following regions were among those which offered the highest inducements: Sakhalin, Kamchatka, the lower Amur, Khabarovsk, Magadan, Murmansk, Kalinigrad, Kuybyshev, and Simferopol (the former Crimea) *Oblasts*; and Armenia, Georgia, and Azerbaidzhan. Cf. *New York Times*, Oct. 18, 1954, p. 5, Clifton Daniel.
[5] *Pravda* and *Izvestia*, June 27, 1954, pp. 1–4, *Current Digest*, VI, 26, p. 13.
[6] *Pochvovederie*, 4, 1954, as quoted by Volin, "The New Battle for Grain in Soviet Russia," p. 198.

Throughout the region the growing season was short, averaging from only 120 to just under 150 frost-free days with the likelihood of late spring and early fall frosts which would severely damage the rotation crops as well as some grains. But the most limiting factor was the erratic and small amount of precipitation. The region as a whole averaged less than 16 inches a year and in some places less than ten. Frequent spring and summer droughts with high winds made the spectre of a giant dust bowl a distinct possibility. [1] But even under such adverse conditions the stakes made the gamble attractive. Khrushchev obviously was counting heavily upon the multiplying factor. Even if it were possible to obtain merely one third of the planned 15 bushels per acre it would amount to a tremendous addition to the Soviet grainery. [2] His reaction to the dismal failure of the 1955 harvest indicated that he considered the venture worthwhile if in five years there was one excellent crop, and two mediocre ones for two failures. [3]

But it is possible to make a substantial case for the argument that a number of non-agricultural considerations played a significant part in influencing the development of the virgin lands. Undoubtedly the grain crisis was a major factor, but it was not a new development on the Soviet scene and, therefore, did not explain the suddenness of this new program. It is hardly likely that the regime had deluded itself with its own opportunism based on the "biological harvests" rather than "barn yields." Nor is it likely that Stalin's heirs had lost confidence in the ability to raise per acre production in the short period between September 1953 and early 1954 when the basic outlines of the program were drawn up. In fact, when Khrushchev announced the new program in the Central Committee, he conceded that insufficient time had elapsed to fully evaluate these efforts. [4] Primary among the other considerations may have been

---

[1] *Ibid.*, pp. 198–199, and *Economic Survey of Europe in 1954*, p. 75.

[2] Volin, "Khrushchev's Economic Neo-Stalinism," p. 459.

[3] *Pravda*, Feb. 15, 1956, pp. 1–11, Gruliow (Ed.), *Current Soviet Policies*, II, p. 43.

[4] *Pravda* and *Izvestia*, March 21, 1954, pp. 1–5, *Current Digest*, VI, 12, p. 3. Even in September 1953 when the entire emphasis was upon intensification of production, Stalin's much publicized grandiose programs such as the "transformation of nature" by reforestation; gigantic irrigation projects totaling 12,000,000 acres in the Volga, Don, and Dneper river basins; or the Fifth Five Year Plan goal to increase grain production from 40 to 50 per cent with only a ten per cent increase in acreage were never mentioned. Harris, "Growing Food by Decree," p. 270, and Volin, "The New Battle for Grain in Soviet Russia," p. 197.

the Malenkov-Khrushchev struggle. The latter's grim report amounted to a slap at Malenkov for his boast at the Nineteenth Party Congress. Interestingly, Khrushchev attacked the chief government agricultural officials for their failure to plan sufficient grain acreage, but, with the exception of the Kazakh Party Secretaries, he did not level criticism at any members of the Party Central Committee apparatus although it was as closely connected with the problem as its state counterpart. [1] This suggests the existence of a rivalry between the agricultural organizations in the government and the Party and disagreement over how the crisis could best be solved. Possibly in September 1953 Khrushchev had not been strong enough to openly challenge Malenkov's position and had been forced to bide his time.

An important feature of the virgin lands program was the prominence given the *sovkhozy* (state farms). During the first two years they were to account for about one third of the new farms and an even higher percentage by 1956. During 1954 alone 124 of the total 560 were of this type. [2] These were, in fact, the giant grain factories which were attempted first in the 1930's and later in Khrushchev's *agrogorod* program of the 1950–1951 period. At the Nineteenth Party Congress Malenkov (without mentioning Khrushchev by name) had sharply criticized these as being the cause of many of the regime's agricultural failures. The frontier society of the virgin lands gave Khrushchev an excellent opportunity to push his pet idea because the newly formed *sovkhozy* with their high percentage of young people from the cities had none of the traditional ties with the old villages which had been such a major stumbling bloc in the past. But the *sovkhozy* were important for still another reason. They were more directly under the control of the central administration. During a period of emergency they could more easily be forced to carry out

---

[1] Khrushchev criticized by name N. Skvortsov, First Deputy Minister of Agriculture; Kozlov, Minister of State Farms; S. T. Demidov, Vice Chairman of the State Planning Committee; and V. S. Dmitriyev, former chief of the Agricultural Planning Administration in the USSR State Planning Committee, who had been fired. *Pravda*, and *Izvestia*, March 25, 1954, *Current Digest*, VI, 12, p. 3.

[2] Kazakhstan was to have the largest percentage. Over one half of the newly cultivated land there was to be organized in *sovkhozy*. By the end of 1954 93 such farms had been established and another 300 were in various stages of organization. *New York Times*, Nov. 1, 1954, p. 4; Volin, *op. cit.*, 196; Spector, *The Soviet Union and the Muslim World: 1917–1956*, p. 123; and the *Economic Survey of Europe in 1954*, p. 75.

a scorched earth policy and were not as likely to offer the resistance the regime had encountered from some Ukrainian collectives during the Second World War.

The question of internal security seems to have occupied a very important part in the whole program. At the moment it was announced the West was forging the first links in the Bagdad Pact along the USSR's southern flanks. As a result, this new influx of young, non-Moslem pioneers into the Soviet Middle East coincided with the development of a Western-oriented Moslem alliance. The transfer of demobilized soldiers (often under their former officers) to the state farms not only satisfied the need for laborers but also provided a type of "defense in depth" through the creation of numerous potential military strong-points. From the strategic point of view the program was an important step forward in Moscow's efforts to decentralize its economic development. The creation of an important agricultural area far removed from Russia's vulnerable Western boarders and closer to the area's growing industrial complex brought regional self-sufficiency that much nearer. However, it was not exclusively the West which Moscow had in mind when it undertook to colonize Central Asia. Moscow could not have overlooked the similar process being conducted by Communist China in Sin-kiang. [1]

It was impossible for the virgin lands program to be carried through without Khrushchev's earlier plans for the intensified cultivation of existing acreage suffering. Beginning in January 1954 they were suddenly relegated to second place. Despite the fact that his campaign to provide the older farming areas with more machinery and thousands of trained technicians and agri-cultural specialists was less than five months old, by February these were being diverted to the new lands. In fact, the older collectives lost some of their already inadequate machinery and their too few specialists to the new program with very little prospect of having either replaced.

The regime's solution was to supply them with larger quantities of spare parts and to raise the required working norms. [2] This tightening of discipline was apparently the first of its kind since

[1] Cf. Fedyshyn, *op. cit.*, pp. 127–145.
[2] *Economic Survey of Europe in 1954*, p. 76.

arrived in the larger cities they sold for between two rubles ten kopecks and one ruble 75 kopecks each, as compared with four and five rubles each the previous year. (The average wage in the Soviet Union was between 800–900 a month.) However, the regime had acquired them at a mere ten kopecks each. [1]

THE NEW DIPLOMACY

While these domestic questions demanded a good share of the regime's attention they did not prevent it from developing a diplomacy which was a bewildering combination of threats, conciliatory gestures, and imaginative departures into previously unexplored fields, all subtly tied together in a highly flexible global program designed to exploit the slightest advantage. As it maneuvered for time in which to consolidate its position at home, the regime never lost sight of its major foreign policy goals: the neutralization of American political and military influence in Europe and Asia and the eventual transformation of these areas into spheres of Soviet domination.

In Europe Moscow concentrated upon preserving the *status quo* in both Germany and Austria while attempting to aggravate existing differences within the Western alliance. To accomplish this it turned to Asia where it supported outright aggression in Indochina. However, its main interest in the Far East was the neutralization of key Asian countries through offers of economic assistance and the skillful exploitation of nationalism and anti-Western sentiment. In the Middle East it sought to prevent the formation of the Bagdad Pact and to reassert its traditional claims. But in doing so, it was greatly hampered by its dogmatic refusal to compromise – either at home or abroad – with Islam. Moscow also showed definite signs of an awakened interest in Africa.

Germany, Austria, and the Berlin Conference

The first major development in Europe following Malenkov's reassertion in August 1953 that there were no outstanding

---

[1] *Ibid.*, March 17, 1954, p. 11, and cf. Salisbury, *op. cit.*, Chapter 8. As late as 1957 oranges were in such short supply in Moscow that Georgian peasants made sufficient profit from merely what they could carry on their backs to fly with them to the Soviet capital.

questions which could not be settled through negotiation was the Big Four Foreign Ministers' Conference in Berlin. However, it did not materialize until January 1954 and then only after a complicated and confusing exchange of diplomatic notes which lasted for nearly six months. [1]

Immediately after Stalin's death the subject of renewed East-West negotiations was clearly uppermost in the minds of diplomats in Moscow, London, Paris, and Washington, and during the spring both sides cautiously sounded out each other on the subject. However, it was the West which finally took the initiative in July 1953 by proposing that a Foreign Ministers' conference discuss Germany and Austria in the autumn. When the Soviet's replied on August 4 they accepted the general principle of discussing problems of world tension without specificly referring to either country, and indicated that they wanted Communist China to participate in any such conference, but refrained from making this a condition. [2]

Eleven days later Moscow proposed that a German peace treaty conference be held within six months. Its terms were essentially the same as those put forth before:

(1) East and West Germany were to begin direct negotiations immediately;
(2) both German parliaments were to take part in the formation of an all-German government that was to conduct free elections;
(3) after January 1, 1954, all reparation payments were to be ended; and
(4) the all-German government was to refrain from participating in any military alliances directed at any of the World War II allies. [3]

At the very last minute Russia rejected a Big Three invitation to discuss Austria, and implied that she intended to link it to the German problem. [4] The West, therefore, countered with a proposal on September 2 that both be dealt with in mid-October. However, the Soviet answer, which was delayed until the closing

---

[1] For excerpts from this diplomatic exchange cf. Mehnert, "Deutschlandpolitik der Sowjets," pp. 349–355 and pp. 434–442, and "Um die deutche Frage," pp. 27–32.
[2] *New York Times*, Nov. 27, 1953, p. 2, Drew Middleton.
[3] *Ibid.*, Aug. 17, 1953, p. 1, Harrison Salisbury.
[4] *Ibid.*, Aug. 30, 1953, p. 1, Walter Waggoner.

days of the month, neither accepted nor rejected the offer. Once again the West renewed its proposals, setting November 9 as the new tentative date, but again the Soviet response neither accepted nor rejected them. However, it did request that any Four Power conference on Germany and Austria be followed by a Big Five conference (including Communist China) to end the Cold War. [1] An indication of what the Soviets intended to discuss at such a gathering was given in a six-point suggested agenda published in *New Times*, a Soviet periodical devoted to foreign policy:

(1) conclusion of a peaceful settlement in Korea;
(2) restoration of Communist China to her "rightful place in the United Nations";
(3) reduction of armaments and banning of atomic and hydrogen weapons;
(4) liquidation of military bases on foreign territory;
(5) cessation of Cold War propaganda; and
(6) the German problem. [2]

In early November Soviet propaganda took on a renewed toughness. While not as strong as before Stalin's death, it seemed to put an end to the period of moderation and the regime's willingness to negotiate. However, Moscow had apparently miscalculated Western reaction because Molotov took the unprecedented step of calling a press conference to soften the Russian position. (It was the first of its kind with a high Soviet official in six years.) Although he sought to throw the blame for the existing deadlock upon the West, Molotov left the impression that on the question of direct, high-level negotiations the door had not entirely been closed. [3] *Pravda* added another conciliatory note a few days later when it recalled Soviet-American wartime collaboration and declaring that if it could be repeated it

would be a most important factor in the relaxation of tension and the strengthening of peace.[4]

In almost the next breath the USSR replied favorably to yet another Western offer to discuss both Germany and Austria.

[1] *Ibid.*, Nov. 27, 1953, p. 2, Drew Middleton, and Nov. 4, 1953, p. 1, Walter Waggoner.
[2] *Ibid.*, Oct. 4, 1953, p. 2.
[3] *Ibid.*, Nov. 14, 1953, p. 1.
[4] *Pravda*, Nov. 24, 1953, as quoted by *ibid.*, Nov. 24, 1953, p. 8.

Moscow suggested that the Big Four Ministers meet in Berlin but failed to specify a date. The timing of this acceptance (November 23, 1953) was important since it appeared to be a deliberate attempt to disrupt French approval of the European Defense Community and to cause the down-fall of Premier J. Laniel's government which faced a vote of confidence on that issue the following day. [1] (The Soviet desire to meddle in French politics was made even clearer when Moscow later insisted upon postponing the conference from January 4 until January 25, 1954. This meant that it would open in the wake of an anticipated French cabinet crisis that was expected to follow the installation of a new President in mid-January.) [2]

While this exchange was in progress the regime made sweeping changes in its representatives abroad. It was almost as if Moscow hoped to win the confidence of foreign capitals by appearing to make a fresh start in the diplomatic world. The general pattern that began to emerge in late 1953 and early 1954 was the assignment of Party officials to the Satellites and career diplomates to the West and Middle East. The intensification of Soviet interest in this latter area was indicated by the appointment of a Deputy Foreign Minister as Ambassador to Turkey and a man who had formerly held such a post as Ambassador to Iran. This reshuffling also brought the men who had been closest to Molotov when he had been Foreign Minister between 1939–1949 back to Moscow. [3]

Despite Malenkov's New Year's assurance that no obstacles stood in the way of East-West relations, [4] the Soviet attitude at the Berlin Conference showed few signs of departing from its former intransigence. Moscow clearly was determined to maintain the *status quo* in Europe while it exploited the fluid situation

---

[1] *Ibid.*, Nov. 27, 1953, p. 1, Felix Belair, Jr.

[2] *Ibid.*, Dec. 27, 1953, p. 1, Dana Adams Schmidt.

[3] "Soviet Diplomatic Appointments: June 1953–Feb. 1954," BBC, Feb. 19, 1954. Cf. Meissner, "Der Auswärtige Dienst der UdSSR," pp. 49–54 and 112–118 for Soviet diplomatic appointments between 1949 and 1954.

[4] *Soviet News*, 2884, Jan. 4, 1954, p. 1. Soviet diplomacy skillfully exploited local conditions to prove this point. It played on French fears of Germany, and Indian fears of Pakistan; invited British and French commercial missions to Moscow; sold goods to Egypt below cost; released German and Italian prisoners of war; told Italian unemployed their future depended upon increased East-West trade; and ended border incidents along the Greek and Yugoslav frontiers. Cf. *New York Times*, Jan. 17, 1954, p. 1, C. L. Sulzberger.

in Asia so as to strengthen its own position and turn the Western powers against themselves, hoping thus to block the formation of the European Defense Community. The Soviet three-point agenda relegated the discussion of Germany and Austria to secondary importance in favor of

measures for lessening international tension

(i.e., relaxation of the Western embargo, "substantial" disarmament, and abandonment of EDC) and their discussion by a Five Power Conference (including Communist China). [1] Molotov also soon revived an old Russian proposal for a world-wide disarmament conference in which nations outside the UN (again such as Communist China) would participate. [2] When the Western Foreign Ministers abruptly reversed their earlier position so as to avoid an immediate deadlock and agreed to the agenda on the condition that the first item be discussed in private sessions, Molotov presented a series of proposals on Germany and Austria which merely restated the classic Soviet position and left practically no room for compromise without complete capitulation by the West. [3] (One Western observer quipped that Molotov repeatedly put forth new conditions "like rabbits out of a hat.") [4]

With the exception of three amendments his proposed German peace treaty was identical with the one he had submitted on March 10, 1952. [5] It called for the unification of a neutralized Germany which would be forbidden to join any coalition or military alliance directed against a member of the World War II allies, the withdrawal of all occupation forces, and the dismantling of all Western military bases. Molotov also proposed that an "all-German" government have a voice in the final writing of the treaty. The three Soviet amendments were significant. They stipulated that Germany was not to be bound by political commitments made prior to the peace treaty and her reparation debts (but not her commercial obligations) owed the

---

[1] *Soviet News*, 2895, Jan. 29, 1954, p. 4. Cf. Mehnert, "Die Viererkonferenz von Berlin," pp. 104–111 for the German point of view.

[2] *Facts on File*, XIV, 692, p. 34.

[3] By the same token, Russian acceptance of Western proposals would have meant her withdrawal from Central Europe.

[4] Quoted by the *New York Times*, Feb. 14, 1954, Part 4, p. 1.

[5] *Ibid.*, Feb. 2, 1954, p. 1, C. L. Sulzberger.

Big Four were to be canceled. An important limitation was also placed on her future military strength. Whereas the previous draft had provided that Germany

shall be permitted to have such national armed forces ... as shall be required for the country's defense,

this was further restricted to read:

The size of these armed forces shall be in conformity with tasks of an internal nature, local defense of frontiers, and air defense.[1]

According to Molotov's suggested timetable the treaty was to be presented to a peace conference by October 1954. Unification was to be achieved through the merger of both East and West Germany's parliaments into a Provisional All-German government which was to be responsible for conducting

free all-German elections ... without interferences from foreign states.

The government formed as a result of these elections was to assist in the writing of a peace treaty. [2]

Up to this point Molotov had merely presented a rehash of previously unacceptable proposals. But during the third week of negotiations he submitted two new and imaginative proposals (although equally unacceptable to the West) designed specifically to neutralize Germany, EDC, NATO, and force the United States out of Europe. The first called for the simultaneous withdrawal of all but token occupation forces from Germany within six months and the creation of local units to police the respective sectors. At the same time all European nations were invited to form a 50-year collective security system which, in effect, scrapped Western regional defense alliances because it specifically forebade any such arrangement that could be constructed as "contrary" to the general security of Europe. Membership was to be limited to European powers, thus relegating the United States to the role of "observer" and bringing Communist China into European politics by the same ruse. [3]

---

[1] *Soviet News*, 2897, Feb. 4, 1954, p. 6.

[2] *Ibid.*, 2899, Feb. 8, 1954, p. 4. The Soviet proposals for a peace treaty and unification of Germany were in direct opposition to the West's position. It wanted country-wide, free elections (supervised by an international commission) which would select a national Constituent Assembly to govern the nation in all matters except for a few functions retained by the occupation powers until the peace treaty had been ratified. Once this occured Germany was to have complete control over her foreign relations and military development and would be free to join what ever alliance or pact she chose. *Facts on File*, XIV, 692, p. 33.

[3] *Soviet News*, 2901, Feb. 12, 1954, p. 5.

Despite the Western offer to drop its insistence upon international inspection of all-German elections (which Molotov ignored), weeks of negotiation on a German peace treaty failed to reach agreement. The Foreign Ministers then turned to the question of Austria. Again the Soviets indicated that they were not seriously interested in a settlement. Previous Big Four conferences had narrowed the area of disagreement to only five of the 59 articles of the Austrian State Treaty. In an effort to arrive at some form of unanimity the Western Foreign Ministers accepted the Russian version of these last five points. [1] However, Molotov only denounced the West for blocking an Austrian settlement and demanded that three new items be added to the 1949 draft treaty. These concerned:

(1) the neutralization of Austria and the prohibition that it would not enter into any alliances directed against World War II allies;

(2) the withdrawal of the Four Power occupation forces only upon the signature of a German treaty (Moscow raised its familiar cry that this would prevent another *Anschluss*); and

(3) Four Power negotiations over the demilitarization of Trieste. [2]

Acceptance of these conditions would have effectively prolonged indefinitely the *status quo* in Austria.

The joint communiqué at the close of the Berlin Conference spelled out with remarkable clarity the fruitlessness of a month's wrangling and the inability of the Foreign Ministers to come to terms. On the last two items of the agenda it simply stated:

> The four Ministers have had a full exchange of views on the German question, on the problems of European security, and on the Austrian question, but they were unable to reach agreement. [3]

Only on the first item had there been any room for unanimity. Here the West reversed its position and consented to confer with Communist China on April 26, 1956, at Geneva about the questions of a peaceful unification of Korea and the restoration of peace in Indochina. The Big Four, the Chinese People's

---

[1] *World Today*, "Austria and the Berlin Conference," p. 150. These were as follows: (1) Austrian cooperation in preventing Germany from rearming outside her own territory; (2) indemnity for the prewar seizure by Germany of property belonging to UN members; (3) repatriation of displaced persons; (4) and (5) recognition of the prewar and postwar Austrian debts. *Facts on File*, XIV, 694, p. 49.

[2] *Soviet News*, 2906, Feb. 15, 1954, pp. 2–3.

[3] *Ibid.*, 2906, Feb. 24, 1954, p. 1.

Republic, North and South Korea, and any other interested powers who had participated in the Korean War were to be represented. On the question of disarmament the Foreign Ministers agreed that there should be "an exchange of views" at an unspecified future date, using the UN organizations already existing for this purpose.[1]

From the Soviet point of view the Berlin Conference was a brilliant success. It preserved the division of Europe while permitting Russia to play the paradoxical role of champion of European solidarity. For the moment at least, Moscow indicated that the German and Austrian problems were inseparable and could be settled only on its terms. Behind this position was not only a very real fear of German militarism but also the realization that unification on Western terms amounted to the probable loss of the country which held the balance of power in Central Europe. The implications this would have had on its already weakened Satellite empire were all too evident. [2] With both sides unwilling to budge from rigid positions in Europe Russia apparently felt that through repeated negotiations and increased exploitation of Western weaknesses in Asia it could eventually obtain a settlement to its liking. The soundness of this reasoning seemed to be substantiated by the way in which Molotov was able to force the West to agree to future talks with Communist China. It was here that he achieved his greatest success. Despite the fact that the final communiqué specially stated that the negotiations did not

imply diplomatic recognition in any case where it has not already been accorded,[3]

they did mean that the United States had been forced to give ground on a major point in its Asian policy for the sake of Western unity in Europe.

In the interval between the two conferences Moscow sought to exploit its diplomatic advantage by alternately using threats and smiles. The threats were both implied and overt. During February 1954 Moscow celebrated the largest Soviet Army Day in several years and issued charges that the United States was

[1] *Ibid.*
[2] Schnitzer, "German Studies: Soviet Policy on the Reunification of Germany, 1945–1952," p. v.
[3] *Soviet News*, 2906, Feb. 24, 1954, p. 1.

preparing for a new war. [1] In a rising crescendo of denunciations the press placed the full blame for the heightening world tension on Washington. American participation in NATO, its influence in EDC, and its efforts to form a "northern tier" alliance felt the brunt of the attack. However, other governments were not immune. In rapid succession Turkey, the Netherlands, Greece, and Pakistan received diplomatic notes outlining Soviet displeasure with their membership in these pacts and the presence of Western bases in their territory. [2] At the same time the regime held up its all-Europe security plan as the only real solution. To give these claims substance it initiated two important diplomatic moves. The first was the recognition of the German Democratic Republic as a sovereign and independent state. The second was an offer to join NATO and transform it into an all-Europe security pact. [3] The Soviet note making this latter proposal in essence called for an end to the Cold War and implied that refusal would result in the creation of a rival Eastern alliance. It rather graphically painted the spectre of the holocaust which would result if these blocs collided. [4]

The implications of these two moves, which were closely related, were rather far-reaching. An independent East Germany would enjoy an equal voice in any all-European security system. It also suggested the possible creation of an East German Army designed to "liberate" the West. The offer to join NATO and turn it into a general security pact in which the United States could participate gave France an alternative to the rearming of Germany. This sudden Russian desire to become a member of the much denounced Western organization was another device to throw the onus of Europe's continued division upon the United States. In the same vein, Moscow dangled the possibility of large Eastern markets before West European commercial interests. It continually asserted that these could be had if it were not for the intransigence of American policy.

Indochina, Korea, and the Geneva Conference

This more or less cooperative spirit, which was displayed as the

[1] *New York Times*, Feb. 24, 1954, p. 1.
[2] *Ibid.*, March 28, 1954, p. 6.
[3] *Soviet News*, 2920, March 29, 1954, p. 1, and 2922, April 2, 1954, pp. 1–3.
[4] *Ibid.*, 2922, April 2, 1954, pp. 1–3.

occasion demanded in Europe, did not prevail in the Far East where the military campaign against the French in Indochina was at its height. Communist propaganda stepped up its efforts to convince the world – particularly the Asian nations – that the United States was bent upon provoking a major nuclear war with the Chinese People's Republic simply to preserve French colonialism. (Interestingly, while it graphically portrayed the horrors of such a conflict in its foreign press and radio the regime was careful to see that its domestic information media limited this information to the select military audience.) [1]

As the French position in Indochina rapidly deteriorated (a sizeable force was surrounded at Dienbienphu in early March 1954) Moscow strove to drive even deeper wedges into the widening Western disagreement over the ultimate aim of its Asian policy. To the French, who had a considerable portion of their Army tied down in a costly and unpopular war, the Soviet held out the possibility of direct talks with the Viet Minh at Geneva as the first phase of a final settlement. While Communist forces launched a new invasion of Cambodia, Moscow lectured both Britain and America on the dangers of the conflict spreading to the rest of Asia should the United States intervene directly. [2] Moscow's solution was the creation of a Far East Security Pact similar to the one proposed for Europe. This was an obvious attempt to frustrate American efforts – begun after the Berlin Conference – to form a Western oriented defense alliance in Asia. [3]

This was the general situation which faced the 19 participating nations when they assembled for the first session of the Geneva Conference on April 26, 1954. [4] Although the subject of Western recognition of the People's Republic of China as a member of the Big Five was clearly not on the agenda, there was every indication that precisely this topic would directly affect the success

[1] *New York Times*, April 4, 1954, Part 4, p. 3, Harry Schwartz.

[2] *Izvestia*, April 10, 1954, p. 3, and *Pravda*, April 11, 1954, p. 3, *Current Digest*, VI, 15, pp. 15–17.

[3] *New York Times*, April 7, 1954, p. 1.

[4] The Soviet Union, Communist China, and North Korea represented the Communist world while the United States, Britain, France, South Korea, Australia, Belgium, Canada, Columbia, Denmark, Ethiopia, Greece, the Netherlands, New Zealand, the Philippines, Thailand, and Turkey (the UN members who participated in the Korean War) represented the West. *Facts on File*, XIV, 704, p. 133.

or failure of the negotiations. Even before the talks began Soviet propaganda tried to picture them as a meeting of the Big Five while the United States worked just as adamantly to portray them as the general political conference specified by the Korean armistice. [1]

Significantly, the tone of the conference was set in Moscow and not in Geneva. If there was any doubt in the minds of Western diplomats about the Russian position it was quickly dispelled on the opening day when both Malenkov and Khrushchev delivered two of the strongest foreign policy statements to emanate from the Soviet capital since the death of Stalin. Speaking before the two chambers of the Supreme Soviet they did little more than repeat the charges which daily appeared in the Russian press, but coming as they did just as East and West were sitting down at the conference table in Geneva they took on added significance which the negotiators could not fail to overlook.

Malenkov, who apparently had forgotten his earlier counseling that in any future conflict both sides would be destroyed, warned that atomic aggression by the West would be met in kind and

would inevitably result in the disintegration of the capitalist social system. [2]

Simultaneously, Khrushchev's speech contained

the most stinging attack any high Russian spokesman ... had yet made against Secretary of State Dulles. [3]

At Geneva these sentiments were reflected in an almost immediate deadlock on the Korean question once the two Korean delegations had presented their respective positions. Molotov made it clear that his government firmly supported the proposals of North Korea and Communist China. This was particularly true of China's demand that the Asian countries be given a completely free hand in settling their own problems. [4] After weeks of haggling over the question of free elections for a unified Korea – during which neither side budged substantially from its original

---

[1] *Soviet News*, 2923, April 5, 1954, p. 1.
[2] *Ibid.*, 2933, April 28, 1954, p. 4.
[3] *New York Times*, April 27, 1954, p. 1, Harrison Salisbury.
[4] *New Times*, Supplement 19, May 8, 1954, pp. 12–16. Cf. Mehnert, "Die Korea-Konferenz in Genf," pp. 277-284, and "Die Indochina-Konferenz in Genf," pp. 368-379.

position – the Western nations finally broke off the negotiations on June 15. [1]

However, the discussions about Indochina took a much different turn from the very beginning. On May 3 they were enlarged by the issuance of formal invitations to Viet Nam, Laos, and Cambodia by the Western Big Three and to Viet Minh by Russia and Communist China. [2] Although there were repeated deadlocks the pressure of continued French military setbacks [3] and the resulting political instability at home split Western unity and sapped the French will to maintain a rigid position. Their demands (put forth on May 8 and supported by the US and Britain) called for the Viet Nam conflict to be classified as a "civil war" but the fighting in Laos and Cambodia to be labelled "foreign intervention." They also included the declaration of an immediate truce; the disarming of guerillas and the grouping of both French Union and Viet Minh forces in pre-arranged assembly zones; the complete withdrawal of all Viet Minh regulars and irregulars from Laos and Cambodia; and the immediate liberation of prisoners of war and civil internees in the three Associated States. Such a truce was to be supervised by the UN and guaranteed by the Big Four, Communist China, the three Indochinese states, and Viet Minh. [4] The Viet Minh, for their part, demanded an immediate cease fire throughout Indochina; the withdrawal of all foreign (French) troops; complete independence of the three Associated States; suspension of United States foreign aid; and "free general elections" without outside supervision. [5]

While each side was presenting its demands the United States undertook several independent actions which had a direct bearing on the outcome of the talks. Against British opposition, which favored waiting for the conclusion of the Geneva negotiations, it renewed its efforts to form a South-East Asia Treaty Organization and took under serious consideration the possibility

---

[1] *Facts on File*, XIV, 711, p. 1.

[2] *Ibid.*, XIV, 705, p. 146.

[3] The northern French stronghold of Dienbienphu fell May 7, 1954, with the loss of its 16,000 man garrison after having been encircled for two months. *Ibid.*, XIV, 706, p. 153.

[4] The Viet Nam representatives of the Bao Dai government demanded harsher terms which barred partition of the country in any form and called for Viet Minh submission to Viet Nam authority, including the incorporation of its army in the latter's.

[5] Quoted by *Facts on File*, XIV, 706, pp. 154–155.

of direct military intervention in Indochina. It also gave assurances to Viet Nam Emperor Bao Dai that it would not accept partition of his country. [1]

On May 25 the Communist Viet Minh suggested a partition scheme which – while not acceptable to the Laniel government – caused it to instruct Foreign Minister G. Bidault to use it as the basis for a compromise agreement. Direct military truce talks began four days later. [2] But these were stalled by the Communist refusal to accept Western demands that the fighting in Viet Nam be treated as a civil war and that in Laos and Cambodia as invasions by foreign troops. The Red insistence upon a mixed inspection team (similar to one which had not worked in Korea) composed of Sweden, Switzerland, Poland, and Czechoslovakia likewise proved unacceptable to the West. [3]

With France in the throes of a cabinet crisis as the result of Laniel's Indochina policy and Bidault representing a caretaker government, Chou offered a new set of proposals. He dropped his demands that Communist movements in Laos and Cambodia be recognized by the West as "governments," agreed to the withdrawal of Viet Minh troops from both nations under a cease fire, and agreed that the Viet Minh military command represent the Communists in the truce talks. (These new terms may have resulted from indications that Britain intended to stiffen her position in regard to Laos and Cambodia.) [4]

After another month of further negotiations along these lines the new French government of Premier Mendès-France agreed to an armistice. According to the truce terms signed on July 21, 1954, Viet Nam was divided along roughly the 17th Parallel in a manner similar to that of Korea. In addition to providing for the eventual evacuation of the opposing military forces to their respective sides, they specified that within two years an all-Viet Nam election was to be held. The agreements were to be supervised by a commission composed of India, Canada, and Poland which was to refer violations to a meeting of Ambassadors of the nine powers represented at Geneva. [5]

[1] *Ibid.*, XIV, 707, pp. 161–162.
[2] *Ibid.*, XIV, 708, p. 169, and 709, p. 181.
[3] *Ibid.*, XIV, 710, p. 189.
[4] *Ibid.*, XIV, 711, pp. 197–98.
[5] These were the USSR, Communist China, Viet Minh, the US, Britain, France,

Other aspects of the final agreement provided that:

(1) Laos and Cambodia were to be demilitarized and during 1955 to hold elections by secret ballot;

(2) the number of foreign troops in Viet Nam was not to be increased; and

(3) the division of Viet Nam was to be considered a military and not a political one. [1]

Despite Western claims to the contrary, the Communist world had clearly achieved a major victory both in propaganda and in the physical extension of its influence. Russia immediately began to exploit its advantage on all fronts. In Europe, where policy revolved around Western efforts to tie the Federal German Republic to its alliance system, Moscow's immediate goal was the destruction of the proposed EDC. Here it utilized the widening cracks in Western solidarity that had appeared at Geneva as its chief levers. France was the most obvious target because her differences with the United States over the Indochina settlement were potentially transferable to the European scene. However, the Soviets did not overlook the desirability of also wooing Great Britain and the smaller nations.

With increasing frequency the USSR reasserted that "peaceful co-existence" was the only real solution to outstanding international disputes. With this firmly established as a point of departure it elaborated in greater detail on such issues as the destruction of the American sponsored embargo on strategic goods. This was an extremely effective issue with which to sow seeds of discontent since the alleged Russian willingness to normalize trade relations had struck a responsive cord in a number of West European capitals.

Soviet diplomats took the position that only the egoistic motives of the United States deprived the West of access to a potential market of 800,000,000 people – amounting to one third of the world's population – in the Soviet bloc. This issue not only provided the Russians with an opportunity to cast the United States in the role of an international ruffian but also with the powerful new weapon of economic penetration which

Viet Nam, Laos, and Cambodia. (*Ibid.*, XIV, 716, p. 241.) Viet Nam never accepted nor signed this truce agreement. *New York Times* (*Int. Ed.*), Feb. 6, 1958, Greg Mac Gregor.

[1] *Soviet News*, 2974, July 26, 1954, pp. 2–3.

they later used with such great success in the underdeveloped
areas of the world. [1]

The Soviet All-European Security Plan

Soviet efforts to identify the United States as the chief villain
of the Cold War were the key-stone of its propaganda. While the
other Western countries also felt Moscow's wrath, it was not as
strong as that directed against the US. Russia was more interested in wooing Europe than in driving it into closer collaboration with America. Its chief lure was the all-European security
plan. While it had been modified to permit US participation, its
theme remained largely "Europe for the Europeans" and offered,
in effect, something for everyone. With one hand it played on
French fears of German militarism while with the other it held up
the prospect of a unified Germany. To the smaller countries it
promised relaxation of international tension with reductions in
arms budgets and standing armies; the eventual withdrawal of
American troops; and an equal voice in European affairs. Above
all, it held out the promise that the unnatural economic barrier
cutting through the heart of Central Europe would be removed.

Immediately after the Geneva Conference the USSR took
steps to press this plan by proposing to London, Paris, and
Washington that within four months all interested European
nations (as well as the United States) should meet to discuss it.
(Communist China was invited to attend as an observer.) [2] Two
weeks later Moscow suggested that any such gathering should be
preceded by another Foreign Ministers Conference. [3]

[1] The extent to which Moscow had shifted its emphasis on this issue was most
clearly illustrated by M. Nesterov, President of the Soviet Chamber of Trade, who
had written in mid-1953:
"There can be no doubt that realities will more and more compel the capitalist
countries to re-establish and expand trade with the countries of the socialist camp."
  Less than six months later he declared:
"Regarding [the development of East-West trade] as an integral part of their
struggle for relaxation of international tension and for peace, the countries of the
socialist camp are prepared to make every possible effort to bring it about. We say
that our 1954 motto in the sphere of foreign trade will be: 'welcome'."
New Times, 36, 1953, and 6, 1954, as quoted by "Soviet Foreign Trade Propaganda:
A Change of Emphasis," BBC, Feb. 15, 1954.
  [2] Pravda, July 26, 1954, p. 1, Current Digest, VI, 30, pp. 13–14. A similar but more
vague proposal for further negotiations about Asian problems had been made by the
central press two days earlier. Pravda and Izvestia, July 23, 1954, p. 1, ibid., VI, 29,
p. 15.
  [3] Pravda and Izvestia, Aug. 6, 1954, p. 4, ibid., VI, 31, p. 30.

To make its plan more enticing Russia included additional proposals which obligated the participants to improve their economic relations with one another and hinted strongly that its acceptance by the West would facilitate the settlement of the Austrian State Treaty. Editorial comment in the Soviet press went to great pains to stress the plan's conformity not only with the spirit of the United Nations Charter, but with its legal interpretation as well. This was part of a skillful effort to characterize it as an instrument of peace open to all as contrasted to NATO and EDC which Moscow claimed were closed military organizations having aggressive intentions. [1]

This round of Soviet diplomatic notes was well timed to take advantage of Western disunity. The French government, which had yet to ratify EDC, was beset by chronic political instability at a time when there was considerable opposition to it. Even in Britain there was a sizeable segment of public opinion that also questioned the wisdom of rearming Germany. [2] Nevertheless, despite the strains imposed during the summer of 1954 the West formally rejected both of Moscow's proposals in mid-September. [3]

Soviet foreign policy, which became extremely flexible during the summer of 1954, did not rely entirely on diplomatic notes. The regime sought to "humanize" its relationships with the rest of the world and remove the stigma of Stalin's remoteness. As a result, it initiated a new approach which could best be described as "cocktail diplomacy." The cordial reception given the British Labor Party delegation headed by former Prime Minister Clement Attlee was in marked contrast to the isolation and the aloftness of the past. [4] But such occasions were far more than mere social functions. They were calculated to provide extensive forums for emphasizing new policies.

[1] *Pravda*, July 26, 1954, p. 1, and *Izvestia*, July 30, 1954, p. 3, *ibid.*, VI, 30, pp. 13–15.

[2] The note to the United States was more strongly worded than the ones to Britain and France. *New York Times*, July 25, 1954, p. 1, and July 26, 1954, p. 3.

[3] *Ibid.*, Sept. 11, 1954, p. 1.

[4] At the height of this cordiality Radio Moscow's home service carried a scathing denunciation of life in the United States. This type of attack had not been as frequent as before. Also the British were criticized by both the press and radio for their policy in Iran and Suez. This was apparently the regime's method of letting the Russian people know that its policy was basicly unchanged while permitting it to exploit the friendly gestures as much as possible for foreign consumption. *Ibid.*, Aug. 17, 1954, p. 4, Harry Schwartz.

As the question of French ratification of EDC reached a climax, Soviet pressure was intensified. *Pravda* editorialized in late August against the consequence of rearming Germany. It called such action incompatible with the obligations of the Franco-Soviet Friendship Treaty of 1944, pointing out that as far as the USSR was concerned the

creation of a closed military alignment in the form of EDC and the inclusion of a remilitarized Western Germany would render Germany's unification ... impossible. It would set up new insurmountable obstacles to agreement on the German question

and seriously impair the settlement of other international questions. [1] Adroitly Moscow approached the subject from still another tack. In the closing days of August 1954 Poland offered France a treaty of friendship and mutual assistance which would have pledged her

not to take any part in any coalitions,

thus automatically excluding her from NATO. [2]

To what extent the defeat of EDC can be ascribed to Soviet pressure is impossible to determine. Unquestionably purely domestic issues played a significant role. In any case, it was the USSR's second major victory during the summer of 1954 and clearly illustrated how badly the Western powers had been outmaneuvered. Where Stalin's policy of the mailed fist had failed, his successors' willingness and ability to cover it with the silken glove at the most opportune moment achieved much that he had sought but could not obtain. The regime's more subtle policy was a

combination of hard threats designed to frighten even those of strong nerves and soft allurements calculated to attract the naïve, the wishful-thinkers, and the frightened.[3]

At both the Soviet Army Day and May Day celebrations the regime unveiled new weapons – including what appeared to be tactical atomic artillery and new jet bombers – which highly impressed Moscow's most sober critics with its ability to back up these threats. This flexing of its military muscles and the pure fright propaganda about the holocaust of nuclear destruction,

[1] *Pravda*, Aug. 28, 1954, p. 3, *Current Digest*, VI, 35, p. 12.
[2] Quoted by the *New York Times*, Sept. 5, 1954, Part 4, p. 5, Harry Schwartz.
[3] *Ibid.*

when blended with the implied threat that the Soviet bloc would go to war over the rearming of Germany, was a skillfully manipulated counter-point to the main theme of peace, security, and trade. [1]

Nevertheless, while Soviet achievements were considerable, they did not prevent the Big Three from turning to an alternate program to bring the Federal German Republic into the Western alliance. Consequently, the Russians maintained their propaganda barrage. When Foreign Minister Molotov visited East Berlin on October 6, 1954, he used the occasion to renew the proposal for an immediate Four Power conference. Speaking more to the West German people than to the diplomats, he held out the prospect of reunification, neutralization, and evacuation of foreign troops, warning that rearming meant Germany must forever forgo all hope of unification. [2]

Two weeks later Moscow formally presented his proposals in new notes to France, Britain, and the United States which called for discussion of essentially the same topics that had been dealt with in January at Berlin. [3] This was followed by yet another series of notes (this time issued jointly by the Czech, Polish, and Russian governments) formally inviting 23 European countries and the United States to an all-European security conference on November 29. (The Chinese People's Republic was to participate as an observer.) These notes made the unusual suggestion that the Big Three issue similar invitations to Spain and the Federal Republic, countries with whom the Soviet bloc did not have diplomatic relations. As in the past the timing of this diplomatic fusalage was important, because France had again turned its attention to approving German rearmament. [4] Each time that the West moved one step closer Moscow countered with another conference invitation and new threats – in much plainer words – of what would happen if it was ignored. By late November the incongruous mixture of threats and smiles had reached a frantic pitch. [5]

---

[1] *Ibid.*

[2] *Soviet News*, 3017, Oct. 12, 1954, pp. 1–4.

[3] *Ibid.*, 3027, Oct. 26, 1954, pp. 1–3.

[4] *Ibid.*, 3041, Nov. 15, 1954, pp. 1–2.

[5] *Pravda* repeated its threats five times in one article and *Izvestia* hinted at the formation of a rival Communist military organization. (*New York Times*, Nov. 17,

Moscow's reaction to Western plans was based on more than simply a calculated evaluation of the resulting shift in the balance of power. On its part there was a genuine fear of a militarized Germany which was magnified almost to the point of hysteria by the experiences of two World Wars. Also domestic economic and political problems were coming to a head. Despite its boisterous shouting the regime was in no position to launch the country into foreign adventures, but such threats made an excellent screen behind which to hide its internal squabbles.

When Moscow's efforts to convene an all-European conference were spurned by all but the Soviet bloc, it went through the motions of calling a rump gathering known by the grandiose title of the

Conference of European Countries for Safeguarding Peace and Security [1]

which heard the first stages of a much stiffer Soviet propaganda line that concentrated on the increased dangers of war. The Conference's final communiqué rehashed previous Russian proposals and added the expected threat that if the Federal Republic were rearmed the Eastern bloc would unify its military forces in a collective defense organization of its own. [2] Such a move was in line with earlier Soviet efforts to strengthen and consolidate its ties with Eastern Europe and Communist China. [3]

The Moscow Conference also repeated the warning that efforts to rearm Germany were inconsistent with the Anglo-Soviet and Franco-Soviet Treaties. Inclusion of the Federal Republic in the Western alliance

---

1954, p. 1.) About the same time *Trud* published a letter from a reader calling for an Eastern counter-part to NATO. (*Soviet News*, 3049, Nov. 25, 1954, p. 1.) This method was usually employed to give policy decisions the appearance of grass-roots origin.

[1] The possibility that Moscow never seriously wanted Western participation is suggested by the early date named in the original note and the presence of Communist China which automatically precluded American acceptance. *New York Times*, Nov. 22, 1954, p. 22, C. L. Sulzberger.

[2] This was in addition to the existing series of bilateral military treaties already linking the Soviet orbit. *Soviet News*, 3055, Dec. 3, 1954, p. 5.

[3] Soviet participation in Hungarian, Bulgarian, Rumanian, and Chinese joint-stock companies had been terminated in October 1954. Reparation payments from East Germany were ended, occupation costs were eased, and special Soviet companies were handed back to the Germans. The Russians press also began to speak warmly of Yugoslavia and both the USSR and its Satellites opened trade relations with Belgrade. *New York Times*, Dec. 5, 1954, Part 4, p. 5, Clifton Daniel, and the *Economic Survey of Europe in 1954*, p. 109.

would wreck the possibility for settling outstanding European problems, and above all the German ... [one].[1]

A new Soviet note to the Big Three on December 10 used even stronger language. Such action, it said, would make further Four Power negotiations on German unification "pointless" and would "preclude" the possibility of reaching agreement. [2] Previously, Russian policy had stopped just short of taking such a firm stand from which it would find retreat difficult.

Africa, the Middle East, and Asia

While Soviet diplomacy in Europe dominated the headlines there were definite signs that the regime was taking a renewed interest in Africa, the Middle East, and Asia. However, it was severely handicapped by the negative position which Stalin had taken toward the growth of nationalism in underdeveloped areas, and it took great effort to break out of the rigid lines he had followed. As a consequence there was a considerable amount of backing and filling while the regime sought to develop a consistent policy. The fact that this policy was more clearly and forcefully stated after Khrushchev took a personal hand in Soviet foreign policy in early 1955 suggests that it may have been an issue in the Malenkov-Khrushchev struggle.

Soviet knowledge of Africa up until Stalin's death was very sketchy. A small group of Africanists existed at the Institute of Ethnography of the Academy of Science, but

their writings showed great ignorance of Africa past or present. Africa was simply another name in a list of 'colonial and semicolonial countries.' It seemed that little original thinking had been done since 1917, Lenin's *Imperialism* remaining the text.[3]

But from the middle of 1953 there was a pronounced spurt in Soviet interest in that vast continent and serious steps were taken to remedy the years of neglect. As a result the omissions in the two major works which appeared in 1954 and 1955 resulted from policy rather than ignorance. [4] During the 1953–54 period work on dictionaries in Swahili, Hausa, and the Bantu languages was

[1] *Soviet News*, 3055, Dec. 3, 1954, p. 5.
[2] *Ibid.*, 3060, Dec. 10, 1954, pp. 1–3.
[3] *World Today*, "Soviet Interest in Africa," p. 356.
[4] They were *Narodi Afriki* and *Formirovanie Nationalnoi Obshchennosti Yuzhno-Afrikanskikh Bantu. Ibid.*

begun in conjunction with similar programs for Asian and Middle Eastern languages. School geographies of Lybia and Ethiopia as well as popular pamphlets on various other areas were also prepared. The Institute of Oriental Studies which was activated and enlarged was given responsibility for research on Egypt and the Magrib while Africa below the Sahara was assigned to the Institute of Ethnography. [1]

The Soviet position in the Middle East was somewhat different. Russia had long maintained an active interest in the area and periodically both the Czarist and Soviet governments had made unsuccessful forays in the hope of establishing a sphere of influence. The latest of these was Stalin's attempt between 1939 and 1947 to carve out a Russian domain in both Turkey and Iran. When his intervention in Iran was thwarted by the United Nations in 1946 and his designs on Turkey blocked by the Truman Doctrine, he withdrew from active participation in Middle Eastern affairs. Nevertheless, he kept a sizeable finger in the pot so as to be able to stir up trouble whenever it was to Russia's advantage. As a result, the Soviet Union voted for UN partition of Palestine (the first time it had supported Zionism against the Arabs since 1917); permitted her Satellites (primarily Czechoslovakia) to sell arms to both sides in the ensuing civil war; and enflamed the Arab displaced persons against both Israel and the West. [2] Consistently Moscow worked to prevent the formation of the Middle East Defense Command, which would have unified the Arab world around British military establishments in the Mediterranean, and sought to create trouble in Iran by supporting political discontent.

Mass organizations, appealing primarily to the intellectuals, rather than the very weak Communist Parties (illegal except in Israel) were the major vehicles of Soviet propaganda. Many of these were affiliated with international front organizations such as the Partisans of Peace, the Women's International Democratic Federation, the World Federation For Democratic Youth, etc.

---

[1] *Ibid.*

[2] The Soviet reversal on the Palestine issue may have been prompted by several motives: (1) a desire to woo Jewish sentiment in the West; (2) the hope of "Balkanizing" the Middle East; and (3) the realization that, since the West was more deeply involved, Arab hatred would vent itself against it rather than against the USSR. Lenczowski, "Middle East," p. 59.

Also popular front coalitions between extreme right-wing and pro-Communists left-wing political parties were common. [1]

As long as the USSR could neutralize the Middle East from its position on the side-lines and provoke unrest, which in an emergency might deny its resources (i.e., oil fields, air bases, and the Suez Canal) to the West, Stalin seemed content to relegate it to a secondary position in his diplomacy. But his heirs were faced (as he would have been had he lived) with a new situation. During 1953 the West (primarily as the result of prodding by Secretary of State Dulles) shifted its attention away from the Egyptian-oriented defense plan to the concept of a "northern tier" defense pact along the Soviet Union's southern flank linked to NATO through Turkey. The new regime faced the necessity of devising a program which would not only counter this alliance but also give it greater freedom of movement in the Middle East. But here Moscow was at a severe disadvantage because Soviet ideology was fundamentally opposed to Islam as well as the nationalism which sparked the political life of the area. At the same time it was faced with the unresolved question of how any new *rapprochement* with the Moslem world would be received by the huge Islamic minorities in Soviet Central Asia and the adjoining Chinese empire, whose independent cultures had been so vigorously suppressed by Stalin's ruthless Russification policies.

During most of 1954 it was evident that the USSR was attempting to work out some compromise on this question. The regime became increasingly aware of the potentialities of using the Soviet Moslems as a bridge between Russia and the Middle East, but this did not fully materialize until early 1955. [2] As it became aware that its blustering propaganda did not prevent the formation of the key links in the Bagdad Pact, it began maneuvering to hurtle this barrier by wooing the Syrian-Egyptian axis, Afghanistan, and India.

In Eastern Asia Stalin left a much different legacy: Communism was well established in China; the Korean adventure had become a war of attrition; Malaya and Indochina were both

---

[1] Cf. Laufer, "Communist Party Strategy and Tactics in the Arab World," pp. 40 and 43–44.
[2] Wheeler, *op. cit.*, pp. 13–14.

fighting undeclared civil wars; but elsewhere Soviet meddling in local politics had achieved little in concrete results. There were strong local Communist Parties which drew their greatest support from the universal poverty that held Asia in its grip, but they were heavily tinged with the growing spirit of nationalism that prevailed in the wake of the decay of Western colonial empires.

The flexibility of the regime's Asian policy permitted it to be skillfully coordinated into a program of global diplomacy which had several objectives. The first, of course, was to expand the area under Communist domination either through a negotiated political settlement or military conquest. The second was to destroy Western solidarity in Europe by exerting pressure on the already existing cleavages in its Asian policy. A third goal was to enhance the position of Communist China in the eyes of the world by forcing the West – particularly the United States – to parley with it on a basis of equality. A fourth was to discredit the United States in the eyes of the new Asian nations by saddling it with the blame for creating a near-war situation merely to preserve European colonialism. While Russia was pursuing a belligerent policy toward the French in Indochina and the Nationalist Chinese on Formosa, it began a new effort to win over the rest of Asia. Its key features were the reversal of the traditional Soviet hostility toward local nationalism and Moscow's systematic enterance into the field of economic diplomacy. Both of these trends developed gradually during 1953 and 1954 and did not become fully apparent until the following year when they assumed major importance in Soviet policy. They reflected changes that had taken place on the Russian domestic scene since Stalin's death as well as new, inviting circumstances which presented themselves in Asia. [1]

To the Soviets the most important country in South Asia – both because of its size and its leadership among other Asian

---

[1] Some authorities ascribe the shift more to changes in Asia than within the Soviet Union:

"If these developments are related to general policy pursued by the Soviet leadership since the death of Stalin, it must be emphasized that the actual turn which ... has been dated from the year 1954 was due rather to changes in the situation in non-Soviet Asia than to an alteration in Moscow's response to circumstances which remained the same. *The ideological preparation for the turn goes back, indeed, to Stalin's lifetime and if the policy switch did not take place earlier, it was only for lack of opportunity.*" (Italics added.)
Hudson, "Soviet Policy in Asia," p. 2.

nations – was India. Soon after Stalin's death the USSR's first Ambassador to New Delhi, K. N. M. Novikov, who was noted for being stiff and correct, was replaced by I. A. Benediktov. However, the latter suffered from his inability to speak English, and he was soon recalled to Moscow. His successor, M. A. Menshikov, immediately attracted attention because of his informality and his command of English. But as subsequent events soon indicated Menshikov's qualifications as an expert in foreign trade (he had been Minister of Foreign Trade before Stalin's death) were Moscow's prime considerations. Within three weeks of his arrival the Soviet Union agreed to accept India's trade terms, [1] and a five year bilateral trade pact was concluded in early December 1953. In exchange for raw materials and handicrafts India agreed to receive 39 Soviet items which included wheat, crude oil, petroleum products, iron and steel manufactured goods, heavy industrial equipment, boring and mining machinery, industrial electrical equipment, textiles, tractors, all types of machinery, as well as films and printed matter. [2]

This was a significant departure from the past, because, with the exception of a 1951 barter agreement, trade between the two countries had been negligible. It paved the way for the much more important Soviet technical assistance program – the construction of a 1,000,000 ton steel mill in 1955. These Russian successes were greatly facilitated by two factors on the Indian domestic scene. One was New Delhi's dire need of economic assistance to ensue the completion of its planned industrialization and the other was the development of Indian antagonism toward the United States and Great Britain during 1953 and 1954 because of their efforts to draw Pakistan into what eventually became the Bagdad Pact. India tended to view this alliance with its military provisions as a threat to her claims in Kashmir. The Soviet Union quickly sought to exploit this opportunity by staunchly supporting India's position before the United Nations and in other ways building ties of friendship. [3]

---

[1] Payment was to be based upon the rupee with the difference settled in sterling.

[2] *New York Times*, Nov. 14, 1953, p. 2, Robert Trumbull, and Dec. 3, 1953, p. E. 2.

[3] During 1954 the Soviet press carried an appreciably increased amount of material stressing friendship with India. Particular emphasis was placed upon the expanded cultural exchange program.

Russia's goal in Asia was not the creation of a military organization but the establishment of a large bloc (with India as the pivotal nation) devoted to "neutralism." Because this was the Soviet Union's first thrust into the heart of South Asia such a grouping by nature would be anti-Western but not necessarily anti-Russian. Rather than attempting to dictate a uniform, alien foreign policy, the Soviet regime sought to identify itself with the Asian reluctance to be drawn into what was generally regarded in the Far East as a Western-made conflict. Moscow's skill and understanding of the Far Eastern political scene was illustrated by its superficial adoption of Nehru's famous Five Principles as part of its own policy at just the moment that the West sought to whip up enthusiasm for its ill-conceived and unpopular South-East Asia Treaty Organization. [1]

In formulating its Asian policy Moscow could never forget the existence of Communist China whose presence was something of a mixed blessing. On one hand it provided the USSR with important new opportunities to spread its doctrine, but at the same time posed the threat of becoming a rival center for Asian Communism. In a few short years Mao's rag-tag armies had not only fought their way out of the barren interior of the Chinese mainland but established remarkably firm control over the entire sprawling country. From the moment his regime joined the ranks of the Communist bloc it clearly enjoyed a unique relationship with the Soviet Union. At no time was it a Satellite. From the very beginning it was treated as a junior partner. Aside from its size and geographical importance there were other reasons for this. For one thing it had come to power largely without the help of the Soviet Union. It was not a regime which had been artificially created in the wake of the Russian Army. For another, its leadership had developed an ideology which retained a certain degree of independence from Moscow while

---

[1] The *Panch Shila* (Five Principles) which were originally formulated in negotiations between Nehru and Chou during June 1954 as the basis of future Sino-Indian relations were as follows: (1) mutual respect for territorial integrity and sovereignty; (2) non-aggression; (3) non-interference in each others affairs for any reasons (economical, political, or ideological); (4) cooperation for mutual benefit; and (5) peaceful co-existence. These were made part of the Bandung Communiqué in 1955 and the Soviet Union officially accepted them the following June. However, they figured prominently in Soviet propaganda during 1954. *World Today*, "Soviet Political Strategy in Asia," p. 196.

still being part of the international Communist movement. As a result Stalin dealt with it primarily through the normally accepted Party and government channels and did not attempt to gain control of the internal chains of command as he had done throughout Eastern Europe. [1] As Peking's influence in the Far East increased and as it began tapping its vast reservoir of untouched resources, it could justly claim a large role in the Sino-Soviet partnership. However, its major weakness remained its economic dependence upon Moscow.

But with Stalin's death Mao's bargaining position was greatly improved. During 1953 there were repeated signs that Moscow was acutely aware of the problems involved in harmonizing its own interests in Asia with those of Communist China. The Soviet press gave stepped-up coverage to developments on the Chinese mainland, particularly in regard to the drive for industrialization and the role the USSR was playing in it. Mao's stature, which had been more or less in eclipse while Stalin lived, was considerably increased. His selected works were published in Russian and the fourth volume received considerable praise in the press. Also his birthday in December 1953 was given more attention than in the past. The Soviet illustrated weekly *Ogonyok* devoted a greater share of one issue to him and his government. Likewise, the traditional congratulatory telegram from the CSPU Central Committee was more cordial than it had been for a number of years. [2]

Outwardly, there seemed to be a high degree of cooperation between Moscow and Peking, particularly in the coordination of foreign policy. Almost as soon as international tension in Asia had diminished over Korea the Communist bloc shifted the spotlight to Formosa and Indochina where it was whipped up to a new fever pitch. This may have been the result of joint action on the part of the Sino-Soviet partnership or an independent decision by the Chinese People's Republic. In any case, Moscow was quick to adroitly exploit the situation for the mutual benefit of both members. At Geneva in the spring of 1954 the Communist nations gave every appearance of being in complete harmony and

[1] Rostow, *The Prospects for Communist China*, p. 217.
[2] *The Economist*, Jan. 9, 1954, p. 101.

achievied their greatest successes because they presented a united front to a divided West.

Nevertheless, there were important internal differences which severely strained the alliance. These hinged primarily upon Communist China's continued economic dependence upon the USSR. Moscow was anxious to use this as a lever to keep Peking from outstripping her as the leader of Asian Communism. Consequently, the announcement of Soviet economic assistance to North Korea in mid-1953 was made with more fanfare than much more important similar grants to Mao's regime made public at the same time. The Sino-Soviet negotiations which preceded this announcement were reported to have been characterized by hard-headed bargaining and to have been conducted in an atmosphere of only the minimum cordiality dictated by diplomatic protocol. The Chinese themselves later revealed that they received only enough assistance to raise the level of their major industries by 1959 to that enjoyed by the USSR in 1932. [1]

By the autumn of 1954 the internal strains had become important enough to force Russia to send a high-level delegation headed by Khrushchev and Bulganin to Peiping to repair the alliance. Aside from illustrating the importance which Moscow attached to the relationship with Mao's regime, its composition [2] foreshadowed the change which was to come within five months in the Soviet Union.

In the negotiations Russia succeeded in obtaining unity of action in the field of foreign policy in return for considerable economic concessions and recognition of Communist China's growing nationalism. One of these was the promise to relinquish control of ice-free Port Arthur in May 1955. For ten years it had been a key establishment in the Soviet Far East defense system. In 1950 Moscow had agreed to give up its exclusive control in favor of joint occupation with Peking. This was to last until a peace treaty was signed with Japan or, at the latest, 1952. However, when the agreement expired it was extended for another five years. [3] Despite the repeated pledges of "fraternal

[1] *New York Times*, Oct. 12, 1954, p. 9, Harry Schwartz.
[2] It consisted of the following: Khrushchev, Bulganin, Mikoyan, Shvernik, G. F. Alexandrov, Shepilov, E. A. Furtseva, V. S. Nasriddinova, V. P. Stepanov, P. F. Yudin.
[3] *Soviet News*, 3018, Oct. 13, 1954, pp. 1–2, and the *New York Times*, Oct. 12, 1954, p. 1, Clifton Daniel.

cooperation" the Chinese Communists apparently found the presence of any foreign troops galling.

Another concession which was also obviously meant to placate the traditional Chinese xenophobia was the dissolution of the four Sino-Soviet joint stock companies originally created in 1950 and 1951. [1] These had been organized along the lines of similar ones in Eastern Europe which had played such an important part in bringing Hungary, Bulgaria, and Rumania into the Russian orbit after World War II. Available evidence seems to indicate that until the close of the Korean War the Sino-Soviet companies were little more than paper organizations. As in Eastern Europe Moscow was the chief beneficiary, receiving more than she contributed. The ending of its participation in the Chinese companies followed close on the heels of similary action in the Satellite states. Possibly when Moscow found itself hard pressed by Mao's demands to withdraw it dissolved the others to save face. [2]

Other provisions pledged the USSR to provide a total of 520,000,000 rubles of long-term credits to build 15 additional industrial establishments and to increase the delivery of equipment to the 141 other establishments envisaged in earlier agreements. When calculated in terms of actual Soviet purchasing power and the tremendous cost of industrialization, this was a rather niggardly sum. The two countries also planned the construction of two additional railroads to supplement the Trans-Siberian line which was the only rail link between them. [3]

[1] These had been established to develop the production of non-ferrous and "rare" minerals (possibly uranium); to develop mine and oil resources in Sinkiang; to construct ships at Daran; and to operate civil air lines. *New York Times*, Oct. 12, 1954, p. 9, Harry Schwartz.

[2] Fedyshyn, "Soviet Retreat in Sinkiang? Sino-Soviet Rivalry and Cooperation, 1950–1955," pp. 130–133. The joint-stock companies in Hungary and Rumania were terminated in September 1954 and those in Bulgaria only the day before the Sino-Soviet agreements were announced. (*New York Times*, Oct. 12, 1954, p. 9, Harry Schwartz.) However, the Soviet-North Korean companies continued in existence until May 31, 1955. (*Soviet News*, 3175, May 31, 1955, p. 3.) Mikoyan is reported to have confirmed the Chinese objections at the July 1955 Central Committee session. Bialer, *op. cit.*, p. 12.

[3] *Soviet News*, 3018, Oct. 13, 1954, pp. 1–2. One line from Tsining through Ulan Batar, Erlien, and Dzamyn was to parallel the Trans-Siberian and be finished by 1955. The second was to originate in Alma Ata and extend through Urunchi, terminating in Lanchow. (The Lanchow-Yunan section had been started in 1953.) Each country was to be responsible for construction in its own territory with the sections in Outer Mongolia being built by the USSR. *New York Times*, Oct. 12, 1954, p. 1, Clifton Daniel.

What was probably more disturbing to the Soviets than the actual terms of these agreements was the way they had been forced on Moscow when it was wrestling unsuccessfully with its own economic problems. Moreover, the Russian delegation could hardly overlook the stark reality that even these concessions provided only a temporary respite from even greater demands that were certain to be made within five to ten years. Even at this relatively early stage Peking was having a profound influence upon the course of the USSR's domestic policy. The concessions which were made to Mao's regime in October 1954 played a significant part in bringing the internal struggle for power to a head five months later. Possibly they were even the deciding factor in the shift back to the unquestioned supremacy of heavy industry.

There were a number of reasons why Peking was in such a much stronger position *vis-à-vis* the Soviet Union in 1954 than it had been only two years before. Firstly, the termination of the Korean War had reduced its immediate dependence upon Moscow for weapons and military supplies. At the same time the presence of Communist Chinese troops in North Korea made that country more a Satellite of the Chinese People's Republic than of the USSR. Secondly, in Asia as a whole Peking's influence was steadily on the increase, and its presence at the Geneva Conference had done much to improve its prestige in the non-Asian world. Nor should it be overlooked that after Stalin's death Mao (despite his recognition of Moscow's leadership) was the senior theorist in the Communist world. [1]

Economic Diplomacy

The whole question of economic diplomacy – both in its own orbit and in the free world as well – was under intensive study by Moscow during 1953 and 1954. During 1952 Russia had only three trade agreements with underdeveloped countries in Asia and the Middle East. Offers of both economic assistance and increased trade had been made in the later years of Stalin's life, but they had never materialized. The new regime soon altered this policy. By the end of 1953 seven new trade agreements had

[1] Mehnert, "Peking und Moskau," p. 20.

been negotiated with low-income countries, and a year later there were ten more in force. However, this is not the entire story. An important feature of Moscow's new diplomacy was the careful integration of the economic activities of the entire Communist bloc in such a way that the Soviet Union remained in the background while the Satellites carried on most of the activity. In December 1953 the Afro-Asian countries had a total of 39 trade and payment agreements with the USSR, Eastern Europe, and Communist China. The following year the number rose to 48. [1]

A significant feature of this economic diplomacy was the Soviet bloc's willingness for the first time to provide capital goods in exchange for indigenous raw materials, something that the Western foreign aid programs had difficulty in doing because of domestic surplusses. Also Communist transactions were conducted on a government-to-government basis rather than through the media of private capital as preferred by the United States. America usually attempted to get guarantees (such as pledges against confiscation) which were not always possible to obtain. In countries where socialist economic doctrines prevailed this US insistence upon private capital and its protection often caused irritation. The Soviet approach did not encounter such difficulties.

[1] Cf. *Foreign Assistance Activities of the Communist Bloc and Their Implications for the United States*, p. 7.

CHAPTER IV

DOMESTIC POLITICAL AND ECONOMIC CRISES

THE POLITICAL CRISIS

The Background

Malenkov's resignation from the Premiership at the February 1955 Supreme Soviet session marked the close of the second period of the post-Stalin era. [1] It would be an oversimplification to consider this merely the climax of personal rivalries, although that element was present. His downgrading actually symbolized the destruction of the coalition which had ruled Russia for the 18 months following Beria's unsuccessful bid for power and the formation of a new one oriented around Khrushchev, but not completely dominated by him.

This re-alignment, with its subsequent changes in both domestic and foreign policy, was precipitated by several closely inter-related problems which came to a head about the same time. One was the economic crisis. Although it had been aggravated by the post-Stalin investment policy, it was deeply rooted in the past and resulted primarily from the nature of the Soviet economy. Another was the international situation, which, from the USSR's point of view, had deteriorated badly during the previous year despite increased flexibility in Russian diplomacy. A third was the changing relationships within the coalition itself resulting from the competative efforts to fill the vacuum left by the destruction of the secret police and the subsequent parcelling out of its vast "empire."

By the fall of 1954 the regime could no longer postpone the necessity of re-appraising both its domestic and foreign policy. The economic situation was critical. The failure of the collective farm system, poor harvests, a nationwide labor shortage, popu-

---

[1] The first lasted from Stalin's death to Beria's arrest (March-June 1953). The second comprised the year and a half between the presentation of the new regime's economic program in late summer 1953 until February 1955.

lation pressures, rapid urbanization, changing consumer demands, and expanded purchasing power, kept agriculture in a
perpetual state of crisis. The industrial sector was not much
better off. It depended upon agriculture for both a constant food
supply for its labor force and raw materials for its machines,
neither of which the collectives were able to provide in the
desired quantities. Also industry was plagued by the fundamental
question of allocating resources to both heavy and light industries at a time when productivity was falling off, labor was
in short supply, and mounting inflation generated by the 1953
concessions, beset the economy.

Despite Soviet successes in negotiating a favorable settlement in
Indochina and blocking the ratification of the European Defense
Community, the regime had not been able to destroy Western
unity nor reverse the sentiment in favor of rearming West Germany. Also its efforts to stem the formation of the Balkan Pact,
the "northern tier" alliance, and the South-East Asia Treaty
Organization had failed. Of equal seriousness were the economic
concessions which the Russians had been forced to make to the
other members of the Communist orbit – particularly China – to
solidify their own camp. At the same time, the Soviets were just
discovering the inherent possibilities of economic diplomacy in
underdeveloped areas.

These factors had to be considered in the light of changes
which had taken place in the ruling coalition during 1954. The
military had emerged as a powerful force, willing to remain
behind the scenes as long as its interests were taken care of but
ready to express itself when it felt them in jeopardy. Such a
situation existed in the closing months of 1954. The "new course"
had stabilized military expenditures in mid-1953 and then cut
them by ten per cent nine months later. They were further pared
down by the mounting inflation which took a substantial toll in
the amount of equipment that could be procured within these
financial limitations. This squeeze came at precisely the moment
when the Ministry of Defense was experiencing the agonizing
strains of modernization. Its huge stock-piles of conventional
weapons were rapidly becoming obsolete in the face of swift
technological advances. In this respect, it faced an even greater
problem than the West. The oxcart and horse-drawn Army that

fought its way into Berlin ten years before had become one of the best equipped military organizations in the world. In fact, it was the only major fighting force that had been completely re-equipped with new conventional weapons in the decade following World War II. Yet it was precisely the armament industries that were the first to feel the pinch when plants were ordered to convert to consumers' goods. These facts were brought into sharp relief by the failure of Soviet diplomacy to destroy Western unity and block German rearmament. Viewed from the Russian steppe, this combination of circumstances could hardly have presented an encouraging picture to the professional soldiers charged with the responsibility of fighting a potential war. Despite the military's increased stature, it still did not enjoy a seat on the inner-most councils of the Party Presidium where the final decisions were made. It had to be satisfied, for the moment at least, in forging a close relationship with Khrushchev, who, as First Secretary, had risen with even greater rapidity within the regime.

Outward signs of an internal conflict began to multiply during the fall of 1954. Initially, they appeared to be merely elements of a personal rivalry between Khrushchev and Malenkov. It was not until late December that occasional statements in the Soviet press verified Western speculation that disagreement on fundamental issues was at the bottom of the rapidly developing political crisis. [1] But before this happened, it was only possible to catalogue the growing list of events which pointed to Khrushchev's rising influence and Malenkov's corresponding decline.

One of the earliest of these was the Khrushchev-Bulganin trip to Peking in October 1954. It clearly indicated that he had recovered from any setback he might have suffered a few months before. While the trip was important because of the economic and political concessions the regime as a whole made to Peking, it was personally important to Khrushchev because it marked his

---

[1] The first hints came from Hungary when Dravas, the Minister of Culture, (November 21, 1954) and M. Rákosi, Party First Secretary, (December 3, 1954) both "expressed alarm at the tendency of prominent officials under the pretext of 'self-criticism' to attack fundamental regime policies and institutions." Published in Free Europe Press, "The New Line in the Soviet Sphere: A Chronology of Major Events, November 16 – March 19, 1955," and Free Europe Press, "The Second Analytical Survey of Major Trends in the Soviet Orbit (July 1954–June 1955)." (Hereafter referred to as the "Second Analytical Survey.")

first public participation in the formation of Soviet foreign policy. Also it gave him an excellent opportunity to mend his political fences in the remote Siberian and Central Asian Republics where he found it necessary to whip several recalcitrant local leaders into line. [1]

By late November there were additional indications that something was developing. One was Khrushchev's signature of the Central Committee's decree ending the excesses of the anti-religious propaganda campaign. This broke the principle of anonymity which had governed the issuance of both government and Party decrees under the regime's "collective leadership." Another was the curious press coverage given several of Khrushchev's speeches. A major one on cotton growing and the role of animal husbandry in Central Asian agriculture which he delivered at Tashkent received only passing mention in the central press and was only published in full by the local press. [2] Later there was a marked difference in *Pravda's* and *Izvestia's* reporting of his remarks before two national conferences. In each case, he interjected comments which were given prominence by *Pravda* (the Party organ) but omitted entirely by *Izvestia* (the government organ) despite the fact that the stories were otherwise identical. [3]

During December evidence began to mount that the regime's investment policy – and not merely personal rivalries – was the crucial issue on which the domestic controversy was being fought out. Apparently during the closing days of 1954 the Presidium voted to reverse the course of the previous 18 months and to return to increased concentration on the development of heavy industry, particularly those segments related to military needs. [4] However, this did not amount to a complete return to the eco-

[1] U. Yusupov, Uzbek Premier, was replaced by N. A. Mukhitdinov after Khrushchev personally denounced him, his cabinet, and the Uzbek Party's Politburo for their failure to deliver cotton. *New York Times*, Dec. 29, 1954, p. 5.

[2] *Pravda* printed only a 1700 word Tass dispatch which mentioned the speech in four of the last five paragraphs but gave no more than a hint of its subject. *Pravda*, Nov. 21, 1954, p. 2, *Current Digest*, VI, 46, p. 17, and the *New York Times*, Dec. 24, 1954, p. 12.

[3] *New York Times*, Dec. 24, 1954, p. 4, Harry Schwartz.

[4] Malenkov had never publicly challenged the hegemony of heavy industry. His program was more a change in degree than in direction. However, even this was too much at a time when outside economic pressures were clamoring for capital goods, and when the regime was particularly conscious of what even a slight change would mean in terms of the Sixth Five Year Plan then under consideration.

nomics of the Stalin era. Much later the Hungarian newspaper *Szabad Nép* characterized the mood of the new period with special reference to local conditions but in terms which were applicable to thinking in the Communist bloc as a whole.

The [1953–54] regrouping [of the economy] was necessary, but it did not indicate a basic change in the policy of our Party, as some people tried to present it. The regrouping served the purpose of restoring the proper proportions to the People's economy. [But] the fact that light industry develops at a faster rate than heavy industry for a year or two should not be taken to mean that we thereby have abandoned the principle of giving preference to the development of heavy industry. [At the same time] our enemies like to point out that we are now returning to the situation which existed prior to June 1953. No, this is out of the question. We do not want to, and we shall not commit the faults revealed in the June 1953 resolution of the [Hungarian] Central Committee.[1]

As late as December 21, 1954, the Soviet press treated its readers to one of those rare differences in semantics which traditionally indicated the presence of an unsolved controversy within the regime's inner-circle. The occasion was the 75th anniversary of Stalin's birthday. [2] In its eulogy *Izvestia* barely touched on his role in the industrialization of the USSR while *Pravda* devoted a significant portion of its article to praising precisely this contribution, because, it argued:

Unlike the capitalist method, [of organizing the economy] the Soviet method proceeds from the fact that it is necessary to begin industrialization of the country with heavy, not light industry.[3]

But the accompanying editorials contained the greatest difference of opinion. *Pravda* enumerated all of the measures, especially those dealing with agriculture, associated with Khrushchev but refrained from mentioning the importance of material self-interest as an incentive for labor. Of light industry it simply said:

The measures which have been carried out will considerably improve the supplies of raw material for light industry.

However, its treatment of heavy industry was much different.

At the present time, when the problem of perfecting the building up of socialism and of the gradual transition to Communism is being solved,

---

[1] *Szabad Nép*, June 12, 1955, as quoted by the "Second Analytical Survey," *op. cit.*, p. xi.

[2] With the rise of Khrushchev there was a noticeable but still restrained resurrection of Stalin. His image was used to obtain support not only in economic matters but also for revision of other aspects of the "new course."

[3] *Pravda*, Dec. 21, 1954, pp. 2–3, *Current Digest*, VI, 51, p. 3.

the Party calls upon the Soviet people to concentrate their attention on carrying out the plans for the further growth of heavy industry. The party considers heavy industry to be the very foundation of a socialist economy and a firm basis for the further development of the national economy.

But *Izvestia* on the same day wrote:

The principal task of the Party and government is the maximum satisfaction of the constantly increasing material and cultural needs of all members of society. In order to carry out this task, the Party and government are leading the struggle . . . for the best utilization of all economic reserves.[1]

(By January 5, 1955 — only two weeks later — *Izvestia* had switched to a considerably different line.

Only by the all-out development of all branches of heavy industry can our country successfully fulfill the great historic tasks it faces.[2]

The regime's new position was even more clearly stated in *Pravda* by A. Kursho a few days later when he wrote:

At the present time the interests of a further mighty expansion of the socialist economy require that the production of the metallurical and coal industries be increased by all means and that power resources be quickly expanded inasmuch as the level of output already attained in these industries still does not sufficiently guarantee the growing requirements of the national economy.)[3]

On the same day (December 21, 1954) *Tägliche Rundschau*, one of the official organs of the East German regime, published a picture showing Stalin, Voroshilov, Bulganin, Khrushchev, and Zhdanov together. It was soon established by Western observers that it was another example of the skillful "doctoring" of photographs practiced in the Communist world for political purposes. In this case Malenkov had been removed from the original and Khrushchev and Bulganin substituted. The official association of these two with Zhdanov in this manner interjected a new and somewhat ominous note to the developing crisis. [4]

Three days later the Soviet central press carried the news that V. S. Abakumov, the former Minister of State Security before his mysterious disappearance in 1952, and three of his police associates had been tried and executed. The announcement

---

[1] *Pravda* and *Izvestia*, Dec. 21, 1954, as quoted by the *Bulletin of the Institute for the Study of the USSR*, "Post-Stalin Domestic Policy," p. 33.
[2] *Izvestia*, Jan. 5, 1955, as quoted by the *New York Times*, Jan. 17, 1955, p. 36, Harry Schwartz.
[3] *Pravda* as quoted by *ibid.*
[4] Löwenthal, "Stalinism Without Stalin?", p. 218.

came precisely one year after Beria's fate had been officially confirmed in the same manner. The interesting feature of Abakumov's case was that aside from the expected assertion that he had been in league with Beria's plots there was the new charge that he had been responsible for fabricating the so-called "Leningrad case." [1] This was apparently a reference to the removal of Zhdanov's supporters from the Leningrad Party organization after his sudden death in 1948. Although Malenkov's name was not mentioned, the announcement appeared to be aimed directly at him since his protégé's had stepped into the vacancies created by the purge.

These two events gave added meaning to Khrushchev's personal purge of Andrianov and his associates from the Leningrad Party organization during the closing days of 1953. It appeared that Khrushchev was attempting not only to remove Malenkov's followers but to win support among what remained of the "Zhdanov wing" of the Party. This also explained why a few scattered stories in the press during 1954 made reference to the wartime activities of Khrushchev, Bulganin, Shcherbakov, and Zhdanov "at the front" and ignored the State Defense Committee in which Malenkov participated. [2]

The same day that *Pravda* and *Izvestia* announced Abakumov's execution (December 24, 1954) they also published the text of an interview the British scientist Professor J. D. Bernal had had with Khrushchev the previous September. This was the first of two important economic statements by Khrushchev which emphasized in no uncertain terms the continued hegemony of heavy industry and clearly slighted consumers' goods that appeared in late December. In both cases they had been made earlier and their publication had been withheld. In his interview with Professor Bernal Khrushchev denied the existence of a bread crisis but admitted that increased purchasing power, changing tastes, and lower prices were indirectly placing a great strain on the available grain supply. [3] He concluded with his

---

[1] The others were A. G. Leonov, former chief of the Investigation Department; his two deputies, M. T. Likhachev and V. L. Komarov (all of whom were shot); and I. A. Chernov and Ya. M. Broverman (who were sentenced to 15 and 25 years, respectively). *Pravda* and *Izvestia*, Dec. 24, 1955, p. 2, *Current Digest*, VI, 49, p. 2.

[2] Löwenthal, *op. cit.*, p. 221.

[3] Four years later Khrushchev admitted the existence of a bread crisis even in

first public assertion of the absolute priority of heavy industry that he had made since the so-called "new course" had been inaugurated by Malenkov in August 1953. [1] Four days later (December 28) Khrushchev's speech to a gathering of construction engineers earlier in the month was made public. In it he gave the impression of speaking with considerable authority on economic questions and of being the regime's chief exponent of improved housing. (At the Nineteenth Party Congress Malenkov had associated himself with this rather popular issue.) Khrushchev also linked the two major issues which became the dominant themes of Soviet propaganda until after the regime had resolved its internal difficulties in February 1955: the mounting world tension and the need to provide the Soviet military with a powerful industrial base. [2]

Thus, within one week all the main ingredients of the coming change had become visible. There was the alliance between Khrushchev, heading the Party machine, and Bulganin, heading the political generals and the political commissars; ... the invocation of Zhdanov's name and the rehabilitation of his followers; ... the return of the orthodox Stalinist emphasis on heavy industry first and last; ... the attempt to saddle Malenkov with the blame for continued difficulties in agriculture; and to take from him the merit of initiating the 'new course.' [3]

With the new investment program firmly established (although still not officially announced) and the budget in preparation, Soviet foreign policy during January 1955 took on an increasingly belligerent nature. In the middle of the month it made one more last minute attempt to block German approval of rearmament, issuing a statement to the Western press obviously aimed at swaying popular sentiment in the Federal Republic. It rehashed all of the previous threats and promises, holding out the lure of unification, neutralization in an all-European security pact, and normal diplomatic relations if ties with the West were rejected. Ominously, it added one new note: the German people were at the crossroads where they had to choose between East and West. As Moscow pictured it, once the decision was made there could be no recourse. [4] At the same time the Soviets took up

the major cities during 1952. *Soviet News*, Supplement to 3992, Jan. 23, 1952, pp. ii–iii.
[1] *Pravda* and *Izvestia*, Dec. 24, 1954, p. 1, *Current Digest*, VI, 51, p. 7.
[2] *New York Times*, Jan. 4, 1955, p. 20.
[3] Löwenthal, *op. cit.*, pp. 218–219.
[4] *Pravda* and *Izvestia*, Jan. 16, 1955, p. 1, *Current Digest*, VII, 3, pp. 23–24.

Communist China's diatribes against American "occupation" of Formosa, presenting the issue to the United Nations Security Council. Taken with the breast-beating of the Soviet military leaders in the domestic press, the Soviet man-in-the-street could not be blamed if he felt a little anxious about the possibilities of war. [1]

There were a number of reasons why this "hard" line in Soviet diplomacy developed after more than a year of emphasizing its desire for cooperation. It first appeared in late November and early December when the efforts to block German integration into Western defense plans were frustrated. It, therefore, may have been a purely tactical return to "black-mail diplomacy" or a true expression of the very real Soviet fear of a militarized Germany. These developments unquestionably entered the economic debate which raged at just this time and were undoubtedly used by the military leaders to strengthen their arguments for larger expenditures in heavy industry. [2] (This raises the conjecture whether or not the "heavy industry" group artificially whipped up international tension to provide itself with a better bargaining position in the Presidium.) Once the decision had been made to abandon the "new course" for a period of greater austerity, the program had to be "sold" to the people. This was especially important because Malenkov's policy of increased consumers' goods was very popular. The threat of war was an issue with which even the most devoted advocates of his program could not argue. At the same time it provided an excellent screen to hide the internal instability from the outside world.

The appearance of a lengthy commentary in *Pravda* by Shepilov on January 24, 1955, signaled the beginning of the last phase in this drama. Vigorously attacking those who

proposed setting an identical rate of development for light and heavy industry or even providing for predominant development of light industry

during the transition of socialism to Communism, he denounced such views as heresies of the "rightest reactionaries" and those

---

[1] *Soviet News*, 3082, Jan. 14, 1955, p. 2.
[2] The military press supported the renewed emphasis upon heavy industry before, as well as after, Malenkov's resignation. Garthoff, *op. cit.*, p. 22.

who held them as "vulgarizers of Marxism" and adherents of "petty bourgeois economics." To carry out this program, he asserted, would mean leaving the USSR

unarmed and helpless economically.

According to Shepilov, the only course open to the economy was the unquestioned hegemony of heavy industry. If Russia were to allow itself the luxury of consumers' goods when capital goods were more vitally needed, then it must be prepared to take a back seat to Western technological development, particularly in those fields closely related to defense. [1] This was the severest and most direct attack yet leveled at Malenkov's "new course." Its full implications were not immediately apparent until it became evident that Shepilov was merely parroting the statement Khrushchev delivered to the Party's Central Committee the following day. [2]

During the next six days it heard him outline the regime's problems and gave its endorsement to Malenkov's removal and the new investment program. [3] For the fourth consecutive time it devoted a sizeable share of its attention to the agricultural crisis. The grave figures which Khrushchev presented indicated that despite improvements, conditions were not appreciably better than when the first measures to spur production were authorized in September 1953. Again his answer to the problem was the launching of still another grandiose program – this time the transformation of Soviet agriculture to a corn-hog economy. [4]

---

[1] *Pravda*, Jan. 24, 1955, pp. 2–3, *Current Digest*, VI, 52, pp. 4–6.

[2] On January 25, 1955, Mikoyan resigned as Minister of Trade. (*Pravda* and *Izvestia*, Jan. 25, 1955, p. 4, *ibid.*, VI, 52, p. 6.) This was originally interpreted as the first move against the "new course" because the domestic trade network had been closely associated with actually putting goods on the shelves. However, Soviet officials discouraged this view, and his subsequent promotion on March 1 to First Deputy Premier seemed to support the argument that his resignation was actually a preview of the forthcoming reorganization. *New York Times*, March 1, 1955, p. 1, Clifton Daniel.

[3] The exact role of the Central Committee in these events is unknown. Despite its increased influence after Stalin's death there was nothing to indicate that it played as significant a part in 1955 as it did in July 1957. Everything points to the 1955 changes having originated in the Presidium. The purpose of the meeting was apparently to brief local officials in much the same manner as Soviet diplomats stationed in Western capitals had been briefed two weeks earlier. *Ibid.*, Feb. 13, 1955, Part 4, p. 1.

[4] *Pravda* and *Izvestia*, Feb. 3, 1955, pp. 1–5, *Current Digest*, VII, 6, pp. 3–11.

Malenkov's Resignation and Its Aftermath

While the Central Committee was meeting, the regime issued a call for a special session of the Supreme Soviet to convene on February 3, 1955, (considerably earlier than usual) on only a week's notice, the purpose being to legitimize the changes which had been hammered-out well in advance. Before the Soviet parliament ended its meeting the "new course" had been officially repudiated in favor of increased capital investment and military expenditure; Malenkov had been removed as Premier; the military had emerged from behind the scenes to take an active part in the government; and Khrushchev had forged a new ruling coalition in which he occupied the most important position.

Care was taken to create the proper background for these changes. On February 2 the Central Committee's decree outlining the sweeping new programs in agriculture (with their focus on improving the supply of meat and expanding the virgin lands) was published. The next day when the delegates convened *Pravda* printed the full 29,000 word text of Khrushchev's Central Committee report which firmly established the predominance of heavy industry and heaped scorn on the "pseudo-theoreticians" who challenged it. Their

vulgarization of the basic economic laws of socialism

was labeled

profoundly incorrect reasoning, alien to the spirit of Marxism-Leninism ... and nothing but slander of ... [the Communist] Party. [It was] regurgitation of the right deviation ... of views hostile to Leninism, views which Rykov, Bukharin, and their ilk once preached.[1]

Thus the stage was set for the presentation of the new budget by Finance Minister Zverev. It contained a decided increase in the allocations for defense and heavy industry and reductions in agriculture and light industry.

The wholesale price cuts (effective the following July 1) which were also announced at the same time gave added significance to the 12 per cent increase in military expenditures. But despite Soviet huffing and puffing about the increased danger of war,

---

[1] *Ibid.*, p. 3.

Soviet Budgets
(In billions of rubles)

Item	1953	1954	1955	%
Total expenditures	514.7	553.9	563.5a	+ .02
National Economy	180.4	213.4	222.3	+ .04
Heavy industry ⎫	82.6	{ 79.7b	101.2b	+ .27
Light industry ⎭		{ 14.2c	11.5d	− .23
Agriculture and forestry ⎫ Agricultural procurement ⎭	39.9	62.5	55.1	− .12
Defense	110.2	100.3	112.1e	+ .12

a = Expenditures revised to 533.0 after the July 1, 1955, wholesale price reductions.
b = Includes construction.
c = Includes domestic trade.
d = Of which 0.9 was for domestic trade.
e = The defense appropriation was the largest officially announced for any year since World War II, including the Korean War years of 1951 and 1952 when it was offically placed at 93,900,000,000 and 108,600,000,000 rubles, respectively.

(Source: Economic Survey of Europe in 1955, p. 184.)

Zverev soft-pedaled the idea by merely observing that there was no sign of a lessening of international tension. [1]

The fate of light industry was symbolized by two features of the budget report. The annual retail price cuts were not mentioned [2] while the 1955 "voluntary" bond sales were doubled (i.e., 30,500,000,000 rubles as compared with 15,900,000,000 in 1954). In terms of take-home pay, this meant automatic deductions of four weeks' wages during the year rather than the two taken out since April 1953. It reversed what was, without doubt, the most popular single measure of the short-lived Malenkov regime.[3]

Once the budget had been presented and approved, Malenkov's removal was only a question of time. However, it came in a matter which broke sharply with Soviet tradition. Instead of being arrested, tried, and executed as an enemy of the state as would have been the case under Stalin, Malenkov was permitted

[1] Pravda, pp. 2–3, and Izvestia, pp. 4–5, Feb. 4, 1955, Current Digest, VII, 4, pp. 7–13.
[2] During July the prices of television sets, phonograph records, cameras, and aluminium kitchen utensils (all luxury items out of the reach of the vast majority of consumers) were cut by 20 per cent. In December television set prices were slashed a further 20 per cent. Economic Survey of Europe in 1955, p. 168. Cf. pp. 339–340.
[3] Herman, "Soviet Economic Policy since Stalin," p. 10.

to tender his resignation and retain his membership in the Central Committee, the Presidium, and the Council of Ministers. In it he sought to portray himself as incompetent, stating that his

inadequate experience in local work and in direct supervision of particular branches of the national economy, in a ministry or other economic body ... [had] had a detrimental effect upon the fulfillment of the complicated and important duties of Chairman of the Council of Ministers.

He also then went on to shoulder a sizeable share of responsibility for failures of agricultural policy.

I see particularly clearly my fault and responsibility for the unsatisfactory state of affairs in agriculture, because, over a number of years before this, I was entrusted with the duty of control and leadership of the work of central agricultural bodies and the work of the local Party and organization in the sphere of agriculture.

Leaning over backwards, he included praise for the Central Committee's (i.e., Khrushchev's) leadership in this field as well as reaffirming the supremacy of heavy industry. [1] For doing public penitence Malenkov was shunted to the head of the Ministry of Electric Power which was an important but not decisive position. [2] In the Council of Ministers he was reduced in rank to Deputy Minister. [3]

The method in which Malenkov was downgraded was significant for two major reasons. Firstly, it illustrated the sophistication the regime had acquired since Stalin's death, making it an even greater menace. Secondly, although maintaining the outward appearance of "monolithic unity," it exposed the deep fissures which existed beneath the surface. Neither Malenkov's "defeat" nor Khrushchev's "victory" were as complete as the official picture attempted to portray. Malenkov's ability to retain

[1] *Soviet News*, 3100, Feb. 9, 1955, p. 1. Malenkov's record belies these assertions: March 1939–October 1952 member of the Orgburo; February 1941–March 1946 alternate member of the Politburo and a full member after that date; March 1939–March 1953 member of the CPSU Secretariat; member of the wartime State Committee of Defense; and Chairman of the Council of Ministers from Stalin's death until his 1955 "resignation." It was Khrushchev and not Malenkov who had been most closely identified with agriculture since 1950. In the explanation circulated to the Cominform Malenkov was charged with taking part in the "Leningrad affair" and opposing Beria's arrest. Bialer, *op. cit.*, pp. 8–9.

[2] The importance of this ministry had been diminished by the creation of the Ministry of Electric Power Station Construction on November 22, 1954. However, if it still retained authority over atomic power installations then Malenkov retained significant importance. Mosely, "How 'New' is the Kremlin's New Line?", p. 376.

[3] *Soviet News*, 3101, Feb. 10, 1955, p. 3, and 3105, Feb. 16, 1955, p. 3.

both his position in the Presidium and the Council of Ministers as well as control over a relatively important ministry indicated that he remained a force with which Khrushchev still had to reckon.

Once Malenkov had stepped down Khrushchev lost little time advancing Bulganin's candidacy for the Premiership. More than likely he was a compromise choice made by the Party and the military. The latter's influence in these events was immediately apparent when Marshal Zhukov was elevated to fill the vacant post of Minister of Defense, the highest government position a professional soldier had ever held in the Soviet Union. If anything else were needed to publicly confirm this it came just one month later when ten generals were promoted to the rank of Marshal and one Marshal of Aviation was made Chief Marshal. Never before, except when the rank was originally created, had so many been authorized at one time. It appeared that Zhukov was loosing no time in rewarding the "second generation" of wartime generals who were gradually filling the important commands. [1] (These promotions had interesting repercussions in Communist China where similar ones were announced almost simultaneously. In the Communist world the rank of marshal was a sign of special position. The only other members of the Soviet bloc to use it were Poland and Mongolia. In the latter country it had lapsed with the death of Mou Choibalsan in 1952 and of the two in the former one, K. K. Rokossovsky, was actually Soviet and the other, Rola-Zymierski, was in disgrace. Thus it appeared that Mao's regime was determined to assert its equality with Moscow even in the manufacturing of titles. In fact, Peking stole the march on the USSR through the creation of the rank of General-Marshal, the equivalent to Stalin's title of Generalissimo which lapsed with his death.) [2]

[1] The following Army Generals were promoted to the rank of Marshal of the Soviet Union: I. Kh. Bagramyan; S. S. Biryuzov; Grechko; Yeremenko; Moskalenko; and Chuikov. The elevation of two colonel generals, S. I. Rudenko and V. A. Sudets, to the rank of Marshal of Aviation indicated the importance of the air force. Colonel Generals S. S. Varentsev and V. Kazakov were both made Marshals of the Artillery. Later in the year six more professional soldiers with important commands were promoted to the rank of General of the Army. (*New York Times*, March 12, 1955, p. 1, Clifton Daniel and Garthoff, *op. cit.*, pp. 24 and 49.) Between 1950 and 1954 ten of the 23 military district commanders had been replaced. Five others had been transferred to different areas of the Soviet Union. Meissner, "*Verwaltungsumbau*," p. 289.

[2] "Communist Marshals," BBC, March 14, 1955.

But it would be a mistake to assume that the "military" was a cohesive bloc. Its internal differences reflected those in the Party and had been successfully manipulated by Stalin while he lived. Khrushchev showed signs of doing the same. In fact, four of the promotions went to Ukrainians – Grechko, Yeremenko, Moskalenko, and S. I. Rudenko – who had become increasingly important since Beria's arrest. [1]

Before the Supreme Soviet adjourned both Bulganin and Molotov utilized it as a forum to re-emphasize the regime's belligerent foreign policy. Once again the West felt the sting of Moscow's fire-breathing invectives at their worst.

During March Bulganin moved rapidly to reorganize the Council of Ministers. In the first of these changes Mikoyan, Pervukhin, and Saburov joined Molotov and Kaganovich as First Deputy Premiers, leaving Malenkov the lowest ranking member of the Presidium. At the same time Colonel General A. P. Zavenyagin, V. A. Kucherenko, P. P. Lobanov, and Lieutenant General M. V. Khrunichev, were named Deputy Premiers. Little was known outside of the Soviet Union of the Party standing of any of these men in the second group. As a class they were all civil servants or experienced administrators. In some cases the appointments represented tremendous advances. [2] Neither of the men holding military rank were line officers. Zvenyagin was a secret police official who was placed in charge of the Ministry of Medium Machine Building (generally believed to be the Soviet atomic energy program) and Khrunichev's experience had been in the production of aircraft, indicating the increased stress upon arms production. [3] Two days later, on March 3, Bulganin ousted Kozlov from the Ministry of State Farms and A. F. Zayadko from the Ministry of Coal Industry. Benediktov was transferred from the Ministry of Agriculture to Kozlov's former post and a comparatively unknown official, A. N. Zademidko, was brought in to head the coal industry. No appointment was made for the Ministry of Agriculture, which remained vacant for most of 1955 and was apparently filled personally by Khrushchev. [4] A third

---

[1] New York Times, March 12, 1955, p. 3, Harry Schwartz.

[2] Pravda and Izvestia, March 1, 1955, p. 1, Current Digest, VII, 9, p. 30; and the New York Times, March 1, 1955, p. 1, Clifton Daniel.

[3] New York Times, March 2, 1955, p. 6 and March 1, 1955, p. 3, Harry Schwartz.

[4] Pravda, March 3, 1955, p. 2, and Izvestia, p. 1, Current Digest, VII, 9,

change took place on March 22 when G. F. Alexandrov was dismissed as Minister of Culture after only a year in office. His replacement of Ponomarenko in 1954, when the ice-jam in the regime's cultural policy was beginning to break up, had attracted much interest because as a philosopher his views on the origins of Marxism had been pillored by Zhdanov. The new Minister of Culture was N. A. Mikhailov, whose carreer indicated that he was an orthodox Party man. Before his last post as Ambassador to Poland (March 1954) he had been a former First Secretary of the Komsomol organization, a Secretary of the Moscow *oblast*, and, interestingly, a member of the special court that tried Beria. [1] However, this did not mean that the regime was completely reverting to the tactics employed during Stalin's lifetime. Actually it was groping for a new position somewhere between the two extremes.

While these changes were taking place Molotov indirectly came under fire. There had been nothing to suggest that the downgrading of Malenkov had effected him. In fact, the Soviet Union's belligerent foreign policy was more closely associated with him than with any other individual. It was precisely this point which made him vulnerable. For some time the regime had indicated its desire for a *rapprochement* with Yugoslavia, but the gulf still separating the two countries was formidable. Molotov commented in his February 9 speech before the Supreme Soviet that:

> As we know, progress has lately been made in the relations between the Soviet Union and Yugoslavia. We do not consider that everything has already been done in this respect, but we believe that this no less depends upon Yugoslavia herself. Evidently, in these past years Yugoslavia has to some extent departed from the position which she held in the early years following the Second World War. That, of course, is exclusively her internal affair. [2]

In March the Soviet central press surprised the world by printing Tito's retort.

> Unquestionably, Mr. Molotov's formulation regarding Yugoslavia ...

---

p. 30. Not until October 18, 1955, was V. V. Matskevich, the Deputy Minister made Minister of Agriculture. *Bulletin of the Institute for the Study of the USSR,* "Chronicle of Events – October 1955," p. 48.

[1] Slusser, "Soviet Music since the Death of Stalin," p. 123, and the *New York Times,* March 22, 1955, p. 1.

[2] Supplements to *News,* 4, Feb. 16, 1955, and *New Times,* 7, Feb. 12, 1955, *Current Digest,* VII, 8, p. 11.

does not correspond to fact and in some respects coincides with those assertions [made by leaders in the Communist bloc that Belgrade was recanting its errors]. We consider this an attempt to conceal the facts from his own people, again at our expense. It is time to describe things as they are and as they developed, instead of stopping half way toward normalization and raising new doubts among the people. Manifestations of this kind do not encourage improvement of relations but on the contrary hinder the process which, as is evident, does not go easily after what was done to our country and after all the insults we have had to bear without any guilt on our part.[1]

Considering the venomous invectives which this would have evoked at an earlier date, *Pravda's* editorial response two days later was surprisingly mild. While it defended the Soviet position, it did not reply to his attacks against Molotov. [2] The net result was to make his position appear a little less secure than before. The question that at once came to mind was whether Khrushchev would be willing to sacrifice the Soviet Foreign Minister for an effective settlement with Yugoslavia.

Another sidelight to the February reorganization was the apparent influence it had upon the regime's relations with Peking. Two days after the Supreme Soviet session closed Moscow concluded a trade agreement with Communist China which had been under negotiation since the previous October. This sequence of events was remarkably similar to that which took place in March 1953 when the new regime suddenly came to terms following Stalin's death. Mao's precise influence in dethroning Malenkov cannot be ascertained, but it was certainly in his interests to support the Khrushchev-Bulganin faction because its economic policies meant Moscow would be in a better position to assist China's industrialization, than under the "new look's" consumers' goods program. [3]

Despite the recurring indications that Khrushchev was assuming more and more the posture of Stalin, [4] there were numerous signs that the principle of collective leadership was very much alive and being actively debated within the regime. *Pravda* made this clear in a major editorial in mid-April.

[1] Quoted by *Pravda* and *Izvestia*, March 10, 1955, p. 4, *ibid.*, VII, 8, pp. 11.
[2] *Pravda*, March 12, 1955, p. 4, *ibid.*, VII, 8, pp. 11–12.
[3] "The Great Friendship of Russia and China," BBC, Feb. 18, 1955.
[4] For example, in early January N. S. Patolichev, Party chief in Belorussia, asserted that the Republic was to become a flax producing area in accordance with "Comrade Khrushchev's instructions." The implication was that they had the same authority as those of Stalin's. *Pravda* as quoted by the *New York Times*, Feb. 5, 1955, p. 4, Harry Schwartz.

The collective experience and collective wisdom of the Central Committee, which bases itself on Marxist-Leninist theory and on the broad initiative of the directing personnel, on the creative energies of the popular masses, guarantees the correct direction of all the business of Communist construction.[1]

THE CONTINUING ECONOMIC CRISIS

In Agriculture

While there was no question that the motivating factor behind this internal reshuffling was the regime's precarious economic position, its seriousness was forcefully brought home by the third round of sweeping agricultural reforms Khrushchev initiated during the first quarter of 1955. The year opened with the departure of the second great wave of pioneers to the virgin lands, but this time they were directed to the Soviet Far East rather than Central Asia where the program had originated. Then in rapid succession Khrushchev pushed through a number of important new measures. The entire emphasis of agriculture was shifted away from traditional lines to a corn-hog economy which was to produce 164, 000, 000 metric tons of grain and to double the number of livestock by 1960. Agricultural planning was partially decentralized and the regime began the gigantic task of replacing nearly one third of the 94,000 collective farm directors with experienced Party administrators from the city.

There was a desperateness boardening on panic in the rapidity with which the regime turned from one program to another in its search of a cure-all. This was certainly justified because, as Khrushchev admitted to the Central Committee in January 1955, Soviet agriculture could not meet the demands being placed upon it. What went unsaid was that the system of collective farming was a failure. [1] This was the crux of the whole problem, but because the regime was sworn to its preservation the proposed remedies dealt with the problem at the periphery rather than at the center. It was not enough simply to narrow the gap between

[1] *Pravda*, April 14, 1955, p. 1 as quoted by *ibid.*, April 17, 1955, p. 22, Harry Schwartz.

[2] In 1957 after four years of intensive efforts to raise production the average Soviet farmer was producing approximately the same quantity of grain (eight quintals per hectare) as Czarist peasants had. This was one sixth the output of his American counter-part. Even Polish peasants under Gomulka's policies averaged 14 quintals per hectare. "Grain Yields," BBC, Jan. 13, 1958.

the existing supply and demand because the latter was constantly rising at a rate greater than the modest increases achieved by the grandiose programs requiring such tremendous expenditures of resources.

There were three major pressures: the mass migration of peasants to the cities; the changing tastes fostered by urbanization; and the rapidly increasing population. The first two resulted from Stalin's industrialization program. One of his goals in forcing collectivization on the Russian peasant was to create a vast reservoir of labor for industry. Until his heirs sought to stem the tide of this migration from the land to the factories, it had the regime's official blessing. [1] The seriousness of the problem was indicated by Khrushchev when he told the Central Committee in January 1955 that 9,000,000 of the 17,000,000 new residents in urban centers since 1950 had come from the country. [2] But this did not reflect the full scope of the problem. The people who migrated to the cities were, by and large, the younger, able-bodied men most needed in the fields. Thus, much of the field work was actually done by the less productive women and old men.

Stalin was also partially responsible for changing the tastes of his laboring class. Of course, much of it was the result of the rapid urbanization of a peasant society in which factory workers no longer were willing to adhere to the alternating periods of abundance and famine that were an inherent feature of life on the land. However, his insistence upon squeezing the peasants to provide the cities with a guaranteed supply encouraged the trend. Even so, at best the workers enjoyed a minimal diet. Before his lieutenants initiated their program of concessions they consumed more fish, potatoes, and possibly more grain than in 1928, but much less milk, meat, and animal products than before. [3] But even two years after Stalin's death there was little more than a thin façade of good living in Moscow and one or two other major cities. Off the beaten track there were serious shortages of even staple food items. For example, a random survey of 12 grocery

---

[1] There had been a few earlier efforts to reverse it. Beginning in 1950 demobilized military personnel were ordered to return to their native villages and were denied permission to work in factories. *New York Times*, Jan. 6, 1954, p. 1, Drew Middleton.
[2] *Pravda* and *Izvestia*, Feb. 3, 1955, pp. 3–5, *Current Digest*, VII, 6, p. 4.
[3] Bergson, "The Russian Economy since Stalin," p. 212.

stores in the Armenian SSR capital of Ervian in late 1955 disclosed that none had butter, eggs, sugar, or milk, and only one had meat, but that was water buffalo. [1]

But the most serious problem was the rapidly increasing population. Khrushchev revealed for the first time in January 1955 that each year it rose by 3,000,000. According to official Soviet statistics over-all agricultural production had increased only ten per cent between 1940 and 1952 while the population rose slightly more. [2] Between 1952 and 1955 grain production was almost static. [3] In the light of these figures only one conclusion was possible: the Soviet Union had been running out of food for a long time. Should the population trends continue unchecked for a decade without sizeable improvements in agricultural production, the only consequence would be mass hunger and starvation.

It was these grim facts Khrushchev had in mind when he addressed the Central Committee in January 1955. He reviewed with candor the reasons for immediately improving grain production and startled his audience with the announcement that by 1960 the USSR had to raise 164,000,000 metric tons of grain annually if it hoped to meet the projected level of consumption. Even assuming that the regime was capable of reaching its 1955 goal of 114,000,000, [4] the planned expansion was staggering. In five years the regime wanted to add 50,000,000 metric tons,

[1] *New York Times*, Nov. 8, 1955, p. 3, Harry Schwartz.

[2] *Ibid.*, April 24, 1955, Part 4, p. 9, Thomas Whitney. Even this modest increase is open to question. Volin, "The Malenkov-Khrushchev New Economic Policy," p. 197.

[3] At the Twentieth Party Congress Khrushchev gave the following index figures for grain production between 1950 and 1955:

1950—100		1952—113	1954—105
1951— 97		1953—101	1955—129

(*Pravda*, Feb. 15, 1956, pp. 1–11, Gruliow [Ed.], *Current Soviet Policies*, II, p. 43.) No absolute statistics were released until December 1958 when Khrushchev disclosed that in 1952 and 1953 the state had procured 33, 870, 983 and 30, 629, 032 metric tons, respectively. (*Soviet News*, Supplement to 3992, Jan. 23, 1959, p. iii.) If these figures were the basis of his 1956 index than it may have represented – with one exception – a fairly realistic picture of Soviet grain production. The exception is the 24 per cent increase during 1955. In January 1956 P. Kozhevnikov, Deputy Minister of State Farms, stated that during the previous year (1955) the Soviet Union produced only 2,407,800 metric tons more than it had in 1954. (*New York Times* [*Int. Ed.*], Jan. 20, 1956, p. 5, Welles Hangen.) In mid-1955 the regime claimed for the first time that the number of cattle (67–68,000,000) had exceded the previous 1928 high of 66,800,000. *New York Times*, Aug. 21, 1955, p. 1, Welles Hangen.

[4] The original Fifth Five Year Plan goal of 130,000,000 metric tons (in terms of 'bar yields') had been scaled down by 1955 to 114,000,000. *New York Times*, Aug. 21, 1955, p. 1, Welles Hangen.

increasing its current output by nearly one half. But even more breathtaking was the way in which this was to be achieved. Traditional crops were to be more or less ignored in favor of a giant expansion of corn acreage even though it was a relatively new crop in the Soviet Union. [1] The ultimate goal was the creation of a corn-hog economy similar to the one in the United States which could produce sufficient fodder to support a rapid rise in meat production. (The failure to increase fodder output had always been a retarding factor in the regime's plans.) By 1960 there was to be twice as much milk and pork, two and two tenths times as many eggs, 70 per cent more beef, and 80 per cent more wool. [2]

Although he acknowledged that Russia's climatic limitations – short growing seasons and uncertain precipitation in marginal lands – were serious problems for corn production, Khrushchev was willing to gamble on its success because he believed it would relieve the serious meat shortage. He argued that corn would reach lactic maturity in any area where wheat could be grown and that green silage provided the same nutritional value as fully ripe ears. (These were premises which were seriously questioned by Western agricultural observers.) Consequently, he reaffirmed his belief in the virgin land program — even though in some areas up to a quarter of the harvest had been lost — and proposed harnessing it to the effort to produce corn. [3]

A direct consequence of Khrushchev's appearance before the Central Committee was a shake-up of the government's top agricultural administration and a series of sweeping decrees

[1] Before 1955 it occupied only 10,000,000 acres but by 1960 there were to be 70,000,000 acres. Forty million of these were planted the first year despite a very late spring. Volin, "Khrushchev's Economic Neo-Stalinism," p. 462.
[2] *Pravda* and *Izvestia*, Feb. 3, 1955, pp. 1–5, *Current Digest*, VII, 6, pp. 6–7. This reflected the regime's incessant drive to improve the Soviet diet as a means of winning popular support. It is especially significant in the light of the grain shortage because "in a real crisis verging on a famine it would be much more economical from the standpoint of national food management to feed grain [rather] than animal products, since the former would yield about seven times as many calories as the latter." Volin, *op. cit.*, p. 462.
[3] *Pravda* and *Izvestia*, Feb. 3, 1955, pp. 1–5, *Current Digest*, VII, 6, pp. 4–5. The strain that this agricultural expansion placed on the economy was illustrated by Benediktov's announcement a few days later that all of the farm machinery manufactured in 1955 was earmarked for the virgin lands. ("Second Analytical Survey," *op. cit.*, p. 49.) By April 3, 1955, Poland, Czechoslovakia, Rumania, Hungary, and Bulgaria, had issued orders adjusting their agricultural policies to similar corn-hog programs. *New York Times*, April 3, 1955, p. 16.

during the next three months which set about to radically change the face of Soviet farming. [1] In mid-April a limited degree of decentralization of agricultural planning was authorized. Officials of the government's State Planning Committee, the Ministry of Agriculture, and the Ministry of Producement were criticized for serious errors which had resulted in "excessive centralization." Under the new program the collectives and MTS were to be given increased responsibility for determining how the over-all quotas (still fixed by the central administration) were to be adapted to local conditions. While in theory the farmers themselves were to have a larger voice in determining this, it was the MTS which actually benefitted most. With each apparent relaxation of the regime's control of agriculture Khrushchev strengthened the MTS's grip on the countryside. [2]

While this was an important step toward a more realistic management of agriculture, it had to overcome the vested interests of a well-intrenched bureaucracy composed of two parallel organizations operated by the Party and the government. Since the Second World War their staffs had grown at a phenomenal rate. Between 1945 and 1954 there was a 63 per cent increase in the personnel of the All-Union Ministry of Agriculture in Moscow and the 32 similar ministries in the Union and Autonomous Republics. [3]

[1] When Khrushchev launched the virgin lands program in 1954 he sharply criticized a number of government officials dealing with agriculture, but, with the exception of the leadership of the Kazakh Party, he did not mention any Party officials even though they were just as responsible. In March 1955 Kozlov, one of those attacked the year before, was ousted as Minister of State Farms, and in the reshuffling Khrushchev apparently assumed responsibility for the Ministry of Agriculture. At the same time Lobanov was elevated to the Council of Ministers and apparently was assigned the function of coordinating the government's huge agricultural apparatus. This series of events strongly suggested that there may have been a basic disagreement between the Party and the government agricultural apparatus which divided the Presidium and became part of the Malenkov-Khrushchev struggle. Khrushchev's charges in 1958 that the "anti-Party group" (Malenkov, Molotov, Kaganovich, and Shepilov) had tried to bloc the development of the virgin lands program appeared to substantiate this. (*Soviet News*, Supplement to 3992, Jan. 23, 1959, p. ii.) However, there exists the possibility that he was merely attempting to rewrite history in his favor.

[2] Previously the central administration had established rigid acreage quotas for each collective. (*Pravda* and *Izvestia*, March 11, 1955, p. 1, *Current Digest*, VII, 7, pp. 16–17.) Future distribution of foodstuffs was to be based not only upon a region's needs but also its original contribution. *Pravda* and *Izvestia*, Feb. 3, 1955, pp. 1–5, *ibid.*, VII, 6, p. 10.

[3] *Dengi i. Kredit*, 6, 1954 as quoted by "Russia's Agricultural Bureacracy," BBC, Nov. 3, 1954.

While no precise official figures are available the following estimates give some idea of the magnitude of the two agricultural apparatus.

Party Officials in Agriculture

Central Committee of the CPSU	300	
Republican Committees of the CPSU	2,000	
Krai and *Oblast* Committees of the CPSU	4,500	
Personnel of *Rayon* and MTS Committees	30,000	
Total		36,800

State Planning Officials

State Planning Commission of the USSR	300	
Republican Planning Commissions	6,400	
Rayon Planning Divisions	75,000	
Total		81,700

State Farm Officials

Ministry of State Farms of the USSR	1,600	
Republican State Farm Ministries	10,000	
State Farm Trusts	3,480	
State Farm Administrators	90,000	
Total		105,080

Ministry of Agriculture Officials

Ministry of Agriculture of the USSR	4,600	
Republican Ministries of Agriculture	41,600	
Krai and *Oblast* Agricultural Administrations	46,900	
Total		93,100

Ministry of Agricultural Deliveries Officials

Ministry of Agricultural Deliveries	4,000	
Plenipotentiaries of Ministry of Agricultural Deliveries in the Republics	1,600	
Plenipotentiaries of Ministry of Agricultural Deliveries in *Krais* and *Oblasts*	5,700	
Plenipotentiaries of Ministry of Agricultural Deliveries in Districts	100,000	
Total		111,300

Total full time officials in agriculture	427,980

These do not include among other things the 9,000 MTS with their large managerial staffs. By comparison the Ministry of Agriculture and Fisheries in the United Kingdom employs a total staff of 12,500. [1]

The third drastic change came on April 5, 1955, when *Pravda*

[1] *Ibid.*

announced the regime's decision to launch a wholesale turnover of local agricultural leaders. By the following July 30,000 of the 94,000 collective farm chairmen were to be replaced by experienced Party administrators from the urban cadres. (While the regime warned it would not accept misfits unwanted by others, later press comment indicated that this was precisely what had happened.) [1] After the selection had been completed the candidates were to be given short courses in agricultural production and management followed by three months of practical training. [2] Also during the spring there were indications in the press that a modified *agrogorod* program was being revived. The emphasis was on remodeling existing villages rather than the actual resettlement of collective farmers. [3] The drastic nature of these measures could not but convey a suggestion of desperation on the part of Khrushchev and his associates.

From the outset the corn-growing program was thwarted by two major obstacles: peasant resistance and bad weather. The peasants were not only suspicious of a new crop but their long experience on the land had endowed them with an understanding of agricultural realities that made them reluctant to jeopardize their livelihoods by gambling on a risky venture. The regime attempted to overcome this with both threats and promises. On May 21 it authorized both farmers and tractor-drivers to receive 15 per cent of all the corn they harvested in 1955 as a bonus above their normal pay. Simultaneously, another decree penalized those who failed to complete planting by May 22 or obstructed it in any way. [4] While these accomplished the immediate purpose, later press comment seemed to imply that acreage records were achieved at the expense of good quality field work. Plowing was often shallow and apparently large quantities of poor seed had been sown. [5]

An unseasonably late spring throughout the Soviet Union

---

[1] *Pravda*, April 5, 1955, p. 1, *Current Digest*, VII, 14, pp. 11–12. At the Twentieth Party Congress the following year Khrushchev stated that over 20,000 such transfers had been completed, but he failed to explain why the program was not completed as originally announced. Laird, "Decontrols or New Controls? The 'Reform' of the Soviet Agricultural Administration," p. 29.

[2] *New York Times*, April 6, 1955, p. 4.

[3] Intelligence Report No. 6922, U.S. Department of State, May 11, 1955.

[4] *New York Times*, May 23, 1955, p. 1.

[5] *Ibid.*, July 1, 1955, p. 2, Harry Schwartz.

delayed field work as much as six weeks in some areas. In mid-May an alarmed *Pravda* reported a mixed forecast of agricultural progress. Conditions in the new Siberian areas were favorable but those in the older farming regions of European Russia were highly discouraging. [1] By the following July and August when a delegation of American farmers toured Soviet fields the serious-ness of the 1955 crop failures was apparent. [2] Nevertheless, the central press gave its readers an optimistic view of the progress in Kazakhstan. [3] However, when the US farmers visited the area, Soviet officials confided that precipitation had been only one tenth of normal (generally less than 16 inches but in some parts less than 10), threatening 1,800,000 acres of corn. Only a few months earlier Western observers who visited the same fields during spring planting had been confidently assured that since there had been only one drought in the previous ten years it was safe to assume that a climatic change was in progress. [4] But by August dust-bowl conditions were reported throughout Kazakh-stan and Western Siberia (from Karaganda to Novosibirsk) where little or no rain had fallen since May. Despite late planting (but with normal rainfall), the new lands the previous year had produced 18 to 20 bushels per acre. The 1955 drought reduced the expected yield by at least half, if not more. [5] The only bright spot in the agricultural picture was the Ukraine where more favorable climatic conditions helped to balance the losses, by producing a substantial increase over the previous year. However, it failed to do little more than just counter-balance the catastrophic failures in the rest of the country. [6]

But while 1955 was an exceptional year in terms of weather, the regime's agricultural program faced serious obstacles un-related to nature's whims. In the last analysis, the crux of the

[1] *Ibid.*, May 19, 1955, p. 6.

[2] The American delegation was a counter-part to a Soviet one invited to the United States by the *Des Moines* (Iowa) *Register* after Khrushchev had admonished the Central Committee in January 1955 to look to American experience in corn production for guidance.

[3] *New York Times*, Aug. 20, 1955, p. 35, Harry Schwartz.

[4] *Ibid.*, May 23, 1955, p. 11, Clifton Daniel, and Volin, "The New Battle for Grain in Soviet Russia," p. 198.

[5] *New York Times*, Aug. 20, 1955, Welles Hangen, p. 35. The 1955 cotton crop was also adversely effected by the weather. In Tadzhikistan torrential rains and hail followed a late frost. Altogether two or three resowings were required on three quarters of the plantations. *Economic Survey of Europe in 1955*, p. 170.

[6] Cf. p. 178.

problem was the nature of the collective farming system. Although minute peasant holdings with the accompanying subsistance concept of agriculture were not the answer to Russia's needs, neither were the giant super-collectives rigidly controlled from the center. Khrushchev tacitly acknowledged this at the Riga farm conference in mid-June 1955 when he suggested that some of them should be broken up into smaller units. [1] This was the first hint since he launched the virgin land program in 1954 that he had begun to have second thoughts about the wisdom of his expansionist drive. However, it was not a retreat from his basic position because he did not discredit either the cultivation of the new lands or collective farms.

In Industry

In the industrial sector of the economy the situation was also critical. After the regime publicly reasserted the hegemony of heavy industry, it was still faced by the necessity of solving a number of other acute problems which threatened to stymie the fulfillment of the Fifth Five Year Plan. Bulganin's report to the July 1955 session of the Central Committee testified to the seriousness the Soviet leadership assigned to the situation. It was, in effect, the industrial counterpart to Khrushchev's January review of agricultural difficulties. As such it was a studied analysis of the shortcomings of Soviet industry.

While Bulganin began with praise for its accomplishments, he soon developed his major thesis that as it stood Russian industry was antiquated, inefficient, over-centralized, and highly wasteful of both human and material resources. If these conditions were to be remedied, drastic action had to be taken immediately. He gave example after example of industry's failure to utilize technological advances already known in the Soviet Union but not practiced despite their successful use for several years by other Communist countries. As Khrushchev had done in January, he also told his audience to emulate the methods employed in the United States. [2] Among other things, he called for the extension

---

[1] *New York Times*, June 18, 1955, p. 1, Clifton Daniel.

[2] This "learn from the West" campaign was first discernable in early 1954 when Soviet technicians were advised to take lessons from the Satellites. "The New Soviet Line – 'Learn From the West'," BBC, Aug. 25, 1955.

of industrial specialization and the adaption of mass production concepts. But he reserved a considerable share of his criticism for the failure of industry to increase labor productivity at a faster rate. This was a serious enough matter to warrant him saying:

If we do not rectify this situation in the near future ... we will encounter difficulties in supplying the economy with labor.

The over-centralization and bureaucratization of the industrial administration drew his pointed barbs and a number of officials were publicly called on the carpet for actions which previously had received tacit official blessing. The practices of substituting quantity for quality, perennial non-fulfillment of quotas, and the lack of sufficient Party supervision of industry were other subjects which also came in for strong criticism. [1]

The remedies authorized by the Central Committee decree, which translated his proposals into directives, reflected a continuation of the steps the regime had taken during the first half of 1955. The adaption of the latest technological advances – including automation – was ordered throughout industry, and a number of ministries were specificly told to improve their mass production techniques. However, it was in regard to increasing the rate of labor productivity that the regime's action was felt most directly by the man-in-the-street. The Central Committee decree rebuked those industrial concerns which put such a great emphasis upon fulfilling production quotas that they offered higher wages and created artificial work norms which could easily be over-fulfilled. It ordered the newly created State Committee on Questions of Labor and Wages (under the direction of Kaganovich in his familiar role as "trouble-shooter") to re-examine the whole question of the relationship of wage rates and realistic production norms. [2]

This was a drastic attempt to bring labor productivity into line with wages. If productivity could be increased while purchasing power was curtailed the regime would be able to solve both its critical labor shortage and its mounting inflation. During the Fifth Five Year Plan the Soviet Union had continuously lost

[1] *Pravda* and *Izvestia*, July 17, 1955, pp. 1–6, *Current Digest*, VII, 28, pp. 3–20.
[2] *Pravda* and *Izvestia*, July 13, 1955, pp. 1–3, *ibid.*, VII, 26, pp. 6–12, and the *New York Times*, July 18, 1955, p. 13, Harry Schwartz.

ground in its efforts to raise its man-hour output faster than the West. By 1955 the Soviet rate of increase was a little more than half of what had been attained in 1950. [1] However, the regime was still able to meet its Plan goals by expending more labor than it had originally intended. [2] Until 1950 it continued to draw heavily from the countryside for this surplus, but about that time there were signs that the regime realized that it was no longer an unlimited supply which could be tapped at will. [3] While Khrushchev acknowledged this in 1953 his agricultural programs in 1954 and 1955 only aggravated the labor shortage even more because they required hundreds of thousands of workers for entirely new enterprises.

Aside from the regime's obvious desire to improve both agricultural and industrial production as soon as possible, the fact that 1955 was the closing year of the Fifth Five Year Plan and the start of an even more ambitious one gave an added sense of urgency to these efforts to alleviate the economic crisis that gripped the country. The balance sheet which was issued on January 30, 1956, was a measure of its success. By and large the regime had made very substantial gains in fulfilling the targets established five years before. However, it was necessary for it to make a number of important qualifications. Fourteen ministries failed to meet their goals, the capital investment plan was not fulfilled, every major construction administration except that of the Moscow authority fell short of its target, and the situation in agriculture – while improved – was obscured by vague generalities that suggested that it still suffered from serious shortcomings. [4]

The gross national output of Soviet industry rose by 12 per cent in 1955. This was approximately the same as the 1954 increase, but there was a significant difference. Whereas the 1954 figure was divided about equally between producers' and consumers' goods the 1955 rates were 16 and nine per cent, respectively. This reflected the greater priority given heavy

[1] *New York Times*, Oct. 18, 1955, p. 7.

[2] During mid-1955 it was estimated that by the end of the year the regime would be employing 48,000,000 persons to do the work originally intended for 45,000,000. *Ibid.*, Aug. 21, 1955, Part 4, p. 5, Harry Schwartz.

[3] *Ibid.* Between the fall of 1953 and the close of 1954 the regime's agricultural reforms had reversed the existing migration to the point where the farm population rose by 1,500,000. *Ibid.*, Aug. 21, 1955, p. 1, Welles Hangen.

[4] *Ibid.* (*Int. Ed.*), Jan. 30, 1956, p. 3.

industry as a result of the February 1955 revision of the government. It was the first year since the early years of the plan that

Soviet Industrial Production
in the Fifth and Sixth Five Year Plans

Commodity	Unit	1950 (Actual)	1955 Plan Original[a]	1955 Plan Revised 1953	1955 (Actual)	1956 (Plan)
Coal [e]	Million tons	261	372	...	396	593
Crude oil	Million tons	37.8	70	...	70.7	135
Electric power	Million MWh	91	163	...	170	320
Pig iron	Million tons	19	34	...	33	53
Crude steel	Million tons	27	44	...	45	68
Rolled products	Million tons	21	34	...	35	53
Bicycles	Million	0.64	2.29	3.45	2.88	4.23
Sewing machines	Thousand	0.49	1.18	2.62	1.61	3.78
Washing machines	Thousand	N.A.[c]	N.A.	196	87	528
Refrigerators	Thousand	N.A.	200	330[b]	151	635
Radios	Million	1.05	N.A.	3.77	3.53 ⎱	10.2
Television sets	Million	0.03	N.A.	0.76	0.49 ⎰	
Cameras	Thousand	260[d]	N.A.	1000	1020[d]	N.A.
Clocks and watches	Million	7.6	16.1	22.0	19.7	33.6
Cotton fabric	Billion meters	3.90	6.18	6.27	5.90	7.27
Linen fabric	Million meters	420	N.A.	406	305	556
Wool fabric	Million meters	155	239	271	251	363
Silk fabric [f]	Million meters	130	400	573	526	1074
Knitwear	Million	213[f]	N.A.	470	431	580
Ready-made clothing	Billion rubles[g]	30[d]	49	50	51.3	78
Leather footwear	Million pairs	226	318	318	299	455
Meat [h]	Million tons	1.27	2.43	2.55	2.22	3.95
Sausage products	Million tons	0.48	N.A.	0.85	0.83	N.A.
Fish	Million tons	1.7	2.7	3.2	2.7	4.2
Dairy produce [i]	Million tons	8.5	N.A.	....	13.5	25
Butter	Thousand tons	319	550	560	436	680
Cheese	Thousand tons	48.2	112	135	105.3	N.A.
Margarine	Thousand tons	194	350	450	364	N.A.
Vegetable oil	Million tons	0.78	1.38	1.50	1.12	1.84
Granulated sugar	Million tons	2.53	4.5	4.8	3.42	6.53
Macaroni products	Thousand tons	442	N.A.	1030	994	N.A.
Tinned foods	Billion tins	1.48	3.0	...	3.14	5.58

a = As adopted by the Nineteenth Party Congress, October 1952.
b = Cf. p. 88.
c = N.A. = Not Available.
d = Estimated by the Economic Commission for Europe secretariat.
e = Hard coal, brown coal, and lignite on a ton-for-ton basis.
f = Including artificial fabrics.
g = At July 1, 1955, prices.
h = State industry only.
i = In whole milk equivalent.

(Source: *Economic Survey of Europe in 1955*, Table XXX, pp. B 34–B 35.)

such a large difference in the rates had existed. [1] However, it was necessary if the targets for heavy industry were to be met.

What this meant in terms of the production of individual items can be seen from the table on page 187. From these figures it is clear that the short-lived effort to rapidly improve the consumers' position barely got off the ground before it was stiffled by the re-emphasis of the unquestioned supremacy of heavy industry. Only the production of cameras and ready-made clothing equaled or surpassed the revised target figures for 1955. In fact, the regime had difficulty in some cases even fulfilling the original Five Year Plan quotas set in 1950. This was particularly true of such basic necessities as food items, leather footwear, and cotton cloth. Here again the regime was forcefully reminded of the reliance of light industry upon the raw materials supplied by agriculture.

Despite intensive efforts to improve agriculture during the Fifth Five Year Plan it still remained the most critical sector of the economy. Even the few concrete figures regarding the number of livestock were not very encouraging. Superficially, at least, they showed an improvement, but, as Western observers were quick to point out, the rate of increase was not sufficient to achieve the promised doubling of meat and other animal products promised for 1960. In the two years preceding 1955 cattle had increased at an annual rate of three point one per cent, cows by six per cent, and hogs by four point seven per cent. If the number of cattle increased by only 15.5 per cent by 1960 then more than 80 per cent of the projected increase in meat, milk, and hides had to come from the increased productivity of the existing animals. [2]

Another major departure from the economic pattern of the immediate past was that real wages lagged substantially behind the rise in productivity. This was the reverse of what had happened in 1953 and in 1954 when productivity had not increased much faster than real incomes. [3] (During 1955 real wages rose one point five per cent as compared to the yearly average of eight per cent for the 1951–1954 period.) [4]

[1] *Economic Survey of Europe in 1955*, pp. 168–169.
[2] *New York Times (Int. Ed.)*, Jan. 31, 1956, p. 3, Welles Hangen.
[3] *Economic Survey of Europe in 1955*, p. 168.
[4] Herman, *op. cit.*, p. 13.

Productivity and Real Wages in the Soviet Union
(percentage increase over preceding year)

	Average real wage of workers	Average real wage of collective farmers	Labor Productivity Industry	Building
1949	12	14	13	..
1950	15	19	12	..
1951	10	10	10	10
1952	7	8	7	7
1953	10	13	6	4
1954	5	4	7	8
1955	3	7	8	10
1956 (Plan)	..	..	8	10

(Source: *Izvestia*, Dec. 27, 1955, and *Pravda*, Jan. 15, 1956, as quoted by *Economic Survey of Europe in 1955*, Table 78, p. 168.)

CHAPTER V

SOVIET FOREIGN POLICY: 1955

THE NEW APPROACH

These were the domestic problems which the regime had to take into consideration during 1955 as it formulated its diplomacy. The seriousness of the economic situation and the inherent possibility of further political instability were heavy liabilities. What was needed was a period of consolidation. However, it would be mistaken to contend that Soviet foreign policy was dictated solely by these liabilities. On the other side of the ledger it possessed impressive assets. Chief among these was the regime's remarkably increased subtleness in diplomatic affairs. While the basic goals remained the same, adaptability was made the key to success. The technique initiated during the previous year and a half of playing on Western shortcomings was polished to perfection, giving Russia's foreign policy a finesse which it had not had in the past. Using a diplomatic sleight-of-hand, Moscow focussed the spotlight of world attention upon European politics while it stepped up its efforts to convert Asia, the Middle East, and Africa to Communism.

The extent of Russia's flexibility was graphicly illustrated in the period immediately following the February internal realigment. Within four months the "hard" line which had suddenly sprung to life in December 1954 was dramaticly shelved and completely reversed. By mid-May 1955 Moscow was preparing for a Summit Conference and had announced its intensions of patching up its rift with Yugoslavia.

The first serious indication that Soviet policy was seeking to break out of its self-created log jam was the treatment *Pravda* gave Marshal Tito's criticism of Molotov in March. In the month that had followed the latter's Supreme Soviet address almost every indication had pointed to it as having outlined the guiding principle of the regime's foreign policy. [1] Marshal Zhukov's

---

[1] Exceptions which went largely unnoticed were the January 25, 1955, decree that

Soviet Army Day (February 23) Order of the Day in the central press did little to dispel this notion:

led by the US monopolists, the aggressive forces of the imperialist countries are establishing political groupings and military blocs ... are trying with all of their strength to restore German militarism ... [and] they are openly preparing a new war against the Soviet Union, the people's democracies, and the Chinese People's Republic.[1]

However, by late March and early April there could be no doubt that changes were in progress: Tass quoted Bulganin as favoring a Four Power conference without tacking on the usual conditions;[2] Moscow praised the forth-coming Bandung Conference;[3] agreement was reached on the long sought after Austrian State Treaty; and the Russian propaganda line began advocating cordiality and affability. As April slipped into May there was a noticeable relaxation of tension in both Europe and Asia, indicating that for the first time the Soviets had launched a coordinated peace offensive with Communist China.[4]

When the West took cognizance of these changes and formally proposed a Summit conference on May 10 the regime immediately countered with a new series of disarmament proposals.[5] While the details for such a meeting were being ironed out both sides began consolidating their respective positions. The West formally tied Germany to the North Atlantic Treaty Organization and the Soviets created the Warsaw Pact with its coordinated military command and sought to come to an understanding with Marshal Tito.

This *volte-face* in diplomacy coincided with two changes within the ruling coalition. The first was Khrushchev's and Bulganin's active participation in the formation and execution of foreign policy. (This facet of Khrushchev's many-sided role had been first publicly exhibited in Peking during October 1954.) The second was the serious effort on the part of the marshals to bring

formally ended the state of war between Russia and West Germany and the overtures to Japan.

[1] *Pravda* and *Izvestia*, Feb. 23, 1955, p. 1, *Current Digest*, VII, 8, p. 3.

[2] *Soviet News*, 3133, March 28, 1955, p. 1.

[3] *Pravda* had endorsed the idea as early as January 5, 1955, taking the position that it could only weaken Western "imperialist" efforts in Asia. *Pravda*, Jan. 5, 1955, p. 3, *Current Digest*, VII, 1, p. 20.

[4] *New York Times*, May 1, 1955, Part 4, p. 3, Thomas Hamilton.

[5] *Ibid.*, May 11, 1955, p. 1, Harold Callender.

Soviet military doctrine into line with the needs of the thermo-nuclear age.

THE REAPPRAISAL OF SOVIET MILITARY DOCTRINE

Between the Second World War and Stalin's death in March 1953 military thinking had become stagnant as the result of the virtual cannonization of the "Stalinist" military science. In the period between 1947 and 1953 practically no creative work was done by the men who were charged with the regime's defense. Just how far Stalin had made himself omnipotent in military matters was illustrated by a Soviet colonel who wrote in 1947 that

there is not a single aspect, not a single problem, of military art which has not received its further development from Comrade Stalin.[1]

Had he actually possessed even a fraction of the genius attributed to him in the last years of his life this would not have been a bad situation, but as Major General N. V. Pukhovsky declared as early as November 1953 the "cult of the individual" had adversely affected military science and the habit of citing sterile, repetitious quotations as authority (Stalin was not mentioned by name)

voluntarily or involuntarily ... hindered the development of military-theoretical thought.[2]

One of Stalin's major weaknesses in this field had been his preoccupation with the past rather than the future. Speaking *ex cathedra* in February 1946 he declared in a special order that

the further development of Soviet military science must be conducted on the basis of a skillful mastering of the experience of the recent war [3]

and there the matter stood until his death. Consequently the strategy of 1950 was primarily that of 1940 despite the fact that in the same ten year period the USSR had forged ahead in the development of the most up-to-date weapons, which, in some cases, were superior to their Western counter-parts. Thus, when Stalin died, there was the incongruous situation of the Soviet

---

[1] *Istochniki Voennogo Moguchestva Sovetskogo Soiuza*, pp. 82–83 as quoted by Garthoff, *op. cit.*, p. 63.
[2] *O Sovetskoi Voennoi Nauke*, Nov. 16, 1953, pp. 84–85 as quoted by *ibid.*, p. 61.
[3] *Krasnaya Zvezda*, Feb. 23, 1946, as quoted by *ibid.*, p. 62.

Union having atomic weapons in its arsenal which its military forces did not know how to use. However, the marshals soon moved to remedy this situation. One of the first signs was Admiral Kuznetsov's statement in *Pravda* during July 1953 that

the experience of the Great Fatherland War alone is no longer sufficient.[1]

A few months later the first small-scale maneuvers to test defenses against atomic attack were carried out. [2] Also, in late 1953 a serious debate on the "laws of military science," the first of its kind in nearly three decades, was begun in the pages of *Voennaya Mysl,* the authoritative military journal restricted in circulation to the higher echelons of the Soviet officer corps, by its chief editor Major General N. A. Talensky. The disputed point was the nature of military science. Did it include,

in addition to military questions, a whole complex of questions on war as a social-historical process

or should it,

basing itself on Marxist-Leninist teachings on war and the armed forces, ... [study only] the laws of war as armed conflict?

The conclusion, which was reached only after a year and a half in which 40 articles and letters on the subject were aired in the pages of *Voennaya Mysl,* was in favor of the later view. [3] In effect, this excluded

from the competence of Soviet military scientists the basic issue of peace and war, and ... by implication ... [excluded] *from the competence of the Soviet political leadership the questions of military doctrine, of how to wage a war.*[4]

At the same time there was a systematic effort by the military press to inform its officers and men on the development, use, and implications of new weapons. During 1954 and 1955 *Krasnaya Zvezda* alone published approximately 50 articles about atomic energy and nuclear weapons. This was in sharp contrast to the Stalin period when during 1945 and 1946 three were known to have been published in military organs, and between 1947 and 1953 when

not a single article on atomic energy or atomic weapons [was] ... known

---

[1] *Pravda,* July 26, 1953, as quoted by *ibid.,* p. 61.
[2] *Ibid.,* p. 156.
[3] *Voennaya Mysl,* 4, April 1955 as quoted by *ibid.,* pp. 66–67.
[4] *Ibid.,* p. 67.

to have appeared in ... the Soviet military daily and periodical press, open or restricted in circulation.[1]

Also there was a serious re-appraisal of Western military strength. Whereas in the past the regime's propaganda had refused to admit the existence of a serious threat from Western armed forces, the military began to tell its officers and men that the potential enemy possessed a formidable (although not superior) striking force. It even suggested that it would be well to devote more effort to developing strategy and tactics to counter those the Soviet Army could expect to meet in case of war. [2] Another important development during early 1954 was Malenkov's declaration before the Supreme Soviet that nuclear war could result in the "destruction of world civilization" instead of just the capitalist world. [3] The following year just prior to the February reorganization Zhukov addressed a secret gathering of the regime's military leadership at which he emphasized the necessity for increased flexibility, personal initiative, and imagination in the practical application of strategic thinking. In short, he called for a revitalization of military doctrine. [4]

Then, coinciding with the culmination of the debate in *Voennaya Mysl*, the downgrading of Malenkov, and the further rise of the professional military men in the regime's inner circle, the divergent threads of political and military strategy, which had been developing during the previous two years, were brought together. Major General Korniyenko confirmed in *Sovetsky Flot* on May 6, 1955, that the impetous for this had come from above.

The leaders of the Party and the government have given detailed directives as to the aims and ways of future development of Soviet military science .... [They] require the military leaders to reject all outdated ideas and systems of battle preparations and everything that does not correspond to the new conditions of armed struggle.[5]

The relationship of the professional military *vis-à-vis* the Party in the formation of policy at the highest level was illustrated by a *Voennaya Mysl* editorial just after the February 1955 reorganization.

---

[1] *Ibid.*, 64.
[2] *World Today*, "The Soviet General Staff Takes Stock," p. 498.
[3] Quoted by the *New York Times*, Dec. 20, 1955, p. 1, Welles Hangen.
[4] Garthoff, *op. cit.*, pp. 68–69.
   Sovetsky Flot, May 6, 1955, as quoted by *World Today*, *op. cit.*, p. 492.

The missions of [military] strategy ... are set by politics, but political leaders must also know the potentialities of a strategy, in order to set tasks before it skillfully at each concrete historical stage.[1]

The line of thinking that emerged in 1955 was primarily a modification of previous doctrine rather than a radical departure from the past. The strategic concept continued to adhere to the classic military belief that the primary task in a future war would be the destruction of the enemy's armed forces rather than the destruction of his economic and population resources. [2] Consequently it completely rejected reliance upon strategic bombing as a decisive means of winning but did accept it as a means of preventing retaliatory blows and as a supplementary phase of the general effort which had to be carried out primarily on the ground in direct combat. [3] This had several important implications. Firstly, the Soviets retained their traditional emphasis upon a balanced striking force. Despite the acquisition of the atomic bomb in 1949, the development of thermonuclear weapons in 1953, and the growth of a sizeable fleet of intercontinental bombers by 1954, they continued to reject any strategy based upon the predominant reliance on a single weapon system as being the "ultimate." In fact, Major General G. Pokrovsky, a nuclear physicist and military expert in the field of atomic weapons, declared in 1955:

Atomic and thermonuclear weapons at their present stage of development only supplement the fire power of the older forms of armament. Artillery, small arms, tanks, aviation, and the other armaments were and remain the basic fire power of the Army.[4]

Secondly, this view tended to minimize the importance of American strategy – particularly that phase of it built around the "nuclear deterrent" of which the Soviets did not seem aware – with its predominant emphasis upon strategic bombing, overseas bases, and heavy expenditures upon aircraft. [5] Despite the fact that Russian military leaders tended to disregard these bases as decisive factors because of their vulnerability, extended supply lines, and proximity to the Soviet Union, they were apprehensive

---

[1] *Voennaya Mysl*, 3, March 1955 as quoted by Garthoff, *op. cit.*, p. 8.
[2] *Ibid.*, p. 71.
[3] *Ibid.*, pp. 72–75.
[4] *Marksizm-Leninizm o Voine i Armii*, 1955, p. 168 as quoted by *ibid.* p. 78.
[5] *Ibid.*, pp. 118–132.

about the initial destruction their planes could cause before they were neutralized in the first few hours of the attack.

It was this fact which precipitated the major innovation of the 1954–1955 period: revision of the role assigned to the element of surprise in strategic planning. Previously it had been generally held that the vast resources of the Soviet Union prevented it from being knocked out by a surprise attack. This doctrine of "rolling with the punch" long had been credited with playing a major role in defeating the Germans in World War II. Traditionally Russian generals had traded space for time, luring the enemy deep into the Russian hinterland and destroying him there. This had been the fate of Napoleon as well as Hitler. Now, it was felt that warfare had reached the stage where the speed and capacity to destroy made it no longer possible to rely upon resilience after the initial attack as a sufficient guarantee for survival. In short, the war would most likely have to be fought with the forces in existence at the outset. This was one of the reasons why the Soviets retained huge standing armies in the face of a critical labor shortage. Assuming mutual, massive destruction in the initial stage, the side which could still field a sizeable force would posses what might be a decisive advantage. While space retained importance in the new concept, the emphasis was on it as a valuable factor for dispersal to lessen the dangers of the initial blow. The most important change was that the war had to be taken to the enemy so that he would be destroyed in his homeland before he had an opportunity to launch an attack on Soviet territory. Thus, surprise was recognized as being a possible decisive factor. [1]

But this concept had several important qualifications. Its principle exponent, Marshal P. A. Rotmistrov, a tank officer, stressed that

surprise cannot yield a conclusive result, cannot bring victory, in a war with a serious and strong enemy.[2]

In short, surprise alone did not justify going to war. He was also careful to emphasize that he was not advocating a "preventive war." What his strategy did purpose was a "preemptive" or "forestalling" strike against air bases, communications, and

[1] *Ibid.*, pp. 84–85, and *World Today, op. cit.*, 498–499.
[2] *Krasnaya Zvezda*, March 24, 1955, as quoted by Garthoff, *op. cit.*, p. 84.

other strategic targets at the very last moment to throw an enemy, who was *known* to be preparing an attack, off balance and to seize the initiative.

While emphasizing the importance of surprise the Soviet marshals refused to place much faith in *blitzkrieg* warfare. Rather their plans were for a long, drawn-out conflict fought primarily on the ground in which the major task, after the mutual neutralization of long range striking forces, would be the destruction of the Western land armies and the occupation of Europe, the Middle East, and Asia. An important part of their planning was the harnessing of the industrial capacity of the occupied areas to the Soviet economy to replace the losses suffered in the early stages of fighting. [1]

Such a view raised an interesting secondary question: was the morale of the Soviet soldier prepared for aggressive operation outside of the USSR. While there was little question in the minds of the military leaders that any conflict on Soviet soil would be taken in stride, they admitted that the rank and file were not prepared to participate in offensive actions in foreign countries. The professional soldiers sought to improve discipline by strengthening the undivided authority of military commanders at the expense of the Party's political officers. [2] Because of the presence of professional officers in the regime's inner-council for the first time this had important implications in the relationship of the military and the Communist Party which went far beyond mere questions of command.

An important factor in Soviet strategy was the continued emphasis upon the building and maintenance of armed forces capable of fighting both nuclear and non-nuclear wars. Consequently, the regime enjoyed a wide latitude of choice in the planning of its future operations. Available evidence suggests that the marshals believed that it would be advantageous to avoid the use of nuclear weapons in an all-out war but at the same time create the impression that the USSR had achieved parity with the West. Such a policy had a two-fold purpose. On one hand it hoped to create doubt in the minds of the smaller powers that the US would risk virtual suicidal destruction merely

[1] *Ibid.*, pp. 73 and 87–88.
[2] *Ibid.*, pp. 154–157, and *World Today, op. cit.*, 498–502.

for them. On the other, it wanted to force American officials to think twice before employing nuclear weapons against a Soviet move. If the Russians could prevent the use of nuclear weapons in an all-out war their large, well-equipped land armies would give them a substantial advantage over the West, whose strategy was built around a small, nuclear striking force. [1] Interestingly, both Soviet political and military leaders rejected both the possibility of limiting the use of nuclear weapons in an all-out war to tactical operations and the likelihood of future "brush-fire" wars such as the one in Korea despite the fact that their armed forces were better equipped than the West for precisely this type and that such wars have played an important part in Soviet military tradition. [2]

One Western military analyst concluded from this:

> There are good reasons for doubting that these statements represent the real Soviet expectation or foreshadow future Soviet behavior .... They generally deny the possibility of future local wars ... because they want to deter the United States from initiating such wars and, perhaps, even from preparing defensively for them. But this present denial in no way limits future Soviet initiative or response.[3]

However, another observer felt that this inconsistency was better explained by the inability of Soviet marshals to adapt their doctrine to reality

> because the Party still impose[d] severe restrictions on their intellectual freedom. The conceptual framework within which the professional strategists ... [were] compelled to work ... [was] quite inappropriate both to the size and nature of the Soviet armed forces and even more to the known capacity and doctrine of the USSR's only serious opponent in global war.

This was illustrated by the Soviet image of American military strategy that was

> ludicrously at variance with facts which ... were common knowledge to anyone who can read English.

This was particularly true of the refusal to admit the existence of the concept of a deterrent strategy even though this was a fundamental part of Western planning.

> The one factor which may ultimately save the [Soviet] generals is that their organization and doctrine, however unsuitable for conflict with the

[1] Garthoff, *op. cit.*, pp. 98–101.
[2] *Ibid.*, pp. 112–113.
[3] *Ibid.*, p. 113.

United States, may be exactly what is needed for a situation in which the main enemy is China .... Nearly everything ... which makes nonsense in the context of the current Cold War would then make impressive good sense.[1]

While military doctrines were undergoing review during 1955, foreign policy questions closely related to them were also scrutinized. The establishment of Communist China in 1949 had raised doubts about the continued validity of the "capitalist encirclement" thesis which dictated the corollary that the Soviet Union should never fight a two-front war. Nevertheless, the terminology had been retained and transfered to the Western bases which gradually came to encircle the USSR as the various alliances were welded together. The result was that

the East-West orientation of Soviet strategy ... [was] replaced by a North-South orientation of expansion[2]

in which the anti-colonial program played a significant role. Its purpose was not so much to add territory to the Russian empire but to neutralize the existing bases and deprive the West of other potential ones and to turn the Western flanks in such a way that it would encircle those who sought to contain it. In fact, the most consistent feature of the regime's foreign policy during 1955 was the renewed attempt to destroy Western alliances and to create a belt of neutral states along the entire perimeter of the Communist world from Finland to Japan. In Asia and the Middle East its inital efforts were centered around the Bandung Conference while at the same time Austria was the focus of attention in Europe.

THE BANDUNG CONFERENCE

The political sentiments which spawned the ten day Afro-Asian Conference in mid-April forced the Soviets to crystalize their position on the issue of nationalism in the underdeveloped areas. Since Stalin's death there had been repeated signs that a change was in progress, but despite its new diplomatic flexibility the regime continued to be hampered by backing and filling on the crucial question of how the tremendous revolution taking

[1] Healey, "Arms and Doctrine," p. 46.
[2] World Today, op. cit., p. 497.

place in Asia could be fitted into the Soviet scheme for world domination. The emergence of the so-called "third force" or neutral bloc posed as great a challenge to Moscow as it did to the West, although the USSR had somewhat of an edge over its opponents, because, through historical accident, it was not considered to be guilty of traditional imperialism despite the Czarist conquest of parts of Central Asia and Siberia. It also possessed an ideology which was conveniently anti-Western.

Nevertheless, in Stalin's last years he had personally enforced a policy dominated by the belief that:

> The 'third line' or 'third force' concocted by the right-wing socialists is in fact nothing other than a cover for the policy of defense of capitalism and fight against Communism. . . . Two forces, two camps, exist throughout the world.[1]

There were some in Moscow who recognized the basic falicy of such an uncompromising position. Among them was the economist E. Varga, who, during the closing years of World War II, had recognized the changing relationship between Europe and Asia. However, the purging of his book in 1947 and his forced recanting put an end to any movement in this direction until after Stalin's death. [2] Then the regime developed a more active interest (referred to by some observers as a " 'pre-occupation' with Asia") [3] that attempted to mobilize these areas for its own purposes by identifying their objectives with those of Communism. This was done with careful regard for the special sensitivity which is so highly characteristic of people emerging from colonial rule. Every effort was made to prevent the USSR from acquiring the stigma of imperialism, either in the old-fashioned political sense or the newer, but equally effective, economic sense. As a result, Moscow went to great lengths to stress the principle of equality in its relationship with these countries, thus flattering their egos. Even if it meant a radical departure from long held tenants of Communist ideology, the Soviet Union continuously attempted to portray the idea of "oneness" of purpose and goals as the natural consequence of

---

[1] *Voprosy Filosofii*, 2, 1948, p. 87 as quoted by Tucker, "The Psychology of Soviet Foreign Policy," p. 3.

[2] *Ibid.*, p. 4.

[3] Kirkpatrick (Ed.), *Target: The World – Communist Propaganda Activities in 1955*, p. 158.

two groups travelling in the same direction toward an identical destination. In short, the heavy-handedness which had hammered the minorities of Soviet Central Asia into the Slavic mold was conspicuous by its absence. Communist China and, to a lesser extent, the minority groups within the USSR were important instruments in the fulfillment of the Russian program. Operating through them, Moscow remained at a discreet distance in the background while Asians dealt with Asians.

This adaptation of Soviet policy to the changing political climate of the Afro-Asian world necessitated a shift in ideology. While it did not fully materialize until 1956, it was increasingly evident during 1955. The general "line," when it finally did emerge, discarded the traditional condemnation of nationalism as the staunch and faithful ally of imperialism and praised it as an inevitable step in the development of low-income countries in their search for Communism. It admitted that the fight for sovereignty had developed under the "national bourgeoisie" rather than the workers and peasants and had been achieved through peaceful means and not class warfare. Strong religious and nationalist sentiments, the Soviets said, had joined with various ideas taken from the Western past to create the foundation of national liberation movements. However, the argument continued that the absence of modern means of production in most underdeveloped countries was reflected in their political ideologies. This was a very important shift because it justified Soviet dealings with the Afro-Asian countries but did not represent a deviation from the fundamental position that these regimes were merely a transient stage on the eventual road to Communism. Nor did the fact that Moscow now spoke of the "national bourgeoisie" as being "sincere and lasting" rather than "conditional and provisional" (as it had in the 1920's) mean that it envisaged a longer period of collaboration. It merely meant that phases of its ideology had once again been modified to bring it into line with practice in order to obtain the same goal. [1]

---

[1] Cf. *Sovetskoye Vostokovedenie*, 1 and 5, 1956; *Kommunist*, 18, 1956; and *Partiynaya Zhizn*, August 1956 for examples of the fully developed position. (Laqueur, "Soviet Prospects in the Middle East," p. 21.) For a view contemporary with the Bandung Conference which retains the emphasis upon the workers and peasants cf. Zhukov, "The Bandung Conference of the African and Asian Countries and its Historical Significance," pp. 18–32.

The Bandung Conference presented Moscow with an important opportunity to demonstrate these new trends. Therefore, one of the most interesting features of the Afro-Asian gathering was the fact that the Soviet Union did not participate. Since representation was supposedly based solely upon a geographical basis, [1] the USSR was certainly entitled to take part. While it may be argued that a large percentage of its "Asian" population was actually of European descent, the Uzbeks, Turkmens, Tadzhiks, and Kazakhs had long histories as indigenous Asian peoples. Why, then, was the USSR not at the conference table? The answer depends largely upon the interpretation given to the motivating factors behind the meeting. If it is regarded as simply the product of a truly independent movement directed toward greater regional solidarity then the exclusion of Moscow must be considered a very serious rebuff. If, on the other hand, the gathering resulted partially from the adroit manipulation of this growing political consciousness by the Sino-Soviet partnership through the international Communist movement, then the absence of the Soviet regime was a shrewd gambit in the game of power politics. The weight of the evidence is in favor of the second interpretation, [2] but as in so many situations it is impossible to ascertain precisely which factors were the most influential. Without question both elements were present. The initial impetus for convening the Conference came from Indonesia, the host country. Clearly, it had much to gain in terms of domestic and foreign prestige by holding such a gathering. However, its regime was politically dependent in domestic politics upon the large, influential local Communist movement, and

it is extremely unlikely in the circumstances of its political situation that ... it would have made such an important move in foreign policy without the knowledge and consent of its Communist supporters, and the attitude of the latter would undoubtedly have been determined not so much by local ... considerations as by the wishes of Moscow and Peking.[3]

From the beginning it was clearly Indonesia's intention that Communist China should participate, and Peking's willingness to attend apparently was ascertained at an early date. Throughout

[1] The exclusion of Israel was a flagrant violation of this principle.
[2] Hudson, "Balance Sheet on Bandung," pp. 563–564.
[3] *Ibid.*, p. 564.

the negotiations leading up to the Conference the Soviet Union gave no public indication of having taken offence at not being invited, an indication that the question may have been cleared with Moscow in the early stages.

The participation of other Asian countries, particularly India, appears to have been the result of outside circumstances such as Pakistan's rearmament and membership in the "northern tier," the creation of the South-East Asia Treaty Organization, and the rising anti-colonial sentiment rather than local Communist pressure. Initially Nehru hesitated to give the idea his support. His change of heart may have resulted from the feeling that it would provide him with a sympathetic audience before which to reassert India's neutralist position and moral leadership of Asia. The participation of Pakistan with its Western commitments and the Moslem countries of the Middle East was probably obtained through political log rolling involving the exclusion of Israel, the inclusion of a hostile reference to it in the final communiqué, and the special mention of Algeria, Morroco, Tunesia, and Aden in the general denunciation of Western colonialism. [1]

Therefore, at the conference table there were three diverse elements: the two Communist nations (the Chinese People's Republic and North Viet Nam); the eight pro-Western countries (Iran, Iraq, Japan, Pakistan, the Phillipines, Thailand, Turkey, and Viet Nam); and the 18 so-called "uncommitted" states (Afganistan, Burma, Cambodia, Ceylon, Egypt, Ethiopia, the Gold Coast, India, Indonesia, Jordan, Laos, Lebanon, Liberia, Libya, Nepal, Saudi Arabia, Syria, and the Yemen). [2] This latter group was largely responsible for the anti-Western attitude which dominated most of the sessions. In fact, Chou En-lai's conduct at the conference table was exemplary. His conciliatory attitude achieved more than had he ranted and raved against the West. This he adroitly left to the non-Communist countries. While the West came in for considerable attack, the Soviet world hardly felt the sting of criticism. Its severest critic among the leaders of the "uncommitted" states was Sir J. Kotelawala, Prime Minister of Ceylon, who spoke out against Communist activities in his own country and in favor of linking the anti-

---

[1] *Ibid.*, pp. 564–565.
[2] *Soviet News*, 3157, May 4, 1955, p. 1.

colonial strictures with conquest through internal subversion. Although his views were supported by a substancial minority they were largely kept out of the final communiqué. [1]

In fact, there was little in it with which the Soviets could find fault. [2] The Dutch, the British, and the French were directly criticized for their colonial policies while there was no hint of criticism for Russian activities in Central Asia. [3] The wording of the equivocal section dealing with the testing and use of nuclear weapons was, by implication, adverse to the United States. This also applied to the declaration that each nation had the right to independent and collective self-defense as long as it resulted in the

abstention from the use of [such] arrangements . . . to serve the particular interests of any of the big powers.[4]

This was clearly directed at American efforts to organize alliance systems in Asia and the Middle East.

The one serious setback for the Communist bloc was the failure of the Conference to include the Peking regime in the long list of nations it deemed worthy of membership in the United Nations. (However, a "United Viet Nam" was included.) [5] But this was offset by the incorporation of the *Panch Shila* (or Five Principles) into the closing ten points of the communiqué, a significant accomplishment for Communist diplomacy. These five points – 1) mutual respect for territorial integrity and sovereignty; 2) non-aggression; 3) non-interference for whatever reason; 4) cooperation for mutual benefit; 5) peaceful co-existence – had become the basis of Russia's new diplomatic approach in both Europe and

---

[1] Hudson, *op. cit.*, pp. 564–565.

[2] *The Economist* took a different view. It felt that the final communiqué represented the first expression of the position of a new power bloc. It wrote that it contained no reference to the "misty concept" of peaceful co-existence

"but a set of terse warnings against aggression, threats of force, and racial discrimination; insistance on the rights of small nations and on peaceful settlement of disputes; and specific recognition of every country's right to join in arrangements for collective self-defense, provided that these . . . [did not] serve the private interests of any great power."

The Economist, April 30, 1955, p. 362.

[3] The only reference which might be construed as criticism was the admonishment that

"colonialism in all its manifestations is an evil which should speedily be brought to an end."

Soviet News, 3157, May 4, 1955, p. 2.

[4] *Ibid.*, p. 3.

[5] *Ibid.*, p. 2.

Asia. Under these principles all countries striving for socialism were to be gathered in under Moscow's protective, but not dominating, wing. The Yugoslavs forced the Russians to spell this out more precisely a few weeks later when they demanded and received the right to proclaim the existence of more than one road to socialism. Rather than alienating those who could not accept the position that the Soviet Union provided the exclusive model, the USSR sought to attract potential converts with this version of an international united front in which conformity was not mandatory.

The effect of this policy in Asia was primarily twofold. Firstly, it undercut American warnings against the dangers of Soviet encroachment [1] and, secondly, made it easier for Moscow to deal with Peking. Despite the apparent high degree of Sino-Soviet cooperation at Bandung the men in the Kremlin could not have found the arrangement entirely to their liking. Despite the officially expressed pleasure with the way the Chinese presented the Communist case, no member of the Soviet inner-circle could have overlooked the fact that while Moscow was on the outside looking in, Peking sat at the conference table. [2] The spectre of a Communist Asia oriented toward China rather than the Soviet Union must have haunted the Presidium's deliberations. The brand of Communism practiced by Russia's Far Eastern partner was admittedly different from that found on the steppes of the great Eurasian land mass. For the USSR to have demanded conformity from the under-developed countries leaning toward socialism would have forced a showdown which would have been disastrous for Moscow. However, the "many-roads" doctrine provided a workable solution in which there was room for all. It put off momentarily the inevitable question of the acute rivalry between the Goliaths of the Communist world, permitting the Soviet Union to marshal its forces and remain in the race.

[1] *World Today*, "Soviet Political Strategy in Asia," pp. 196–198.

[2] This was particularly true of Chou's statement that Communist China was an Asian power while the Soviet Union was a European one. (Wirsing, "Die Konferenz von Bandung," p. 335.) When Prime Minister U Nu of Burma visited Moscow the following November he proposed that the USSR should participate in any future Afro-Asian conferences, an idea Khrushchev immediately endorsed. *The Times*, Nov. 2, 1955.

THE AUSTRIAN STATE TREATY

While the Soviet Union was thus busily occupied behind the scenes in Asia, its more dramatic maneuvers in Europe held the spotlight. They were part of a well coordinated program designed to give Russia its own "position of strength" at the summer Summit Conference. The first was the offer to negotiate an Austrian State Treaty. This provided the West with one of the "deeds" it had insisted on as a condition for any Four Power meeting. It also successfully neutralized a key area in the heart of Central Europe.

At the Berlin Conference in January-February 1954 the Soviets had linked the withdrawal of occupation troops from Austria to the solution of the German problem, declaring that it was the only way to ensure the prevention of an *Anschluss*. There was no great departure from this position until Molotov's speech before the Supreme Soviet a year later. At that time he made ambiguous references to the possibility of disassociating the two if satisfactory guarantees to quiet Russian fears could be obtained from the West. The price was Austria's neutralization and a Four Power conference on both Germany and Austria. However, he quickly dampened any enthusiasm he might have generated by stating in the same speech:

> It should, however, be borne in mind that, in the event of the Paris agreements [to rearm Germany] ... being ratified, a serious danger of *Anschluss* would be created and consequently a threat to Austria's independence.[1]

The West considered this merely to be another propaganda statement, but when Austria pressed the Soviet Foreign Ministry on its sincerity, it received an affirmative answer. In fact, Moscow even accepted the Austrian position that it was unnecessary to link the discussion of both issues (i.e., Germany and Austria) and unreasonable to expect the West to be willing to negotiate before the ratification of the Paris agreements was completed. The Russians went as far as to invite Vienna on March 24, 1955, to send a delegation to the Soviet capital to conduct preliminary negotiations. Between April 12 and 15 the two governments speedily dealt with the knotty problems which

---

[1] *Soviet News*, 3106, Feb. 17, 1955, p. 4.

had blocked the signing of a treaty for so many years. [1] The terms which the USSR offered on the most hotly disputed points were more favorable than those which the West had been prepared to accept in Berlin the previous year and were designed to emphasize the new Russian generosity. They gave up virtually all of the economic concessions envisioned by the 1949 draft treaty and, instead of demanding payment in American dollars for the $ 150,000,000 [2] worth of assets seized by Germany during World War II, agreed to take payment entirely in Austrian goods. Also the oil concessions and the assets of the Danube Shipping Company were to be returned for proper compensation. Earlier drafts had provided for them to remain in Russian control. The price demanded of Austria for these concessions was the withdrawal of all foreign troops from the country no later than December 31, 1955, and her promise not to take part in any military alliance or to permit foreign bases in her territory. [3]

This last point had special importance to both sides from a purely strategic point of view. It forced Western troops in Austria to withdraw to northern Italy and complicated the communication and supply of lines between NATO forces in Germany and Italy. On the other side of the Iron Curtain, it deprived the Russians of their excuse for maintaining troops in her Satellites. To continue to do so without some other justification would have been in violation of the respective peace treaties. This probably was a contributing factor to the formal creation of the Warsaw Pact the following month.

With the Austrian problem resolved except for the formalities of acceptance by the Big Three, who had already expressed on April 5 their desire to sign a treaty as soon as possible, the Soviets next turned their attention toward Germany. The first step to annul the wartime treaties with Britain and France, on the grounds that both countries had approved its rearmament, were taken on April 10 and the action was officially completed on May 7. [4] On the surface it seemed that Moscow was acting in a peak of temper, but actually it was a shrewd move to ensure that

---

[1] *World Today*, "The Hard Road to an Austrian Treaty," pp. 193–195.

[2] Actually, the demand had been for "fully convertible currency."

[3] *New York Times*, April 16, 1955, p. 1, Clifton Daniel, and *Soviet News*, 3145, April 15, 1955, p. 1.

[4] *New York Times*, April 10, 1955, p. 1, and *Soviet News*, 3160, May 9, 1955, p. 3.

the USSR would be the only country participating in any Four Power negotiations which could deal directly with both East and West Germany. In a little noticed decree the previous January the Supreme Soviet had ended the state of war which technically existed between Russia and the Federal Republic. Consequently, the regime was in a position to threaten the West with direct negotiations, by-passing any Four Power conference table it chose to ignore.

By mid-May 1955 the movement within the Soviet ice pack was so great that a whole chronicle of major diplomatic moves was telescoped into less than a week. Taking cognizance of the concessions made to Austria the West felt that the climate was right for the much talked about Heads-of-State Conference and formally issued an invitation to the USSR on May 10. [1] The same day, in what was evidently a counter-maneuver, Moscow's representatives at the London United Nations disarmament talks presented a new series of proposals. Three days later, May 14, 1955, the Austrian treaty was signed by the Big Four and the Russians indicated a willingness to attend a Summit Meeting in Geneva. This coincided with the Soviet bloc's efforts to strengthen its bargaining position by formally creating the long-threatened Warsaw Pact. [2] Poland, Czechoslovakia, Hungary, Rumania, Bulgaria, Albania, and East Germany joined with the Soviet Union in an organization similar to NATO but much less complicated. The integration of the respective armed forces under Marshal Konev, the third ranking military man in the USSR, was looser than in its Western counterpart and the participation of an East German Army was left open, apparently in one last bid to stem the rearming of the Federal Republic. Also on the same day, May 14, 1955, the Soviet leadership announced that it intended to fly to Belgrade at the end of the month to heal the long standing rift with Yugoslavia. [3]

---

[1] *New York Times*, May 11, 1955, p. 1, Harrold Callender.

[2] The meeting coincided with the granting of complete sovereignty to the Federal Republic by the West.

[3] *New York Times*, May 14, 1955, p. 1; May 15, 1955, p. 1, Clifton Daniel; and May 15, 1955, p. 1, John Mac Cormac.

THE DISARMAMENT NEGOTIATIONS

Two of these maneuvers – the disarmament proposals and the bid to Yugoslavia – require much closer scrutiny. For ten years disarmament negotiations had been deadlocked in direct proportion to the intensity of the Cold War. In 1952 the United Nations, hoping to overcome this, had merged its Atomic Energy Commission and its Commission for Conventional Armaments into one body. Membership in the Disarmament Commission, as it was called, consisted of nations sitting on the Security Council plus Canada. During that year the West proposed numerical ceilings of between 1,000,000 and 1,500,000 men for China, the USSR, and the United States and between 700,000 and 800,000 for France and Britain as well as a program of verification of the size of each country's armed force and atomic stockpile. The Soviets, on their part, proposed immediate prohibition of atomic weapons and other means of mass destruction with effective international controls which were to be "initiated simultaneously." They also included a one third reduction in conventional armaments within one year. However, they provided no details, but did raise another question – the prohibition of chemical and bacteriological warfare through the acceptance of the 1925 Geneva Protocol (which the United States had not yet ratified). The basic positions of these deadlocked negotiations were as follows: The West advocated the establishment of control; the reduction of conventional armaments and armed forces; and then the prohibition of nuclear weapons. The Soviets reversed the order so that prohibition came first, followed by reduction, and then concluded by inspection. [1]

In 1953 the French attempted to break the deadlock by advocating the dovetailing of the various stages in such a way that no country would be placed in jeopardy at any stage in the process. Also the West as a bloc suggested that future discussions be held in private. In December 1953 President Eisenhower proposed the creation of an international atomic energy organization to promote the peaceful use of atomic energy. The Soviets replied by agreeing to take part in negotiations and

---

[1] *World Today,* "Disarmament: Proposals and Negotiations, 1946–1955," pp. 335–336.

called for a solemn pledge that all nations refrain from using atomic or hydrogen weapons. This they envisaged as the first step toward eventual complete elimination of all nuclear weapons. [1]

In 1954 the UN Disarmament Commission established a sub-committee of those powers (Canada, France, the USSR, Britain, and the United States) most directly concerned with the problem. This action followed on the heels of the release by the United States of data on the destructive capacity of hydrogen bombs and the resulting public clamor (including a proposal by Nehru to ban testing) for some form of agreement. Also during the same year the French and British joined forces to develop a new departure in Western proposals which advocated a "phased" disarmament scheme in the following sequence: (1) a limitation of military expeditures in national budgets; (2) a reduction of conventional forces by one half of an agreed figure; (3) the reduction of the remaining one half; and (4) the prohibition of nuclear and other means of mass destruction. A control group was to be established and "positioned" before the first stage could be begun and was to report the progress as each subsequent stage was entered. The Canadian and American governments, while not actually accepting the program as presented, indicated their general support, but the Soviets rejected it. The West, in turn, refused to accept the Russian unconditional and unsupervised prohibition of nuclear weapons. Although the result was still deadlock, two important changes in the Western position resulted from the British and French plan. These were the dropping of the principle of disclosure and verification prior to any disarmament and the substitution of the principle of a "freeze." Also international inspection and supervision replaced the "Baruch Plan" provision for international ownership of atomic energy facilities. [2]

The Soviets surprised the United Nations in September 1954 by agreeing to accept the Anglo-French program as the basis of further negotiations. However, they added conditions and modifications which nullified a good share of it. However, their willingness to reverse the order of procedure offered the first indication in many years that there might be an eventual – if only

[1] *Ibid.*, pp. 337–338.
[2] *Ibid.*, pp. 339–340.

limited – agreement. This hope was kept alive by two resolutions the General Assembly unanimously passed in November 1954. These called for the establishment of an international organization for the peaceful uses of atomic energy and the drafting of a disarmament convention covering limitation of conventional forces; the banning of atomic weapons; and the creation of international inspection and control. They were the first two resolutions on atomic energy to be passed unanimously since 1946. [1]

The Disarmament Sub-Committee again met in London during the first months of 1955, holding 28 private sessions between February 25 and May 18. Both sides began developing their respective positions. The West, this time including the United States and Canada, restated on March 8 the plan previously put forth by France and Britain. It offered two compromise proposals – troop levels of Britain and France were to be limited to 650,000 men each and prohibition of nuclear weapons should begin when 75 rather than 100 per cent of the reduction was complete – which the Soviet Union rejected. Moscow's delegates restated their September 1954 program. They still insisted on temporary control for Phase One and permanent control for Phase Two but appeared to advance further towards accepting the principle that the control body exercise permanent supervision

to the extent necessary to ensure implementation of the convention by all States

and that

the international control organ . . . [should] have its own permanent staff of inspectors, having unrestricted access, within the limits of the supervisory functions they exercise, to all establishments subject to control.[2]

However, the Soviets still appeared to insist upon a one third across-the-board-reduction of big power forces rather than accepting the Western proposed ceilings. [3]

The new proposals, which the Soviets made on May 10, 1955, were in three parts and important because they not only contained significant departures from the previous Russian position

[1] *Ibid.*, pp. 340–341.
[2] Quoted by *ibid.*, p. 342.
[3] *Ibid.*, p. 343.

but also broached a number of new ideas. The first part covered relaxation of international tension and the ending of the Cold War;[1] the second outlined an international disarmament treaty; and a third set forth the principles of international control.

In effect, the Soviets continued to demand the acceptance of their two-stage proposals, each scheduled for one year, but agreed to the Anglo-French compromise which placed the prohibition of nuclear weapons into effect after only 75 per cent of the conventional disarmament stage had been completed. Moscow also abandoned its insistence on a one third reduction in favor of the Western proposed limitations. However, it insisted that foreign bases be liquidated within two years. The new USSR plan also made prohibition of nuclear testing one of the first steps of any agreement but did not make it a condition. Likewise, it accepted the use of such weapons in defensive war as the West had asked but added the restriction that this could be done only with the sanction of the Security Council where it had a veto. However, again this was not made a preliminary condition to an agreement.

Concerning the control phase of disarmament, Moscow accepted the creation of a single permanent organ but doubted its effectiveness to prevent a surprise attack resulting from the clandestine manufacture of arms. Therefore, it added that such a body should have inspection points at principal harbors, airports, and rail and road junctions to check on troop concentrations. Also, it suggested empowering the organization with complete access to all budgetary information on military expenditures. During the second stage the control group was to have the right of permanent inspection with

unimpeded access at all times, within the limits of the control functions they excercised, to all objects of control.[2]

In case of violations, the Soviets wanted the inspection body to

---

[1] It contained the following recommendations: (1) the elimination of Cold War propaganda; (2) the withdrawal of occupation forces in Germany, with the exception of strictly limited contingents; (3) the limitation of foreign military bases by the Big Five; (4) the prohibition of attaching either political or economic conditions to assistance given to low income countries for the development of the peaceful uses of nuclear energy; (5) the ending of discrimination in international trade; and (6) the elimination of obstacles to international cultural relations. *Ibid.*, p. 343.

[2] Quoted by *ibid.*, p. 343.

merely notify the Security Council while the West desired it to notify the General Assembly and the various states concerned and to have power to take interim action by itself. [1]

One of the many reasons for this substantial shift in the Soviet's position was the very real desire to lessen the financial burden of armaments on their already strained economy. Such a reduction would also have released badly needed man-power for both agriculture and industry.

THE 'RAPPROCHEMENT' WITH YUGOSLAVIA

The magnitude of the changes taking place in Russian diplomacy was apparent from the lengths Moscow was willing to go in order to normalize relations with Yugoslavia. A settlement with Tito was vital if the USSR were to negotiate from its own "position of strength" at Geneva. Psychologically his successful defiance of the Kremlin personified the irrational foreign policy pursued during the Stalin era. A reconcileation would serve Moscow's purpose of removing this stigma in the eyes of the non-Communist world and graphically portraying the members of the regime as rational, reasonable men who were seriously interested in lessening international tension even if it meant making concessions. In its own orbit, Moscow could never feel confident that as long as Tito remained a "heretic" one of the other Satellites might not try to mimic him. Therefore, it was essential that Yugoslavia be brought back into the fold as soon as it was feasible. Only then could Moscow convincingly justify its claim of speaking for all of the Communist world. This point was of particular importance in light of the Western insistence upon discussing the legality of the Eastern European regimes. A rebellious Yugoslavia presented the West with an inviting point of departure. It was also necessary for Russia to end, if possible, Tito's flirtation with Western military alliances, particularly NATO. Geographically, his country occupied an important position in the "neutral" belt desired by the Soviets. With Finland neutralized politically, and militarily by her proximity to the USSR; Sweden and Switzerland by tradition; Austria by treaty; only Yugoslavia and Germany were needed to complete

[1] *Ibid.*, p. 345.

it. If Tito could be made to fall into line, Moscow's arguments for a neutralized Germany would be substantially strengthened. Domestically, it gave Khrushchev and his associates a specific issue upon which to attack their more conservative opponents – Molotov in particular.

None of these factors had escaped the attention of Stalin's lieutenants. Being shrewd politicians, they realized that the Soviet Union only stood to loose as long as the rift continued. But while Stalin lived nothing could be done. However, he

had hardly been laid to rest in the Red Square Mausoleum before his heirs ... launched a campaign to re-establish warm and close relations with Yugoslavia.[1]

Within two days of his death, the secret police, who had constantly harassed Belgrade's representatives in Moscow, disappeared. The Soviet press, which had frequently printed articles such as the one entitled "The Tito Fascists are a Tool of the Warmongers," lessened the quantity of its abusive material but continued to publish it for several months. [2] The lines were too sharply drawn in this struggle for such slight gestures to bring about reconciliation. It required two years of constant maneuvering by both sides before it became evident that neither could gain more advantage.

To appreciate fully the importance of the regime's pilgrimage to Belgrade it is necessary to survey briefly the events of the previous two years. [3] The news of Stalin's death was received with "ill-concealed glee" in the Yugoslav capital because Tito's followers were convinced it meant a change in Moscow's attitude toward them. They did not have to wait long. On April 29, 1953, the Russians approached Tito's envoy in Moscow on the re-establishment of complete diplomatic relations which culminated in the July appointment of V. A. Valkov as the new Soviet Ambassador and the dispatching of D. Vidié as his Yugoslav counter-part the following September. Belgrade's diplomacy also reflected the changing climate. Observers in Rome felt that its support of the creation of a Free Territory in Trieste was merely a

[1] New York Times, May 14, 1955, p. 2, Harrison Salisbury.

[2] Ogonyok, 2, Jan. 1953 as quoted by Staritzky, "The Soviet-Yugoslav Talks," p. 3.

[3] For a detailed chronology of developments between July 1953 and February 1954 cf. Bauer, "Tito und die Sowjetunion," pp. 100–101.

reiteration of the Soviet thesis. [1] However, Tito was careful to indicate that this did not mean his return to the Soviet bloc. Apparently, it was more a reflection of his desire to look out for his own self-interests should there be a general East-West partitioning of Europe.

As 1953 progressed the Trieste issue continued to be a thorny one which provided the Soviet Union with an excellent opportunity to show its new friendliness for the Yugoslavs. On October 8 the United States and Britain announced the end of the Allied Military Government in Zone A. Both Italian and Yugoslav troops were immediately mobilized on their respective boarders and the West's position in Tito's country suffered a severe setback. Moscow entered the frey with diplomatic notes to both London and Washington four days later charging that it was a gross violation of the Italian Peace Treaty. On October 13 Vishinsky demanded a special meeting of the Security Council to discuss it. However, Tito's regime dealt with the situation with amazing coolheadedness. In fact, Pijade declared that as far as the Yugoslav government was concerned, the Soviet move was not made in the interests of its people or those in Trieste. [2]

While this issue was simmering Tito sought to improve relations with the Cominform. A large number of Yugoslavs who had been jailed after the 1948 break for supporting it were freed by the July 8, 1953, amnesty. Negotiations over border questions were begun with Hungary and Rumania, and by the end of the year diplomatic relations with Albania, Bulgaria, and Hungary had been resumed. Also an agreement between Moscow and Belgrade on problems concerning the Danube was signed during 1953 and the Yugoslav representative was elected Chairman of the Danube Commission. [3]

During 1954 these trends of improved relations with the Satellites continued, but the "normalization" of relations with Moscow lagged. They amounted to little more than the exchange of diplomatic representatives, primarily because of Tito's insistence upon maintaining a "middle position" and his dissatisfaction with the USSR's failure to produce economic gestures.

[1] *World Today*, "The Russo-Yugoslav *Détente*," pp. 13–15.
[2] *Ibid.*, p. 16.
[3] Staritzky, *op. cit.*, pp. 3–4.

These, he insisted, had to come from the Soviet capital because it, rather than Belgrade, had been responsible for the original break.

These gestures materialized gradually in the form of barter agreements with East Germany, Poland, and Bulgaria. Finally, on September 5, 1954, Moscow sent a trade delegation to the Yugoslav capital which returned three weeks later with agreements calling for the exchange of Soviet crude oil, cotton, manganese ore, coal, and newsprint in exchange for meat, tobacco, ethyl alcohol, hemp, caustic soda, and calcium soda. About the same time there was also a noticeable change in Moscow's propaganda campaign against Tito. Cominform radio stations ended their jamming of Radio Belgrade and the "clandestine" radio station calling itself "Free Yugoslavia" ceased its transmissions from Moscow.

However, during 1954 Tito played a cautious game. On August 9 he finally signed a new agreement with Greece and Turkey which converted their earlier (February 1953) tri-partite friendship treaty into a military organization. He also dropped strong hints that he might be willing to participate in some form of European organization if the problem of Germany could be resolved. These were deliberately vague to give him room to maneuver. On September 19, 1954, he indicated he was willing to participate in an European community but made it clear that NATO had too much of a political coloring. Significantly, the Soviet press reported his remarks on this occasion.

About a month later when the Trieste issue was settled by a compromise, the Soviets did a complete *volte-face* and praised the agreement which only a year before they had denounced as a violation of the Italian Peace Treaty. [1] This was only one of an increasing number of Soviets efforts designed to curry favor with Belgrade. Two of the more obvious came in November. At the 37th anniversary of the October Revolution Saburov declared:

Our country's relations with Yugoslavia have improved of late. Some obstacles which hindered [their] normalization ... have been removed, and steps have been taken to resume trade and the organization of relations in cultural and other matters.... On its part, the Soviet government will continue to give every encouragement to complete normalization ... to strengthening the old friendship of our peoples with the fraternal

---

[1] *World Today, op. cit.*, pp. 17-19.

peoples of Yugoslavia, and hopes that it will meet with complete mutual understanding on the Yugoslav side.[1]

These were the first warm words of this kind since the rupture in 1948. On November 28 Malenkov, Molotov, and Khrushchev attended the celebration of Yugoslavia's national holiday at its Embassy in Moscow where they drank the health of "Comrade" Tito, his Party, and his country. [2] But again such gestures were insufficient to entice Belgrade from its position on the fence. While it had rejected NATO it likewise refrained from taking part in Moscow's European Security Conference which was attended only by the Soviet orbit.

An official version of how the May 1955 *rapprochement* was arranged was never published. However, there were indications that the Soviets made the initial overtures sometime in October or November after Khrushchev's return from China. At that time Tito was invited to Moscow. Simultaneously, discussions of the ideological difficulties which separated the two Parties were begun. Both of these matters were dealt with by the Central Committee session of the Yugoslav Communist League just prior to Tito's departure for India and Burma. Although the agenda and decisions of this meeting were not published, the Yugoslav's presumably replied that the Soviets would have to come to Belgrade. At the same time the Yugoslavs took the position that their internal reforms had created a social system so different from that of the USSR that only a relationship on a state-to-state basis was possible. In other words, they were demanding "co-existence" rather than "fraternal solidarity."

The Russians may have been encouraged to make their initial gestures by internal developments in Yugoslavia. At the time the Djilas heresy was at its height – although unpublished – and there were indications of a swing back toward a more conservative position. However, any assumption by the Soviets that Tito was voluntarily coming back into line should have been dampened by the way in which the Djilas affair was handled once it was made public.

During the subsequent negotiations the Russians accepted both the principle of a public apology and a pilgrimage to

---

[1] *Pravda* and *Izvestia*, Nov. 7, 1954, pp. 1-2, *Current Digest*, VI, 42, p. 13.
[2] *World Today*, *op. cit.*, p. 19.

Belgrade but stuck to their demands of discussing Party relations. In the early spring of 1955 the Yugoslavs decided to meet such a request not with a complete refusal (as they had first planned) but by pressing their demand for Soviet recognition of each country's right to select its own road to socialism. As the Yugoslav's saw it, this was to be a broad enough interpretation so as to also include the paths selected by Western labor movements. [1]

The composition of the Soviet delegation illustrated the gap which still existed between the two countries on the eve of the talks. While the presence of foreign policy experts and trade officials showed the directions the negotiations were to take, the announcement that Khrushchev, in his Party capacity, rather than Bulganin was to head the group indicated that Moscow had not ruled out the question of an ideological *rapprochement*. Tito kept insisting this was not to be a subject of discussion. *Pravda*, however, left little doubt that it could not be avoided. In fact, just prior to the regime's departure, it went so far as to stress the "ideological affinity" which it insisted existed between the people of both countries. [2]

The omission of Molotov, the third ranking member of the Soviet inner-circle and the nominal foreign policy spokesman, was a major victory for Tito. No other member of the Presidium had been so closely linked to Stalin's negative diplomacy and the 1948 rupture which drove Yugoslavia from the Cominform. Molotov's Deputy Minister, A. A. Gromyko, represented him in Belgrade while Shepilov, editor of *Pravda*, looked after the Party's interests in these matters in his capacity as Chairman of its Foreign Affairs Commission.

Thus the stage was set for the strange scene which took place at Zemun airport outside of Belgrade on May 26, 1955, when Khrushchev stepped from his plane and delivered his opening speech, which was received with stony silence by the Yugoslavs. The fact that he made a public apology was not unexpected, but the position he took was a complete surprise. In one sweeping paragraph he sought to saddle

Beria, Abakumov, and other exposed enemies of the people

[1] *World Today*, "Yugoslavia between Independence and Orthodoxy," pp. 326–327.
[2] *Pravda*, May 18, 1955, p. 1, *Current Digest*, VII, 20, p. 20.

with the rupture of relations between Moscow and Belgrade. He also tried to pretend that no serious differences had ever existed between the two countries. The explanation for this strange behavior was to be found in a later paragraph where he publicly called for a resumption of full Party relations.

As representatives of the Communist Party of the Soviet Union ... we consider it desirable to establish mutual confidence between our Parties .... The most enduring bonds develop between the peoples of those countries where leadership is given by the Parties which base all their work on the teachings of Marxism-Leninism. The Parties which rely for guidance upon Marxist-Leninist theory ... have a common aim – the struggle for the interests of the working class and of the working peasantry, for the interests of the working people.

. . . .

Steering the new, socialist course, the peoples of these countries are strengthening their forces through enduring, unshakeable friendship.

. . . .

In the interests of the workers and peasants, in the interests of the international labor movement and of the common aims of the struggle for strengthening peace, for mankind's better future, the leaders of the Communist and Workers' Parties must develop mutual confidence between these Parties.[1]

The total absence of comment in the Yugoslav press the following day echoed Tito's silence at the airport. Privately his senior officials spoke of it as "provocation." [2] Not until May 28 did *Borba*, the official organ of the Yugoslav regime, reply to Khrushchev's appeal and then only in an indirect but drastic way which left little doubt exactly where it stood. The article expressed Belgrade's approval of specific passages of his speech, reiterating in nearly every paragraph the importance of "inter-state relations," but pointedly omitting any reference to either the strange apology or the bid for closer Party ties. In fact, it went to great pains to clearly place even the "inter-state relations" in the proper framework of Yugoslavia's "very good" relations with the Afro-Asian bloc; her "good relations" with the West; and her "relations of alliance" with the members of the Balkan Pact. It concluded with the solemn declaration that

the partition of the world into ideological blocs ... [was] not the path which leads to peace.

[1] *Soviet News*, 3174, May 27, 1955, p. 2.
[2] Quoted by *World Today*, p. 329.

What Yugoslavia wanted, it added, was "active co-existence" which was

not co-existence in the sense of some sort of a temporary truce between two hostile blocs, created by an ideological division ... [but] the active cooperation of all countries regardless of differences in their internal systems.[1]

For the next few days this difference was thrashed out behind closed doors. On the day that the final communiqué was signed (June 2, 1955) another editorial in *Borba* indicated that Khrushchev had not succeeded in winning over the Yugoslavs on this point.

It is apparent that the concept of the division of the world into two ideological blocs starts from the inevitability of the ultimate conflict between these two blocs. Therefore, those who start from such a point of view do not accept the possibility of a full and permanent world peace, but only the possibility of postponing the ultimate conflict. Willy-nilly, such concepts must inevitably be reflected in practical policy, even in well-intentioned efforts to solve international problems; hence these efforts cannot achieve satisfactory results. ... Those who consistently work for the preservation of world peace must approach this task with the deep conviction that peace can be preserved not only temporarily, but permanently. They must be convinced that a world armed conflict, no matter when it came, would represent a general catastrophe for mankind and that, accordingly, it is not enough to prevent it today, but that one must endeavour to prevent it for ever.

The same article also asserted that

it is quite wrong to believe that the progress of the world depends on the expansion of this or that ideological bloc.[2]

However, this was exactly the position Khrushchev tried to drive home. It was unofficially reported that when he criticized the Yugoslav deviations from the Soviet pattern in the closed door sessions, Tito answered him personally with straight-from-the-shoulder talk, uninhibited by Marxist-Leninist polemics. [3]

The sum and substance of these discussions, which were published in a joint communiqué, indicated that Tito had succeeded in driving a hard bargain. Nowhere did it even mention the Communist Parties of either country but concentrated on the inter-state nature of their relationship. If this needed additional emphasis, it was driven home when Khrushchev relinquished the

---

[1] *Borba*, May 28, 1955, as quoted by *ibid.*, p. 330.
[2] *Borba*, June 2, 1955, as quoted by *ibid.*, pp. 330–331.
[3] *Ibid.*, p. 331.

limelight to Bulganin for the first time at the signing ceremonies.[1]

While Tito spurned Moscow's plans for Party solidarity, he did publicly accept its position on foreign policy. In the communiqué both nations advocated peaceful co-existence as the basis of international cooperation; an ending of trade embargos; the banning of nuclear weapons; the reduction and limitation of conventional forces; the admission of Communist China to the United Nations; the latter country's "legitimate rights" to Formosa; the use of nuclear energy for peaceful purposes; German reunification

on a democratic basis and in conformity with the interest and wishes of the German people

as well as the

requirements of general security;

support of the position adopted by the Afro-Asian nations at Bandung; the abolition of military blocs; and approval of an European security system. [2] In this long list neither side made extensive concessions because their foreign policies had closely paralleled each other for some time. Yugoslavia probably made the biggest concession by endorsing the European security system which she had previously rejected. However, the condemnation of military blocs was a two-edged sword. It prevented Tito from further flirtation with NATO but also blocked his membership in the Warsaw Pact as well.

On inter-state matters there were considerable signs of concessions by Moscow. It formally acknowledged full respect for Yugoslavia's sovereignty, independence, and territorial integrity as well as recognizing that its relations with Belgrade had to be on a basis of equality. In effect, this meant that Tito could maintain his ties with the West without interference from the Soviet hierarchy. It also agreed to those other principles which were at variance with its previous policy. These were

---

[1] However, the Soviets were not content to drop the issue. On July 16 *Pravda* made another bid for renewed Party relations. This time it was reprinted by *Borba* in full but without comment. Western observers in the Yugoslav capital reported that a *rapprochement* on the basis of equality was expected. *Pravda*, July 16, 1955, p. 1, *Current Digest*, VII, 26, p. 3, and the *New York Times*, July 22, 1955, p. 8, Jack Raymond.

[2] *Soviet News*, 3178, June 3, 1955, pp. 1–2.

1) the elimination of propaganda and similar action which would impede the development of harmonious relations;

2) the condemnation of aggression and all attempts to subject countries to economic and political domination; and

3) the non-interference in internal affairs of other countries, recognizing that different forms of socialist development were possible and that these were the exclusive concern of each country.[1]

This last point was the Soviet Union's greatest concession. Although its policy in Asia and the Middle East (particularly after the Bandung Conference) had skirted the edges of this question, there remained only one acknowledged "road to socialism" – the USSR's. Now Moscow was forced to admit publicly that its ultimate goal could be reached from a number of directions. This sowed a myriad of dragon teeth not only in the Soviet orbit but throughout the uncommitted world also. [2]

Khrushchev went to Belgrade prepared to grant Yugoslavia independence within the Communist world, but he was forced to acknowledge the established fact of its independence *outside* of it. He had to be satisfied with creating a climate of renewed contacts which he apparently hoped would eventually create internal pressure for closer affinity with Moscow. [3]

Although *Pravda* hailed the new relationship between the two countries, [4] there was little reason to doubt that the regime privately did not share its enthusiasm. In the first place, by being forced to go to Belgrade, it publicly demonstrated that it was possible to defy Moscow and get away with it. The other Satellite leaders could not fail to see the importance of this and ponder it. Even if the same communiqué had been negotiated in the Soviet capital there would have been an element of penitence

---

[1] *New York Times*, June 3, 1955, p. 1, Jack Raymond. Another important phase of the agreement delt with economic relations. Russia wrote off the $9,000,000 Yugoslav debt accumulated before the break. In September it announced that a $70,000,000-a-year trade agreement (covering a three year period) had been signed and that the Soviet Union was granting Tito's government loans totaling $84,000,000. By the close of 1955 Belgrade's trade with the USSR and the rest of the Soviet bloc was about $40,000,000 and $130,000,000, respectively. In both cases this was less than the pre-1948 level. Cf. *World Today*, "Soviet Yugoslav Economic Relations," pp. 38–46.

[2] An interesting point of conjecture is the influence of Mao's doctrines upon Tito's position with the Soviets. Yugoslavia and Communist China exchanged Ambassadors for the first time shortly before the Russian trip to Belgrade. *New York Times*, June 4, 1955, p. 1, Clifton Daniel.

[3] *World Today*, "Yugoslavia between Independence and Orthodoxy," p. 333.

[4] *Pravda*, July 16, 1955, p. 1, *Current Digest*, VII, 26, p. 3.

in Marshal Tito's journey. As things stood, he remained defient to the last. Previously the USSR had equated Western aid with enslavement, but now Tito's economic negotiations outside the Soviet sphere were given Moscow's blessing. Again this point could not be lost upon the Eastern European countries, particularly Czechoslovakia and Poland, to whom Russia had denied American economic assistance in 1947 when they had been struggling to force their weakened and unmanageable economics into the Soviet world.

THE NEGOTIATIONS WITH JAPAN

While these events were transpiring in Europe, Russian diplomates were working on another phase of their Asian policy. Beginning in December 1954 the Soviet Foreign Ministry held conversations with Japanese officials on the possibility of a peace settlement. [1] These overtures were constantly pressed in 1955 and were accompanied by Tass articles from Tokyo pointing out the economic advantages which normalization would bring. In this case, not only were the Japanese offered Soviet orders but also the opportunity to regain their traditional markets on the Chinese mainland. To further strengthen the Russian's case 86 Japanese nationalists were released from Siberian prisons and repatriated in mid-April 1955. These were sufficient enducements to cause Tokyo to agree to hold formal discussions the following June in London on the resumption of diplomatic relations.

However, when the negotiations opened, it was soon clear that the two sides remained far apart. On June 14 the Soviets put forth their terms for a peace treaty that immediately dashed Japan's over-optimistic hopes. The conditions, which were not merely bargaining points but firm demands, would have effectively neutralized the Japanese islands by barring Tokyo's participation in any military alliances and closing the sea between Japan and Korea to all warships except those of Communist China and the USSR. [2] On other vital issues which were more closely linked to Japanese domestic issues, the Russians proved

[1] The Soviet overtures were in response to the declaration by Japanese Foreign Minister Shigemitsu that the new Hatoyama government wished to normalize relations with both the Soviet Union and Communist China.
[2] *New York Times*, June 17, 1955, p. 1, Robert Turmbull.

equally intransigent. They insisted that diplomatic envoys be exchanged before any discussion could begin of the 12,000 unrepatriated Japanese nationalists which Tokyo claimed still remained in Soviet territory. Their return was generally considered by the Japanese as the *sine qua non* for the signing of any peace treaty rather than the subject of diplomatic discussions. Moscow was equally uncompromising on the question of the territories she had seized in the closing days of the Second World War. Also dashed by the USSR's firmness was the hope that it might be possible to negotiate a comprehensive fishing agreement to end disputes which usually culminated in the seizure of Japanese fishing boats and their crews. [1]

With these concrete moves in both Europe and Asia there was also a perceptible change in the tone of Soviet propaganda. It was noticeably more affable toward the West in general and the United States in particular. A campaign to convince Soviet refugees to return home was launched in April. Originally directed toward those in Western Europe, by May it was being addressed to those in the United States. [2] An increasing volume of material appeared which apparently sought to prove that the difficulties involved in the improvement of cultural and political relations were not the fault of the Soviet Union but of the West. In short, Moscow piously began proclaiming that it was not responsible for the Iron Curtain which separated the East and West. [3] For their part the Russians sought to renew past relationships which had been broken off for years. They accepted the invitation of the *Des Moine* (Iowa) *Register* to send a delegation of farmers to study American corn production; [4] proposed that American veterans join their Soviet counter-parts at a celebration of the anniversary of the two armies meeting at the Elbe; and made elaborate overtures to President Eisenhower by emphasizing his wartime comradship with leading Soviet marshals.

---

[1] *World Today*, "Soviet-Japanese Peace Talks", pp. 358–360.
[2] *New York Times*, May 22, 1955, p. 7, Harry Schwartz.
[3] *Ibid.*, May 7, 1955, p. 1, and *Pravda*, May 8, 1955, p. 2, *Current Digest*, VII, 17, pp. 3–5.
[4] Cf. p. 183.

THE MILITARY AND FOREIGN POLICY

This latter move was significant because it symbolized the emergence of the military leaders – particularly Marshal Zhukov – into the realm of foreign policy. In the spring and summer of 1955 Zhukov replaced Molotov as the mouth-piece of Soviet diplomacy, at least in its relationship to the United States and Western Europe. For example, on April 19, 1955, Zhukov addressed a letter to the American Overseas Press Club in New York containing an informal peace bid. It was typical of the new approach because it was directed toward a mass audience and appealed to the "wisdom" of the people to stop "certain politicians" who were bent upon a new war. [1]

Despite these efforts to convey the impression that the Soviet Union was a respectable member of the family of nations, the regime did not intend to imply that it would be negotiating from a position of weakness at the Summit Conference. Repeated Western assertions to this effect brought vehement denials and a checkered pattern of strongly worded statements which were out of place among the milder ones that set the pace of Moscow's propaganda mill. May Day and the tenth anniversary of the end of World War II provided two excellent opportunities for the Soviets to dispel the notion of weakness. At the same time that Zhukov was assuring his readers that "peaceful co-existence" was possible irrespective of differences in social systems and forms of government, Marshal Chuikov, commander of the Kiev military district was writing in *Pravda* that the US was slandering the USSR by degrading its role in winning the Second World War. [2] Ten days later on the anniversary of Germany's defeat, the tone was much more harsh but still checkered with an occasional conciliatory word for the West. Zhukov, writing in the central press, accused the "ruling circles" in the West of plotting a new war against both Russia and China and also denounced the ring of American bases which surrounded the Soviet Union. [3]

[1] *Pravda* and *Izvestia*, April 21, 1955, p. 6, *Current Digest*, VII, 16, p. 17. The next month Marshal Sokolovsky sent "friendly greetings and best wishes" to President Eisenhower. *New York Times*, May 13, 1955, p. 1.
[2] *Pravda*, May 2, 1955, pp. 1–2, *Current Digest*, VII, 18, p. 20, and the *New York Times*, May 3, 1955, p. 10.
[3] *Pravda*, May 8, 1955, p. 2, *Current Digest*, VII, 17, pp. 3–5.

In his speech in Berlin on the same day he declared that the Soviet people had

no hostile feelings toward West Germany. We are for a lasting friendship with the whole German people and for the establishment of neighborly relations with all European states.[1]

While Zhukov was saying this, Marshal Konev in Moscow was denouncing the rearming of the same country because of its aggressive intents in Central and Eastern Europe. In a strange reversal of itself, the central press carried another article, this time by Marshal Vasilevsky, which generously praised the West for its contribution to the winning of the Second World War. However, it carefully made a distinction between the people who fought the war and the financial and political circles allegedly responsible for starting it. [2]

This sudden emergence of the marshals into the sphere of diplomacy strengthened the tendency in the West to think of the Soviet military leadership as a cohesive group. However, this was not the case. In fact, immediately following Malenkov's downgrading in February 1955 there was a period of "intense maneuvering" at the top of the military pyramid. Either Khrushchev, seeing the potential dangers of a unified military, sought to build up certain marshals to counter-balance Zhukov's genuine popularity, or they themselves felt that they needed political patrons. In any case, Marshals Konev and Moskalenko, as well as some of the senior political officers, were the ones who soon became most closely identified with the Khrushchev group. Zhukov and most of the other professional military leaders refused to align themselves with the various factions. [3] Zhukov was unquestionably the strongest of the marshals, but Western observers disagreed as to the extent of his influence. Some who were stationed in Eastern Europe felt that his importance was being magnified by those outside the Soviet Union and that the regime itself was making a studied attempt to reduce his prominence before the Russian public. To back up this argument they pointed to the tenth anniversary celebration of Germany's defeat. Marshal Konev and not Zhukov delivered the primary

---

[1] Quoted by the *New York Times*, May 8, 1955, p. 1.
[2] *Pravda* and *Izvestia*, May 9, 1955, p. 2, and *Izvestia*, May 8, 1955, p. 2, *Current Digest*, VII, 18, pp. 3–5.
[3] Garthoff, "The Role of the Military in Recent Soviet Politics," p. 18.

speech in Moscow. In fact, the latter was in Berlin as a member of a relatively minor delegation headed by Pervukhin, a lesser member of the regime's hierarchy, and his Berlin speech received relatively secondary attention in the Soviet press. [1] On May 8 *Pravda* carried Zhukov's special article and *Izvestia* printed Vasilevsky's. The following day both newspapers and *Krasnaya Zvezda*, the Army's official organ, published Konev's speech with his picture, an unusual honor for a military man. [2]

Khrushchev's influence in this split was evident from the content of Konev's various writings on the history of the Second World War. Khrushchev had been engaged in re-appraising and improving his role during most of 1954, but it was only after Malenkov's downgrading and the flurry of new articles which followed that Konev became the first senior, professional officer to take part. He not only presented both Khrushchev and Bulganin as being front-line figures but substantially altered the list of others mentioned so that their names appeared first. This was contrary to the "collective leadership" listing in Cyrillic alphabetical order which had otherwise been maintained after February. In the 20 key articles on military affairs which appeared in early May Konev and Colonel General A. S. Zheltov, head of the Chief Political Administration, again repeated this new listing but only Marshals I. Kh. Bagramyan and Chuikov and two lesser political officers even mentioned their role. All the other officers refrained from mentioning living individuals. However, none of the marshals contributed to Khrushchev's subsequent efforts to rewrite his contribution to the Battle of Stalingrad and his role as one of "Lenin's associates" during the Civil War. [3] But in other matters concerning the revision of history the marshals did take a hand. With the deterioration of the Stalin myth the credit for the various military victories was redistributed. In the process Zhukov, Konev, Vasilevsky, and Rokossovsky gained the most prestige but not without some internal squabbling. Probably the most blatant example was Konev's abortive attempt in June 1955 to deprive Zhukov of the credit for liberating Berlin. [4]

[1] *New York Times*, May 30, 1955, p. 2, Harry Schwartz.
[2] Garthoff, *op. cit.*, p. 20.
[3] Garthoff, *Soviet Strategy in the Nuclear Age*, p. 25.
[4] Garthoff, "The Role of the Military in Recent Soviet Politics," pp. 19–20.

Another bone of contention between the Army and the Party was the restoration of the principle of individual command and the lessening of the authority of the political commissars. It was generally felt in the West that Zhukov exerted strong influence in the effort to re-establish the concept of unity of command which resulted in the abolition of political officers on the company level by late 1955. [1]

One Western analyst writing in mid-1955 summed up the position of the military in Russian politics in the following words:

straws in the wind indicate that the struggle for power in the Soviet Union has been extended to the Army chiefs, that the political commissar system is again a bone of contention between the 'professional' soldiers and the 'political' soldiers, and that the Army, like the Party, is probably factionalized with no one man or group of men able to control it. [2]

THE PRE-GENEVA MANEUVERING

It was evident from the long and imposing list of diplomatic overtures which eminated from Moscow just prior to the crucial Geneva negotiations that Soviet foreign policy was radically reshaping the whole appearance of East-West relations. The world situation in which the Western Big Three found themselves by mid-July bore little resemblance to the one they had been so accustomed to only six months before. Russian foreign policy was so fluid that a complete cataloguing of its diplomatic activities proved a monumental task. In addition to the major developments which captured the headlines there were trade fairs, loans, technical assistance programs, and exchange delegations almost without number. Moscow was rapidly becoming one of the busiest capitals in the world.

Two visitors invited in June 1955 warrant special mention. The first was Prime Minister Nehru of India, who was given a welcome unprecedented since the 1917 Revolution. The second was West German Chancellor K. Adenauer, who delayed his trip until the following September. Both invitations were undisguised attempts to win over and neutralize two key areas before the regime faced the West across the bargaining table.

[1] Ibid., p. 16. During 1955 Krasnaya Zvezda was actively restoring the prestige of military commanders. New York Times, June 5, 1955, p. 2, Hanson Baldwin.

[2] New York Times, June 5, 1955, p, 2, Hanson Baldwin.

Nehru's visit was part of the campaign of personal flattery which the Russians had found so successful. Playing upon his personal ambitions directly or indirectly by greatly enhancing the role of India in world affairs, they hoped to channel his substantial influence in Asia toward their efforts of creating a neutral buffer zone around the Communist world. (The interesting feature about this buffer area was that it was to be composed of states which were either "uncommitted" or definitely pro-Western in their orientation. In no case did the Soviets show any desire to neutralize their own Satellites.) [1]

Their efforts with Nehru met with a large measure of success and culminated in his formal acceptance of a wide range of Soviet diplomatic principles. This included re-statement of the famous Five Principles, recognition of Communist China's right to Formosa, the seating of Mao's regime in the UN, acceptance of Soviet policy in Yugoslavia and Austria, immediate prohibition of nuclear weapons, disarmament, and a control system based upon the Soviet proposals. To a casual reader not aware of the intricaties and reservations of diplomatic language, the joint communiqué issued by Nehru and Bulganin gave the appearance of complete unanimity on the major principles of foreign policy. [2]

The invitation issued to Chancellor Adenauer on June 7, 1955, contained a bid to normalize Soviet-West German relations and once more held out the lure of increased trade. [3] Again the purpose of presenting the Summit Conference with a *fait accompli* was clear. All Soviet notes to the West since the prospects of a Heads-of-State Conference materialized had avoided mentioning Germany as a subject for negotiating, although it was unquestionably the outstanding problem between East and West in Europe. [4] Despite Soviet efforts, the Chancellor of the Federal

---

[1] The tactics utilized to obtain this were as follows: Japan – peace treaty talks and delegations to Moscow; India – exchanges, technical assistance, and personal flattery of Nehru; Afghanistan – backing of Afghans in dispute with Pakistan and greatly increased technical assistance; Iran – increased trade, a border agreement, payment in gold for settlement of a long, outstanding dispute; Turkey and Greece – overtures during Yugoslav talks, suggestion made to widen the Balkan Pact to include Communist members; Yugoslavia – "normalization" of relations; Austria – neutralization by treaty; Germany – trade proposals and offers of settlement; and Scandinavia – trade, exchanges, and political pressures, particularly on Finland.

[2] *Soviet News*, 3192, June 23, 1955, pp. 1–2.
[3] *Ibid.*, 3181, June 8, 1955, p. 1.
[4] *New York Times*, June 8, 1955, p. 1, Clifton Daniel.

Republic refused to accept without first awaiting the outcome of the Geneva Conference.

While there was agreement among the Big Four that the Heads-of-State Conference should be held in Switzerland, there was less unanimity on what should be discussed. Moscow's official acceptance of the West's invitation was couched in very general diplomatic language which left the USSR virtually uncommitted on the question of an agenda. In fact, it concluded that the agenda was a matter which the Heads-of-State should define for themselves across the conference table. However, the Soviets did give a few hints as to the line the discussions would take. The easing of international tension and the strengthening of mutual trust and confidence were to be their points of departure. To this they intended to relate the disarmament question but left it unclear as to whether they expected to deal with it at Geneva or in the London United Nations discussions. Moscow was much more specific about what it did not intend to discuss. One of these points was Eastern Europe which it found unacceptable in any form. Economic and political conditions in this area, it declared, were "internal" questions. In mid-June a Tass statement in reply to remarks made by Secretary of State Dulles added "activities of international Communism" as another matter which did not meet its approval. [1]

However, this same statement greatly clarified what Moscow considered to be "truly vital questions" for discussion. These it listed as the reduction of arms; prohibition of nuclear weapons; creation of an European security pact; ensuring the peace and security of the Far East; and the recognition of Communist China by the United Nations. About a week later Molotov made substantial additions to this list when he addressed the tenth anniversary session of the United Nations in San Francisco. The new items were the ending of war propaganda; agreement of the Big Four to give up foreign military bases; development of the peaceful uses of atomic energy; the withdrawal (except for small temporary contingents) of Four Power troops from Germany and the creation of strictly limited German police forces; the ending of restrictions of international trade; and wider

---

[1] *Soviet News*, 3174, May 27, 1955, and 3185, June 14, 1955, pp. 1-2.

extention of exchange delegations and increased tourism. [1]
Nevertheless, he insisted that the Heads-of-States should still be
free to draw up their own agenda once the Conference began. [2]

The absence of Soviet comment on the question of German
unification caused Secretary of State Dulles to quip that Moscow
had "lost interest" in it. This was obviously a tender point with
the regime because it brought the immediate retort that such
was not the case and that Russia was just as interested as before
in unifying the country. [3] A week later in mid-July it was still
smarting from this charge of indifference and authorized Tass to
release a statement proposing the step by step unification of
Germany within the framework of the general European security
pact. It asserted that the West was responsible for determining
whether or not this was achieved, and insisted that the question
of elections – a cardinal point in Western thinking – was subordinate to the issue of German militarization. It also recommended that a *rapprochement* between the two Germanies would
speed unification. This statement reflected the failure of Soviet
efforts to entice West German Chancellor Adenauer to Moscow
before the opening of the Geneva Conference. [4]

With the exception of an additional challenge to the West to
enter a contest of peaceful economic competition to test the
relative merits of the respective systems, this was the USSR's
position on the eve of the departure of its delegation from
Moscow. [5]

Why was the Soviet Union going out of its way to create a
climate suitable for a Summit Conference? [6] It clearly wanted a
lessening of the international tension, but before the conference
opened Western observers were not in agreement as to its
motives. Many felt that domestic economic problems and political
pressures still unresolved from February were forcing the regime

---

[1] *Ibid.*, 3194, June 27, 1955, pp. 2–4.

[2] *Ibid.*, 3199, July 4, 1955, pp. 2–3.

[3] *Ibid.*, 3202, July 7, 1955, p. 1.

[4] *New York Times*, July 13, 1955, p. 1, Welles Hagen. At the signing of the Austrian
State Treaty Molotov had indicated that the Soviet price for German unification was
its neutralization *Ibid.*, May 16, 1955, p. 1, M. S. Handler.

[5] *Soviet News*, 3209, July 18, 1955, p. 1.

[6] The regime not only promptly granted visas to American correspondents; attended the July 4 celebration at the American Embassy; but also expressed regret and
paid damages for an American plane shot down over the Bering Sea the same month.
New York Times, July 10, 1955, Part 4, p. 1.

to the conference table to bargain. This view held that the USSR's position *vis-à-vis* the West was one of weakness. This reasoning was based upon a number of factors which had manifested themselves during the previous year. On the international scene events had worked against Soviet doctrine. Rather than falling at each others throats under the pressure of increased economic competition as prophesied by Stalin, the West, despite constant hammering from Moscow, had solidified its alliances and dealt the USSR a historic defeat by approving West German rearmament. At the same time it had enjoyed a period of great prosperity, particularly in the United States. Internally, the Soviet empire was faced with a hydra of economic and political problems. The leadership question remained unresolved at a time when the Party was being challenged by a rising military faction. The food situation throughout the Communist bloc was dangerous. Near famine conditions existed in North Vietman and meat and sugar shortages were present in Eastern Europe and the Soviet Union itself. Every increase in food production was immediately challenged by the continuous increase in population. The high costs of armaments took a heavy toll on the various economies, resulting in widespread discontent over the failure of the promised improvement of the inadequate standards of living. The rate of industrial growth – while still high – showed signs of tapering off. In such critical areas as machinery the Soviet Union had to make up the difference when its Satellites were unable to meet their industrial plans if it wanted them to increase their economic growth at the specified rate. This was not such an important factor in Eastern Europe as it was in the Far East where the demands of the Chinese industrialization were exorbitant. However, in this critical case, this was the price which had to be met if the alliance was to be maintained. [1]

The tenacity with which the Soviet press and radio hammered away to disprove these arguments only made Western observers more certain of their validity. Moscow's official reasons for desiring to hold a conference and its domestic press coverage of the Western position did nothing to discourage this line of reasoning.

[1] *Ibid.*, July 10, 1955, Part 4, p. 5, Harry Schwartz.

Officially, the regime claimed that its reason for going to Geneva was to create an international climate in which all "peace-loving countries" would be able to finish building their societies. Therefore, the Soviets argued, peaceful co-existence was more desirable than conflict. However, they left no doubt that their eventual goal of destroying capitalism remained un-challenged. But for the time being, and for the foreseeable future, there was nothing to prevent the two systems from living side by side. [1]

The domestic press went to unusual lengths prior to Geneva to give its readers a comprehensive picture of both sides of the issues at stake. On June 8, 1955, *Komsomolskaya Pravda* carried the first description intended for mass distribution of the de-structive force of atomic and hydrogen weapons. With the exception on a one-sentence statement (buried in a long speech) made by Malenkov in 1954 that nuclear warfare would destroy both sides, information of the subject had been limited to the select military audience of *Krasnaya Zvezda*, the official organ of the Soviet Army. [2] Also in late June and early July the central press, in an extraordinary and unprecedented reversal of its previous policy, began publishing Western views on the subjects most likely to be discussed by the Heads-of-State. It went so far as to report without criticism or comment one of President Eisenhower's press conferences in which he advocated that Eastern Europe be on the agenda. Only on the following day did *Pravda* carry editorial rebuttal. [3]

While the significance of the internal stresses could not be overlooked, Moscow also possessed a number of assets which materially strengthened its bargaining position. Chief among these was the amazing degree of flexibility of its diplomacy. It had realized that much of the Western alliance's cohesion had been produced by the icy blasts which had emanated from the Soviet Union. Under the warmth of smiles the USSR sought to undo its own handiwork. By pressing for disarmament the Russians not only wanted to maintain military superiority, but they also hoped to create havoc in Western economies which they

---

[1] *Ibid.*, June 19, 1955, Part 4, p. 5, Clifton Daniel.
[2] *Ibid.*, June 14, 1955, p. 1, Harry Schwartz.
[3] *Pravda* and *Izvestia*, July 1, 1955, p. 3, *Pravda*, July 2, 1955, p. 1, *Current Digest*, VII, 26, p. 13.

seriously believed maintained their stability only from defense expenditures. Another strong point which could not be ignored was the huge, well armed military force which the Communist bloc maintained in a higher state of integration than was ever possible in the West. (Here, as in economic and political questions, the advantages of a centralized dictatorship were apparent.)

As if to emphasize the state of its military preparedness, the regime staged an impressive air demonstration on July 3, only a matter of days before the Heads-of-State were scheduled to meet. The appearance in quantity of heavy and medium jet bombers (equivalent to both American B 52 and B 47 models), as well as more advanced prototypes, at least a year before anticipated by Western experts provided a sombre setting for Khrushchev's remark the following day at the American Embassy that the USSR did not go to Geneva from weakness.

THE SUMMIT CONFERENCE

For six days (July 18–23, 1955) under the glaring spotlight of world attention the Heads-of-State met at the "Summit." [1] When it was over and the last delegation had departed from Geneva it was difficult to say what had been accomplished. Nothing concrete had been negotiated. Every point of disagreement had been immediately referred to the Foreign Ministers who had dealt with them unsuccessfully before. Little remained but the highly illusive "spirit of Geneva" which sent international tension plummeting to its lowest level since the beginning of the Cold War. In effect, the Conference had been an effort by the Russians to improve their public relations. After years of playing the ruffians it required only a little on their part to achieve the major propaganda victory they wanted and needed.

The Heads-of-State spent their time making pledges of good will and tabling their respective proposals (some old and some

---

[1] The composition of the Soviet delegation to Geneva re-emphasized the importance of collective rule. It was as follows: Bulganin as its nominal head; Khrushchev as a member of the Supreme Soviet; Molotov as Foreign Minister; and Zhukov as Minister of Defense. (The latter's presence reflected the rise of the military to the inner-circle.) Others were Gromyko, Y. A. Malik, S. A. Vinogradov, G. N. Zarubin, G. M. Pushkin, and V. S. Semyonov *Soviet News*, 3208, July 15, 1955, p. 1.

new), but they made no serious effort to debate them. This was apparently the Russian intent from the beginning, because they showed great restraint in commenting on Western proposals and did not condemn them out of hand as had happened on previous occasions. Nor did they insist on items which they knew were completely unacceptable. Their proposals were marked by gradualness, indicating they expected no immediate shift in the world situation. Without being contrary they made clear that on some issues – interference in Eastern Europe, withdrawal of American troops from Europe, and the ending of world-wide subversion – they would not retreat. The real work was done by the Foreign Ministers who had to formulate a workable plan for future East-West negotiations. On this level, where the real test of the Geneva spirit was to take place, the atmosphere was less pleasant than at the Summit. [1]

The opposing positions on the three issues referred to the Foreign Ministers (Germany and European security, disarmament, and increased East-West contacts) were clearly staked out from the beginning. In his opening remarks Bulganin indicated that he had not come to Geneva to unify Germany. The new series of proposals which he presented (referred to as "variation on a theme" by Western journalists) skirted the major Western demand for this. [2] The Soviet Union, he stated, was more interested in European security. As a result, he again insisted upon acceptance of an all-encompassing pact which would guarantee it. His specific proposals were only slightly modified from those of the past. He related the plan to the disarmament issue by suggesting that the occupation forces withdrawn from Austria be demobilized as a first step. For the rest of Europe he called for a two-stage program which would begin by retaining the *status quo* in both the level of armaments and current treaty commitments. However, the signatories would pledge not to use force to settle differences. In the second phase all foreign troops (presumably American) were to be withdrawn and an all-European security system would replace both NATO and the Warsaw Pact, which were to be gradually dissolved. While insisting that

---

[1] *New York Times*, July 16, 1955, p. 14, C. L. Sulzberger, and July 24, 1955, Part 4, p. 5, Clifton Daniel.
[2] *Ibid.*, July 19, 1955, p. 1, Clifton Daniel.

the Soviet Union was still vitally interested in German unification, the Soviet Premier said that at the time it was "mechanically" impossible. In his plan the two halves of the divided country were to exist side by side on a basis of equality for some time. The Soviet reasoning behind this indefinite postponement was quite clear. Moscow had no intention of continuing multilateral negotiations on a question which it was confident could be settled directly with Bonn. Even if it had to wait, the USSR was certain that in the end it could obtain a settlement more to its liking if it by-passed the Big Four conference table. [1] On other issues the Soviets announced their willingness to contribute to President Eisenhower's proposed pool for the peaceful utilization of atomic energy and insisted that their acceptance of the Western disarmament quotas justified their calling for the Big Three to agree to the prohibition of nuclear weapons.

These were in contrast to the Western proposals that reaffirmed the belief in a unified Germany (created by supervised, free elections) free to choose which bloc it desired. (The Big Three were convinced that any German government established under these condition would align itself with the West.) The British and French sought to calm Russian fears by offering them a five power treaty (including a unified Germany) which committed the signatories to take action against any aggression in Europe. They also put forth a reciprocal agreement on the level of armaments of the new German state. The British added a third suggestion which would have created a demilitarized zone between East and West (presumably in East Germany) which could be gradually expanded to include all of Europe. The French also introduced the concept of a budgetary control of armaments. [2] While it was not technically a disarmament program, the United States put forth its important "open skys" plan for aerial inspection and the exchange of military blueprints. Its purpose was to reduce international tension by eliminating the possibility of a surprise attack. Once this had been accomplished it was hoped serious disarmament negotiations could then be conducted in a much freer atmosphere.

Eisenhower's plan must have taken the Soviets by surprise

[1] *Ibid.*, July 24, 1955, Part 4, p. 1, and *Soviet News*, 3214, July 25, 1955, pp. 1–2.
[2] *New York Times*, July 24, 1955, Part 4, p. 1.

because Bulganin, who had immediately made non-committal comments on the British and French proposals, made no mention of it for two days. However, the Soviet central press soon published it along with the text of its own collective security plan. [1]

It was not until the Soviet leaders had returned to Moscow and Bulganin addressed a special session of the Supreme Soviet that Russia made any official comment on the American proposal. However, when it came it appeared to dismiss the idea out of hand, but when the Western press reported this Bulganin took the unusual step of informing the world that he had been misinterpreted. The Soviet Union, he said, was in fact giving Eisenhower's suggestion careful study. In other respects Bulganin's report on the conference was a moderate one containing praise for Eisenhower's sincerity and in keeping with the illusive atmosphere which had become known as the "spirit of Geneva." [2]

THE "SPIRIT OF GENEVA"

During the interval between the Heads-of-State conference and the Foreign Minister's meeting the following October Soviet diplomacy enjoyed one of its most successful periods since the end of World War II. [3] During those three months the USSR skillfully manipulated its propaganda in such a way that the West was placed on the defensive at embarassing moments. Just when the Russians themselves were stirring up international politics with an even bigger stick, the West was made to appear to be standing in the way of making the Geneva good will a reality. For example, it announced in mid-August that it was cutting its military strength by 640,000 men by December 15, 1955,

---

[1] *Ibid.*, July 23, 1955, p. 1.

[2] Bulganin's speech was another part of the eight-month-old campaign to win international respectability through extensive *pro forma* use of the Supreme Soviet in foreign relations. The regime in the past had (1) stressed adherance to legislative prerogatives as defined by the Constitution; (2) summoned a special session to hear Bulganin's Geneva report; (3) published works of legislative commissions dealing with foreign affairs; (4) issued a call for exchange of parliamentary delegations; (5) joined the Inter-Parliamentary Union; (6) begun to enhance the formal roles of the Republic Supreme Soviets in foreign affairs. It was also used extensively as a platform for propagating the regime's diplomacy. *Ibid.*, Aug. 5 and 6, 1955, p. 1, Clifton Daniel, and "USSR Seeks International Prestige for the Supreme Soviet," US Department of State, Oct. 7, 1955.

[3] *New York Times*, Oct. 9, 1955, Part 4, p. 3, Drew Middleton.

as a result of the new climate of international relations. The process was dramatized by the earlier order to demobilize the 44,000 troops being withdrawn from Austria before October. [1] The Soviets had called for this type of action at Geneva as a "first step" toward disarmament. Therefore, when the American occupation forces in Austria were simply withdrawn to northern Italy for regrouping the Russians obtained the propaganda advantage. Of course, what the Communists chose to overlook was that despite the cuts the USSR maintained the largest standing army in Europe – Western estimates placed it between 3,000,000 to 4,000,000 men – and that technological advances more than made up for the cut in combat efficiency. Neither was the near-crippling labor shortage in the Soviet Union mentioned in this connection. [2] Interestingly, the same day on which Moscow announced the demobilization, the Rumanian government invited the Soviet Army to remain in its country after the Austrian withdrawal had been completed on the grounds that world tension was at a new high. This contradictory note was understandable in light of the internal instability of the Communist regimes in both Hungary and Rumania. [3]

Another example of this type of propaganda was the September announcement that the Soviets intended to withdraw their troops from the Porkkala naval base in Finland. [4] This enclave which the USSR had been able to carve out of Finnish territory as a result of that country's defeat in World War II was no longer valuable as a strategic base. However, this gesture gave the Russians another opportunity to "demonstrate" that they were taking the initiative on an issue raised (by themselves) at Geneva. During their November and December tour of Aisa Bulganin and Khrushchev could honestly boast that the USSR had liquidated two of its overseas bases. To the uninitiated in Asia this was accepted at its face value without taking into consideration the

---

[1] *Ibid.*, Aug. 13, 1955, p. 1, and July 31, 1955. By the time that the Foreign Ministers' Conference opened the other Eastern European countries had also announced similar cuts totaling 168,000 men. The only exception was East Germany where an increase was planned. *Economic Bulletin for Europe*, VII, 3, p. 23.

[2] In December 1955 Moscow Radio confirmed that the demobilized troops had been "transferred to agriculture." Quoted by the *New York Times*, Dec. 13, 1955, p. 24.

[3] *Ibid.*, Aug. 14, 1955, p. 13, Harry Schwartz.

[4] *Ibid.*, Sept. 18, 1955, p. 1, Clifton Daniel.

political facts of life in Eastern Europe or Communist China and North Korea.

Soviet press coverage of the Summit Conference went a long way to give substance to the widely held belief that the USSR actually desired an end to the Cold War. Pictures of the regime's inner-circle in friendly conversation with Western leaders were printed; the texts of several Western statements were published; and accurate, unslanted summaries of Western proposals appeared. It was the first time in years that Soviet citizens had been furnished with such a comprehensive picture of the West's position. The bulk of comment in the domestic press seemed aimed at telling its readers that "A New Era in International Relations Has Begun." [1] It developed the theme that the people outside the Communist bloc were peace-loving and pictured Eisenhower as one of the leading advocates of peace. [2]

This new "internationalism" which suddenly became fashionable after so many years of isolation was of two types:

1) the studying of foreign methods (particularly scientific) and their adaption to the Soviet scene, and

2) the creation of strong bonds between the people in all countries (particularly the proletariat) to further Communist goals. [3]

In the light of subsequent events this turn-about on the part of the Russian press appeared to represent merely another tactical maneuver designed to lull the West into believing that the Soviet change of heart was genuine. When compared with the official American reaction of "wait-and-see" skepticism, it was even more striking and this contrast itself served an useful purpose. However, this may not be the entire explanation. The dangers inherent in suddenly relaxing censorship and building up public support for an admittedly very popular cause purely for a momentary propaganda advantage were quite great. This raises the question whether the regime merely took a calculated gamble or if it actually was seeking to prepare the Russian people for any major shift in foreign policy should the international situation take an unexpected turn.

---

1 The title of *Izvestia's* first post-Geneva editorial.
2 *New York Times*, July 31, 1955, Part 4, p. 5, Harry Schwartz.
3 *Ibid.*, Aug. 19, 1955, p. 1, Clifton Daniel.

During the "Era of Good Feelings" which existed between the two conferences Moscow turned a good share of its attention to improving its relations with Germany and extending its influence in the Middle East. Its goal in Central Europe was to pull West Germany out of NATO with the bait of unification. For these efforts the Russians unexpectedly found support in a considerable part of the German people. Adenauer long had been under a variety of domestic pressures which the Soviets alone could ease. These were: 1) reunification; 2) revision of the temporary Potsdam settlement that gave a substantial part of Eastern Germany to Poland; and 3) the return of an estimated 100,000 war prisoners who still remained in Soviet camps. The West knew that the Soviet hierarchy was counting heavily on these to force the hand of the Bonn government and was content to wait patiently for time to remove the staunchly pro-Western, 80-year old Chancellor from the scene. In the meantime, Moscow was willing to drive the stiffest bargain it could with the existing regime so as to bolster its hand for the October meeting of the Foreign Ministers.

The Chancellor's mid-September visit to the Russian capital was in marked contrast to that of Prime Minister Nehru the previous June. It was arranged only after a complicated diplomatic duel in which the USSR finally agreed to discuss unification rather than merely trade, diplomatic recognition and cultural exchanges. For prestige reasons, the German leader flew to Moscow in the largest plane available and demanded extraterritorial rights for the special train which served as his headquarters. But this was a small concession for the Soviets with such important issues at stake.

Almost immediately the negotiations between the two powers were deadlocked. The Soviets insisted that the first step was the establishment of diplomatic relations. These channels could then be used to discuss the question of prisoners, trade, and cultural exchanges. The West Germans made settlement of the prisoner issue the condition for the exchange of diplomats. The Russians countered with the argument that this was impossible without the presence of East Germany. However, this was unacceptable to the representatives of the Federal Republic since they refused to recognize the Communist regime and insisted that they spoke

for all Germans. In these stormy sessions the question of unification was not pressed by either side. [1] Then suddenly after eight
days of hard-headed bargaining agreement on the establishment
of diplomatic missions was reached. It resulted only after
compromises by both sides which reflected not only the domestic
pressures in West Germany but also the Soviets desire for future
bilateral negotiations on the issue of unification. While Moscow
made a verbal agreement on the prisoner question, the Soviets
would not accept the German contentions that the Federal
Republic spoke for all Germans or that the existing borders
were not permanent. [2]

The results of these negotiations gave the Western Big Three
more than a little to ponder for the future. While Chancellor
Adenauer might be able to withstand the pressure of accepting
Soviet enducements his days on the political scene were numbered. His successor, who was nowhere in sight, might find it
less easy not to yield when faced by the hard facts of domestic
politics. In October, immediately before the Foreign Ministers
gathered in Geneva, one observer commented:

> Since the Big Four meeting in July the situation in Europe has changed
> so greatly as a result of West Germany's agreement to enter into diplo-
> matic relations with the Soviet Union, that it is now accepted that the
> Foreign Ministers' conference represents the last chance of the West
> obtaining German reunification in freedom along lines it has advocated
> for a decade.[3]

As soon as the officials from the Federal Republic had departed
from Moscow their opposite numbers from East Germany, who
had been hovering in the wings, were called to the Soviet capital
where they signed a series of agreements designed to enhance
their prestige. The most important aspect of these stipulated
that the Communist regime was free to handle all of its own
diplomatic relations. Besides allowing the East Germans to
police their own borders and control traffic to Berlin, the
Soviets abolished the office of Soviet High Commissioner and
established relations based on equality. [4] This was the final step

---

[1] *Ibid.*, Sept. 13, 1955, p. 1, Clifton Daniel. For a detailed account of Adenauer's
Moscow visit cf. *Osteuropa*, "Der Kanzler in Moskau," pp. 448–454.

[2] *New York Times*, Sept. 14, 1955, p. 1, Clifton Daniel.

[3] *Ibid.*, Oct. 23, 1955, Part 4, p. 5, Drew Middleton.

[4] *Ibid.*, Sept. 16 and 21, 1955, p. 1, Clifton Daniel. Undoubtably the Russians
also used the occasion to reassure the East Germans that they were not being sold out
to Bonn.

in the Soviet effort to supply supporting evidence for its insistence that the two Germanies should enter the proposed Russian security pact as equals. It also created a situation where not only the Federal Republic but the West as well found it increasingly difficult to avoid dealing directly with the puppet regime in East Germany.

THE MIDDLE EAST AND SOVIET DIPLOMACY

At the same time that Chancellor Adenauer was visiting Moscow Soviet diplomacy showed marked signs of stepping up the tempo of its activities in the Middle East. Although there had been repeated indications of increased Russian interest in the Arab World since Stalin's death, it had previously not reached the magnitude it did after the Summit Conference. The successful Soviet-Egyptian arms negotiations were the climax of these efforts and were responsible for a good deal of Western disenchantment with the "spirit of Geneva." To the man-in-the-street who wanted to believe in its sincerity this Soviet maneuver looked very much like an effort to fish in troubled waters behind the screen of pious pronouncements of friendship.

The immediate chain of events leading up to this agreement, which mortgaged the Egyptian cotton crop for several years, dated from April 16, 1955, when the Soviet Foreign Ministry issued a statement to the effect that Western success in establishing a military alliance in the Middle East had greatly imperiled its peace and tranquility. However, its roots were much deeper. Changes had been in progress since Stalin's death in March 1953, but the critical period was 1954, since his heirs had to decide several basic questions before a coherent policy could be formulated. Three of these were: 1) how the Western "northern tier" alliance should be blocked; 2) what ideological shifts were necessary to accomodate the local emphasis on both nationalism and Islam; and 3) the role the Moslem minorities in the Soviet Union were to play.

The one in need of the most immediate attention in 1953 and 1954 was the Western intention of creating a defense alliance bordering the Soviet Middle East. Moscow immediately adopted three lines of attack. Domestically the regime sought to strengthen its hold on Central Asia through another mass Slavic migration. In foreign policy, the Soviets alternatively wooed and threatened its perspective members. At the same time it tried to turn the flanks of the alliance before it was created. In this Afghanistan was an important pivotal country because it bridged the gap between Iran and Pakistan along the Russian frontier. Moscow had no intention of permitting Western influences in a country bordering Soviet Kirgizia where extensive atomic research was reported in progress. The Russians did their best to fan the flames of the Pushtoonistan dispute between Afghanistan and Pakistan. [1]

But they were not satisfied with driving a wedge between Iran and Pakistan by neutralizing Afghanistan. The regime turned its attention toward the other end of the alliance where it selected Egypt as the country providing the greatest possibilities for disrupting the area behind the "fence." From the point of existing indigenous Communist influence, Syria would have been a better choice but it lacked Egypt's dominant position in Arab politics and significant geographical position. Astride the Suez Canal, Egypt not only was the gateway to both Africa and the Middle East but also a vulnerable link in Europe's communication with Asia. Its fervent nationalism and its desire to dominate Arab politics made the country even more inviting. Moscow hoped to channel this driving force toward its own objectives and wreak havoc in the oil fields. If such a program succeeded, the "northern tier" alliance would not only be rendered impotent, but its pro-Western members would be cut off and surrounded.

One of the chief stumbling blocks to these ambitious designs was the Soviet long-standing aversion to both Islam and nationalism which were the dynamic forces behind Middle Eastern politics. For Moscow to adopt its ideology to meet these conditions was not simply a question of an abrupt *volte-face* (Stalin had accomplished greater ones in his time) but a much more complicated problem involving important domestic consequences. An estimated 30,000,000 Moslems lived in Soviet Central Asia and

---

[1] The central issue of this dispute was the effort of the nomadic Pathan tribesmen' who live on both sides of the ill-defined border, to create an autonomous Pushtoonistan. An estimated 7,000,000 live in West Pakistan and another 5,000,000 in Afghanistan. Sulzberger, *op. cit.*, p. 212.

in the Urals where the USSR was developing a new industrial complex. [1] Across the frontier their neighbors (and co-religionists) lived in newly independent countries with pro-Western orientations. Since the 1917 October Revolution the Soviets had systematicly crushed every spark of "bourgeois nationalism" among these peoples and just as vigorously surpressed the Islamic religion until it amounted to a mere shadow of its former strength. In suddenly embracing both of these in its diplomacy the regime had to carefully calculate what effect this would have on this large domestic minority. Stalin had solved the problem by simply sealing off the Soviet Moslems from their brethren in the free world. The world had been encouraged to simply forget their existence. However, his heirs almost immediately sought to alter this policy. They realized that in their campaign to exert influence in Asia and the Middle East the Soviet Moslem Republics could serve the useful purpose of bridging the gap between the Slavic culture of the Great Russians and that of the Afro-Asian world. If correctly manipulated this could prove an important advantage over the West which was separated from these non-European areas by a wide cultural gulf. However, the implementation of this policy was such a delicate matter that there was considerable backing and filling on the part of the Soviets during 1954.

The rapidity and vigor with which the virgin lands program was launched in the opening days of 1954 suggested that the Soviets were in no measure certain of the loyalty of the Moslem minority. [2] The influx of tens of thousands of young, highly indoctrinated Komsomol members and demobilized military personnel (often under the command of their former officers), as well as the subsequent political changes in which local leaders

---

[1] This does not take into account the Moslem population of the Chinese mainland. Its precise size is difficult to state accurately. French scholars put it at 4,000,000 in 1915. The China Islamic Association (created by Peking in 1953) declared that it was 10,000,000. American scholars put it at five per cent of a 400,000,000 population (i.e., 20,000,000). In light of the 1955 Communist Chinese census of 600,000,000 this would mean between 20–30,000,000 Moslems. Spector, *op. cit.*, p. 128.

[2] The regime's experiences in World War II must have given them cause to ponder. Besides successfully enlisting thousands of Soviet Moslems in labor battalions, the Germans organized 180,000 men under Kayum-Khan into military units which were intrical parts of either the *Wehrmacht* or the *Waffen-SS*. Three such battalions fought to the last man in the Stalingrad campaign and six held up the Soviet advance into Berlin. Altogether it is estimated that they lost 50, 000 men. *Ibid.*, 122.

were replaced by outsiders, indicated that the Party had in mind nothing less than an ethnic and political revolution when it initiated the program.

The difficulties which this problem presented made themselves evident in the inconsistencies in the regime's domestic and foreign propaganda. During the Stalin era the Islamic clergy and the ruling classes of all Moslem societies had been considered irrevocably hostile to the Soviet cause and friendly toward the West. Islam was pictured as the factor responsible for the backwardness of Moslem culture. However, in the period after his death this no longer served the Soviet cause. Therefore, it was modified so that Western imperialism became the evil force which had debased Islam and turned it into a tool for its own ends. Having been spared this blight, so the argument went, the Moslem culture in the Soviet Republics had escaped this plague and was, therefore, considerably stronger. Internally, anti-Islamic propaganda continued but was toned down somewhat. [1] The newer Soviet works on Central Asia either ignored Islam except when absolutely necessary or attacked it on grounds which meant little except to scholars. [2]

On the question of nationalism a remarkable change took place both internally and externally. In Central Asia the various cultural heritages were given more credit in a rewriting of history at the expense of the "civilizing" influence of the Great Russians. In fact, a few national heroes and early leaders, previously out of favor, were restored. Former Soviet doctrine on this point had insisted that during the century before the arrival of Russian "civilization" their cultures had been in decay. Since the khanates of this period had been almost exclusively Islamic, the influence of the post-Stalin interest in the Middle East was clear. [3]

Externally, it was possible to chart with even greater clarity a

[1] Wheeler, *op. cit.*, p. 14. In 1956 the carefully selected Soviet pilgrims to Mecca assumed this attitude. (Spector, "Soviet Cultural Propaganda in the Near and Middle East," p. 19.) Interestingly, the domestic repression of Islam in the Soviet Union had not had an effect upon its stature in the Arab World. Apparently, this was the unwritten price for economic assistance. Laqueur, *op. cit.*, p. 23.

[2] Wheeler, *op. cit.*, pp. 14-15. Cf. *Central Asian Review*, II, 4, and III, 1 and 2 for an abstract of the first comprehensive Soviet book on Islam during both the Czarist and Soviet periods – *Ocherki Istarii Izucheniye Islama v SSSR* by N. A. Smirnov (1954).

[3] Wheeler, *op. cit.*, p. 15.

similar shift. This was particularly enlightening in regard to Egypt:

July 1952 – When the Naguib-Nasser regime came to power it was denounced as reactionary, cruel, anti-democratic and terrorist.

1953 – It was called "anti-working class" and Soviet authors claimed
that the "progressive" military leaders behind the revolution
had been excluded.

July 1954 – The Anglo-Egyptian treaty was denounced as "contrary to
the national interests of Egypt and other Arab countries ...
The Egyptian toilers would have to fight many a battle
before the victory of real democracy."

May 1955 – A book published that month still said that the government
advocated "anti-popular measures" such as "restricting the
rights of the workers, defending the big feudal landowners
against revolutionary measures."

June 1955 – But the tone was soon softened and these reproaches disappeared entirely. After the Bandung Conference criticism
turned to praise for its neutral position and efforts to block
the Western defense treaties.[1]

At the same time there was a marked revival in Soviet Oriental studies during the winter of 1954–55. After 18 years of silence *Sovetskoye Vostokovedenie* reappeared in April 1955 as the Orient-alists' own journal. The following month *Kommunist* carried an unsigned article which took scholars to task for the lack of more and better works on the Middle East. [2] Another example, of how extensively the regime was pushing this renewed scholarly interest was the appearance during the first half of 1955 of *Palestivski Sbornik* No. 63. The first 62 issues had been published before the 1917 Revolution. [3]

It is necessary to insert a word of caution when discussing Soviet trade with the Middle East. The figures for Eastern bloc imports and exports from that area (including Greece and Yugoslavia) [4] during 1954 were 56 per cent and 26 per cent higher, respectively. In fact, Communist trade relations during the period under consideration developed more rapidly with Greece and Iran than with the Arab World. In the autumn of 1955 the Soviet bloc took about 16 to 20 per cent of the total

---

[1] Quoted by Laqueur, *op. cit.*, p. 20.
[2] *World Today*, "Soviet Policy in the Middle East," p. 521, and *Kommunist*, 8, May 1955, pp. 74–83, *Current Digest*, VII, 28, pp. 21–24.
[3] *New York Times*, Oct. 15, 1955, p. 14, C. L. Sulzberger.
[4] Their inclusion complicates the picture unnecessarily but is required by the absence of specific figures for each country in the source.

Egyptian cotton exports. This was more than the average of nine per cent for 1953–54 but not much more than that of 1952–53 (16 per cent). However, the arms negotiations radically altered this pattern because Egypt was forced to mortgage a sizeable share of her future cotton production. [1]

The Bandung Conference coincided nicely – either through accident or design – with the sudden surge of Soviet interest in the Middle East, particularly Egypt. It provided an opening wedge. Not only had the regime become "respectable" in the eyes of Nehru who had significant influence in Cairo, but it found common cause with the Arab World in his famous Five Points and its opposition to the "northern tier" alliance. In the months that followed there was a steady stream of delegations travelling between the Communist orbit and the Arab World. While the size of the traffic was not large compared to that between Eastern and Western Europe, it was something of a novelty. [2]

There were other signs that Moscow was concentrating on Egypt. In the United Nations the Russians vetoed a Western proposal that would have forced Cairo to allow Israeli ships to use the Suez canal; arranged a bilateral agreement which swaped Rumanian oil for Egyptian cotton; offered Nasser assistance in establishing his first atomic energy station; sent Shepilov to attend Cairo's Liberation Day; and invited Nasser to visit Moscow in 1956. But these were merely preparatory moves for a much bigger *coup* – the sale of substantial Czech arms in return for cotton. [3]

This was a major victory for the USSR and a correspondingly severe setback for the West. The situation had been festering for over six months as the West stalled Egyptian requests for modern arms. The exact date when Egypt turned to the Soviet Union or Moscow approached Cairo is unknown. Probably the negotiations were conducted in July and Shepilov's presence that month at the Egyptian National Liberation Day celebrations may have played an important part in concluding them. Some reports said that he initiated them. [4] Regardless, on September 27,

---

[1] *World Today, op. cit.*, pp. 523–524.
[2] For a partial list cf. *ibid.*
[3] *New York Times*, Oct. 2, 1955, Part 4, p. 2.
[4] In November 1955 on his 50th birthday Shepilov was awarded the Order of Lenin, the highest Soviet decoration. This was unusual because such awards were

1955, Nasser officially revealed that the agreements had been
signed with Czechoslovakia "about a week ago." However,
Moscow refused to confirm this until *Pravda* carried a short official acknowledgement on October 2. [1]

The manner in which Moscow conducted the negotiations under
the guise of commercial transactions with Czechoslovakia and
her stubborn refusals to admit that any agreement did in fact
exist suggested that the regime realized how delicate the matter
was and attempted to avoid attracting public attention as much
as possible. But once the agreement was exposed, the Soviets
moved rapidly to follow up their advantage. In the second half
of October diplomatic relations with Saudi Arabia were re-
established; the Soviet-Yemen pact of 1927 was renewed; negotiations for diplomatic relations with the Sudan and Libya
were opened; arms were offered to Afghanistan, Syria, and Saudi
Arabia; and Moscow's Ambassador to Cairo, D. A. Solod, made
vague propaganda offers of farm machinery, industrial equipment, and technical assistance to all Afro-Asian countries. None
of these moves was of the same magnitude as the Egyptian arms
deal, but they indicated that the USSR intended to stay in the
Middle East. [2]

The Russians had a number of goals in mind when they
undertook these venturesome maneuvers. The most important
was to neutralize the Middle East and deprive the West of its oil.
By operating from Egypt there was always the possibility that
they could play havoc with the French as they had in Indochina.
The Soviets were well aware of Bismarck's philosophy that
France could be forced to destroy itself as a strong Continental
power by bleeding to death in North Africa. There may have
been one other reason. During 1956 what is usually considered to
have been a shrewdly planned and well coordinated diplomatic

customarily reserved for later occasions, i.e., 55th and 60th birthdays. *Ibid.*, Nov. 5, 1955, p. 6.

[1] In late October 1955 the US Department of State revealed that as early as June 3 (i.e., before the Geneva Conference) that Moscow was prepared to go through with such a deal. About the same time M. Sharett told the Israeli Parliament that the negotiations had been initiated by the Soviet Union rather than Egypt or Czechoslovakia. *World Today*, op. cit., pp. 525–526. Cf. *Foreign Assistance Activities of the Communist Bloc and Their Implications for the United States*, p. 92 for the terms of the agreement.

[2] *World Today*, op. cit., p. 527, and the *New York Times*, Oct. 11, 1955, p. 1, Kennett Love.

and economic penetration by both Communist China and the Soviet Union materialized. It is impossible to determine to what extent this was actually a joint effort. An interesting question for conjecture is whether or not Moscow's activities in the Middle East did not partially spring from the desire to combat stiff competition from Peking and to maintain its place in the race for the allegiance of the underdeveloped world.

Despite the fact the Middle East was not even considered as a topic for discussion at the July Geneva Conference, it had, nevertheless, occupied an important place in determining Soviet policy for the meeting. By diplomatic sleight-of-hand the regime had sought to lull the West into a relaxed state of mind while it stirred up trouble in an area where it had not previously held a serious foothold. At Geneva the Russians obtained two important concessions which greatly facilitated their task. One was a freezing of Europe's *de facto* frontiers and the second was Western assurances that it would never start an aggressive atomic war. This amounted to a *carte blanche* for the Soviets to meddle in any part of the world without fear of retaliation. [1]

It was not until September 5, 1955, that the Soviet press took issue with the United States over the sincerity of the "spirit of Geneva." Then it directed its attack against a speech made by Vice President Nixon ten days earlier. Apparently the Soviets did not want to be open to the charge of being the first to criticize. Shrewdly, they built their article around comment which had already appeared in the American press. [2] A few days later Khrushchev took off the kid gloves and made it clear that regardless of Geneva the goals of Communism remained the same:

We always tell the truth to our friends as well as to our enemies. We are in favor of a *détente*, but if anybody thinks that for this reason we shall

---

[1] *Ibid.*, Oct. 15, 1955, p. 14, C. L. Sulzberger. At the Geneva Conference a member of the Soviet delegation confided to reporters that its most useful feature had been the personal contact between Eisenhower and Bulganin, particularly the former's pledge that the US would "never take part in an aggressive war." Quoted by *ibid.*, July 24, 1955, Part 4, p. 5, Clifton Daniel.

[2] *Pravda*, Sept. 5, 1955, p. 3, *Current Digest*, VII, 36, p. 11. In August the Soviet press published without comment Eisenhower's speech in which he declared that the US did not accept the European *status quo* as the price for peace. It also included a smattering of US press reaction. (*Pravda*, Aug. 26, 1955, p. 3, *Ibid.*, VII, 34, pp. 11–12.) Later it printed without comment excerpts of W. Lippmann's criticism of US reaction to the post-Geneva period. *Pravda* and *Izvestia*, Sept. 2, 1955, p. 4, *ibid.*, VII, 35, p. 9.

forget about Marx, Engels, and Lenin, he is mistaken. This will happen when shrimps learn to whistle. . . . We are for co-existence because there is in the world a capitalist and a socialist system, but we shall always adhere to the building of socialism. . . . We don't believe that war is necessary to that end. Peaceful competition will be sufficient.[1]

THE STIFFENING SOVIET PROPAGANDA LINE

By early October a much harsher tone was emanating from Moscow. In contrast to the period immediately following the Summit Conference when criticism was restricted to "certain circles," the top leadership of both the United States and Britain were singled out once again. Part of the explanation probably was the Soviet Union's failure to prevent Iran from formally joining the Bagdad Pact and its irritation with Secretary of State Dulles' chiding about its activities in the Middle East. The Russians particularly disliked the American assertion that the Geneva spirit was a fraud. Another important reason was the preparation of the Soviet public for the failure of the Foreign Ministers' Conference. This had to be handled rather skillfully because the atmosphere generated by the Geneva Conference had been very popular with the Russian man-in-the-street.

In mid-October the inner-circle of the Soviet leadership met in the Crimea where they most likely discussed preparations for both the Foreign Ministers' gathering which was to convene within a few days at Geneva and the Twentieth Party Congress that had been announced a few months before for February 1956. [2] The diplomatic situation they surveyed must certainly have vindicated their earlier belief in the wisdom of a Summit Conference. The relaxation of international tension had created important chinks in Western unity. Before Moscow had begun generating the Geneva spirit Western solidarity had reached its peak: the Federal German Republic had been brought into NATO, despite ideological differences the Balkan alliance had been created, and the "northern tier" (or Bagdad Pact) had been formed. But with the coming of expressions of good will and mutual trust at the Summit a new climate developed in the West. There were second thoughts about rearming Germany. As a

[1] Quoted by Healey, " 'When Shrimps Learn to Whistle' – Thoughts After Geneva," p. 2.
[2] *New York Times*, Oct. 16, 1955, p. 1.

result, the implementation of the hard fought for treaty lagged. The French, pre-occupied with their own problems in North Africa, pulled their best troops out of Europe, leaving the total number in the NATO command fewer than six months before, and the Italian defense program remained uncertain. In both these countries the local Communist Parties again became respectable. Nearly all NATO members were cutting their defense budgets. The Soviet gestures toward demobilization and withdrawal from the Porkkala Finnish naval base put pressure on the United States to do likewise. The *détente* with Yugoslavia had caused Belgrade to have second thoughts about the Balkan Pact and it showed indications of wanting to turn it into a loose, ineffective organization with the possible inclusion of Soviet Satellites. The Greeks and Turks had more important worries over Cyprus where they were at loggerheads over the island's future, and the Bagdad Pact members, particularly Iraq, were meeting strong opposition from the Syrian-Egyptian axis, which was being encouraged by Moscow's new interests in the Mediterranean.

Whenever possible (such as in Germany where Moscow posed the threat of bilateral negotiations) the Soviets did their best to add to the West's problems though the shrewd exploitation of local difficulties. Only once did the Russian diplomatic offensive seem to stub its toe. That was when the USSR voted in the UN to debate the Algerian question. This resulted in French Premier E. Faure and Foreign Minister A. Pinay cancelling their scheduled visit to Moscow. [1]

Molotov was conspicuously absent from the group which reviewed these developments. [2] This was only one of an increasing number of indications that he was slipping from power. Apparently, his downgrading began just after Malenkov had been removed and the Khrushchev-Bulganin faction had consolidated its position. At a Presidium meeting soon after the February reorganization he was sharply criticized for the conduct of his

[1] During the six months which preceded October 1955 an ever-increasing number of Russians travelled abroad, yet there were no major defections. This could have been explained by hostages at home but might have been an indication that the slight improvement of the domestic situation was having the desired effect. *Ibid.*, Oct. 9, 1955, Part 4, p. 3, Drew Middleton.

[2] Those present were Khrushchev, Bulganin, Zhukov, Mikoyan, Voroshilov, Kirichenko, and Admirals Kuznetov and S. G. Gorshkov. *Ibid.*, Oct. 16, 1955, p. 1.

Foreign Ministry. After *Pravda* published Marshal Tito's March rebuke the signs multiplied that he was no longer the driving force behind the Soviet foreign policy. It was all too clear in April and May 1955 that Khrushchev and Bulganin had assumed responsibility for the regime's diplomacy. Nowhere was this more evident than in Molotov's exclusion from the Russian delegation to Belgrade. At the July Central Committee session his opposition to the creation of a new *détente* with Yugoslavia was made the subject of a blistering personal attack by Khrushchev who sought to thoroughly discredit him just prior to Geneva. (While Molotov had favored the re-establishment of inter-state relations – as advocated by Tito – he apparently opposed not only the Khrushchev-Bulganin visit but the creation of a *rapprochement* between the CPSU and the Yugoslav League of Communists for ideological reasons.) To save what he could from the situation Molotov capitulated to the Central Committee's verdict against him. [1] Although he participated in the Summit Conference a few days later, *Pravda* took pains to exclude him from the picture it printed of the departure of the regime's delegation. Afterward he returned directly to the USSR while Khrushchev and Bulganin visited East Germany to reassure its puppet government of Soviet intentions. Also, it was Shepilov, and not Molotov, who represented Russia in Cairo during July. [2]

The crowning humiliation came in the first week of October when an editorial in *Kommunist* attacked him for putting forth erroneous views on the status of the development of socialism in the USSR during his speech the previous February. The same issue also printed a letter in which he admitted his "error." The ideological point on which the criticism hinged was so small and of such minor importance in the context of the entire speech that it immediately aroused suspicion that the article's real object was to discredit him and his foreign policy only three weeks before the Geneva Foreign Ministers' Conference. (By implication it lauded the Khrushchev-Bulganin diplomacy when it praised the ability to combine theory and practice in foreign affairs.) [3]

[1] Bialer, *op. cit.*, p. 11.

[2] *New York Times*, Aug. 7, 1955, p. 6, Harry Schwartz.

[3] *Kommunist*, 14, Sept. 1955, pp. 3–12 and 127–128, *Current Digest*, VII, 38, pp. 3–6. The fact that the point criticized dealt with the progress of socialism may have been related to the re-interpretation of the USSR's relationship to other Communist

In the eyes of his Western counter-parts he had been clearly downgraded and there was the temptation for them to think of him as little more than a mere spokesman who was not free to negotiate. Moscow's action a month later at the height of the Conference did nothing to dispell this notion. At that moment *Pravda* published its first comment on Molotov's "error," supporting the position taken by *Kommunist* and adding a few additional critical remarks. Obviously, the regime desired this material to have mass circulation rather than being confined to the ideological journal's more select audience. Why the Party organ chose just the moment when its columns were filled daily by Molotov's speeches to discredit him with two pages of devastating criticism puzzled Western observers. *Pravda* gave one significant clue when it linked the denunciation with a reaffirmation of collective leadership. In the past this had been a sign that the internal struggle for power was once again a central issue in the Presidium. Significantly, *Pravda's* criticism coincided with an increased number of attacks against the "cult of the individual." [1]

Probably the central controversy between Molotov and the Khrushchev-Bulganin faction was not the regime's East-West policy. If such had been the case he would not have represented Moscow at Geneva. Most likely it involved the USSR's relationship with the other members of the Communist world. Khrushchev's 1954 trip to Peking and his junket to Belgrade the following spring may have been attempts to tighten the ideological links of the Sino-Soviet orbit and place increased emphasis upon firmer Party ties. The systematic replacement of career Soviet diplomats in these countries over the previous two years by Party men without diplomatic training apparently was one of the moves in this direction.

THE FOREIGN MINISTERS' CONFERENCE

The agenda for the Foreign Ministers' Conference, which opened on October 27, 1955, had been clearly stipulated in the

countries – particularly Yugoslavia and China – and the Asian nations whose economic philosophies were strongly influenced by socialist thinking. *New York Times*, Oct. 10, 1955, p. 9, and Oct. 11, 1955, p. 16, Harry Schwartz.

[1] *Ibid.*, Nov. 5, 1955, p. 5, Welles Hangen.

communiqué issued by the Heads-of-State the previous July, and the positions of the two sides on the respective issues – European security and Germany, disarmament, and the development of East-West contacts – were well marked out by previous statements. On the first item, which was the key to any really workable agreement on the second, the Four Powers were committed to discuss the possibilities of an European security pact; limitation, control, and inspection of both arms and troops; and the establishment somewhere between the two power blocs of a zone for mutual inspection. At the Summit the Heads-of-State also pledged their delegates to comply with the injunction that

reunification of Germany by means of free elections shall be carried out in conformity with the national interests of the German people and the interests of European security.[1]

Despite this agreement in principle, the big powers were deadlocked even before the Foreign Ministers had begun their discussions. Molotov's first speech did nothing but reiterate the time-worn arguments which Bulganin had used three months before. The German issue, he said, could only be discussed as a subordinate issue of an European security treaty that did away with opposing military blocs. The Western representatives, on the other hand, felt that the Summit Conference had intended the two questions to be discussed simultaneously and as interdependent issues. Moscow's position on Germany was also unwilling to see the country firmly tied to a Western military alliance. [2] Molotov did seem to make two changes in the Soviet conditions for unification, but both were the kind which worked against it rather than for it. In the past Moscow had been willing to accept a politically neutral but armed Germany. However, in October 1955 he seemed to imply that it also had to remain demilitarized. For the first time at the conference table he raised the demand that in any unified state East Germany be allowed to retain her economic and social pattern. As West German observers pointed out, this amounted to a Trojan horse that could easily prove fatal to any democratic state. [3] For two weeks both East and West presented security proposals centering

[1] *Soviet News*, 3215, July 26, 1955, p. 1.
[2] *New York Times*, Oct. 28, 1955, p. 3, M.S. Handler.
[3] *Ibid.*, Oct. 29, 1955, p. 5, M. S. Handler, and *Soviet News*, 3283, Oct. 28, 1955, pp. 1–2.

around Germany which were mutually unacceptable. [1] The West offered a plan to keep an unified Germany in check if it choose to join NATO and the Soviets countered with the familiar all-European security plan, which had been rejected the previous July. Molotov then brought out another proposal (similar to the so-called Eden plan) for a demilitarized zone between the two halves of a divided Germany. Through all of these plans ran the basic disagreement over the continued division or unification of the country. The West called unification the keystone to any workable security system while the Soviets insisted on the opposite. These difficulties were not eased by Molotov's insistence, and the West's equally vehement refusal, to have both Germanies present at the conference table. The high point of the debate was the West's challenge to the Russians to approve free elections in September 1956. This also brought a negative response. [2] This rejection amounted to a withdrawal of the ambiguous offer the Soviets themselves had made for elections at Berlin in January 1954. In fact, the Soviet position on Germany was unchanged from 1950 and on the security question unchanged from 1954. This hardening of what originally had been conces sions seemed to be a veiled way of telling the German people that direct negotiations and not the Big Four conference table were the only path to final settlement. [3]

The other two items on the agenda brought exactly the same negative reaction from the Soviets. Molotov launched a sharp, detailed attack on Eisenhower's program for aerial inspection. He said that the USSR would not consider it except as part of a bigger plan. [4]

Even on the third item (increased East-West contacts) no agreement was possible, marking the conference as a complete failure. [5] The reason was that, as in other fields, the Soviets were obtaining what they wanted without having to negotiate. Following Geneva Western European Communist Parties again became respectable, especially when they began advocating a

[1] For a brief chronology with excerpts from important documents cf. Gelbe-Haussen, "Die Aussenministerkonferenz von Genf," pp. 61–68.

[2] *New York Times*, Oct. 29, 1955, p. 1, Ellie Able; Nov. 1, 1955, p. 1, Harrold Callender; and Nov. 3, 1955, p. 1, Drew Middleton.

[3] *Ibid.*, Nov. 13, 1955, Part 4, p. 3, Thomas Hamilton.

[4] *Ibid.*, Nov. 1, 1955, p. 1, Drew Middleton.

[5] *Ibid.*, Nov. 15, 1955, p. 1, Drew Middleton.

new united front movement. By the end of 1955 exchanges across the Iron Curtain reached proportions of a mass movement. In the 18 months following January 1, 1954, two persons visited the USSR for every one who went West, but in the second half of 1955 this trend dramaticly shifted to a one to one ratio. [1]

THE NEW TREND IN SOVIET DIPLOMACY

The tenacity with which Molotov refused to budge was a sign of the Soviets' growing confidence that time was on their side, not only in Europe but in the rest of the world as well. They felt no need to negotiate because their immediate goals had been obtained simply by exploiting the Geneva spirit with a series of adroit diplomatic maneuvers. This was particularly true in Asia where the regime's methods underwent significant alteration during 1955. It postulated the existence of four "Asias" and developed policies to meet the needs of each. The first was the one directly under Communist control – Soviet territory, the Mongolian People's Republic, Communist China, North Korea, and North Viet Nam, totalling 700,000,000 people. As members of the Communist bloc these countries were given unqualified Soviet support as they had been in the past. The next category was the politically independent but economically dependent countries comprising 500,000 people in India, Burma, and Indonesia. The third "Asia" was composed of what Moscow referred to as "formerly independent countries" such as Pakistan, Philippines, Thailand, Iraq, and Turkey, who, in Soviet eyes, had "sold out" to the West. The fourth grouping covered the remaining dependent areas such as Malaya and New Guinea. [2]

Moscow concentrated its attention upon the nations in the second category because they provided the most fertile grounds for conquest, but it did not entirely write off those in the third group which it hoped to pry away from the West. It took the position that countries adhering to a friendly or neutralist foreign policy could count upon unqualified Communist support, but those who aligned themselves with the West could expect to

---

[1] *Ibid.*, Nov. 21, 1955, p. 1, and Dec. 12, 1955, p. 2, Dana Adams Schmidt.
[2] "The Three Asias," BBC, Sept. 6, 1955, and "Moscow Takes a New Doctrinal Look at Asia," USIS, Nov. 25, 1955.

be the subject of diplomatic and non-diplomatic pressures until they moved toward a more neutral position.

A significant feature of this new Soviet friendship toward Asia was an important modification of the role of the local Communist Parties.

> At no previous point ... [in the past] including the United Front period after 1935, [had] Communist Parties been forced to subordinate their individual struggles for power so completely to Soviet or Chinese Communist diplomatic interests; and at no previous juncture [had] the activities of the Parties been consistently so submerged in the pursuit of a brand of 'people's diplomacy' ... necessary to support ... [Moscow's] formal policies and which was best carried on by mushrooming mass fronts.[1]

This was particularly true of Communist activities in India, Japan, Indonesia, Burma, Malaya, and Thailand. However, the operation was not accomplished without some difficulty, particularly in India and Burma where the local organizations found themselves unwilling or unable to quickly accommodate to Moscow's apparent guidance. [2]

In close coordination with this new respectability of the local Communist Parties Moscow launched a sizeable program of economic penetration. From the Nile to the Indies the Russians offered economic inducements: in Egypt, besides the arms deal, there were vague hints about financing the Aswan High Dam, Syria was offered long term loans and markets for her surpluses, and in Afghanistan the USSR proposed undertaking public works programs in addition to arms aid. Already there were 500 Soviet technicians in the country and 35 per cent of its exports went to Moscow. On December 15, 1955, the Afghan government accepted additional Soviet credits for $ 100,000,000 which were almost five times the country's total state revenue during the previous fiscal year. [3] Similar offers of technical assistance were made to India, Burma, and Indonesia. In each case the Communist bloc offered either long term loans or badly needed capital equipment in exchange for local agricultural surpluses and raw materials.

Nothing emphasized the Soviet pre-occupation with the Middle East and Asia better than the Khrushchev-Bulganin 5,000 mile junket through India, Burma, and Afghanistan during November

---

[1] "The Soviet Party Congress and a Possible 'Evolutionary' Trend in Asian Communism," p. 1, USIS, Feb. 21, 1956.

[2] *Ibid.*, p. 6.

[3] Sulzberger, *op. cit.*, p. 209.

and December 1955. With a party of 100 trade and diplomatic experts, the Soviet entourage took on the appearance of a giant Roman circus. Riding elephants, inspecting temples, and shaking hands with the man-in-the-street, these two Russian medicine men made their way through the Orient drumming up support for the Soviet Union. Their object was to obtain the greatest propaganda value from gaudy offers of foreign aid requiring a minimum outlay of hard cash. [1] Their stock in trade were conspicuous projects immediately visible to the masses rather than long term bolstering of economic development through less tangible methods.

Preaching hatred for Western colonialism in one breath and the love and brotherhood of the socialist world in the other, with the missionary zeal of evangelists, their journey in Western eyes took on comic relief. But despite the contempt in which these unorthodox methods were held by the more sophisticated Western diplomats, even the most traditional minded among them were forced to admit that they were extremely shrewd politicians. Well planned and skillfully executed, the Russian tour of Asia presented Communism to the masses at the grassroots in a highly palatable form.

Aside from the unquestioned success of the Khrushchev-Bulganin junket one other aspect seriously disturbed Western observers. This was the growing tone of confidence with which they challenged the free world to a contest of peaceful economic competition. Despite their past belligerence, Soviet pronouncements had always contained underlying tones of insecurity. With Khrushchev and Bulganin's personal direction of foreign policy there was a perceptible change. They no longer spoke as harried revolutionaries but as the directors of a successful corporation. This new assurance probably emanated from several factors: Soviet advances in the scientific fields – particularly nuclear energy; Eisenhower's pledge that the United States would never start an atomic war; the reaction of the Soviet

[1] Another may have been to counter Communist China's growing influence in Asia. Despite the claims of "fraternal brotherhood" the Soviets could hardly have been unperturbed about Mao's increased activities in the Afro-Asian world. During 1955 5,833 Chinese Communists visited 33 countries – an increase of 66 per cent over 1954 – and 4,760 people from 63 countries visited the Chinese People's Republic – an increase of 64 per cent over the previous year. Kirkpatrick, *op. cit.*, p. 100.

people since Stalin's death; and the belief that time was on their side, especially in Asia and Africa. [1] The Soviets had become exceedingly adapt at understanding the climate of international relations – possibly even better than the West. At the 1955 Geneva Conference they had received political confirmation of a fact of which they were well aware – the suicidal nature of global war. Taking a lesson from American successes, Moscow switched to economic diplomacy as the major battle ground. This required two things: 1) the strengthening of its economy to meet the burden of expanded foreign operations, and 2) an ideology to justify its action. Both of these were "maturing perceptively" during the year. Malenkov's economic policy was designed to produce consumers' goods rather than the capital goods needed in underdeveloped areas. In the ideological sphere, the regime abandoned Stalin's concept of socialism developing in isolation, exchanging it for a more flexible doctrine of several roads to the same end. In practice, if not in theory, it accepted the views of the Yugoslav theorist, E. Kardelj, that

history has decided the quarrel between revolutionary and evolutionary socialism, approving both.

By giving at least verbal adherence to the doctrine of non-interference, the Soviet Union was able to make common cause with such widely divergent elements as Nasser's "progressivism"; Nehru's "socialism"; Tito's and Mao's versions of Communism; as well as the brand it practised at home and in Eastern Europe. [2]

[1] New York Times, Dec. 4, 1955, p. 6, Welles Hangen.
[2] Ibid., Dec. 10, 1955, p. 20, C. L. Sulzberger.

CHAPTER VI

THE TWENTIETH PARTY CONGRESS

THE ANNOUNCEMENT

On July 14, 1955, the Central Committee announced that on February 14, 1956, the Twentieth Party Congress would be called into session. [1] This was another example of the regime's post-Stalin efforts to introduce more regularity into political life and to rejuvenate Party meetings in particular. Aside from desiring to revamp the CPSU's Central Committee in the light of changing conditions, the regime's most important reason for calling a Party Congress eight months before the full four years specified by its statutes had elapsed was its need to obtain a new mandate for its authority. Technically, it still operated under the one issued to Stalin in late 1952. Normally this would have continued to be sufficient since it was under no compulsion to present its program to a Party Congress for ratification despite the statutory requirements. However, in this case a new one was necessary because under the pressure of modifying Stalin's policies it was progressively undercutting the very factors upon which it based its claim to speak for the Soviet state.

From the moment Stalin's death was announced his lieutenants began an intensive campaign to prove that their right to assume control was derived from their close association with the late dictator and that it did not need even formal ratification. They were, according to their earliest statements, merely continuing unchanged his policies and programs. To back up this contention (which was not borne out by their actions) they began propagating the concept of an unbroken continuity which stretched from the past through the present and into the future. One of the chief reasons was to prevent their authority from being challenged before it was firmly established. Therefore, no Party Congress was called to ratify the drastic changes made in the membership

[1] *Pravda* and *Izvestia*, July 14, 1955, p. 1, *Current Digest*, VII, 26, p. 6.

and organization of both the Presidium and the Secretariat. In fact, a Central Committee plenum was not convened until March 14, 1953, and then only to accept Malenkov's resignation from the Secretariat. The strange way this was announced a full week after it supposedly took place raised the question whether a full plenum was actually ever held. [1]

As more and more of Stalin's policies were repudiated in one form or another the regime's reliance upon its ties with him became less secure. As long as it was willing to keep within the confines imposed by his legacy and preserve the sanctity of his person, there was no basic conflict. However, after the general policy review which accompanied the February 1955 reorganization, there were increasing signs that the regime was beginning to chaff under the inflexible limitations imposed upon it by the pre-1953 period. Apparently this pressure was sufficient by mid-1955 to warrant it feeling a sharp break with the past was necessary. As a result the decision was made to call the Twentieth Party Congress for the following February.

THE INTERNAL STRUGGLE FOR POWER

The ever-present struggle for power must have also played a part in this decision. The outcome of the February conflict had momentarily stabilized the power relationship in Khrushchev's favor. But he did not have a decisive edge since he was actually the leader of only a majority faction rather than in unquestioned control. Malenkov, despite his fall from grace, remained a power which had to be reckoned with in both the Presidium and the bureaucracy.

Khrushchev was probably among the first to realize that the precarious balance might easily swing against him by the fall of 1956 when the next Party Congress was scheduled to be held. Therefore, it was decidedly in his favor to hold a Party gathering as soon as feasible, thus ensuring that he would reap the benefits while he still retained the advantage. From the available evidence it is impossible to determine whether his original intention was to obtain a position similar to Stalin's or if he would have been satisfied to remain as merely the dominant figure in a collective

[1] Cf. p. 40.

leadership. It is entirely possible that his gradual assumption of more and more power and the purging of his opposition was dictated by his desire for survival rather than by personal ambitions. [1] However, there can be no doubt that in the year between Malenkov's removal and the Twentieth Party Congress there were serious rumblings of disunity and intensive maneuvering beneath the outward show of "monolithic unity."

The mere fact that the central press began emphasizing collective leadership so soon after Malenkov's downgrading indicated the unsettled nature of the situation. These was evidence of a movement to thwart Khrushchev's efforts to press his advantage by attempting to circumscribe the authority of the Secretariat. A *Pravda* article on Lenin's birthday April 20, 1955, by Petrovsky, an Old Bolshevik and former Politburo member who had been purged from the Ukraine in 1938 as the Great Purges were drawing to a close, gave support to this. [2] He closed his commemorative remarks with the significant injunction:

> Lenin taught us collectivity of work, frequently reminding us that all Politburo members are equal and the Secretary is chosen for fulfillment of decisions of the Central Committee of the Party.[3]

This same theme was echoed by a number of other articles in the next few months. One in *Kommunist*, which reached its subscribers shortly after Petrovsky's article, also invoked Lenin's name in regard to the virtues of collective leadership and quoted him as having said that the Secretariat's functions were limited to the execution of policies formulated by the Politburo, Orgburo, or the plenum of the Central Committee. [4] Two months later an article in the latest edition of the *Bolshaya Sovetskaya Entsiklopediya* enhanced the Presidium's role even more at the complete exclusion of the Secretariat. [5] As late as August (a month after the Central Committee session) N. G. Alexandrov, writing in *Sovetskoye Gosudarstvo i Pravo*, repeated this theme by

---

[1] Even after Khrushchev had purged Malenkov, Molotov, Kaganovich, Shepilov (July 1957), Zhukov (October 1957), and Bulganin (March 1958), well-informed Western diplomats in Central Europe were divided on his motives. Cf. Rush, *op. cit.* for a circumstantial case constructed from the Soviet press supporting the argument that it was a deliberate effort on his part.

[2] Cf. pp. 54 and 176.

[3] *Pravda*, April 20, 1955, as quoted by Rush, *op. cit.*, p. 14.

[4] *Ibid.*, pp. 15 and 100.

[5] *Bolshaya Sovetskaya Entsiklopediya* (2nd Ed.), XXXIV as quoted by *ibid.*, p. 34.

stating that only the Party Congresses, the Central Committee, and the Presidium were the Party's policy making organs. In late October 1955 a new edition of a basic textbook for use in the Party's political schools made its appearance. What gave it relevance to this apparently undeclared debate was a Party organization chart that failed to show any indication that in its relationship to the Central Committee the Secretariat was subordinate to the Presidium. This was, of course, an old question which Stalin had fought out at early Party Congresses and settled through his control of both. After the Seventeenth Party gathering in 1934 the relative authority of the Politburo, Orgburo, or the Secretariat was no longer discussed. Following his death and Malenkov's unsuccessful attempt to assume his commanding role, the Secretariat was, in practice, made subordinate to the Presidium. However, it increased in importance in proportion to Khrushchev's rise. [1] Although it is not possible to know precisely how these articles fitted into the regime's internal politics it would appear that for the first time in a quarter of a century the sensitive subject of the Secretariat's position vis-à-vis the Presidium was being publicly questioned.

One other indirect contribution to the power struggle should also be mentioned. During 1955 a new biography of Lenin was published in which Khrushchev was made to appear to be in the line of direct succession of the Leninist-Stalinist heritage. This was accomplished by reproducing at the end a full page of his January 1955 Central Committee speech in which he leaned heavily upon Stalin for support. [2]

While this apparent maneuvering was taking place on the periphery, more important moves were being made at the center. The July 1955 Central Committee session which set the date for the Party Congress heard Molotov soundly attacked not only by Khrushchev but also by Bulganin, Mikoyan, Kaganovich, Suslov, and Shepilov in what was the forerunner of the public criticism in *Kommunist* and *Pravda* the following October and November. [3] At the same time it announced the first promotions to the Party

---

[1] *Ibid.*, pp. 31–35.
[2] The same long quotation also appeared in the political textbook *V Pomoshch' Slushateliam Politshkol-Uchebnoe Posobie* of which 3,000,000 copies were printed at the close of October 1955. *Ibid.*, pp. 19–20 and 100–101.
[3] Bialer, *op. cit.*, p. 11.

Presidium and Secretariat since the membership of these bodies had been stabilized shortly after Stalin's death two and one half years before. A. I. Kirichenko, First Secretary of the Ukrainian Communist Party, and Suslov, who already was a member of the Secretariat, were elected directly to full membership in the Presidium without passing through candidate status. [1] Suslov had been a member of Stalin's short-lived Presidium but had been dropped in the initial March 1953 reorganization. His promotion came as no great surprise because since the end of the Second World War he had been one of the rising young figures in the Communist Party. As a consequence of his advancement he shared with Khrushchev the distinction of occupying positions on both the Secretariat and the Presidium. Kirichenko had likewise been closely associated with Khrushchev in the past in the Ukrainian Party organization and had, in fact, been re-elected First Secretary in early 1954 at a time when extensive changes in the Republic Secretariats strongly suggested a Khrushchev-led purge. However, as head of the largest single Communist Party organization (outside of the CPSU) in the USSR there were strong reasons, aside from this association with Khrushchev, for his promotion. Customarily, the Ukrainian Party Secretary held a position in the Presidium as either a candidate or full member. Since Melnikov had been forced out in the spring of 1953 the Ukraine had been unrepresented. Kirichenko had the added advantage of being a native Ukrainian.

The net effect of these appointments was to strengthen the position of the Secretariat within the Presidium. Three of its 11 members were full-time Party Secretaries. One surprising feature about these changes was that both men leaped over Shvernik, a much older and more distinguished Party official who continued to hold merely candidate status.

In the same *Pravda* announcement Shepilov, its editor, N. I. Belyayev, Party Secretary in Altai *Krai*, and A. B. Aristov, the head of the government in Khabarovsk *Krai*, were named to the Secretariat. Thus its membership was brought back to six. After Malenkov's abortive bid for control of both the government and the Party in March 1953 the Secretariat had officially consisted of

---

[1] *Pravda* and *Izvestia*, July 13, 1955, p. 1, *Current Digest*, VII, 26, p. 6. One of these filled the vacancy left by Beria's arrest in 1953.

Khrushchev, Suslov, Pospelov, Shatalin, and Ignatyev. Within a few days Ignatyev had been dismissed as a result of his implication in the so-called Doctors' Plot. Shatalin, whose career was closely associated with Malenkov's during Stalin's lifetime, was apparently dropped early in 1955 as a result of the Malenkov-Khrushchev struggle. [1] This left only Khrushchev, Suslov, and Pospelov by mid-1955 when the new promotions were announced.

Shepilov was the best known of the new men because of his recent emergence in the realm of foreign policy and his editorial support of Khrushchev in *Pravda*. Little was known about the others. Aristov came to the attention of the West during the short interlude between the Nineteenth Congress and Stalin's death when he was a member of both the Presidium and the Secretariat. After that he became chairman of the executive committee governing the Khabarovsk *Krai* in the Soviet Far East, an area important to Khrushchev's resettlement program. As Party Secretary in the Altay *Krai*, a fertile area important to the campaign to increase grain production, Belyayev was also closely associated with one of Khrushchev's pet projects. [2]

An interesting feature of these promotions was that they all involved only relatively young men (about 50) who had come up through the ranks, who were familiar with current problems, and who were in some way linked with Khrushchev (although this latter point may not have been the deciding factor). Despite the evident influence of the military in the February 1955 reorganization, no marshals joined the ranks of the Presidium, not even as candidates. Such a promotion would not have been surprising considering the military's steady rise following Stalin's death.

While these shake-ups were taking place at the peak of the Party pyramid similar convulsions were being transmitted to every level of its apparatus and to the diplomatic corps where an increasing number of career Ambassadors were replaced by staunch Party members. This trend first became apparent in late 1953 and early 1954 during the general reshuffling of diplomatic

[1] The exact course of events is unclear. There was no official notice of Shatalin's removal. He reappeared in the Primorskii *Krai* in Siberia. During the last years of Stalin's regime he had been Chief of Cadres under Malenkov. Rush, *op. cit.*, p. 24, and "Soviet Presidium Changes," BBC, July 13, 1955.
[2] "Soviet Presidium Changes," BBC, July 13, 1955.

assigments which accompanied the inauguration of the regime's "new course." [1] By the end of 1955 all but one of the 11 Russian envoys in Communist countries were men whose careers had been made in the Party rather than in the Foreign Ministry. This was true even of N. P. Feryubin, the new Soviet Ambassador appointed to Belgrade during the second half of the year as a part of Moscow's continuing efforts to achieve an ideological *rapprochement* with Marshal Tito. The one exception was G. M. Pushkin, who represented the USSR in the German Democratic Republic. He had been the first Soviet envoy to Hungary after World War II and was generally credited with having been largely responsible for the successful Communization of that country. This appearance of Party officials in diplomatic posts clearly pointed up the decline of Molotov and the emergence of Khrushchev in the fields of foreign policy. [2]

Throughout the Soviet Union itself the pattern of changes was remarkably similar and strongly suggested that Khrushchev was "packing" the lower ranks of the Party organization with his trusted followers in anticipation of the election of delegates to the Twentieth Party Congress. Most of the attention seemed to be focused upon the Republic Party organizations, but in a number of instances important *oblasts* felt the initial effects of the purge as well as its subsequent shock waves.

The 1954 Republic Party Congresses had resulted in a substantial turnover in Party Secretaries, but this was to be expected since they were the first to be held in the post-Stalin period. [3] However, almost as soon as these newly elected three-man Secretariats had taken office a movement was begun to enlarge all 15 with one or two additional hand-picked men. Considering Khrushchev's firm hold on the All-Union Secretariat he almost certainly was behind this campaign, which continued well into mid-1955. [4] By the time the Republic Congresses gathered to

[1] Cf. p. 111, and Meissner, "Der Auswärtige Dienst der UdSSR," pp. 43–44 for Soviet diplomatic appointments during 1954.

[2] "Party Men Replace Soviet Diplomats," Voice of America, Jan. 2, 1956, and "Party Man to Yugoslavia as Ambassador," BBC, Aug. 26, 1955.

[3] Cf. p. 334 for the composition of the Republican Secretariats in 1952, 1954, and 1956.

[4] The Ukrainian and Kazakh Party Congresses were the only ones to have elected more than three Secretaries in 1954. As early as September 1953 a similar program of increasing the number of Party Secretaries was begun on the *rayon* level in connection with the strengthening of the MTS. Rush, *op. cit.*, p. 24 and the *New York Times*, Aug. 29, 1955, p. 6, Harry Schwartz.

re-elect their officials and delegates to the CPSU session the principle was firmly established throughout the Soviet Union. [1] What made this of such great importance was that on the Republic level the Party Secretaries (unlike their All-Union counterparts) were automatically voting members of the Politburos. [2]

However, simply the enlargement of the Republic Secretariats were not the only changes. Between the 1954 and 1956 elections Secretaries in seven of the 15 non-Russian Republic organizations were removed. [3] These followed no general pattern but struck down First Secretaries and less important members alike. Several of the most important purges took place only after the Twentieth Party Congress had been announced. In Kazakhstan the regime completed a "political revolution" to go along with its earlier "ethnic revolution" set in motion by the virgin lands program. In late June 1955 the Kazakh leader, Shayakhmetov, was ousted from his second Party post in less than a year. In February 1954, just before the great influx of young people from European Russia began, Moscow had deposed him as First Secretary of the Kazakh Party. He was at that time the most high ranking Kazakh and non-Russian Party official in the Soviet Union. However, he was not completely purged but shunted to the less important post of First Secretary of the southern branch of the Republic's Party organization. This was the post he lost in mid-1955.

What gave these events the mark of a "political" revolution were the prominent positions given to Slavs in the wake of both demotions. Ponomarenko and Brezhnev, who had been imported by Moscow in 1954 to reorganize the Party, were both "foreigners." When Ponomarenko was dispatched to the Soviet Embassy in Poland in April 1955 the question of a new First Secretary again arose. The regime left little doubt of its intentions by the further demotion of Shayakhmetov and the promotion six weeks later of Brezhnev and I. R. D. Yakovlev, another Slav also trained in the Ukrainian apparatus under Khrushchev. [4]

---

[1] With the exception of the Estonian and Karelo-Finnish Secretariats, which elected only four Secretaries, all of the Republics elected five-man Secretariats. Cf. p. 334.

[2] Rush, *op. cit.*, p. 24.

[3] Cf. p. 334.

[4] *New York Times*, June 27, 1955, p. 7; Aug. 12, 1955, p. 3; and Aug. 15, 1955, p. 2, Harry Schwartz.

As August drew to a close A. N. Yegorov was removed from his post as First Secretary of the Karelo-Finnish Republic and replaced by L. L. Subennikov of the Minsk *Oblast*. In the Ukraine changes were made about the same time in the leadership of the Chernigov and Poltava *Oblast* organizations.[1]

In November six more Georgian secret police officials were reported by *Zarya Vostoka* to have been executed and two others imprisoned because of their connections with Beria. This was the third in the series of executions since 1953.[2] Western observers saw several possible explanations for this new announcement. Some felt it was merely a "house cleaning" being conducted by Georgian officials, while others felt it had a direct bearing on the forthcoming Twentieth Party Congress. They reasoned that inside Russia it would be interpreted as yet another discrediting of the secret police and at the same time a stern reminder that the regime had no intention of brooking any opposition from dissident elements at the Party gathering. There was also the possibility that it was another phase of a larger effort by Khrushchev to secure his position.[3]

In December, as the time for the important Republic Congresses approached, the purges took a mounting toll. A. I. Niyazov, First Secretary of the Uzbek Party, was removed and replaced by N. A. Mukhitdinov, the Uzbek Premier,[4] apparently as a result of Niyazov's failures to meet cotton production goals. The changes followed closely on the heels of Khrushchev's and Bulganin's visit to the Republic on their way back from their Asian tour. About three weeks later the Premier of the Lithuanian SSR since 1943, M. A. Gedvilas, was ousted and replaced by

[1] In the former P. F. Kumanko (Second Secretary) replaced V. S. Markov, and in the latter M. M. Stakhursky was replaced by N. M. Rozhanchuk, former government head of the *oblast*. These men may have been merely reassigned rather than purged. This was suggested by their former close association with Khrushchev. *Ibid.*, Aug. 26, 1955, p. 6, Harry Schwartz.

[2] Those reported executed were: N. M. Rukhadze, former Georgian Minister of State Security; A. N. Rapava, former Georgian Minister of Internal Affairs; Sh. O. Tsereteli, former Georgian Deputy Minister of State Security; and K. S. Stavitsky, A. S. Khazan, and N. A. Khrinan, all former Georgian investigators for the NKVD. Two others, G. I. Paramonov, and S. N. Nadarai, were sentenced to 25 and ten years, respectively. The former had also been an NKVD investigator, and the latter was simply identified as an "enemy of the people." *Zarya Vostoka*, Nov. 22, 1955, p. 2, *Current Digest*, VII, 45, pp. 14–15.

[3] *New York Times*, Nov. 23, 1955, p. 4, Harrison Salisbury; Nov. 24, 1955, p. 28; and Nov. 25, 1955, p. 5.

[4] *Ibid.*, Dec. 29, 1955, p. 22.

M. Shumauskas, one of the Secretaries of the Republic's Party organization.[1] The same week the Premier of the RSFSR, the largest Republic in the USSR, A. M. Puzanov, was replaced by M. A. Yasnov, the mayor of Moscow. Similar changes were reported from Gorky, Syerdlovsk, and Vologda during late December.[2]

Only two weeks before the Party Congress was scheduled to meet Colonel General Kruglov was removed as head of the Ministry of the Interior (MVD). He had succeeded Beria after the latter's arrest in June 1953 but had never enjoyed as much power because the regime had moved rapidly to circumscribe his authority. He was replaced by N. P. Dudorov, an official of the Moscow City Communist Party who, significantly, was known for his Party work rather than any association with either the police apparatus or Beria. (His last known position had been Deputy Mayor of Moscow.) His appointment seemed to further emphasize the determination of the regime to make a clean break with the past in at least this respect.[3] Dudorov's appointment may have a much deeper significance: Khrushchev's successful control through his protégés of the complete police apparatus. Serov, who headed the important KGB, had been his subordinate for a time in the Ukraine, and his political fortunes after Stalin's death paralleled those of Khrushchev in important aspects although there was no direct link between the two. The office of Procurator General, which since 1954 had controlled the secret police, was occupied by R. A. Rudenko, also a former member of the Ukrainian apparatus. Dudorov had been a member of the Moscow City organization which Khrushchev had directed until March 1953. As in other cases, the precise importance of these former associations with the First Secretary was impossible to establish.[4]

Other important changes were revealed when the composition of the ruling bodies of the 15 Republic Parties was published during January as each organization held its own Congress. Changes similar to those already mentioned in the Secretariats also took place in the Politburos. Not a single one elected in 1954

[1] *Ibid.* (*Int. Ed.*), Jan. 20, 1956, p. 1.
[2] *Ibid.*, Jan. 25, 1956, p. 1, Welles Hangen.
[3] *Ibid.* (*Int. Ed.*), Feb. 1, 1956, p. 1, Welles Hangen.
[4] Rush, *op. cit.*, p. 98.

was returned intact. The changes varied from simply the removal of candidates in some Republics to the purging of four or five full members in others. This represented a considerable turnover.[1] A similar turnover was also noticeable in the membership of the various Central Committees. In all but one Republic these bodies were enlarged. However, in every case there was an impressive influx of both new members and candidates.[2] The expansion might be partially explained as the recognition of increased Party membership which was particularly heavy in the non-Russian Republics, but the widespread removal and demotion of former members and candidates within less than two years strongly suggested a purge similar to the one that took place when the CPSU Central Committee was elected in February 1956.

THE STALIN IMAGE BEFORE THE CONGRESS

Deeply immeshed in this pattern of internal politics was the Stalin image. Its periodic rise and fall was not only a partial barometer of the power struggle taking place in the Presidium but also an important index of the progress the regime as a whole was making in its efforts to revise his outmoded dogmas and archaic policies. After the first few months when his heirs overnight relegated his image to the limbo of silence they realized that it had a positive advantage as a symbol of stability and continuity, especially when the process of change threatened to get out of hand or internal rivalries swept through the system. Therefore, necessity dictated a compromise of a partial restoration.

When Stalin died in 1953 his self-inspired campaign of deification was at its height. Preparations were then under way for the celebration of his 75th birthday in December 1954, which most likely would have outdone the unprecedented spectacle of self-adoration that took place in 1949. The Nineteenth Party Congress in October 1952 with its quasi-religious atmosphere of Byzantine ritual and litany such as

Glory to the Great Stalin

---

[1] Meissner, *The Communist Party of the Soviet Union*, pp. 137–144.

[2] Only in Turkmenia did the net number of full members and candidates remain the same. Cf. p. 336.

and

Hail Comrade Stalin, the great leader of the working people of the world!

gave a good preview of what could be expected.[1]

Against this background the immediate attempt by his successors to consign Stalin to the dust bin of obscurity was even more striking. After the restrained funeral service and the March Supreme Soviet session in which he was pointedly forced to share the spotlight with Gottwald, a secondary figure of the Communist world by any standards, Stalin's image virtually disappeared from the public eye until the following June.[2] The Soviet press which had lavished him with praise suddenly fell silent. It appeared to be guided by a policy of refraining from mentioning his name except when necessary and never more than twice in the same article regardless of its length.[3] In fact, on March 23, only 18 days after his death, an entire issue of *Pravda* appeared without a single reference to him.[4] Such time-tested formulas as the "Stalin Constitution," the "Stalin Five Year Plan" or the "Stalin Plan for the Transformation of Nature" were either renamed or, as in the last instance, completely discarded.[5]

But the downgrading of the Stalin image was a more serious effort than merely removing his name and picture from public view.[6] Precisely six weeks after his death, April 16, *Pravda* criticized individual leaders who

start to act as though they were the only ones who could say anything sound and sensible

and asserted that in the Communist Party it was the principle of "collectivity" which ruled. This attack upon the "cult of individuality" – a heretofore unprecedented phrase – quoted Stalin himself as its authority but took care to mention the

---

[1] *Pravda*, Oct. 15, 1952, p. 1, Gruliow (Ed.), *Current Soviet Policies*, (I), pp. 234–236. Cf. *Pravda*, Dec. 21, 1949, Gruliow (Ed.), *Current Soviet Policies*, II, pp. 1–8 for examples of the tributes by the Politburo members on his 70th birthday.

[2] The notable exception was Malenkov's abortive attempt to bask in his reflected glory immediately after Stalin's death. Cf. p. 37.

[3] Tucker, "The Metamorphosis of the Stalin Myth," p. 39.

[4] Wolfe, *op. cit.*, p. 20.

[5] Tucker, *op. cit.*, p. 39.

[6] The Soviet press failed to print Stalin's picture on May Day 1953, an unprecedented omission. *Ibid.*, p. 40.

precise year (1931), implying that he had been guilty of deviating from his own principle in later years.[1]

Late the following month *Pravda* carried a thinly disguised rebuke on Stalin's last economic work, *Economic Problems of Socialism in the USSR*, which had held the spotlight at the Nineteenth Party Congress. The newspaper attacked "certain propagandists" for promoting Stalin's concept of the transition from conventional trading to a system of "product exchange" in the countryside which would have obliterated the distinction between state-farm and collective farm property.[2] This repudiation drew attention to the fact that the status of this "great work of genius" had become extremely dubious after his death. Despite the praise which had been so lavishly bestowed on it while he lived, it was unceremoniously omitted from the April 14, 1953, list of approved materials to be used by the Party's political study groups and was replaced by the decisions of the March Supreme Soviet session and the statements of the regime's leading members.[3] For the next two months it languished in the limbo of obscurity with other mementos such as the "Stalin Prizes."[4] But near the end of June it was again restored as

an outstanding contribution to the treasure-trove of Marxism-Leninism

and was made an acceptable part of the Party's educational program.[5] While his views were no longer criticized the regime felt no compulsion to give them more than lip service, and, in fact, during June a campaign against "Talmudism" – the mere repetition of quotations – was begun.[6] The problem it faced was best illustrated by his "product exchange" thesis. The Khrushchev-Malenkov 1953 economic program was in obvious contradiction to it, but the regime did not feel in a position to repudiate it completely. *Kommunist* wrestled with this dilemma and finally rationalized away the difficulties by arguing that it remained

[1] *Pravda*, April 16, 1953, p. 1 as quoted by *ibid.* It was merely elaborating upon a *Kommunist* article which had appeared a week after Stalin's death. *New York Times*, April 17, 1953, p. 1.
[2] Tucker, *op. cit.*, p. 41, and the *New York Times*, May 31, 1953, p. 10, Harrison Salisbury.
[3] Leonhard, "Party Training after Stalin," p. 10, and Tucker, *op. cit.*, p. 42.
[4] They were not awarded during the spring of 1953. Tucker, *op. cit.*, p. 39.
[5] Quoted by *ibid.*, p. 42.
[6] Leonhard, *op. cit.*, p. 11.

a long-range prospect ... which can be attained only in the future, upon the foundation of a tremendous growth of productive forces.[1]

This was in line with another shift that was taking place as the new regime formulated its own economic policies. During Stalin's last years there had been a flood of material emphasizing that Communism is not a matter of the distant future, but his successors soon took a much more cautious approach.[2] Here, then, was the basic dilemma which faced the regime: Stalin's image had to be cut down in such a way that the basic tenants of Communism were not challenged but so that his lieutenants could do away with those aspects of his policy which most fettered their actions. They also had to keep in mind that as his heirs their legitimacy depended on the maintenance of the "line of succession." If they tampered too greatly with his fundamental policies, they called into question their own right to continue them.

With these factors in mind a moderate restoration of Stalin's image was begun during late June 1953. It assigned him the role of the great continuer of Lenin's cause which placed definite limitations upon its ultimate size. These were quite evident in the Party Manifesto issued on its 50th anniversary about a month later. This was the first post-Stalin attempt to write a comprehensive Party history and probably could be considered a replacement for the *History of the VKP(b)* (*Short Course*) which Stalin himself wrote in 1938 as the authorized version. In the Manifesto it was the Party rather than any particular individual which received credit for achievements in the post-Lenin period. Stalin was assigned an important but modest role as Lenin's disciple. Aside from Lenin, whose stature grew enormously, the Central Committee was probably the chief beneficiary of this revision.[3] This trend even identified the

---

[1] *Kommunist*, 10, May 1953, p. 32 as quoted by Keep, "Soviet Ideologies on the Treadmill," p. 33. A final negative verdict on the "product exchange" system was given in a 1954 economic textbook:
"Trade will remain the basic form of the distribution of consumer goods during the whole period of the gradual transition to Communism."
Politicheskaya Ekonomiia – Uchebnik, 1954, p. 569 as quoted by *ibid*.

[2] *J. V. Stalin o Stroitelstve Kommunizma v SSSR*, 1950, p. 45 as quoted by *Ibid*., p. 32.

[3] Lenin's name was mentioned 41 times and Stalin's only four. *New York Times*, July 27, 1953, p. 12, Harrison Salisbury.

Party with the *"vozhd* of the Soviet people." [1] Previously, the term *"vozhd,"* which is translated as "leader," had been exclusively reserved for use by Stalin and carried the connotation of *"Führer"* or *"Duce."*[2]

In October 1953 the anniversary of the Nineteenth Party Congress went completely unmentioned in the Soviet press. Nevertheless, the Cominform organ, *For a Lasting Peace, For a People's Democracy*, and all of the Rumanian newspapers made reference to it. However, in the latter only Malenkov's name appeared and there was no mention of Stalin's *Economic Problems of Socialism in the USSR*.[3]

By necessity the rewriting of Stalin's role in Soviet history had to be completed by December 1953 since the anniversary of his birth required not only the mentioning of his name but also a review of his career. The celebration itself was carried out in the most perfunctory manner and added little to what had already been said. (It was in sharp contrast to the major propaganda ceremony that was accorded to the 30th anniversary of Lenin's death the next month.) [4] However, the treatment Stalin received on the first anniversary of his death, March 5, 1954, clearly illustrated the policy the regime had decided upon after wrestling with the problem for a whole year. Both *Pravda* and *Izvestia* carried commemorative, page-one editorials,[5] while the provincial press published a 2,000 word eulogy which had been dictated over Radio Moscow two days before. The headline in *Pravda* – "J. V. Stalin – the Great Continuer of the Cause of Lenin" – clearly set the tone.[6] The press commemorated less the death of the man than a milestone in the history of the Communist Party.

Despite Stalin's greatly reduced stature there was no hint of any criticism even by innuendoes.

In fact, he received what would best be described as "moderately

[1] *Pravda*, March 17, 1953 as quoted by Tucker, *op. cit.*, p. 45.

[2] *Ibid.*, and Wolfe, *op. cit.*, p. 19.

[3] *The Economist*, Oct. 10, 1953, p. 85, and Oct. 24, 1953, p. 238.

[4] Tucker, *op. cit.*, p. 46.

[5] *Pravda's* accompanying three column photograph was the first one of Stalin to appear on the front page since his death. Likewise, it had not devoted a page-one editorial to him since his funeral. *New York Times*, March 5, 1954, p. 6.

[6] Lenin's name appeared more times than Stalin's in both articles. *Ibid.*, March 3, 1594, p. 2, and *Pravda*, March 5, 1954, p. 1, *Current Digest*, VI, 9. p. 13.

laudatory" praise. He was, among other things, a "faithful and worthy disciple" and a "firm follower of Lenin's ideals." The article in the provincial press continued the process begun earlier in the year of revising downward his role in the 1917 Revolution. During Lenin's lifetime he was pictured as having been among his "closest associates" rather than the towering figure of the past. In this version he merely successfully executed the policies of the Communist Party when he was Commissar of Nationalities rather than initiating them himself as it had been customary to claim.[1] *Pravda's* editorial assigned an even larger share of Stalin's past glories to the Party, crediting it with formulating and carrying out the concepts of planned industrialization and the collectivization of agriculture. Again Stalin was portrayed simply as the agent of a higher authority. Changes were also made in his contributions to Communist dogma. While he was still referred to as an

outstanding theoretician of creative Marxism

this was qualified in such a way as to confine his efforts to specific limited categories which were not elaborated in detail.[2]

In order to make the Party's position unequivocally clear *Pravda* published a second article the same day which put its front page editorial in excellent perspective and must have dampened any misplaced enthusiasm. After an opening paragraph of lauditory remarks in the same vein as the editorial it settled down to a lengthy account of the development of Marxism and the growth of the Communist Party. When it had finished, Stalin's contributions were made to appear rather minor by comparison to those of either Marx or Lenin. He was effectively pictured as merely a link in the endless chain of Party leaders who carried on the traditions of the past.[3]

---

[1] Krasov as quoted by Tucker, *op. cit.*, pp. 48–49.

[2] Indicating the care which was taken in formulating this point both articles used identical language:
"He creatively developed Marxist-Leninist teaching, applying it to new historical conditions, and, on a number of questions enriched revolutionary theory with new principles."
Pravda, March 5, 1954, p. 1 as quoted by *ibid.*, p. 50.

[3] *Pravda*, March 5, 1954, p. 2, *Current Digest*, VI, 9, p. 15. Interestingly, the other members of the Soviet bloc did not adopt such a restrained position. Stalin's deification was continued by the Chinese press while the East European Satellites adopted a line somewhere between the two. *World Today*, "Stalinism in the Post-Stalin Regime," pp. 307–308.

While this line was being pursued by the Party the military was conducting its own re-appraisal. During the course of the first year the groundwork was laid in a large number of individual articles by ranking professional soldiers for an eventual re-evaluation of Stalin's part in the Second World War and the cult of the individual came in for its share of criticism for retarding military thinking. The marshals also tended to transfer credit for leadership from his person to the Communist Party. They

managed to tell the story as though Stalin had practically nothing to do with the evolution of the Soviet forces and their combat operations during the war years.[1]

The few noticeable exceptions concerned episodes when he praised the professional soldiers for their ability. Nevertheless, even at this stage the rewriting of history was not without its problems, particularly when it came to redistributing the credit. *Pravda's* commemorative editorial one year after Stalin's death contained just a hint of a rift between the marshals and the politicians on how this should be done. In discussing the political consequences of World War II, it wrote:

Thanks to the might of the Soviet state and the wise leadership of the Communist Party, thanks to the self-sacrificing heroism of Soviet men and women, our people won a world-historic victory over the fascist aggressors and maintained the freedom and independence of their Motherland.

The crushing defeat of the German and Japanese fascists aggressors *provided conditions* for the formation of an invincible camp of peace-loving peoples composed of the USSR and the people's democratic countries of Europe and Asia. *All of these great victories of the Soviet people are indissolubly linked with the name of Stalin, who in the war years headed the State Defense Committee and the Soviet Armed Forces.*[2]

This may have been a way of acknowledging the military's role in the war and its assertion that Stalin's "genius" did not win it, but at the same time emphasizing the point that military victories were not enough. They only prepared the way for the political decisions by the Party's leadership which had a better grasp of the over-all picture. *Izvestia's* editorial the same day made the same point in a different way. Stalin, it asserted,

became head of the Armed Forces of the Soviet state *on the decision of the Central Committee of the Party and the Soviet government.*[3]

[1] Tucker, *op. cit.*, p. 51.
[2] *Pravda*, March 5, 1954, p. 1 as quoted by *ibid.*, p. 52. (Italics added.)
[3] *Izvestia*, March 5, 1954, as quoted by *ibid.*, p. 54. (Italics added.)

During the rest of 1954 the regime continued to whittle down his image and transfer the credit wherever possible to the Party. Consequently, the Komsomols revised their oath so as to pledge their fidelity

to the teachings of Lenin, to defend firmly our Communist Party and the victory of Communism

rather than to Stalin's teachings,[1] and in April *Pravda* revived Lenin's criticism of Stalin's work when he had headed the Workers' and Peasants' Inspectorate as a part of its criticism of the contemporary agricultural bureaucracy.[2]

But on the 75th anniversary of his birth (December 21, 1954) the treatment accorded him was more extensive than it had been the previous year although not as lavish as in 1949 nor that given Lenin the following April.[3] The explanation was that Stalin's image had become directly involved in the internal struggle for power which had greatly intensified during the fall of 1954, and its prestige was being involked by one of the protagonists as a means of obtaining additional support. (At the same time it served the regime as a whole as a national symbol of unity behind which it could hide these factional differences.)[4]

Khrushchev's January 1955 speech to the Central Committee on the hegemony of heavy industry in the nation's economy restored Stalin to new heights. His choice of words and his allusions to events of 1929 and 1930 illustrated his deliberate desire to identify himself as closely as possible with his predecessor's image and, thereby, to receive sanction for his policies.[5]

---

[1] Quoted by the *New York Times*, April 21, 1954, p. 3.

[2] It was taken from "How We Should Reorganize the Workers' and Peasants' Inspection" (Jan. 23, 1923) and "Better Fewer, but Better" (written in February 1923 and published the following March 4). The fact that these were quoted as part of an attack upon the inefficiency of the Ministry of Agriculture's bureaucracy may have been an early effort to shift the blame for the farming crisis to Stalin's shoulders. *Ibid.*, April 18, 1954, p. 13.

[3] The proportions Stalin's cult had reached by 1949 may be judged by the press coverage given his 70th birthday. In December leading Soviet newspapers began publishing the names of prominent individuals and organizations who had sent him greetings. The list was serialized for 22 months before it was discontinued in October 1951 (as his 72nd birthday approached) although it was still incomplete. In 1949 *Pravda* printed a special 12 page birthday issue in which, with the exception of a two inch theater program and a three inch report of a chess championship, every line was devoted to Stalin. Cf. Gruliow, *op. cit.*, pp. 1–7; Fisher, *The Life and Death of Stalin*, pp. 34–35; and the *Bulletin of the Institute for the Study of the USSR*, "Two Anniversaries," pp. 29–32.

[4] Cf. p. 163.

[5] Rush, *op. cit.*, pp. 7–8.

This association was strengthened a few weeks later when a new biographical article described Khrushchev as

one of the closest comrades-in-arms of J. V. Stalin [1]

whereas the previous year he had merely been a "comrade-in-arms." But at the same time the revised article on Stalin in the same publication slighted Khrushchev in two ways. He was the only one of the seven senior members of the Presidium not mentioned and it also revised Stalin's status as "General Secretary" during the period between October 1952 (the Nineteenth Congress) and his death six months later in such a way as to imply that the purpose was to detract from the importance of Khrushchev's leadership of the Secretariat.[2]

Despite this increased emphasis upon Stalin's role those involved in the political in-fighting which preceeded the February 1955 reorganization were careful to keep well within the previously defined bounds. He remained the

great continuer of the cause of V. I. Lenin.

This was the theme of the limited press coverage given the second anniversary of his death. The one article in *Pravda* dealt primarily with the development of Communism in the USSR rather than with his life.[3]

During the following year the regime's policy toward Stalin passed through a strange and somewhat bewildering phase. There seemed to be two distinct and contradictory trends. One concerned the policies most closely linked to his name and the other the public fortunes of his image. After his death these two had moved in the same general direction but at different speeds. In the immediate wake of the 1954–1955 power struggle there appeared to be a momentary reversal of both, but once the dust had finally settled the movement away from Stalin's policies was ressumed at an accelerated pace – particularly in Soviet diplomacy. However, his image began a gradual but perceptible

---

[1] *Entsiklopedicheskii Slovar*, III 1955, as quoted by *ibid.*, p. 8.

[2] The wording used was
"J. V. Stalin worked at this post [General Secretary of the Central Committee] until October 1952, and subsequently until the end of his life was Secretary of the Central Committee."
Entsiklopedicheskii Slovar, III, 1955 as quoted by *Ibid.*, p. 12.

[3] *Izvestia* carried no mention of the occasion nor did either paper publish his photograph. *Pravda*, March 5, 1955, pp. 2–3, *Current Digest*, VII, 9, pp. 17–19 and 41.

upward climb.[1] This was given a boost in the closing days of September by the authorization of a new 200,000-copy edition of his famous *History of the VKP(b)* (*Short Course*) from the unedited 1945 matrices.[2]

Somehow related to this trend was the sudden reappearance of the term "General Secretary" in the press in early November. From the moment Stalin died almost all references to him by this title disappeared from Soviet newspapers. (When it was mentioned in various books or reference works the manipulation of dates that accompanied it indicated that it was part of some unexplained internal controversy.) Oddly enough when the term again made its appearance it was in connection with Khrushchev rather than Stalin. Entirely by accident New Zealand's Deputy Prime Minister K. Holyoake had addressed a thank-you letter to

Mr. N. S. Khrushchev, General Secretary of the Communist Party of the Soviet Union

and it was given the widest possible publicity in the central press, provincial newspapers, and even on Radio Moscow, suggesting that Khrushchev saw an opportunity to manipulate the prestige which had been associated with the term during Stalin's lifetime for his own benefit.[3]

There was no reason why the 76th anniversary of Stalin's birth should have received any special attention, yet he was given as much attention then as the previous year. Part of it came in a *Kommunist* article which identified him as "General Secretary" and concluded with a quotation from Khrushchev on the Party's record of successes and its policies for the forthcoming Twentieth Congress.[4]

During the first two weeks of 1956 the tendency to eulogize Stalin continued. On January 12 Tass announced the imminent publication of the 14th volume of his *Collected Works*, covering

---

[1] Cf. Rush, *op. cit.* for the intricate reasoning behind the argument that after Malenkov's downgrading Khrushchev began a deliberate effort to improve his political fortunes by associating them with Stalin's cult.

[2] Rush, *op. cit.*, p. 106. In 1954 the regime had re-issued three volumes of Party decisions and resolutions – some of which had not previously been available – covering the period from 1889–1953. These and a new economic textbook were the basis for the post-Stalin study of Party history. Leonhard, *op. cit.*, p. 11.

[3] Rush, *op. cit.*, pp. 11–12, 27, and 35–36.

[4] *Ibid.*, p. 37.

the crucial period of 1934 through 1941. The previous 13 had appeared at regular intervals between 1946 and 1951, but this one had probably been held up because it covered the period of the purges. This was a specially knotty problem after Stalin's death and the subsequent rehabilitation of some of his victims. The first issue of *Kommunist* for 1956 also spoke favorably of him.[1]

However, despite this latest upsurge in his popularity about the middle of January he once again slipped into obscurity. His name was rarely invoked in the published accounts of the Republic Party Congresses, and it was completely absent from *Pravda* after January 23.[2] A conference of historians which met for three days during the last week of the month carried on a vigorous debate on his version of Party history, but its proceedings as published by *Voprosy Istorii* only mentioned his name once. Far more important than this single reference were the discussions. The deputy chief editor, E. N. Burdzhalov, in his co-report, called for a re-appraisal of historical writing so that more attention would be given to the "Bolsheviks on whom V. I. Lenin relied"; a new look at the histories of the Ukrainian and Transcaucasus Party organization; and the presentation of the factional fights of the 1920's as fights against

anti-Leninist tendencies and groups supported by backward social strata.

His implied criticism went even farther when he asserted that

some historians of the Party treat many important questions dogmatically, uncritically, limiting themselves to expositions of the *History of the VKP(b)* (*Short Course*), not developing the theses which it presents, remaining on the level achieved by science in 1938.[3]

This mild break with the past – which could either have been sent up as a trial balloon or was the product of individual initiative that correctly foresaw which way the political winds were blowing – met with substantial criticism by other speakers. In the ensuing debate there was a tendency for the academic historians to support Burdzhalov (he was not a Party member) and those working for Party institutions to criticize him.[4] A. M.

---

[1] *Ibid.*, p. 38–39. As of January 1959 volume XIV had not yet been published.
[2] *Ibid.*, p. 39.
[3] *Voprosy Istorii*, 2, 1956 as quoted by *ibid.*, p. 45.
[4] Among his critics were M. A. Dvoinishnikov and M. D. Stuchebnikova of the Marx-Engels-Lenin-Stalin Institute; G. D. Kostomarov of the Institute for Party

Pankratova, member of the Central Committee and editor of *Voprosy Istorii*, avoided these controversial points in her co-report, and in her summation concluded that no "revolution in historiography" was intended.[1]

The same issue of the historical journal carried another article which criticized historians for ignoring the official activities of several of Stalin's victims.[2] This was not the first time that it had helped in rehabilitating the "damned." The previous December it had revived Voznesensky, the economist and former Politburo member, just when the Stalin image was riding on the crest of publicity in the press.

On February 4, ten days before the Party Congress opened, another piece was added to the jigsaw puzzle. The traditional greetings sent to Voroshilov on his 75th birthday by the Central Committee and the Council of Ministers omitted any reference to Stalin. Before it had been customary to praise the recipient as

a pupil of Lenin, a co-worker of Stalin.[3]

Only on the day before the Party gathering convened did *Pravda* break its silence on Stalin's name. The occasion was an article by B. Bierut, First Secretary of the Polish Communist Party, in which he wrote that Poland was

implementing the principle of priority for heavy industry ... which was emphasized by Lenin and later by Stalin and systematicly carried out by the Central Committee of the CPSU.

He also made reference to the "sharpening class struggle," a Stalinist doctrine which was soon to be disavowed.[4] The following day the central press ignored Stalin completely. However, the provincial press followed a mixed pattern. Papers in Armenia, Moldavia, and the Karelo-Finnish Republic made no reference to him and did not print his picture. In Kazakhstan, Turkmenia, Estonia, and Kirgizia his name appeared in editorials. Newspapers

History attached to the Moscow Party organization; and B. D. Datsiuk of the Higher Party School attached to the CPSU Central Committee. *Ibid.*, pp. 46 and 106.

[1] *Voprosy Istorii*, 2, 1956 as quoted by *ibid.*, p. 46.

[2] S. V. Kossior, V. Chubar, P. Postyshev, Marshal Ya. Gamarnik, Manuilsky, Makharadze, and Lunacharsky. *Ibid.*, pp. 46–47, and Wolfe, *op. cit.*, p. 65.

[3] Quoted by Rush, *op. cit.*, p. 47.

[4] *Pravda*, Feb. 13, 1956, as quoted by *ibid.*, p. 48. Bierut died of a "heart attack" while in Moscow for the Party Congress. His death greatly facilitated the return of W. Gomulka to power and the development of the 1956 Polish Revolution. Some Polish Communist believe that his death at such an opportune time was not entirely coincidental.

in Tadzhikistan published merely a photograph. However, in the Ukraine, Belorussia, Uzbekistan, Latvia, and Georgia they gave him favorable treatment.[1]

THE INCREASED FLEXIBILITY OF SOVIET POLICY

While this erratic treatment of the Stalin image and the implied power struggle unquestionably had a direct bearing upon the course of events at the Party Congress, there were other less obscure but equally significant factors involved. One was the marked successes enjoyed by Soviet diplomacy during 1955. The substantial achievements of the Khrushchev-Bulganin tour of Asia had vindicated the decision to shift the regime's policy away from traditional methods of expansion to a more subtle and highly sophisticated program of economic and political penetration. The reception given such moves in both Asia and the Middle East had opened up fertile new grounds previously denied the USSR and caused the regime to cast a covetous eye on the possibility of further expansion in Africa and Latin America. Encouraged by their successes and believing that time was operating in their favor, the Russian leadership spoke and acted with an air of confidence and assurance which had not been present before.

Nevertheless, they were always confronted with the incontestible realization that in the last analysis their ultimate success depended upon a highly industrialized economy with a healthy agricultural foundation. Despite the fact that the Fifth Five Year Plan had been completed eight months ahead of schedule, Soviet economic development remained the regime's Achilles' heel. Important industrial and agricultural targets remained unfulfilled, the rate of growth was slowing, productivity lagged, and consumers' goods production remained negligible. However, these shortcomings did not prevent the regime from boldly establishing even more ambitious goals for the next five year period. While few realistic Western economists felt the

---

[1] Rush believes that this represented an 11th hour disagreement within the Presidium over the "de-Stalinization." He theorizes that Mikoyan informed the Armenian papers that he was going to attack Stalin, but the Presidium as a whole had not concurred otherwise the Ukraine would have been informed by Kirichenko. *Ibid.*, pp. 49 and 106.

Soviet Union could meet these, they did not write them off as merely propaganda nor scoff at the dynamic drive they conceded lay behind the Russian quest for industrial parity with the West. This was a measure of the respect the USSR's economic program had attained among its most sober critics.

One of the fundamental changes that took place immediately after Stalin died was the new attention given to the people's needs. This resulted from the realization that his policy of using unbridled terror to drive the nation was a dangerous and outmoded concept. His successors originally revised it out of fear that smouldering resentment would topple their new regime before it could consolidate its authority. However, despite their internal rivalries they retained this new concern for the people's interests long after the initial crisis had passed because they recognized that they could be made to be more productive if the revolutionary dream, which had worn more than a little thin in nearly 40 years of endless sacrifice, was replenished by a few material incentives and the creation of a way of life that was less demanding and not haunted by the specter of arbitrary arrest and imprisonment. The regime did not intend to allow this concept to upset the regime's fundamental goals or stand in the way of its economic development. But it realized that small concessions such as the promise of an extra pair of shoes, less cramped housing conditions, or simply the availability of more readable books and interesting movies would pay great dividends in improving the nation's morale. However, the great hazard of this approach was that any liberalization of Stalin's totalitarian system had a snowballing effect that was difficult to control. Once terror had been disavowed – even if only partially – there was the danger that the regime might never again be able to fully assert its authority without precipitating a general upheaval.

This principle was constantly being reassessed by the regime in the post-Stalin period and significantly was not repudiated following Malenkov's downfall. In fact, during 1955 there was considerable evidence that it was one of the guiding factors in Soviet domestic policy. Many of the developments at the Twentieth Party Congres, especially the repudiation of Stalin, can be explained in terms of it. By mid-1955 any number of cases could be cited as examples of the relaxation and liberalization that was in progress. Despite the repeated emphasis upon heavy industry during the previous winter and the conclusive figures that it had achieved a decided upswing by June 1955 there was no noticeable decline in the amount of consumers' goods in Moscow stores.[1] *Trud* and other periodicals carried on a campaign to ease labor discipline. Factory managers who mistreated workers, discharged them without cause, or forced them to put in overtime were criticized and held up for public ridicule.[2]

National minority groups were no longer persecuted with the same vigor as in the past. The Party's new position was authoritatively stated by *Partiynaya Zhizn* in July. It argued in defense of the importance of the continued existence of minority groups within the framework of Soviet society and directed surprisingly severe criticism at Great Russian chauvinism (which it mentioned by name) and the persecution of one minority by another. It singled out for particular attention the dangers of anti-Semitism and declared blandly that

the Communist Party has always waged a merciless struggle against anti-Semitism as a phenomenon profoundly hostile to the Soviet system.[3]

This reference was apparently part of a slight rehabilitation of the Jewish community that was begun by the regime in connection with the "Geneva spirit." From 1948 until the Heads-of-State Conference in July 1955 there was no official explanation for the withering away of Jewish cultural life in the USSR. Well-known Jewish writers and intellectuals disappeared, Yiddish newspapers and periodicals suspended publication, and references to cultural institutions rarely appeared in the press. There was every indication of a methodical purge of the Jewish minority, beginning in 1948 and reaching a fever pitch with the 1953 "Doctors' Plot" just before Stalin's death.[4] However, the new

---

[1] *New York Times*, Jan. 4, 1956, p. 49, Welles Hangen. However, according to the United Nations Economic Commission for Europe:
"The rise in [the USSR's] standards of living, which had been very rapid during 1954, seem[ed] to have come nearly to an end, at least in the towns, during the first half of 1955."
Ibid., Dec. 7, 1955, p. 35, C. L. Sulzberger.

[2] *Ibid.*, Aug. 28, 1955, p. 30, Harry Schwartz, and *Trud*, Nov. 18, 1955, p. 1, *Current Digest*, VII, 45, p. 14.

[3] *Partiynaya Zhizn*, 12, June 1955, pp. 71–78, *Current Digest*, VII, 31, p. 5. Cf. Kolarz, "The Nationalities under Khrushchev," pp. 57–65.

[4] In 1957 there was an unconfirmed report reputed to have originated with Ponomarenko, then Soviet Ambassador to Poland, that Stalin's intention of exiling

regime officially remained silent on the subject until the Geneva Conference when a Soviet spokesman hinted that

something not quite above board

had taken place in the World War II Jewish Anti-Fascists Committee.[1] Further facts were revealed by the delegation of Russian newspaper reporters who visited the United States the following October. (The manner in which they dealt with the subject suggested that they had anticipated that it would be raised.) About the same time Warsaw's *Volksstimme* published a poem of L. M. Kvitko, whose works one of the Russian journalists had indicated were to be published in a new edition. During the early weeks of 1956 indications of a revival of Jewish cultural life began to multiply. Interestingly, these reports were published not in Soviet papers but in those of the Satellite press.[2]

This partial rehabilitation of Jewish cultural life did not have the appearance of a conscious effort on Moscow's part. Rather it was the consequence of the general relaxation of the stringent controls on intellectual life and minority groups in general.[3] Nevertheless, anti-Semitism was still present in post-Stalin Russia. Despite the fact that the physicians' conspiracy was repudiated, its anti-Jewish character was never acknowledged except by indirect implication.[4] Discrimination and persecution in jobs and educational opportunities remained the order of the day. However, in all fairness it must be noted that Soviet Jews were permitted to benefit from the increased foreign cultural contacts; they were included in the amnesties; and there was the tacit admission that they had been among those wronged during Stalin's last years.[5]

all Jews to Siberia precipitated an argument in the Presidium which resulted in his fatal stroke. Cf. p. 25.

[1] L. Ilyichev as quoted by Gilboa, "Jewish Literature in the Soviet Union," p. 6.

[2] *Ibid.*

[3] *Soviet Survey, op. cit.,* p. 4.

[4] Even in Krushchev's recitation of Stalin's "crimes" at the Twentieth Party Congress these two were not linked. He made no specific reference to the 1948–1952 purge of Jewish cultural life.

[5] After the Twentieth Party Congress some of the Jewish intellectuals still languishing in Soviet camps were freed. Also the names of several Jewish authors began to appear (at spaced intervals) in the *Literaturnaya Gazeta* in connection with the formation of special committees of the Writers' Union to edit their works, but there was no mention of their fate. However, volume LI of the *Bolshaya Sovetskaya Entsiklopediya*, which appeared in September 1958, did list the date of the deaths (but not the cause) of four. Gilboa, *op. cit.,* p. 6, and the *New York Times (Int. Ed.),* Sept. 15, 1958, p. 2, Max Frankel.

Despite a softening of the regime's attitude toward minority groups during 1955 it was determined not to let local nationalism stand in its way. *Izvestia* made this clear when it commented that

it [local nationalism] strives to forment hatred among peoples and sometimes finds expression in the idealization of backward local traditions that hinder economic and cultural development of national regions.[1]

While this was undoubtably true, it posed a serious dilemma for Moscow. In its simplest terms the regime was forced to choose between maximum efficiency in its internal program or maximum prestige abroad among the non-white population of the Afro-Asian countries.

Religion was another area where relaxation was evident. During 1955 it was given a new lease on life. In the latter part of the year two Roman Catholic bishops in Lithuania were consecrated in accordance with instructions from the Vatican. This was an important step toward normalizing relations with Rome.[2] Religious leaders were treated with a public respect unknown since the Second World War.[3] This had the double advantage of pacifying domestic sentiment and simultaneously providing the regime with effective foreign propaganda. During the summer various church leaders began to appear at the Moscow receptions given in the honor of visiting foreign dignitaries. This first became noticeable when Bulganin entertained Nehru in the Kremlin. Among those present to greet him were Alexei, Patriarch of Moscow and All Russia, Khaletdinov, Chairman of the Moslem Ecclesiastic Administration for European Russia and Siberia, and the Orthodox Metropolitan Nikolai, who had been active in the regime's various "peace offensives."[4] The extent to which the regime was willing to go to impress its guests with religious freedom in the USSR was illustrated the following October when it especially brought the Pandida Kambo Lama, the leader of the Central Spiritual Administration of Buddhists in the USSR, to Moscow to meet the Burmese Premier, U Nu, during his visit.[5]

[1] *Izvestia*, Oct. 28, 1955, as quoted by the *New York Times*, Oct. 30, 1955, p. 13, Welles Hangen.

[2] "Catholics in Soviet Russia," BBC, Sept. 14, 1955.

[3] The head of the Russian Orthodox Church and one of the Moslem leaders were awarded high Soviet decorations during 1955.

[4] "Church Leaders at Soviet Receptions," BBC, Sept. 22, 1955.

[5] Kolarz, "Recent Soviet Attitudes toward Religion," p. 19.

Also funds were diverted from the state treasury for the restoration of certain churches such as the Echmiadzin Cathedral in Armenia.[1] The regime even went so far as to permit the publication of the first new edition of the Orthodox Bible to appear since the 1917 Revolution. Although the first printing was only several hundred copies, it was expected that subsequent ones would go over one million. The Moscow Patriarchate had also prepared the first comprehensive prayer book to be made available under the Soviets. The extent of these concessions can be judged by the fact that the high grade paper being used in the Bible was in extremely short supply and in the past all requests for it had been refused.[2]

These concessions, however, did not mean that the regime had abandoned its efforts to remove religion from Soviet society. *Sovetskaya Kultura* reported in August 1955 that scientific-atheist propaganda had improved noticeably since Khrushchev's remarkable decree the previous November which had called off overt religious persecution in favor of systematic dissemination of "scientific knowledge." However, some areas of the country were sharply criticized for not actively participating. The Soviet Navy was one of the groups taken to task for failing to maintain the indoctrination at a high level. *Sovetsky Flot*, its official organ, stated that it had "visibly weakened" during 1955.[3]

Not to be overlooked were the changes that continued to take place in artistic and intellectual circles throughout 1955. Neither the Second All-Union Writers' Congress which had been held in the closing days of 1954 nor the downgrading of Malenkov two months later had completely reversed the liberalizing trend that had been set in motion by Stalin's death. The situation was extremely fluid with both artists and Party officials searching for a new definition for the regime's doctrine of social realism which would satisfy the requirements of the changing conditions of Soviet society.

Writers who had formerly been branded "rootless cosmopolitans" began to reappear in print, a publication devoted exclusively to foreign literature made its appearance, Western authors

---

[1] *New York Times*, Oct. 15, 1955, p. 13, Harry Schwartz.
[2] *Ibid.*, Dec. 4, 1955, p. 30.
[3] *Sovetskaya Kultura*, Aug. 16, 1955, p. 1, *Current Digest*, VII, 33, p. 33, and *Sovetsky Flot*, Sept. 6, 1955, p. 1, *ibid.*, VII, 36, p. 28.

such as Hemingway who had long been in disfavor were translated and published, and even such Russian classics as Dostojevsky were re-issued for the first time since 1930.[1] However, the development of a new climate was not accomplished without controversy, but, by and large, the movement was toward a more liberal position than had previously been permitted. For example, in the closing days of September 1955 Fadeyev, the former General Secretary of the Writers' Union and usually a staunch advocate of the official position, suggested that it was time for social realism to be re-defined and brought up to date. He went so far as to suggest that Soviet writers might profit by observing Western literature. These proposals went beyond any that had been made the previous December at the Second All-Union Writers' Congress where a milder position had won acceptance. They paralleled similar efforts which were being made to stimulate both Soviet music and the graphic arts.[2]

The key point in this search for a new interpretation of the artist's relationship to the regime was whether it was necessary for him to embody *partiynost* (Party outlook) in all of his works. At the Nineteenth Party Congress in 1952 Malenkov had answered emphaticly in the affirmative. However, in December 1955 *Kommunist* vigorously rejected this assertion. It pointed out that many non-Communist and bourgeois artists who did not accept the need for *partiynost* created powerful works of art

reflecting the life of the working class.[3]

Just prior to the Twentieth Party Congress Khachaturian translated this into more concrete terms by rejecting the contention that it was necessary for creative work to be confined to such subjects as virgin lands, tractors, or production norms to meet the requirements of the Party. In his view:

An honest artist is a mirror reflecting the principle and most important aspects of life. He can concern himself with historical or contemporary subjects, with agriculture, or lyrics.

Khachaturian believed that in the past *partiynost* had been too strictly interpreted. In art he felt it should be defined as

that which is actually going on now and interests the people.

---

[1] *New York Times*, May 25, 1955, p. 8; Sept. 8, 1955, p. 10; and Oct. 23, 1955, p. 35.
[2] *Ibid.*, Sept. 30, 1955, p. 10, Welles Hangen.
[3] *Kommunist*, Dec. 1955 as quoted by *ibid.*, Feb. 13, 1956, p. 9, Welles Hangen.

He also reflected the wide-spread ferment in Soviet artistic circles when he stated that the artist should use his own intuition and not adhere too strictly to the Party's dictates in his creative work.[1]

One of the most significant areas of relaxation concerned the abusive use of arbitrary police power and the inhuman system of forced labor and concentration camps. In speaking about the "liberalization" of the Soviet police state it must be constantly remembered that at no time did the regime basicly alter its control over the population. What it did do was to modify the system in such a way that its most obnoxious features were toned down or removed as a part of the general effort to ease the tension of everyday life and make life a little more livable. This was accomplished in a number of ways. The forced labor camps in the Far East and the far North were reorganized during 1954 in such a way that the economic programs were carried out largely by "free" labor, i.e., workers who had been released under the terms of the 1953 general amnesty but refused permission to leave the area, new deportees, and in some cases genuine volunteers. The process began in the spring and was most advanced in those areas where there had been strikes by prisoners. By June 1955 it was estimated on the basis of reports from former Austrian prisoners of war that 60 per cent of Vorkuta's 500,000 inmates had been released. Conditions for those still under confinement were somewhat improved. The changes closely followed the demands made during the 1953 uprisings. They included the following:

1) release of all invalid prisoners and those under 20 at the time of their "crime" with permission to return to their homes;
2) release without permission to go home of prisoners having served two thirds of their sentence;
3) reduction of a large number of sentences by "Commissions of Revision" from the Ministry of Justice which had been working in the camps for over a year;
4) crediting prisoners with having served three days of their sentence for everyone in which they fulfilled 100 per cent of their norms;
5) sentencing of new offenders to deportation rather than forced labor; and
6) improvement of living conditions (i.e., bars on windows removed, numbers on clothing taken off, pay raised, and leave occasionally granted).[2]

---

[1] Quoted by *ibid.*
[2] *The Observer*, Sept. 18, 1955, p. 1, Richard Löwenthal.

While some camps were actually closed it would be a mistake to consider that forced labor had been done away with as a part of the Soviet penal system. Just how extensive the revision in the number of prisoners was is impossible to accurately determine. A large number of prisoners of war were released as a part of the regime's program to sway political sentiment in Austria, Germany, and Japan. Likewise, a considerable number of Soviet citizens were freed under the 1953 general amnesty and the much more restricted ones that were announced in 1955 and 1956. According to Soviet figures by 1957 there were only 800,000 to 900,000 persons under detention and less than 18,000 of whom were "political" prisoners.[1] In evaluating these figures one Western legal authority commented:

Whether or not these figures bear any relation to the realities, it is very likely that a vast number of political prisoners have been rehabilitated [since 1953].

Another Western source, however, took a different view:

Since Stalin's death no appreciable reduction in the total number of persons confined in camps or prisons is believed to have occured. Although the 1953 amnesty reportedly released large numbers of prisoners it is evident from the Soviet press that many of those released soon took up their former criminal habits and ended up in prison again. This was to be expected as the amnesty applied largely to common criminals, affecting few persons imprisoned for political reasons.[2]

In other aspects of Soviet legal reform there were strange contradictions. Although the new criminal code, which was ordered at the same time as the 1953 amnesty, was the subject of much discussion among Soviet legal authorities during 1954 and 1955, it was not promulgated before the Twentieth Party Congress convened.[3] While

a few of the most unjust laws were ... clearly ... repealed. The fate of the others ... was shrouded in mystery.[4]

For example, Beria's conviction (as officially reported) was rendered in violation of Soviet law. Also the practice of secret decrees continued to be so wide-spread that the actual state of Russian jurisprudiction was impossible to uncover. A striking feature of this practice was

[1] Berman, *op. cit.*, p. 1194, and cf. p. 48.
[2] *Notes – Soviet Affairs*, No. 172.
[3] It was not promulgated until December 1958.
[4] Gsovski, *op. cit.*, p. 16.

that such non-promulgated laws, for the most part, contain[ed] more lenient provisions than those in force previously. It seem[ed] that the government ... [did] not want the population to know of the new, more benevolent treatment of an offender.[1]

For example, a 1947 edict provided harsh penalties of from seven to ten years and sometimes as many as 25 years in corrective labor camps for the theft of public and private property regardless of the value involved. On January 10, 1955, a secret edict reduced this to six months to one year of labor without confinement or three months confinement and made the penalty for repeated acts of petty theft one to two years. The confused situation was summed up as follows:

The liberalizing tendencies of some legal writers ... [were] in conflict with the ... newly created laws. Only a few of them amounted to real changes. The repeal of harsh laws, if any, lack[ed] definitiveness. There ... [were] signs of changes in policies but these ... [had] not sufficiently materialized in law. Taken as a whole, the situation suggest[ed] the picture of traditional Soviet arbitrariness and not of a firm rule of law.[2]

THE TWENTIETH PARTY CONGRESS

It was these general topics – foreign policy, economic development, the improvement of living conditions, and the position of the Stalin image – on which the various speakers dwelt when they presented the regime's programs to the 1436 assembled delegates at the Twentieth Party Congress.[3]

[1] *Ibid.*, p. 17.   [2] *Ibid.*, p. 20.

[3]   *Composition of the Nineteenth and Twentieth Party Congresses*

	1952	1956
Voting delegates	1192	1355
Non-voting delegates	167	81
Age of voting delegates:		
Up to 40	23.6%	20.3%
40 to 50	61.1%	55.7%
50 and above	15.3%	24.0%
Percentage of voting delegates with:		
Higher educations	59.0%	56.2%
Incomplete higher educations	7.0%	8.6%
Secondary educations	15.3%	24.0%
Percentage of voting delegates who were:		
Party officials	n.a.	37.3%
Government officials	n.a.	13.1%
Industrial and transport workers	7.8%	18.8%
Agricultural workers	7.8%	13.8%
Women	12.3%	14.2%

"The Twentieth Party Congress of the Communist Party Soviet Union, "*Notes – Soviet Affairs*, 187, p. 23.

Foreign Policy

In the realm of foreign policy the regime's major objective was to revise its ideology so as to bring it into line with the practices of the post-Stalin period – particularly with those introduced during 1955 – and to create the foundations for future courses of action. To accomplish this it did not hesitate to edit, revise, and completely rewrite previously accepted doctrines and dogmas wherever the occasion demanded. It was hardly necessary to strike out into completely new territory because nearly 40 years of Soviet diplomatic history provided an almost unlimited supply of appropriate examples and quotations from which to cite proof that the new policies were not departures from the fundamental principles of the past but deeply rooted in tradition. Lenin's prolific writings were, of course, the most authoritative source that was invoked. However, the regime's spokesmen did not hesitate to distort the past if it suited their needs and whenever it was necessary they repeated – sometimes almost verbatim but without acknowledgment – principles from Stalin's *Economic Problems of Socialism in the USSR*, despite the fact that it was sharply criticized by Mikoyan on several specific points.[1]

However, the speakers were more interested in justifying their own policies rather than merely preserving *in toto* those of their predecessors. Nothing made this more clear than the Congress's repudiation of the rigidity and inflexibility which had been the hallmarks of the Stalin era. While Khrushchev did not raise the issue specificly in connection with Soviet diplomacy, his introduction of a bold, highly imaginative policy was sufficient to convey the point. However, should this have been lost on anyone, his remark that

the Party courageously exposed shortcomings in various spheres of economies, State, and Party activities, broke obsolete ideas, resolutely sweeping aside everything that had outlived its time and was acting as a break on ... the regime's forward movements

was a general enough indictment of the Stalin era to cover it sufficiently.[2]

---

[1] Mosely, "Soviet Foreign Policy: New Goals or New Manners?", pp. 541–553 argues that the foreign policy put forth at the Twentieth Party Congress was merely a re-statement of Stalin's doctrines, particularly those published in *Economic Problems of Socialism in the USSR*.

[2] Quoted by *Notes – Soviet Affairs, op. cit.*, p. 11. In the text of his speech to the

Other speakers related the problem even more directly to foreign policy. Mikoyan admitted that in the past Soviet diplomacy had made mistakes and "in some cases" had been responsible for the aggravation of international relations. These, he was quick to stress, had been speedily remedied after 1953. As a consequence, "certain hidebound" concepts had been done away with since the Nineteenth Congress, and he particularly praised the maximum flexibility displayed by the regime since 1955. He indicated that the Presidium was particularly concerned about the absence of any methodical study of conditions as they actually existed in the capitalist world. According to him, students were satisfied to limit themselves to specific details for "agitation" (propaganda) purposes and did not approach the subject as a whole. In some of the strongest public criticisms of Stalin to be aired at the Congress Mikoyan said that his thesis did not conform with the facts of the postwar period. The capitalist countries had not fallen at each others throats as the result of intensified economic competition but, in effect, had overcome their differences and formed a solid opposition to the Soviet Union. Mikoyan also criticized the closing down of the 139-year-old Moscow Institute of Eastern Studies at just the moment when the countries of the Afro-Asian areas were emerging as important factors in international politics.[1]

Molotov was even more specific. Indulging in the only self-criticism to be aired by a Presidium member, he was forced to admit that his Ministry of Foreign Affairs was among those elements of the regime that were ·

frequently prisoners of habits and patterns formed in the past, before the Second World War, which now interfered with the development of new, wider and more active forms of struggle against war ... [that] still suffer from an underestimation of the new possibilities which have opened up ... in the postwar period.

closed session of CPSU delegates Khrushchev singled out Stalin's expulsion of Yugoslavia from the Cominform as an example of his detrimental influence upon foreign policy. (Secret Speech, Gruliow, *op. cit.*, p. 182.) The version published by the Italian newspaper *Il Quotidiano* contained similar criticism about his policy toward China and India. (Wolfe, *op. cit.*, pp. 81–82.) Later at the funeral of B. Bierut soon after the Congress Khrushchev was reported to have told non-Soviet Communists that Stalin's insistance upon a veto over China's political development and his price for economic assistance had caused serious discontent in Peking. According to this version, the 1954 trip to Communist China was undertaken to patch up differences and prevent an open split. *New York Times*, June 4, 1956, Sydney Gruson.

[1] *Pravda*, Feb. 18, 1956, pp. 4–6, *Izvestia*, pp. 2–4, Gruliow, *op. cit.*, pp. 82 and 87.

However, Molotov assured his listeners that these serious faults had been corrected in time by the Party's ever-watchful Central Committee, and he exhorted his audience not to repeat these mistakes by continuing to underestimate the potentialities of the situation.[1]

This was precisely what the regime's proposed foreign policy intended to avoid. It was based upon a careful analysis of the current international situation and designed to take the maximum advantage of it. It sought to win support from the largest number of countries through policies which would attract the largest following and at the same time be the least offensive. Therefore, it was primarily oriented toward the so-called uncommitted areas of the world where the opportunities to influence sentiment were greatest. As it moved progressively Westward, its tone became progressively more harsh. The regime was apparently operating on the assumption that the hard core of the Western alliance could not be greatly influenced. Probably the best example of this was its uncompromising position on the fundamental question of German reunification. Khrushchev told the Congress:

> Establishment of a collective security system in Europe, renunciation of the Paris agreements, *rapprochement* and establishment of cooperation between the two German states – this is the right way to settle the German question. Certain circles, of course, want to settle the German problem without the participation of the Germans themselves and to the detriment of the German people's fundamental interests. Such a policy is unquestionably doomed to failure.[2]

Even so, there were noticeable differences in its attitude toward Western European countries and the United States.

The basic point of departure for this discussion of foreign policy was Khrushchev's statement that "it had become an irrefutable fact" that:

> The chief feature of our epoch is the emergence of socialism from the confines of one country and its transformation into a world system.[3]

According to his interpretation, which was merely the familiar repetition of the formula to be found in Stalin's *Economic Problems of Socialism in the USSR*, two world systems were

---

[1] *Pravda*, Feb. 20, 1956, pp. 2–3, *Izvestia*, Feb. 21, 1956, pp. 2–3, *ibid.*, p. 101.
[2] *Pravda*, Feb. 15, 1956, p. 1–11, *ibid.*, p. 35.
[3] *Ibid.*, p. 29.

developing under independent laws and moving in different directions. It was not a new concept, but it had never been put forth with as much vigor and strength as it was at the Twentieth Party Congress. In the past it had been utilized to explain the emergence of the "socialist camp" following the Second World War, but there had always remained an undercurrent of insecurity and disbelief. This, however, now had completely disappeared. When the regime's leaders spoke of two worlds, it was with the note of confidence that had been growing perceptively in the months preceding the Party gathering. Now, when Khrushchev addressed the assembled delegates, he made only perfunctory mention of the traditional "capitalist encirclement" while both Molotov and Mikoyan flatly asserted that it had ceased to exist. The latter illustrated the spirit behind the regime's foreign policy when he declared:

> Not a single major issue can now be decided by the will of the great Western powers alone, without taking into account the views of the Soviet Union, China, and all the countries of socialism.
>
> . . . .
>
> One hundred years ago Marx and Engels said 'A specter is haunting Europe – a specter of Communism'; it is now no longer a specter but is Communism in the flesh, tangible and close to millions and millions of working people. It strides with a firm and relentless tread not only through Europe but through the whole world, and it asserts itself in a loud voice for everyone to hear.[1]

This militant note dominated the entire foreign discussion and was an important psychological factor in the regime's bid for support from the newly independent countries.

When it came to an analysis of these respective "worlds" the regime carefully followed the well-charted path of its predecessors. According to this interpretation the Communist world was a growing, dynamic unit just entering the most fruitful and promising period of its existence. The capitalist world, on the other hand, was a stagnant, decaying society on the verge of both economic and moral bankruptcy. While it would continue to exist for some time its eventual disappearance was inevitable and its days were numbered. Khrushchev presented a comparison of the rates of industrial growth in both societies to "prove" this point. According to his figures, the Soviet Union was assigned a

---

[1] *Pravda*, Feb. 20, 1956, pp. 2–3, *Izvestia*, Feb. 21, 1956, pp. 2–3, *ibid.*, p. 83.

phenomenal rate of 2,049 against 234 and 181, respectively, for
the United States and Britain.[1] (What he failed to mention was
that the index year he selected [1929] marked the beginning of
the Soviet Union major attempt at rapid industrialization and
that the figures were computed from the 1926/1927 price level
which his own economists had discarded in 1950 as an inaccurate
measuring tool.) [2] This clearly showed, he argued, that inherent
contradictions would inevitably sap the capitalist world's
vitality. Its unavoidable collapse was being staved off only
through such temporary measures as increasing military expenditures, cut-throat international competition, the replacement
of worn-out capital equipment, and the steady depression of the
workers' standard of living.

On two points Khrushchev's analysis departed from the
traditional one of the postwar period. He acknowledged capitalist
advancement in specific fields and rationalized this by citing
Lenin's prediction that even though capitalism was on the decline
certain segments of it would continue to expand. The significance
of this point was that Khrushchev advised the Soviet economy to
take lessons from those areas where it was being outstripped by
Western technological advancement. This was a reversal of
Stalin's refusal to admit the superiority of the West and it also
created a theoretical basis for Khrushchev's similar admonishments of the previous year.

The second point dealt with industrial planning in the Satellite
countries. He asserted that conditions in the Communist world
had altered sufficiently to permit each of its East European
members to

specialize in developing those industries and producing those goods for
which it has the most favorable natural and economic conditions.

It was no longer necessary for every country

to develop all branches of heavy industry, as had to be done by the Soviet
Union.[3]

Tenacious insistence upon conformity with the Russian pattern

[1] *Pravda*, Feb. 15, 1956, pp. 1–11, *ibid.*, p. 29.
[2] Even so, the Soviet rate of growth was greater than that of the West but not
to the extent implied by Khrushchev. Royal Institute of International Affairs,
"Current Soviet Policies: An Appraisal of the Twentieth Congress of the Communist
Party of the Soviet Union," March 1956, p. 6.
[3] *Pravda*, Feb. 15, 1956, pp. 1–11, Gruliow, *op. cit.*, p. 30.

had been one of the hallmarks of the Stalinization of Eastern Europe. It had led to economic chaos in country after country where industrialization had been carried out with practically no regard for either its needs or abilities. Hand in hand with this had gone the insistence that deviation for national interests was treason of the worst kind and was unmercifully repressed.

Once the picture of the two-world system had been firmly established and the Communist camp had been clearly painted as the inevitable survivor, the regime's spokesmen began a well-planned and intricate campaign to win support among countries which were not members. This was done by attempting to gather some 1,500,000,000 people, representing all shades of political movements in the ill-defined, nebulous left-of-center in a gigantic "zone of peace" and forceably associating their goals with those of the regime. Khrushchev introduced the topic by asserting that:

> The forces of peace have been considerably augmented by emergence of a group of peace-loving European and Asian states which have proclaimed non-participation in blocs as a principle of their foreign policy. The leading political circles of these states rightly hold that to participate in the closed imperialistic military alignments would merely increase the dangers to their countries becoming involved in the aggressive forces' military gambles and being drawn into the ruinous maelstrom of the arms race.[1]

What, in effect, Khrushchev was doing was revising the traditional Soviet dictum of "whoever is not with us is against us" to read "whoever is not against us is with us." [2] Obviously, the Soviets were anxiously trying to identify Russian policy with that of those Afro-Asian countries who were seeking to avoid committing themselves to either of the world's major power blocs. Also they were attempting to prevent the development of a truly independent "third force" which would represent a serious challenge to Soviet plans. At the same time this maneuver was also directed toward neutralizing as many European countries as possible by appealing to those elements which were anxious not to become involuntary participants in a future atomic war. Conveniently, the regime chose to ignore the existence of the Sino-Soviet treaties and the supplementary Warsaw Pact which controlled the largest system of military alliances yet developed.

[1] *Ibid.*, p. 33.
[2] Mosely, *op. cit.*, p. 550.

While the regime probably adopted this position mainly to attract those countries which preferred to remain aloof from a rigid East-West grouping, there is the possibility that it may have been spurred on by the pressure of Communist China as a rival center of Communist ideology. Moscow was no longer in a position as it had been while Stalin lived to demand absolute, unwavering conformity. Peking was an ever-present alternative should the Soviet Union press its ideology too hard. Whereas Tito's regime was a rebellious outcast, Mao's was a full-fledged partner in the Communist world, an attractive point to those who might not be able to accept Moscow's leadership but were in general agreement with the Communist position. Thus, by propagating the concept of a broad, all-inclusive group in which there was room for numerous points of view, Moscow could still make claim to its leadership without forcing the participating countries to take sides. Peking's mounting prestige among the Asian nations may also have been an important consideration in the Soviet regime's decision to pursue its vigorous attacks against Stalin and the "cult of the individual." By implication these were equally applicable to Mao whose career so closely paralleled that of his Russian counter-part, and the Kremlin may have felt that by destroying Stalin's image it not only could solve its domestic problems but undercut and discredit Communist China at the same time.

The regime's interest in winning over the newly independent countries was made even clearer when speaker after speaker at the Congress referred to the growing importance of Asia and the Middle East. Repeatedly, they went out of their way to praise the struggle for independence and denounce in the most vigorous terms the United States, Britain, and France as exploiting colonialist powers. Khrushchev continued the practice he had so successfully begun in India and Burma of berating British rule by citing for ridicule the worst examples of the colonial mentality.

Frequently the various speakers played on the sensitive political egos of these countries by magnifying their significance in international politics. Adroitly their emergence as important factors in world affairs was associated with the growth of Communism. For example, Khrushchev declared:

The new period in history, *predicted by Lenin*, when the people of the

East play an active part in deciding the destinies of the whole world and have become a new and mighty factor in international relations, has arrived. In contrast to the prewar period, most Asian countries now act in the world arena as sovereign states or states which absolutely uphold their rights to an independent foreign policy.[1]

The identification was strongest with Communist China, the Soviet Union occasionally being willing to take a back seat to its Asian partner. The "Five Points" negotiated between the Chinese Peoples Republic and India were repeated and held up as an example of how relations between members of the Communist world and other countries could be conducted on the basis of equality and integrity. The way in which India was singled out for special attention left little doubt that it was one of the regime's primary targets in Asia. Not only was it listed separately from the other Afro-Asian countries,[2] but it and Communist China were referred to as nations which had emerged as world powers since the Second World War.

Khrushchev emphasized the importance the regime attached to economic diplomacy as a means of drawing these countries into the Communist orbit when he announced that

although they do not belong to the socialist world system, [they] can draw on its achievements in building an independent national economy and in raising their peoples' living standards. Today they need not go begging to their former oppressors for modern equipment. They can get it in the socialist countries, free from any political or military obligations.[3]

Soviet interests were not limited only to those areas where the regime's efforts of economic and political penetration were already achieving substantial successes. Khrushchev's references to "the awakening of the African peoples" and the "national liberation movements" in Latin America indicated that the regime hoped to extend the tactics of economic and political penetration which it had so successfully employed in Asia and the Middle East.[4]

---

[1] *Pravda*, Feb. 15, 1956, pp. 1–11, Gruliow, *op. cit.*, p. 33. (Italics added.)

[2] They were consistently listed as follows: Burma, Indonesia, Egypt, Syria, Lebanon, and, occasionally, the Sudan.

[3] *Pravda*, Feb. 15, 1956, pp. 1–11, Gruliow, *op. cit.*, p. 34.

[4] *Ibid.*, p. 33. Economic penetration was usually foreshadowed by stepped up political activity. During December 1955 and January 1956 Moscow was particularly active in the Middle East and Africa. S. Petrovich, a recognized Middle East specialist, was appointed Minister to Lebanon; D. A. Solod was recalled from Cairo to head the Middle East section of the Ministry of Foreign Affairs; N. I. Generalov arrived in Lybia as the first Soviet Ambassador and promptly made offers of eco-

Another important application of the "peace zone"-formula was the resurrection of the popular front movement which had several times before been a useful vehicle for Soviet foreign policy.[1] This phase of it was directed primarily at those countries where the left-of-center political forces (Communist and anti-Communist as well) enjoyed considerable popular support.

Khrushchev explained the regime's revised attitude when he stated:

> Not a few of the misfortunes harrassing the world today result from the fact that in many countries the working class has been split for many years and its various detachments do not present a united front.... Life has placed on the order of the day many questions which not only demand *rapprochement* and cooperation among all workers' parties, but also create real possibilities for this cooperation. The most important of these problems is that of preventing a new war. If the working class comes out as a united, organized force and acts with firm resolution, there will be no war.
>
> . . . .
>
> Cooperation is possible and essential with those circles of the socialist movement which have different views from ours on the forms of transition to socialism ... many ... are honestly mistaken on this question, but this is no obstacle to cooperation. Today many Social Democrats stand for active struggle against the war danger and militarism, for *rapprochement* with the socialist countries, for unity of the workers' movement. We sincerely greet these Social Democrats and are willing to do everything necessary to unite our efforts in the struggle for the noble cause of championing peace and the interests of the working people.[2]

Hand in hand with this went the regime's re-definition of its views on the transition to socialism. Despite their general leaning toward the socialist economic philosophy, the newly independent countries and the advocates of the independence movement in colonial territories had been reluctant in the past to accept Communism without serious reservations as the blueprint for their development because of Moscow's tenacious insistence that socialism could only be achieved by following unquestionably the Russian pattern. This, in effect, amounted to exchanging domination by one foreign group for that of another. Not until Moscow modified its position and was willing to accept

nomic aid; and the Soviet delegation to the inauguration of President W. V. S. Tubman in Liberia officially proposed the exchange of diplomats and suggested the posibility of economic assistance. *New York Times*, Dec. 17, 1955, p. 5; Dec. 18, 1955; (*Int. Ed.*) Jan. 7, 1956, p. 3.

[1] Cf. Domrach, "Again the Popular Front," pp. 568–579.

[2] *Pravda*, Feb. 15, 1956, pp. 1–11, Gruliow, *op. cit.*, p. 33.

nationalist movements as a step in the right direction rather than as the work of "reactionary" or "fascist" elements that would have to be overthrown before a country was ready to proceed toward socialism was there much hope of cooperation. Recognition of this fact was incorporated into the regime's current body of doctrine by a number of speakers. Khrushchev cited Lenin's assertion that while it was inevitable that every country would eventually reach socialism, each would do it at its own speed and in the process would contribute something unique from its own experiences. To prove the validity of this he pointed to the Eastern European Satellites (although not mentioning the role of the Soviet Army), to Yugoslavia,[1] and to Communist China, which he held up to the free Asian nations as an example of how the transition could be completed in Asia.

Much that is unique in socialist construction is being contributed by the Chinese People's Republic, possessing an economy which was exceedingly backward and bore a semi-feudal and semi-colonial character until the triumph of the revolution ... [it] is pursuing a policy of peaceful reorganization of private industry and trade and their gradual transformation into components of the socialist economy in the course of the socialist revolution.[2]

But Khrushchev desired to make it quite clear that these examples did not represent the only possible alternatives.

It is quite probable that the forms of transition to socialism will become more and more varied; moreover, achieving these forms need not be associated with civil war under all circumstances. ... True, we recognize the need for the revolutionary transformation of capitalist society into socialist society. It is this that distinguishes the revolutionary Marxist from the reformist, the opportunist. ... But the forms of social revolution vary. And it is not true that we regard violence and civil war as the only way to remake society.[3]

It was in these "more varied" forms that the popular front movement was skillfully introduced, because it was one of the most effective means of utilizing democratic institutions as a vehicle for obtaining the revolution.

[1] Marshal Tito's letter of greeting to the Congress indicated that the regime was justified in its belief that its efforts to tie Belgrade more closely to the Communist world through modification of its position would meet favorable response in Yugoslavia. (*Pravda*, Feb. 19, 1956, p. 3, *ibid.*, p. 89.) Just how far the Kremlin was willing to go to woo Tito – despite the inherent risks to its control of Eastern Europe – was illustrated by the warmth of his reception in Moscow, the disolution of the Cominform in April 1956, and Molotov's resignation as Foreign Minister the following June 1.

[2] *Pravda*, Feb. 15, 1956, pp. 1–11, *ibid.*, p. 37.

[3] *Ibid.*, p. 38.

In present-day conditions the working class in many capitalist countries has a genuine opportunity to unite the overwhelming majority of the people under its leadership and to ensure that the basic means of production are placed in the hands of the people. [Uniting with] ... the working peasantry, the intellectual and the patriotic forces ... [it] has an opportunity to win a firm majority in parliament and to turn the parliament from an agency of bourgeois democracy into an instrument of genuinely popular will. In such a case this institution ... may become an agency of genuine democracy ... for the working people.[1]

While he did not specify which countries he had in mind, Krushchev was probably thinking of Western Europe where the French, Italian, and Greek parliaments had sizeable socialist as well as Communist representation. Such methods he explained would not work

in those countries where capitalism is still strong, where it possesses a tremendous military and police machine, serious resistance by reactionary forces is inevitable. The transition ... in these countries will take place amid sharp revolutionary class struggle.[2]

Here, as in all other cases, he was careful to explain that the amount of violence which accompanied the revolution would not be determined by the Communists but by the amount of resistance they met in their attempt to do away with the former system of government.[3]

In the past whenever the Soviets had raised the popular front issue they had shown no willingness to abandon their ultimate goal. Their tactics had been to create a broad organization in which political differences were supposedly abolished in the pursuit of a unified course of action. However, in all cases the Communist element had always retained its identity and attempted to seize control of the organization's leadership. They had openly acknowledged that once they gained control of a government through democratic procedures these were to be sharply curtailed and eliminated to prevent the opposition from regaining its former position. Suslov did not hesitate to tell the Party Congress that this remained the basic concept behind the new popular front movement:

Ensuring a transition to socialism requires the establishment of political leadership of the state by the working class, headed by its vanguard ... Political leadership of the state by the working class is necessary in order

[1] *Ibid.*
[2] *Ibid.*
[3] *Ibid.*

that over a shorter or longer period, depending upon the specific conditions, the capitalist class be deprived of ownership of the means of production and that the means of production be made public property, that all attempts by the overthrown exploiting class to restore their rule be repulsed and the socialist construction be organized.[1]

From this and other statements it was evident at the Party Congress that the regime intended to forestall the possibility of its acceptance of the parliamentary road to socialism being misconstructed as acceptance of any variety of socialism other than that practiced by Moscow. Exactly what the Soviets had in mind when they talked about the peaceful assumption of power through democratic means was made clear when Mikoyan pointed to the 1948 coup in Czechoslovakia as an example of how it could be accomplished.[2]

Another phase of the regime's intricately woven foreign policy program was its restatement of the often avowed belief in the principle of peaceful co-existence. This concept, which had become an increasingly important part of the USSR's propaganda after Stalin's death, was in complete harmony with the other phases of its program. It fitted nicely with the regime's assertion that it was speaking for the "peace loving peoples of the world" when it advocated a "zone of peace" and it strengthened the arguments advanced on behalf of cooperation of both the Communist and socialist movements in popular front organizations. The most glaring contradiction – the conflict between the picture of the two camps living peacefully side by side and the continuously repeated boast that the Communist system would inevitably win out in the contest between the two systems – was answered by Shepilov, the regime's most prominent theorist. He explained that the transition to socialism

matured at different times in different countries

and that while this process was taking place the two systems could co-exist. However, it was not to be considered a permanent relationship because in the end there could be no question about the ultimate supremacy of the socialist system.[3] This was a rather important qualification. After vigorously asserting that peaceful co-existence had always been a fundamental part of

[1] *Pravda*, Feb. 17, 1956, pp. 8–9, *ibid.*, p. 76.
[2] *Pravda*, Feb. 18, 1956, pp. 4–6, *Izvestia*, pp. 2–4, *ibid.*, p. 85.
[3] Cf. *Pravda*, Feb. 17, 1956, pp. 3–5, *ibid.*, p. 72.

Lenin's foreign policy and vehemently denying that its adoption was merely a propaganda tactic, as was repeatedly charged by the West, Khrushchev adroitly summarized the approach the regime was following in its efforts to expand the sphere of Soviet influence.

> When we say that the socialist system will win in the competition between the two systems – the capitalist and the socialist – this by no means signifies that its victory will be achieved through armed interference by the socialist countries in the internal affairs of capitalist countries. Our certainty of the victory of Communism is based on the fact that the socialist mode of production possesses decisive superiority over the capitalist mode of production.[1]

What in fact he was saying was that the East-West struggle had reached a stage where the use of military might had ceased to be the most advantageous means for a country to extend its influence and that economic penetration was a more effective weapon. He was acknowledging the regime's recognition that the fields of economic aid and technical assistance were likely to prove to be the decisive ones in the future. His doctrine of non-interference in the domestic policies of other nations was closely linked to an effort to remove the stigma attached to the forced Sovietization of Eastern Europe and calm the fears of smaller countries that the USSR intended to bring about the Communist revolution at the point of the bayonet. To support this contention he denied that it was possible for revolution to be exported from one country to another.

However, none of the Party's spokesmen completely ruled out the use of force. In fact, they made it clear – particularly Marshal Zhukov – that the threat of nuclear war remained an important weapon in their diplomacy. Since Stalin's death and Malenkov's 1953 announcement that the regime had broken the United States' monopoly of thermonuclear weapons the regime had wrestled with the problem of war in the atomic age. At the February 1955 session of the Supreme Soviet Molotov, in what had been a direct repudiation of Malenkov's statement of the previous year, had declared that

> it is not 'world civilization' that will perish, however much it will suffer from aggression, but the decaying social system of which bloodthirsty imperialism is the core.

[1] *Pravda*, Feb. 15, 1956, pp. 1–11, *ibid.*, p. 37.

Pravda had followed this up with the declaration that assertions about the "ruin of world civilization" in a nuclear war were "theoretically wrong and politically harmful" since only capitalism would be destroyed.[1] However, the Khrushchev-Bulganin joint declaration with Nehru at the close of their visit to India in December 1955 contained seven different references to the inadmissibility of nuclear war. The most important of these was the statement that the results of the Geneva Conference the previous July had produced recognition among the big powers

of the futility of war, which, owing to the development and thermonuclear weapons, could bring disaster to mankind.[2]

The implication was that the regime had recognized the existence of a nuclear statement and had accordingly switched its tactics to other fields. However, at the Twentieth Party Congress several speakers, including Malenkov, repeated Molotov's 1955 assertion that such a conflict would bring destruction only to the capitalist world.

The doctrinaire point of view on the question of war in general was that it was no longer inevitable because the "forces of peace" had grown to such an extent that they had at their disposal

not only the moral but also the material means to prevent aggression.

But, as Khrushchev and others warned,

as long as imperialism exists, the economic base giving rise to wars will remain. . . . As long as capitalism survives in the world, reactionary forces, representing the interests of capitalist monopolies, will continue their drive toward military gambles and aggression and may try to unleash war.

However, rather than concluding his remarks on this pessimistic note, Khrushchev reassured his audience that

war is not a fatalistic inevitability. Today there are mighty social and political forces possessing formidable means to prevent the imperialists from unleashing war and, if they try to start it, to give a smashing rebuff to the aggressors and frustrate their adventurists plans. For this it is necessary for all anti-war forces to be vigilant and mobilized; they must act as a united front and not relax their efforts in the struggle for peace.[3]

[1] Quoted by the *New York Times*, Dec. 20, 1955, p. 1, Welles Hangen.
[2] *Pravda* as quoted by *ibid*.
[3] *Pravda*, Feb. 15, 1956, pp. 1–11, *ibid*., p. 37. This was little more than a repetition of the interpretation given by Stalin at the Nineteenth Party Congress (October 1952). Suslov's and Mikoyan's statements even more closely paralleled Stalin's arguments. The former quoted nearly verbatim – but without attributation – from *Economic Problems of Socialism in the USSR*.

As a result he skillfully once again identified the Soviet Union with the cause of peace and created another important reason for cooperation between Communists and non-Communists.

Significantly, this statement of policy amounted to an ideological *rapprochement* with Peking, bringing Soviet doctrine into general conformity with the line proclaimed and followed for years by the Chinese Communist Party.

This was particularly true of such issues as the transition to Communism without the necessity of a violent revolution and with the participation of non-Communist parties and the possibility of peaceful co-existence and friendly cooperation with non-Communist states. Since the 1940's Mao's "new democracy" had given at least lip service to a united front. Although his regime had not been established through a peaceful take-over of power, it had come about through the collaboration of groups and individuals in all classes and with the cooperation of a number of other than Communist political parties. Peking had also pioneered in the use of peaceful co-existence in its Asian foreign policy.[1]

Economic Growth

The discussion of the national economy centered around the directives of the Sixth Five Year Plan which had been published by *Pravda* in mid-January and whose adoption – virtually unchanged – was a foregone conclusion. The most significant alterations were made by Khrushchev when he announced plans to raise the wages of the lowest paid workers, improve pension programs, and reduce the workweek to 40 hours.[2] The new economic blueprint was in the Stalinist tradition of preferential treatment for heavy industry at the expense of the consumer sectors, but it also embodied the modifications introduced in the three years since his death. This meant that there was greater emphasis upon agricultural development and the gradual improvement of living standards than there had been in previous plans.[3]

[1] *New York Times*, Feb. 25, 1956, p. 4, Tillman Durdin.

[2] Cf. Gruliow, *op. cit.*, pp. 8–26 for the text of the Sixth Five Year Plan in its original and revised form. The necessity for beginning a new Five Year Plan was probably a contributing but not decisive factor in the regime's decision to convene the Twentieth Party Congress eight months ahead of schedule. Stalin had permitted the previous one to operate for nearly two years before he bothered to present it to a Party Congress for formal approval.

[3] *Notes – Soviet Affairs*, 187, p. 26.

The Soviet goal for 1960 was an increase of 65 per cent in overall industrial production above the 1955 level. When this was broken down into its respective categories it meant a 70 per cent increase in heavy industry and a 60 per cent increase in consumers' goods production. To achieve this, total investment during the five year period was to rise by 67 per cent from the 594,000,000,000 rubles spent during the Fifth Five Year Plan to 990,000,000,000 in terms of 1955 prices.[1]

The individual goals for heavy industry emphasized the continuity of Soviet economic development during the previous ten years. They were only slight upward modifications of the targets Bulganin had put forth the previous July when the Central Committee studied the problems besetting industry. But more important was the fact that Bulganin had merely repeated the figures Stalin had established in 1945 as goals to be reached in 15 or 20 years. While they had been termed "visionary" and unrealistic then, they appeared to be within the regime's grasp. Their attainment would amount to a substantial step forward in the USSR's program to catch up with the West.[2]

Growth of Soviet Industrial Production

Units	Stalin's 1945 projected figures for 1960	1950 production (Actual)	1955 production (Actual)	Bulganin's July 1955 projected figures for 1960	1960 production (Sixth Five Year Plan figures)
iron (Million MT)*	50	19	33	50	53
el (Million MT)	60	27	45	60	68.3
led metal (Million MT)		21	35		52.7
l (Million MT)	500	261	391	500	593
(Million MT)	60	38	71		135
ctric Power (Billion KWH)		91	170	250	320
nent (Million MT)		10	22		55
ctors (Thousand units)		109	163		322
eral fertilizers (Million MT)		5.5	9.6		19.6

Metric Tons.

rces: Stalin's 1945 estimates for 1960: *New York Times* (*Int. Ed.*), Jan. 21, 1956, p. 3, Ellie Able. o and 1955: *Pravda*, Feb. 15, 1956, pp. 1–11, Gruliow, *Current Soviet Policies*, II, p. 39. ganin's estimates: *New York Times*, Jan. 15, 1956, p. 1, Welles Hangen. o: *Pravda* and *Izvestia*, Feb. 26, 1956, pp. 2–7, Gruliow, *op. cit.*, p. 9.)

[1] *Ibid.*, pp. 26–27, and *Pravda* and *Izvestia*, Feb. 26, 1956, pp. 2–7, Gruliow, *op. cit.*, pp. 8–9.
[2] *New York Times* (*Int. Ed.*), Jan. 21, 1956, p. 3.

The statistics dealing with oil and electric power were of special interest. Stalin's target figures for oil production had been surpassed by 1955 and the projected goal was well over twice as much as he had anticipated. The 1955 goal for electric power production had also been overfulfilled by 7,000,000 KWH and the Sixth Five Year Plan goals for it differed sharply from that established by Bulganin six months before. In fact, the rate of increase established for 1960 was close to that projected for 1970.

While these production targets – ambitious for even a healthy economy – symbolized the drive and dynamism behind the regime's efforts to reach industrial parity with the West, they could not hide the weaknesses which sapped its vitality. There was nothing new about the difficulties which plagued Soviet industry. They were perennial matters which became more chronic as the USSR approached a higher state of industrialization and the rate of growth showed signs of tapering off. Bulganin's studied analysis of industrial problems had correctly diagnosed the difficulties it faced and contained nearly all of the criticism which he and his colleagues again voiced at the Party Congress. Technical backwardness, managerial complacency and ineptitude, uncoordinated planning, and the uneconomic utilization of resources were only a few of the faults that continued to block efforts to overcome the bottlenecks which consistently stymied production.

The proposed remedies were likewise familiar. The new goals were to be reached primarily by better utilization of existing resources rather than greatly expanding productive capacity. Managers were admonished to shake off their protective lethargy in favor of renewed and strengthened "revolutionary discipline," engineers were instructed to adopt the latest technological advancements regardless of their origin, and planning officials were advised to be more conscientious in their use of resources. In short, as in the past, increased productivity was the watchword of the new plan. In fact, a special section of the Sixth Five Year Plan was devoted exclusively to how this was to be accomplished. Industry as a whole was to increase productivity by "at least 50 per cent" but in the field of construction it was to be 52 per cent. In agriculture the regime had even more ambitious plans.

On state farms it was to rise 70 per cent and a phenomenal 100 per cent on the collectives.[1]

These astounding targets were put forth at just the moment labor in the Soviet Union was in critically short supply. Gone were the days when industrial shortcomings could be solved simply by bringing more people to the cities from the country. This had succeeded in merely denuding the farms of their most productive labor force. The gravity of the shortage facing the USSR was illustrated by one demographer who estimated that the manpower supply from the younger generation during the Fifth Five Year Plan amounted to 10,400,000 but that between 1956 and 1960 it would be no more than 5,300,000 as a result of the Second World War. However, the Sixth Five Year Plan called for the number of workers to be increased by 7,000,000.[2] What was even more astonishing in the light of this tight labor supply was Khrushchev's announcement that beginning in 1957 the regime intended to return to a 40-hour workweek without any reduction in pay. This was the most striking economic development of the Party Congress.[3]

This return to the seven-hour day, which had been abolished in 1940, was probably prompted by the belief that a relaxation of the strict labor regulations would improve the workers' morale to the point where a reduction of absenteeism and loafing, would compensate for the shorter workweek.[4] But it is highly doubtful that by itself this would fully compensate for all of the wasted time (estimated at at least one hour per man per day) since much of it resulted from such factors as production bottlenecks, material shortages, and machinery breakdowns that had little or no relationship to labor discipline.[5] Therefore, it is very likely that strictly "political" considerations played an important part in the introduction of the shorter workweek. After weighing the

[1] *Pravda* and *Izvestia*, Feb. 26, 1956, pp. 2–7, Gruliow, *op. cit.*, p. 19. In the Fifth Five Year Plan productivity on the whole rose by 43 per cent, 41 per cent in the construction industry, and 37 per cent on state farms. Marchenko, "Problems of the Soviet Economy under the Sixth Five Year Plan."

[2] W. Ison estimate quoted by Marchenko, *op. cit.*

[3] *Pravda*, Feb. 15, 1956, pp. 1–11, Gruliow, *op. cit.*, pp. 48–49.

[4] The regime apparently intended to use the new schedule as an incentive to greater work because Khrushchev made its adoption contingent upon the "constant growth of production and an increase in labor productivity." *Ibid.*, p. 49.

[5] *Notes – Soviet Affairs, op. cit.*, p. 28.

various factors the regime must have come to the conclusion that despite the economy's critical need for labor there was a much greater need to ease the pressure on the workers. There were several indications that it was turning to other sources to make up for this loss. Khrushchev implied that more women were to be made a part of the labor force when he called for improvement of public catering services which would free several million for "socially useful work." The expansion of the state-operated nurseries and the development of boarding schools may also have been directed toward this end.[1] One émigré economist summed up the situation with the remark that

the Sixth Five Year Plan ... [had] been conceived in a way involving the maximum drain of all available human resources.[2]

One of the most significant aspects of the new plan was the priority given to the industrialization of Central Asia, Siberia, and the Far East. For example, in Kazakhstan gross output was to rise by 120 per cent as compared to the national average of only 65 per cent. The 78,000,000,000 rubles earmarked for capital investment in Kazakhstan between 1956 and 1960 was 25,000,000,000 rubles more than had been provided during all of the other Five Year Plans combined.[3] Several factors lay behind the decision to so radically expand the development of these formerly neglected areas. One was the recognition that they were very rich in untapped natural resources. To exploit these efficiently it was necessary to process them locally rather than continuing the wasteful process of transporting them to existing industrial centers. Another important consideration was that such an investment program would help to rectify the country's economic imbalance and create a much higher degree of regional self-sufficiency. Aside from the purely economic desire to achieve maximum utilization of resources this had significant strategic implications in an area where dispersal might mean the difference between survival or destruction. The creation of an independent industrial complex outside of European Russian reduced one of the regime's traditionally vulnerable points.

These goals were to be achieved by first developing sources of

---

[1] *Ibid.*
[2] Marchenko, *op. cit.*
[3] *New York Times*, Feb. 5, 1956, p. 1, Welles Hangen.

industrial power – the increased mining of coal and the construction of greater electrical power capacity – by the end of 1960.
Simultaneously a well-rounded industrialization program was to
be undertaken so that within ten or 15 years these areas would
rank third in the production of iron and steel. Khrushchev's
gigantic agricultural gamble was clearly intended as an intricate
part of this massive development program.[1]

While the regime refused to waver from its position that
economic necessity dictated the development of heavy industry
at the expense of consumers' goods production, the Sixth Five
Year Plan made more provision for increased output of light
industry than any of its predecessors. Figures published prior to
the Party Congress revealed how badly the Soviet economy had
failed in its efforts to meet the already inadequate goals of the
original Fifth Five Year Plan and their subsequent upward
revision in 1953. The new plan pledged the regime to targets
which went beyond the "rapid increase" promised by Malenkov
two and a half years before. Khrushchev faced the problem with
more candor than had any Party spokesman since August 1953.[2]

The Soviet people knowingly accepted a curtailment of their needs in
matters of food and clothing, in matters of housing and living conditions,
as well as in many other respects.

However, he did not promise any rapid improvement. In fact, he
admitted that

many important questions connected with the rise of the worker's
material well-being have not yet been solved.... The Communist Party
and the Soviet government will have to do a great deal to raise the living
standard of the population.[3]

The closest he came to promising to alleviate the situation was
his remark that

now that we have a powerful and well-developed industry, a practical
possibility has arisen for rapidly expanding not only production of the
means of production but also production of consumers' goods. ... The
Party is doing and will continue to do everything in order that the
demands of the Soviet people may be satisfied better and more fully.
It sees this as a paramount obligation to the people.[4]

[1] *Notes – Soviet Affairs, op. cit.*, p. 29.
[2] Cf. p. 75.
[3] *Pravda*, Feb. 15, 1956, pp. 1–11 as quoted by *Notes – Soviet Affairs, op. cit.*,
p. 27.
[4] *Pravda*, Feb. 15, 1956, pp. 1–11, Gruliow, *op. cit.*, pp. 40–41.

In absolute terms the goals set for consumers' goods production were the highest ever called for, but they still fell pitifully short of satisfying the Soviet people's needs.[1]

However, any serious attempt at increasing the output of light industry meant a corresponding improvement in agriculture. Taking its cue from Khrushchev, the Sixth Five Year Plan outlined production targets of the same magnitude as he had called for in January 1955. The biggest change was in the already ambitious goal for grain production which was increased from 164,000,000 metric tons to 180,000,000. The others were as follows:

Sixth Five Year Plan Goals for Agriculture
(in per cent of 1955)

Commodity	%
Raw cotton	156
Flax fibers	135
Sugar beets	154
Potatoes	185
Vegetables	218
Meat	200
Milk	195
Eggs	254
Wool	182

(Source: *Pravda* and *Izvestia*, Feb. 26, 1956, Gruliow, *Current Soviet Policies*, II, p. 15.)

These target figures bore strikingly little resemblance to reality. They appeared to have had more significance as propaganda than as serious guides to future production.[2] Khrushchev was so personally involved with the agricultural question that for him

[1] In the summer of 1957 the author found it possible to purchase most consumers' goods in Leningrad although prices in many cases were prohibitive and quality often dubious. Soviet citizens reported that immediately after the Twentieth Party Congress there had been a noticeable improvement in the quantity of goods on sale. For example, white bread was generally available for the first time. However, they reported that such conditions existed only in such principal cities as Moscow, Leningrad, and Kiev and that a consumers' goods "famine" continued to persist in the countryside.

[2] While Western economists seriously doubted the Soviet Union's ability to achieve the 1960 target figures, they did not write them off as merely propaganda. It was felt that they represented a serious effort to simultaneously raise all three sectors of the economy. However, the general consensus of opinion was that before 1960 Moscow would be forced to revise its goals downward. In fact, the regime was forced to scrap the entire Sixth Five Year Plan in September 1957.

to have submitted estimates based upon the economy's true capacity would have amounted to an admission of his failure to deal realisticly with the crisis. It would also have exposed one of the regime's fundamental weaknesses when it was necessary to present a façade of strength and dynamism to both its foreign and domestic audiences.

Khrushchev sought to make the best of a bad situation by using future promises to divert attention away from the past and by attempting to confuse and distort the present situation with almost meaningless percentage figures.

Agricultural Production during the Fifth Five Year Plan
(in per cent of 1950 output)

Commodity	Year				
	1951	*1952*	*1953*	*1954*	*1955*
Grain	97	113	101	105	129
Sunflowers	97	123	146	106	207
Sugar beets	114	107	111	95	147
Raw cotton	105	106	108	118	109
Flax fiber	76	83	64	85	149

(Source: *Pravda*, February 15, 1956, pp. 1–11, Gruliow, *Current Soviet Policies*, II, p. 43.)

As Khrushchev was quick to point out,

while grain and industrial crops hardly increased in the first three or four years of the Fifth Five Year Plan, the gross harvest rose considerably in 1955, thanks to implementation of a number of well-known measures.[1]

He was thus taking personal credit for the improvements he alleged were borne out by the statistics. In fact, however, there was considerable reason to believe that even these ambiguous percentages – particularly the ones dealing with grain yields – had been "doctored" upward to hide the regime's disastrous failures.[2] But it was important for Khrushchev to vindicate his huge gambles in Central Asia and Siberia because of the vast amount of capital and labor that had been expended upon them. He seemed to be anticipating opposition criticism on the wisdom of the program when he reassured his audience that

[1] *Pravda*, Feb. 15, 1956, pp. 1–11, Gruliow, *op. cit.*, p. 43.
[2] They did not tally with the earlier official admissions that agricultural production had failed to meet the Five Year Plan quota nor with the implied absolute figures calculated from the individual percentages assigned the various Republics as their 1960 quotas. *Notes – Soviet Affairs, op. cit.*, p. 30. Cf. p. 178.

a study of available data shows that even with periodic droughts the introduction of grain farming in Kazakhstan, Siberia, and the Urals is profitable and economically justified. If out of five years we have two good harvest years, one average and two poor ones, it is still possible to farm to considerable advantage and to produce grain at low cost, in view of the relatively small outlay required for grain growing in these conditions.[1]

While he endorsed the wisdom of what had already been accomplished, he left the question of future expansion up in the air and did not set new targets beyond 1956. In fact, his only comment on the subject was that in any future extension of the program consideration should be given to promising areas in the Khasnoyarsk Territory, Irkutsk Province and the Khabarovsk and Maritime Territories so that the agricultural needs of the Soviet Far East could be met locally.[2] The directives of the Five Year Plan were more implicit. In the future, development of virgin lands was to be carried out only in those areas where large-scale capital investment was not required.[3] The implication was that the program as it had existed during 1954 and 1955 had been brought to a halt.

Part of the new lands program had been devoted to the introduction for the first time of corn as a major crop, and Khrushchev made a special effort to praise the wisdom of this decision and reprove those who had stood in its way. Adroitly, he linked it to the improvement of the average worker's diet. Between October 1955 and February 1956 there had been a 65 per cent increase in the gross production of milk over a similar period during 1954–1955.

Never before have we had such an increase in milk production during all the years of Soviet rule. It is beyond doubt that corn, the new system of planning, and the enhancement of material incentives of the collective farmers played a decisive part here.[4]

Although the absolute figures would have shattered the illusion

---

[1] *Pravda*, Feb. 15, 1956, pp. 1–11, Gruliow, *op. cit.*, p. 43. However, in 1957 after four harvests the United Nations Economic Commission for Europe could not agree with Khrushchev's evaluation:
"Two bad crops in every five years were part of the calculated risk envisaged when the scheme was launched; ... even if the climate is as benevolent as expected, nothing like the planned average return can be obtained at the present level of current and capital outlay on the virgin lands."
Economic Survey of Europe in 1957, p. 2.
[2] *Pravda*, Feb. 15, 1956, pp. 1–11, Gruliow, *op. cit.*, p. 43.
[3] *Pravda* and *Izvestia*, Feb. 26, 1956, pp. 2–7, *Ibid.*, p. 16.
[4] *Pravda*, Feb. 15, 1956, pp. 1–11, *ibid.*, p. 42.

of abundance, such a decisive percentage increase must have had a significant impact on those in his milk-starved domestic audience who could not remember the earlier years when the per capita consumption was even higher. In 1928 it had been about 440 lbs. per capita as against approximately 365 lbs. per capita by 1956.[1]

While he acknowledged that the introduction of corn had met with considerable resistance in a number of important agricultural areas he continued to defend it as the most profitable crop that could be grown in all sections of the USSR. However, the figures he gave for its future expansion seemed to be in contradiction with his enthusiasm and suggested that Soviet planners had decided to go slow during the next five years. By 1960 the total corn acreage was to reach 11,319,307 acres. This amounted to a drastic curtailment since the five year increase was just a little more than the new acreage planted in 1955 when it had risen from the previous year's high of 1,780,655 acres to 5,503,844 acres.[2]

Head of Productive Livestock in the USSR
(in millions)

| | | Year | | | |
| | | (as of Jan. 1). | | (as of Oct. 1). | |
Livestock	*1951*	*1952*	*1953*	*1953*	*1954*	*1955*
Total cattle	57.1	58.8	56.6	64.9	64.9	67.1
Cows	24.3	24.9	24.3	26.0	27.5	29.2
Pigs	24.4	27.1	28.5	47.6	51.1	52.2
Sheep and goats	99.0	107.6	109.9	135.9	136.8	142.6

(Source: *The National Economy of the USSR*, pp. 115–116.)

Khrushchev's report on the status of animal husbandry indicated that the regime's program of incentives, begun two and a half years before, was making gradual progress but not sufficient to meet the ambitious goals established for 1960. This he recognized when he admitted:

It would be wrong and positively disastrous to present matters as though all the difficulties in animal husbandry development had been surmounted.[3]

Even so he continued to promise an 85 per cent increase in the marketable supply of meat by 1960.

[1] "Background Information" Radio Free Europe, Feb. 7, 1957.
[2] *Pravda*, Feb. 15, 1956, pp. 1–11, *Pravda* and *Izvestia*, Feb. 26, 1956, pp. 2–7, Gruliow, *op. cit.*, pp. 43–44 and 16.
[3] *Pravda*, Feb. 15, 1956, pp. 1–11, *ibid.*, p. 44.

The Congress appeared to confirm earlier Western speculation that there was a movement underway to consolidate the collective farms into even larger production units and to increase the emphasis upon state farms. (In his speech Khrushchev referred to the latter as the highest form of organization in socialist agriculture.) His figures revealed that during 1954 and 1955, aside from the 425 new state farms established in the virgin lands, another 156 had been created elsewhere, presumably in the older farming regions. At the same time the amalgamation of the collectives in some areas appeared to have been stepped up. The speaker from the Stavropol *Krai* reported that there were 264 collectives in the *krai* compared to 1,132 in September 1953 and 6,399 at the beginning of 1950. However, the figures for rural Party organizations indicated that this trend was not taking place at as high a rate throughout the entire USSR.[1]

During January both the central and provincial press devoted considerable attention to a number of questions affecting the collective farms. This revealed that the regime's attitude toward the private sector of agriculture (garden plots and privately owned animals) as well as its position on *agrogorods* was going through a change. Khrushchev was put on record as praising the accomplishments of the collective of his former village which had greatly increased production at the expense of the private plots. At the same time, he suggested that the collective set aside some of its income to provide for the improvements of the farm's buildings and the construction of such additional facilities as homes, nurseries, bakeries, etc.[2] He repeated this point at the Party Congress when he recommended that the collectives manufacture bricks for their local use although at no time did he directly link it to a revival of his *agrogorod* concept. This point had been specificly repudiated as being uneconomic by Malenkov at the Nineteenth Party Congress when Khrushchev's drive for "grain factories" had been out of favor.[3]

[1] *Notes – Soviet Affairs, op. cit.,* p. 30.

[2] The achievements of Khrushchev's Home Collective Farm at Kalinovka were widely publicized in a special pamphlet published in late 1955. Its original press run of one million copies was much higher than would normally have been authorized for anything other than a state document. *Pravda,* Jan. 11, 1956, p. 2, *Current Digest,* VIII, 2, pp. 11–12; *Izvestia,* Jan. 17, 1956, p. 3, *ibid.,* VIII, 3, pp. 21–22; and the *New York Times (Int. Ed.),* Jan. 31, 1956, p. 3, Harry Schwartz.

[3] This point went unmentioned by the other main speakers but was, nevertheless, incorporated into the final resolution. *Notes – Soviet Affairs, op. cit.,* p. 31.

Another question which was under consideration just before the Party gathering met was the system of payment. During January demands for revision of the 20 year-old Collective Farm Statutes became more frequent. The tenor of this discussion, which was carried out in the press, was that the existing basis of work-day units (rather than actual output) impeded production. In 1955 the payment system had been brought closer to that used in factories, an important part of the *agrogorod* idea, by "advancing" farmers each month part of their anticipated year-end income.[1] This new plan – which was already in operation on some farms – would have brought it even closer to the piece-rate system. While the Party Congress did not make a major issue of either of these points, one of the less important speakers, F. I. Dubkovetsky from Cherkassy Province, indicated which way the wind was blowing when he urged that

it is necessary to reconsider the question of the participation of the collective farmers in the commercial economy so that the collective farmer will work not a mere minimum of workdays but throughout the entire year. ... Life itself shows that the small parcels must be reduced to a common denominator, with one tenth of a hectare [about a quarter of an acre] allotted per able-bodied person.[2]

Living Conditions

It was evident during the Party gathering that the regime was seriously concerned about improving the well-being of the people. It had not suddenly acquired a special regard for humanitarianism but was prompted by the entirely selfish urge for self-preservation. In the face of new problems of economic and political development not only their continued support but their energetic participation in the regime's program was a prerequisite for the country's further growth and the retention of its present position. If Soviet society was to regain the dynamism of the early Revolutionary period, which was so necessary to

[1] *New York Times* (*Int. Ed.*), Jan. 31, 1956, p. 3, Harry Schwartz, and *Izvestia*, Jan. 11, 1956, p. 2, *Current Digest*, VIII, 2, pp. 13–14.

[2] Quoted by Wolfe, *op. cit.*, p. 37. The peasants did not have long to wait. On March 10 a decree on collectivized agriculture revised the former statutes on several important points: (1) private plots were to be reduced in size and work on them subordinated to that on collective land; (2) the number of privately owned animals was to be reviewed; (3) obligatory minimum work-day units were to be established on the basis of "conscientious" output; (4) material incentives were to be increased for collective work; and (5) the advance payment system was to be adopted. *Pravda*, March 10, 1956, pp. 1–2, *Current Digest*, VIII, 10, pp. 3–5.

meet the challenge of the post-Stalin years, the regime had to recognize that the people were more than merely another ingredient of industrialization that could be manipulated at will by the central authorities.

While it is impossible to completely unsnarl the intricate motives behind the regime's program, much of what transpired at the Twentieth Party Congress, must be explained in terms of its efforts to come to grips with this problem. The introduction of increased material incentives was, of course, its most obvious effort. It promised stepped-up production of consumers' goods, advocated an upward revision of the lowest wages and a better pension program for the aged, introduction of a shorter workweek with no reduction in pay despite an acute labor crisis and the threat of inflation, outlined a serious effort to solve the housing shortage, and called for an improvement of the amenities of life. It is difficult to say which of these appealed most to the Russian people after so many years of continued sacrifice. Each was carefully calculated to have the maximum impact, but the promise of improved housing probably touched the most responsive cord. Other hardships could be born more easily if the cramped, congested living conditions were alleviated.

While statistics fail to convey the full significance of the situation they give some idea of the size of the regime's problem. During the Fifth Five Year Plan it constructed 1,600,000,000 square feet but this was barely sufficient to keep up with the annual population increase of 3,000,000, let alone enough to overcome the already existing shortage. In the new plan this effort was to be doubled.[1] In 1950 each person in the Soviet Union had approximately 41 square feet of living area. Construction during the next five years raised the average by an additional five square feet. If the regime met its promised goals in 1960 it would have finally reached the 1928 figure of 56 square feet per capita. The inadequacies of even this figure is illustrated by comparing it with conditions in other countries. In 1955 the United States the Federal Bureau of Prisons required a

---

[1] *New York Times*, Nov. 28, 1955, p. 1, Welles Hangen, and *Pravda*, Feb. 15, 1956, pp. 1–11, Gruliow, *op. cit.*, p. 49. These ambitious plans got off to a bad start. Six of the seven major construction ministeries seriously failed to fulfill their quotas for the first half of 1956. "Housing – A Failure of the Soviet System," *Notes – Soviet Affairs*, 203, p. 3, Jan. 16, 1957.

minimum living area of 60 square feet per prisoner. In 1951 the average per capita dwelling area in the United Kingdom and Italy was 215 and 161 square feet, respectively.[1] What these conditions meant in human terms was hinted at by G. Gradov, Secretary of the Board of the Union of Soviet Architects, when he lamented that

one of the evils of the present apartment buildings is that large units of two, three, and four rooms are usually occupied by one family to each room, which sharply lowers the living standards of the working people.[2]

Despite the prominence given the subject at the Party gathering, this was not the first time the regime had tried to deal with the problem. There had been repeated efforts in this direction after it had been raised at the Nineteenth Party Congress in October 1952, but it was not until the new regime was well established that they had achieved any momentum. In August 1955 the Central Committee had issued a decree calling for the standardization of building practices as a further move to reduce waste which was part of a two year old program to mechanize construction and put it on a mass production basis. It set extensive goals for the development of prefabricated parts and the standardization of hospitals, apartment houses, schools, movie theaters, etc. for the 1956–1957 period. Soviet experts believed that these efforts would make it possible to construct 2,000,000 square feet more of living space per year.[3] A short time later both the Central Committee and the Council of Ministers sharply criticized Soviet architecture as being wasteful, over-ornamental, and extravagant, calling the skyscrapers of the Stalin era completely unjustified.[4]

But material incentives were not the only concessions. There were a number of other less obvious but equally important ones which came under the general heading of easing the everyday tension that was so much a part of Soviet life. The chief one in this category was the repudiation of Stalin and a large number of

[1] *New York Times* (*Int. Ed*)., Jan. 21, 1956, p. 3, Elie Able, and *Notes – Soviet Affairs, op. cit.*, p. 1. Even in Moscow, which should have received preferential treatment, there were only about 45 square feet of living area per person. *New York Times*, Nov. 28, 1955, p. 1, Welles Hangen.
[2] *Izvestia* as quoted by the *New York Times*, Nov. 28, 1955, p. 1, Welles Hangen.
[3] *Ibid.*, Sept. 8, 1955, p. 10, Clifton Daniel, and Nov. 28, 1955, p. 1, Welles Hangen.
[4] Khrushchev had voiced similar criticism the previous year. *Ibid.*, Nov. 10, 1955, p. 3.

the things for which he stood. Psychologically it removed a burden that pressed heavily on the shoulders of the Soviet people. Closely connected with it were the regime's renewed pledges to safeguard personal liberties and prevent violations of socialist legality. To give these the appearance of substance the Congress indicated in a number of ways that the secret police had been placed on a much tighter leash and rehabilitated many of its victims. However, it had no intention of jeopardizing its ultimate control and uncompromisingly retained the basic characteristics of a police state, repressing with vengeance the formation of any effective opposition.

Some of its concessions had important international implications. One of these was the regime's continued renunciation of the inevitability of war. While there were significant diplomatic reasons for retaining this as a part of its foreign policy the pressure of domestic sentiment should not be overlooked. As a result of the devastating experiences of World War II there was a genuine desire on the part of the Soviet people for peace. The regime correctly saw, as Stalin had done, that under such conditions to maintain that another war was "inevitable" was self-defeating.

Another concession was the continued gradual loosening of the intellectual controls. Surprisingly little was said at the Congress about art and literature as compared to the previous one in 1952. Khrushchev's remarks on the subject seemed to imply that the regime had little new to add to the already established position that greater freedom should be allowed to the artist in his search for expression as long as he did not stray outside the rather vague limits established by the Party.[1] In the case of science and technology this process was spurred by the economy's desperate need for the fullest utilization of its resources. In education the regime proposed an important new program designed to encourage the development of a new elite through the creation of a system of boarding schools.[2]

[1] *Notes – Soviet Affairs*, 187, p. 32.

[2] The Congress did not clarify their exact purpose or give many details about their operation. As a result there was considerable speculation that they were intended either as a means of perpetuating the existing Communist aristocracy or reforming juvenile delinquents. However, later information indicated that their major purpose was to attack the problem of "hooliganism" at its roots by removing children from environments which might forster it. Cf. "The Soviet Boarding Schools," *Notes – Soviet Affairs*, 196, Sept. 26, 1956.

Destruction of the Stalin Myth

The most surprising feature of the Twentieth Party Congress was the treatment accorded Stalin. Events immediately preceding it had indicated that something unusual was taking place behind the scenes, but there was no firm evidence as to what it was. Although Stalin's image had been considerably reduced in stature during the three years since his death he had been retained as a positive symbol and assigned a sizeable niche in the Communist hierarchy. Therefore, the vigor with which he was attacked – both publicly and privately – had not been anticipated.

The regime utilized two methods to tear down Stalin's reputation. One was his outright repudiation and the condemnation of policies closely linked with his reign. The other was his successor's refusal to associate his name with any of their current programs. Both were employed at the public sessions, which were duly reported in the official press, and in the famous private session addressed by Khrushchev. The way in which the entire process was handled – particularly the public sessions where the attack was ingenuously reinforced and buttressed by deft manipulations of symbols – strongly suggested that it was the result of careful, methodical planning designed to destroy Stalin without participating a major upheaval.[1] Although Khrushchev's private repudiation was much more forceful and went beyond anything even hinted at by others, the cumulative impact of the public denunciations was great enough to set off both domestic and foreign repercussions before the full details of the others were generally known. In short, they dealt the Stalin image a blow from which there was little likelihood of its recovering.

The ironic feature of the public sessions was that, although there could be no doubt about the regime's intention, Stalin's name was hardly mentioned more than half a dozen times. The only four speakers to utter it from the rostrum were Khrushchev, Chu Teh, the Chinese delegate, Mikoyan, and M. Thorez, the French Communist leader.[2] The first of Khrushchev's two re-

---

[1] Cf. Rush, *op. cit.* for a different interpretation.
  Rush, *op. cit.*, pp. 50–51.

ferences was made in his opening remarks when he requested the delegates to stand in memory of three

outstanding members of the Communist movement

who had died since October 1952: Stalin, Gottwald and K. Tokuda.[1] This was a highly effective means of setting the scene for the events to follow since it immediately bracketed him with very minor members of the Communist world and was highly reminiscent of the March 1953 Supreme Soviet session when the same technique was employed to indicate his decline. Khrushchev's second use of his name was also merely a non-eulogistic reference to his death. Interestingly, the two foreign Communists who spoke of him, did so in the previously accepted manner. Chu read the assembled delegates a telegram of greeting from Mao which praised the

invincibility of the Soviet Communist Party created by Lenin and nurtured by Stalin and his closest comrades-in-arms,[2]

and Thorez made a similar reference a few days later. However, in the interval Mikoyan had already made the sharpest attack on Stalin to be aired at the public sessions of Congress, discrediting him by name and criticizing his *Economic Problems of Socialism in the USSR*.[3] This was the first criticism of its kind in over a quarter of a century.

However, much more important accusations were publicly leveled at Stalin without the various speakers invoking his name. Again, Mikoyan bore the brunt of the responsibility for repudiating what had previously been sacrosanct. The central point of censure was Stalin's violation of the principle of collective leadership through the glorification of one-man rule which Malenkov claimed had led to

peremptory one-man decisions and to arbitrariness, and, during a certain period, inflicted great harm on the cause of the leadership of the Party and the country.[4]

---

[1] *Pravda*, Feb. 15, 1956, p. 1–11, Gruliow, *op. cit.*, p. 27. The Russian word Khrushchev used was *deyatel* ("activist") rather than *Vozhd*, the equivalent of *Duce* or *Führer*, that had been associated with him during his lifetime. Significantly, not even *rukovoditel*, the non-charismatic term for "leader" was used. (Wolfe, *op. cit.*, p. 60. Cf. Rush, *op. cit.*, for a different interpretation.) Gottwald had headed the Czech Communist Party and Tokuda the Japanese.

[2] *XX S'ezd Kommunisticheskoi Partii Sovetskogo Soiuza, Stenograficheskii Otchet* as quoted by Rush, *op. cit.*, p. 51.

[3] *Pravda*, Feb. 18, 1956, pp. 4–6, *Izvestia*, pp. 2–4, Gruliow, *op. cit.*, p. 87.

[4] *Pravda*, Feb. 19, 1956, pp. 6–8, *Izvestia*, pp. 2–4, *Ibid.*, p. 92.

As a consequence, the position of the Central Committee was considerably strengthened since it received the major share of the credit for correcting the faults of the Stalin era. The role of the Presidium since 1953 was minimized and the part played by its individual members in formulating the regime's policy went unmentioned. Ironically, while Stalin's "cult" was being repudiated at the Congress Lenin's was appreciably increased. There seemed to be a direct relationship between the rise of one and the fall of the other.

The well-planned series of attacks on Stalin dealt with domestic economics, administrative practices, foreign relations, ideology, law, and justice. Mikoyan accused him of having ignored the basic facts of international politics in formulating his diplomacy and being guilty of not moving with the times. Molotov likewise acknowledged foreign policy mistakes of the past.[1] The ideological shortcomings of his *Economic Problems of Socialism in the USSR* were pointed out, and Mikoyan called for a serious study and critical revision of certain of its tenets. He also took Stalin to task for his revision of history in the famous *History of the VKP(b)* (*Short Course*). According to Mikoyan, if Soviet historians utilized all available sources they would be able to produce a much clearer explanation of many aspects of the Party's history. He particularly decried the absence of truly scholarly works which gave a full picture of the Party's history. The existing ones

arbitrarily exalted some people and even ... [failed] to mention others .... They exaggerated secondary events and belittled other more important events, and they under-estimated the guiding and directing role of the pre-revolutionary Leninist Central Committee.[2]

He was joined in this particular criticism by Pankratova, the editor of *Voprosy Istorii,* who called for a general re-appraisal of the Party's position on the distortions in historical writing. She pointed out that it was particularly important for the corrections to be made in time for the 40th anniversary of the October Revolution in 1957.[3]

Stalin's violations of socialist legality also came in for attention. Both Khrushchev and Voroshilov praised the steps the regime

[1] Cf. p. 293.
[2] *Pravda,* Feb. 18, 1956, pp. 4–6, *Izvestia,* pp. 2–4, Gruliow, *op. cit.,* pp. 88.
[3] *Pravda,* Feb. 22, 1956, pp. 9–10, *ibid.,* pp. 146–149.

had taken since 1953 to protect individual rights and prevent arbitrary acts on the part of the police. Mikoyan, whose criticism repeatedly struck more deeply, cast important doubts on the entire Stalinist legal system when he commented that

during Lenin's life and for a few years after his death ... Soviet jurisprudence and legislative and trial norms developed more rapidly in accordance with the ideas of Marxism-Leninism.
The same cannot be said of the later period.

He also began the process, which Khrushchev continued in much greater detail in the private session, of rehabilitating former Communists who had been purged by Stalin as "enemies of the people." Interestingly, one of the two he selected for mention was S. V. Kossior, Khrushchev's predecessor as Ukrainian Party chief.[1] In this same connection three days after Mikoyan's speech was published, *Pravda* repudiated the purging of the Polish Communist Party before World War II and rehabilitated Bela Kun, the Hungarian Communist, who had been liquidated at Stalin's direction.[2] Other topics provided material for criticism. Belyayev turned to agriculture for his attack. Although he did not specify their cause, he related that the present leadership had discovered

major mistakes and shortcomings in agriculture which ... [had been] tolerated until 1953.[3]

Bulganin and Mikoyan both cited the extreme centralization of planning and administration which plagued the regime as well as the excessive security measures that had been in force while Stalin lived.[4]

While these accusations added up to an unprecedented condemnation of his policies, they did not amount to a complete repudiation. This was never intended even by Khrushchev's much more devastating attack. Despite the severity of the campaign against Stalin, it was carried on within well-defined limits. Mikoyan implied that only the last 20 years of his life – that is his career between roughly 1933 and 1953 – were open to criticism. However, whenever it was necessary his successors borrowed liberally – although without acknowledgement – from

[1] *Pravda*, Feb. 18, 1956, pp. 4–6, *Izvestia*, pp. 2–4, *ibid.*, pp. 88.
[2] *Pravda*, Feb. 21, 1956, pp. 9–10, *ibid.*, pp. 122–123.
[3] Quoted by *Notes – Soviet Affairs*, 187, p. 12.
[4] *Ibid.*, p. 13.

this period. Probably the best example of this was the treatment of his *Economic Problems of Socialism in the USSR*. Although Mikoyan soundly denounced specific parts of it as being distortions of fact and strongly implied that generally it should be discarded, this did not prevent others – among them Suslov – from quoting nearly verbatim sections which supported the regime's foreign policy.

It was against this background of public censure that Khrushchev delivered the strongest attack in a session closed to all but delegates of the CPSU.[1] The format of his midnight address differed from the earlier public criticism by meeting the subject head on. Gone were the indirect references and the more or less hit-and-miss technique that had been employed by the other speakers. Gone also was the reluctance to attack Stalin openly by name. Systematicly Khrushchev catalogued his personal faults, mistakes, and crimes, documenting each accusation with hitherto surpressed facts and details. Nevertheless, he did not stray basicly from the pattern established in the open sessions. His charges fitted precisely into the categories which had either been mentioned or hinted at earlier. It was clear from Khrushchev's first remarks that he intended to stay well within the carefully defined limitations observed by others, adding additional support to the view that the entire campaign was part of a well-planned effort:

> The object of the present report is not a thorough evaluation of Stalin's life and works. Concerning Stalin's merits, an entirely sufficient number of books, pamphlets, and studies had already been written in his lifetime. Stalin's role in the preparation and the execution of the socialist revolution, in the Civil War, and in the fight for the construction of socialism in ... [the USSR] is universally known.[2]

This meant that the Stalin of the 1920's who was responsible for collectivization, the beginning of industrialization, and the early

---

[1] Although Khrushchev warned his audience against spreading the details of his denunciation outside of the Party, the way in which the regime subsequently handled the matter strongly suggested its intention was to let the people know the worst but to allow it to "perculate" down gradually rather than releasing it directly.

[2] Secret Speech, Gruliow, *op. cit.*, p. 172. The text cited here is that released by the United States Department of State, June 4, 1956, with the warning that it had been prepared for the guidance of foreign Communists not in attendance and might, therefore, represent an edited version of the original. Textual evidence indicates that it had been translated from a Slavic language other than Russian. (Cf. Wolfe, *op. cit.*, pp. 81–82.) A strong circumstantial case can be made for the arguement that this version was supplied by the Polish Communist Party.

intra-Party fighting was not the legitimate subject of question. Repeatedly Khrushchev indicated that the crucial dividing point was the years 1933–1934 and the Seventeenth Party Congress. Before this arbitrary date there could be no criticism of Stalin's brutal treatment of the peasants, his use of the Secretariat to seize power, or the elimination of his opposition. After it he could be denounced without fear for his arbitrary abusive use of terror and disregard for law; his willful destruction of collective leadership; and the growth of the cult of the individual. The regime did not want to tamper with the earlier period for fear of undermining too many of the fundamental principles upon which its continued control depended.

The picture Khrushchev painted of Stalin during the early 1930's was one which had not previously ever been hinted at publicly in the Soviet Union. It was one of a power-hungry dictator whose only object was the gratification of his personal goals, a ruthless ruler who would brook no opposition or let any obstacles stand in his way.

According to Khrushchev,

Stalin acted not through persuasion, explanation, and patient cooperation with people, but by imposing his concepts and demanding absolute submission to his opinion. Whosoever opposed this concept or tried to prove his viewpoint and the correctness of his position was doomed to removal from the leading collective and to subsequent moral and physical anihiliation.[1]

By the close of the 1930's these tendencies had become more pronounced and were accompanied by an insistence upon self-glorification which reached new heights in the publication of the *History of the VKB(b)* (*Short Course*) which he personally edited.

Khrushchev's recitation of the facts behind the purges and Stalin's conduct of the Second World War implied the presence of a psychotic condition. In fact, he described him as not only being obsessed by the idea of his own power, but possessed by a persecution complex which had reached "sickly" proportions before his death in 1953.[2] In the course of this discussion of Stalin's personality Khrushchev presented a detailed catalogue of how these abnormalities had impaired Soviet policy. In doing so he concerned himself primarily with the issues raised at the

[1] Secret Speech, Gruliow, *op. cit.*, p. 173.
[2] *Ibid.*, pp. 179 and 183.

public sessions, but also touched on a number of matters not previously mentioned. However, his selection of examples was not hit or miss. He raised only those issues where the regime felt pressed to repudiate the past. (A number of Stalin's equally serious "crimes" went unmentioned because they were still being practiced by the regime and subsequent revelations revealed that Khrushchev did not give an entirely truthful account of the cases he did choose to unveil.)[1]

Therefore, it was not surprising that one of Khrushchev's major efforts was to disassociate the present regime from Stalin's reliance upon terror and his violation of "socialist legality." He outlined in some detail the arbitrary use of police power and the complete absence of concern for individual rights which had characterized the Stalin era. With graphic clarity he showed the ludicrous nature of Soviet "justice" – the widespread use of torture to obtain false confessions, the liquidation of thousands of staunch Communists under the vague accusation of being "enemies of the people," and Stalin's insistence upon punishment irrespective of the facts. In the course of these revelations Khrushchev thoroughly and methodically discredited the secret police. He pictured them as depraved agents of an even more depraved superior. Beria and his senior officers were made Stalin's all too willing accomplices. On them he sought to shoulder the full responsibility of actions which could not be personally ascribed to Stalin, thus relieving himself and his associates of guilt.

Khrushchev also found it convenient to rehabilitate a number of Stalin's more prominent victims as a further indication of the regime's desire to set the record right. Among these were the large number of professional military officers who had been purged on the verge of World War II. This led to repudiation of Stalin's claim to fame as a military genius who had almost single-handedly master-minded the Soviet campaigns in battles against Hitler. The extent to which Khrushchev felt it necessary to redistribute the credit for victory to the professional soldiers

---

[1] This was most forcefully brough home by the publication of volume LI of the *Bolshaya Sovetskaya Entsiklopediya* in September 1955. Among other things, the purge of the Red Army continued until Russia entered World War II rather than being called off in 1938. *New York Times (Int. Ed.)*, Sept. 15, 1958, p. 2, Max Frankel and Harrison Salisbury.

who actually deserved it was a measure of their influence within the regime's inner circle.[1]

Not surprisingly, Khrushchev sought to shift responsibility for some of the regime's worst problems to Stalin's shoulders. This was the case with the crisis in agriculture which he blandly stated was the result of Stalin's isolation from the people and his complete ignorance of the facts. Likewise, the harsh repression of national minorities was layed to Stalin's abnormalities.

But these explanations always seemed to beg the question because they failed to explain how such conditions could have continued to exist without the active cooperation of his lieutenants. It was clear from Khrushchev's remarks that he was aware of these inconsistencies, and he tried to stave off the inevitable implication that this was precisely what had happened by using a number of devices to divert his audience's attention. One of these was to picture Stalin in such complete control that even his closest associates had no freedom of action. While there was probably considerable truth in his revelations that even the Presidium could not function properly without Stalin's personal approval, Khrushchev failed to mention that he and the others had been only too anxious to be his accomplices if it advanced their personal careers. A second method was to throw the blame for all excesses which could not logically be attributed to Stalin himself on Beria and his police organization. Still another device was to shift attention away from the present leadership's past failures to act by emphasizing the changes they had initiated immediately after Stalin's death in 1953. Nevertheless, Khrushchev could not completely remove the implication that Stalin was not alone responsible for the "crimes" he itemized.

While busily destroying Stalin, Khrushchev did not overlook the opportunity it provided to improve his own political fortunes at the expense of his rivals. At several points in his speech he represented himself as the only one of the present leadership who had had the courage to stand up to Stalin. The others he portrayed as weaklings in fear of their lives or in the case of his

---

[1] Significantly, when Khrushchev attempted to use the speech to further his personal ends, one of his chief methods was to identify himself with actions at the front during World War II and as a supporter of Marshal Zhukov in the face of Stalin's wrath. Cf. Secret Speech, Gruliow, *op. cit.*, pp. 180–182.

most formidable opponent, Malenkov, as being closely associated with Stalin's mistakes.[1]

Collective Leadership

On this point – the regime's internal rivalries – the Congress proved to be an interesting barometer. One of its most impressive features was the repetition of the collective leadership theme with its emphasis upon the equality of individual members. In terms of Communist symbols this was expressed in the unprecedented attention given the Central Committee as the Party's policy making body. Both the Presidium and its individual members were forced to take a back seat as far as public recognition was concerned. However, in reality the Presidium clearly remained the center of power. This was candidly acknowledged by one of the minor speakers, Z. I. Muratov, when he described the relationship of the two as follows:

> Plenums of the Central Committee were for us a school for study, a training school, and a tempering school. At plenums and meetings the Central Committee, its First Secretary, Comrade Khrushchev, and other members of the Presidium ... corrected [us] when individual ones of us ... committed errors, corrected [us] in a fatherly way ... regardless of post occupied or of record, taught and reared us ... and demanded a profound knowledge of affairs and concreteness in leadership.[2]

Nevertheless, there was considerable substance to the regime's declarations of collective leadership. The Congress revealed that the Presidium members operated as a well-organized and highly integrated body. No individual commanded a decisive majority although it was equally clear that Khrushchev enjoyed a distinct advantage over the others. Probably the best analogy would be to compare his position to that of the president of an influential board of directors.[3]

Khrushchev's position of "first among equals" was confirmed by the manner in which he conducted himself during the Congress. Aside from giving the two most important speeches – the report of the Central Committee and the repudiation of Stalin –

---

[1] *Ibid.*, pp. 180–181.

[2] Quoted by *Notes – Soviet Affairs, op. cit.*, p. 17.

[3] In July 1956 Khrushchev partially clarified the inner-workings of the Presidium when he acknowledged that the minor differences that existed were resolved through majority votes. *New York Times*, July 5, 1956, p. 1, Jack Raymond.

he interrupted lesser speakers at least four times to interject comments, a privilege not granted the others. The other members of the Presidium repeatedly made reference to his opening address in the course of their own speeches but they did not fill their remarks with the superlatives that had been so common during the Stalin era.

Another indication was the influence he was apparently able to exert in having his protégés elected to the Party's most powerful organs. He himself was made head of the newly created Central Committee Bureau in charge of supervising the affairs of the RSFSR. Belyayev was named his deputy with eight other members,

virtually all of whom [could] ... be identified as Khrushchev followers.[1]

His part in the election of five new candidates for the Presidium – Marshal Zhukov, Brezhnev, Mukhitdinov, Shepilov, and E. A. Furtseva – was also apparent. (Ponomarenko, one of the two former candidates, was dropped. The other, Shvernik, was retained but demoted to last in the new listing which did away with alphabetical order apparently to give Zhukov additional prestige.)[2] The latter's rise probably resulted more from the recognition of his stature among the professional soldiers and his great personal popularity rather than his allegiance to any one man. But the alliance between the military and the Party, which came to light with the arrest of Beria, was also an important factor. Brezhnev had been apparently hand-picked for his position as First Secretary of Kazakhstan by Khrushchev as had Mukhitdinov, Party First Secretary in Uzbekistan. Their promotions also reflected the increased economic importance of these two republics. Shepilov had been closely connected with Khrushchev's foreign policy and had taken his side in the pages of *Pravda* during the winter of 1954–1955. Furtseva was the first woman to reach the top rung of the Party leadership. She

[1] Quoted by *Notes – Soviet Affairs, op. cit.,* pp. 18–19. The others were M. A. Yasnov, V. I. Kapitonov, F. R. Kozlov, V. M. Churayev, A. P. Kirilenko, V. P. Mylarshchikov, A. M. Puzanov, and N. G. Ignatov. *Pravda* and *Izvestia,* Feb. 29, 1956, p. 1, Gruliow, *op. cit.,* p. 202.

[2] All of the full members of the Presidium – including Malenkov and Molotov – were re-elected. Cyrillic alphabetical order was retained in the listing of the full members, as it was in the Secretariat with the exception of Khrushchev whose name appeared at the top of the list. *Pravda* and *Izvestia,* Feb. 29, 1956, p. 1, Gruliow, *op. cit.,* p. 202.

had risen rapidly under his guidance in the Moscow City organization. At the same time Brezhnev and Furtseva were added to the Secretariat, bringing its total membership to eight. (Only the previous July it had been increased from three to six.) This continued the trend of adding much younger blood to the Party's highest bodies,[1] and also recreated the interlocking directorship which had been such a familiar feature of Stalin's control.

The Central Committee also underwent considerable change. While it is impossible to accurately ascribe these changes to any specific individual, the large turnover coincided with the appearance of men usually considered to be Khrushchev's protégés. All told, 60 full members and candidates had been associated with him at one time or another. There was also a noticeable number of men believed to be loyal to Malenkov among those who failed to be re-elected. The total number of full members and candidates was raised from 236 to 255.[2] However, more significant was the rate of turnover. Approximately, 44 per cent of those elected at the end of the Twentieth Party Congress were new. Analysis of the changes showed that there was a slight increase in the representation of both full-time Party and government officials at the expense of military and police officers.

Composition of the Central Committee

Occupation	Year 1952	1956
Party	103	117
Government	79	98 ⎫
Police	9	3 ⎬119
Military (holding command posts)	26	18 ⎭
Others and unidentified	19	19
	236	255

(Source: *Notes – Soviet Affairs*, 187, pp. 17–18.)

(Significantly, at least 12 of the 119 civil servants were former Party officials who had switched to government or diplomatic posts since 1952.)[3]

[1] Cf. *Notes – Soviet Affairs, op cit.*, pp. 15–16.

[2] There were 133 full members and 122 candidates. *Ibid.*, pp. 17–18.

[3] Forty full members and 71 candidates were new. This was a larger turnover than Stalin created between the 1924 and 1938 Party Congresses but not as great as between the Seventeenth and Eighteenth (1934–1952) Party Congresses. (*Ibid.*) For a detailed analysis of the fate of those not re-elected in February 1956 and a comprehensive break-down

The speeches of the most important Party leaders revealed sufficient variation on common topics to provide further evidence of individuality within the Presidium. Whether or not this reflected differences in substance or merely in approach could not be determined. The treatment accorded Stalin provided the best examples of this. Khrushchev, Mikoyan, and Suslov (in that order) were the most outspoken.[1] Malenkov, Molotov, Bulganin, Kaganovich, and Shvernik were more moderate in their criticism. Kirichenko, Voroshilov, and Belyayev all paid tribute to the principle of collective leadership but made no reference to its "restoration" or to any precise period when it had been ignored. Aristov, Shepilov, and Saburov

cast virtually no reflection on the Stalin period

and only Aristov mentioned collective leadership. However, that was in connection with the July 1953 plenum of the Central Committee which seemed to connect the reference more with the destruction of Beria than with Stalin's death.[2]

On other topics both Kaganovich and Molotov appeared to have reservation on the wisdom of certain policies. The former accepted the Central Committee's position on leadership as correct, but conceded that the struggle against the cult of the individual was "no easy question." He went on to describe the status of agriculture as being "difficult" and added that

measures for correcting the matter ... were elaborated and carried out to a certain extent.[3]

In his own field he appeared to be hesitant about a revision of the wage policy. While Bulganin advocated more speed, Kaganovich said that it was a question for careful study. Neither seemed prepared to accept the more egalitarian proposal Mikoyan appeared to imply.

Molotov's speech gave "indications of continued differences" between his approach to foreign policy and that advocated by the rest of the regime. Also he was the only member of the Presidium

of the new Central Committee in terms of its members' Party offices as well as a comparative study of the military's position in 1952 and 1956 cf. Meissner, "Partie und Personnelles," pp. 182–186.

[1] If only the public sessions were considered the order would have to be altered to Mikoyan, Suslov, and Khrushchev. *Notes – Soviet Affairs, op. cit.*, p. 19.

[2] In his remarks on agriculture Belyayev had, however, specified that the mistakes had been tolerated "until 1953." *Ibid.*

[3] Quoted by *ibid.*, p. 20.

to indulge in self-criticism or who did not characterize the doctrinal revisions as creative additions to Marxism. While he discussed the Party's position on the inevitability of war he did not mention the non-violent seizure of power.[1]

Both Molotov and Malenkov were unmistakenly attacked (although not by name) in Khrushchev's Central Committee report.

The Central Committee has had to correct persons who introduced disorder and confusion into certain clear issues which had been settled by the Party a long time ago. Take, for instance, the question of building socialism in the USSR and the gradual transition to Communism. The speeches of some people contained erroneous formulations such as the one that so far only a basis for socialism ... has been erected.

. . . .

We also have persons who understood the thesis of the gradual transition from socialism to Communism as an appeal for immediate realization of the principles of Communist society at the present stage ... Some wiseacres began to counterpose light industry to heavy industry, assuring us that preponderant development of heavy industry had been essential only at the early stages of Soviet economic development, that the only task remaining is to speed up the development of light industry.[2]

Their re-election to the Presidium inspite of this criticism and their earlier defeats by Khrushchev was probably the strongest indication of the limitations which still existed on his power.

[1] Ibid., pp. 17–20.
[2] Pravda, Feb. 15, 1956, pp. 1–11, Gruliow, op. cit., p. 60.

APPENDIX I

The Secretariats of the Non-Russian Republic Communist Parties

1952	1954	1956
The Ukrainian SSR		
1. L. G. Melnikov (F. S.)	1. A. I. Kirichenko (F. S.)	1. A. I. Kirichenko (F. S.)
2. A. I. Kirichenko (S. S.)	2. N. V. Podgorny (S. S.)	2. N. V. Podgorny (S. S.)
3. I. D. Nazarenko	3. I. D. Nazarenko	3. I. D. Nazarenko
	4. N. D. Bubnovsky	4. N. D. Bubnovsky
		5. O. I. Ivashchenko
The Belorussian SSR		
1. N. S. Patolichev (F. S.)	1. N. S. Patolichev (F. S.)	1. N. S. Patolichev (F. S.)
2. M. V. Zimyanin (S. S.)	2. N. Ye. Avkhimovich (S. S.)	2. N. Ye. Avkhimovich (S. S.)
3. T. S. Gorbunov	3. T. S. Gorbunov	3. T. S. Gorbunov
		4. P. A. Abrasimov
		5. N. D. Bubnovsky
The Estonian SSR		
1. I. G. Kebin (F. S.)	1. I. G. Kebin (F. S.)	1. I. G. Kebin (F. S.)
2. V. V. Kosov (S. S.)	2. L. N. Lentsman (S. S.)	2. L. N. Lentsman (S. S.)
3. L. N. Lentsman	3. — Merimaa	3. E. V. Ristmägi
		4. F. S. Ushanev
The Latvian SSR		
1. J. E. Kalnberzins (F. S.)	1. J. E. Kalnberzins (F. S.)	1. J. E. Kalnberzins (F. S.)
2. V. N. Yershov (S. S.)	2. V. K. Krumins (S. S.)	2. F. I. Kashinkov (S. S.)
3. A. J. Pelse	3. A. J. Pelse	3. A. J. Pelse
		4. N. J. Bisenieks
		5. A. J. Migliniks
The Lithuanian SSR		
1. A. J. Sniečkus (F. S.)	1. A. J. Sniečkus (F. S.)	1. A. J. Sniečkus (F. S.)
2. V. P. Aronov (S. S.)	2. M. J. Sumauskas (S. S.)	2. B. S. Sharkov (S. S.)
3. V. J. Niunka	3. V. J. Niunka	3. V. J. Niunka
		4. M. A. Afonin
		5. J. A. Maniusis
The Karelo-Finnish SSR		
1. A. N. Yegorov (F. S.)	1. A. N. Yegorov (F. S.)	1. L. I. Lubennikov (F. S.)
2. I. M. Petrov (S. S.)	2. I. M. Petrov (S. S.)	2. I. I. Senkin (S. S.)
3. N. P. Vtorushin	3. N. P. Vtorushin	3. N. P. Vtorushin
		4. V. F. Smirnov
The Moldavian SSR		
1. L. I. Brezhnev (F. S.)	1. Z. T. Serdyuk (F. S.)	1. Z. T. Serdyuk (F. S.)
2. D. S. Gladky (S. S.)	2. D. S. Gladky (S. S.)	2. D. S. Gladky (S. S.)
3. A. M. Lazarev	3. M. V. Skurtul	3. M. V. Skurtul
		4. D. G. Tkach
		5. A. N. Gavrilov
The Armenian SSR		
1. G. A. Aryutinov (F. S.)	1. S. A. Tovmasyan (F. S.)	1. S. A. Tovmasyan (F. S.)
2. Z. T. Grigoryan (S. S.)	2. G. Kh. Margaryan (S. S.)	2. G. Kh. Margaryan (S. S.)
3. B. A. Grigoryan	3. Ya. N. Zarobyan	3. Ya. N. Zarobyan
		4. G. V. Oganesyan
		5. B. Ye. Sarkisov

The Georgian SSR

1. A. I. Mgeladze (F. S.)	1. V. P. Mzhavanadze (F. S.)	1. V. P. Mzhavanadze (F. S.)
2. V. G. Tskhovrebasvili (S.S.)	2. M. P. Georgadze (S. S.)	2. M. P. Georgadze (S. S.)
3. V. D. Budzhiashvili	3. D. V. Mchedlishvili	3. D. V. Mchedlishvili
		4. G. I. Kadagidze
		5. Z. A. Kvachadze

The Kazakh SSR

1. Zh. Shayakhmetov (F. S.)	1. P. K. Ponomarenko (F. S.)	1. L. I. Brezhnev (F. S.)
2. I. I. Afonov (S. S.)	2. L. I. Brezhnev (S. S.)	2. I. D. Yakovlev (S. S.)
3. M. A. Suzhikov	3. F. K. Karibzhanov	3. F. K. Karibzhanov
	4. M. A. Suzhikov	4. I. T. Tazhiyev
	5. I. T. Tazhiyev	5. K. U. Uspanov

The Azerbaidznan SSR

1. M. D. Bagirov (F. S.)	1. I. D. Mustafayev (F. S.)	1. I. D. Mustafayev (F. S.)
2. V. Yu. Samedov (S. S.)	2. V. Yu. Samedov (S. S.)	2. D. N. Yakovlev (S. S.)
3. Yu. M. Abdullayev	3. M. A. Iskenderov	3. M. A. Iskenderov
		4. G. Sh. Efendiyev
		5. A. S. Bairamov

The Uzbek SSR

1. A. I. Niazov (F. S.)	1. A. I. Niazov (F. S.)	1. N. A. Mukhitdinov (F. S.)
2. R. Ye. Melnikov (S. S.)	2. R. Ye. Melnikov (S. S.)	2. R. Ye. Melnikov (S. S.)
3. S. Kamalov	3. S. Kamalov	3. A. A. Alimov
		4. M. A. Abdurazakov
		5. Z. R. Rakhimbabayeva

The Turkmenian SSR

1. S. Babayev (F. S.)	1. S. Babayev (F. S.)	1. S. Babayev (F. S.)
2. A. Sennikov (S. S.)	2. F. A. Grishayenkov (S. S.)	2. F. A. Grishayenkov (S. S.)
3. O. Shikh-Muradov	3. N. Durdiyeva	3. N. Durdiyeva
		4. V. K. Akulintsev
		5. R. A. Chariyev

The Tadzhik SSR

1. B. G. Gafurov (F. S.)	1. B. G. Gafurov (F. S.)	1. B. G. Gafurov (F. S.)
2. P. S. Obnosov (S. S.)	2. P. S. Obnosov (S. S.)	2. P. S. Obnosov (S. S.)
3. Z. A. Khalikova	3. T. Uldzhabayev	3. A. Imamov
		4. A. V. Nosenkov
		5. M. Rakhmatov

The Kirgiz SSR

1. I. R. Razzakov (F. S.)	1. I. R. Razzakov (F. S.)	1. I. R. Razzakov (F. S.)
2. V. N. Churkin (S. S.)	2. V. N. Churkin (S. S.)	2. V. N. Churkin (S. S.)
3. K. K. Karakeyev	3. K. K. Karakeyev	3. K. K. Karakeyev
		4. V. N. Ostaplyuk
		5. M. Abdykulov

(Source: 1952 = *Pravda*, Sept. 20–30, 1952, p. 2, Gruliow (Ed.), *Current Soviet Policies*, (I), pp. 53–88.

1954 = Meissner, "Neuwahl des obersten 'Sowjetparlaments' und Parteisäuberungen," pp. 221–222.

1956 = Meissner, *The Communist Party of the Soviet Union*, pp. 137–144.)

Changes in the Composition of the CPSU and Republic Central Committees
as the Result of the 1956 Party Congresses

	Total Number of Members	Total Number of Candidates	Number of New Members	Number of New Candidates	Number of Members Not Re-elected	Number of Candidates Not Re-elected	Number of Candidates Promoted to Full Membership	Number of Members Demoted to Candidate Status	Net Change in Number of Full Members	Net Change in Number of Candidates
CPSU	131	122	41	71	37	49	12	4	+12	+14
Ukraine	111	63	22	30	28	23	8	1	+ 1	0
Belorussia	127	75	15	20	13	11	8	4	+ 6	+ 5
Estonia	85	29	31	13	20	6	2	2	+11	+ 9
Latvia	85	33	26	13	22	7	6	2	+ 8	+ 2
Lithuania	99	41	35	17	22	19	6	3	+16	− 5
Karelo-Finland	75	25	33	20	27	20	1	1	+ 6	0
Moldavia	89	29	22	14	24	8	6	0	+ 4	0
Georgia	89	43	20	20	17	10	5	0	+ 9	+ 4
Azerbaidzhan	85	35	31	17	22	11	5	2	+12	+ 3
Turkmenistan	95	45	13	20	18	15	6	1	0	0
Uzbekhstan	145	55	24	21	16	16	8	4	+10	+ 1
Kazakhstan	123	57	46	31	30	21	9	0	+25	+ 1
Kirgizia	79	29	21	16	25	10	6	1	+ 1	+ 1
Tadzhikistan	97	57	25	37	15	13	9	7	+12	+22
Armenia	75	25	16	9	18	4	5	0	+ 3	0

(Source: Meissner, *The Communist Paty in the Soviet Union*, pp. 105–136.)

Glossary of Communist Periodicals and Books

The Soviet Union

1. Periodicals

Bakinsky Rabochy (*Baku Worker*)	Daily	Azerbaizhan Party Central and Baku Committees
Bloknot Agitatora (*Agitator's Notebook*)	Trimonthly	Propaganda and Agitation Department of the Moscow City and Province Party Committees
Bolshevik (*The Bolshevik*)		Renamed *Kommunist*, October 1952. (See below.)
Bratsky Vestnik (*Brother's Journal*)		All-Union Council of Evangelical Christian-Baptists
Dengi i Kredit (*Money and Credit*)	Monthly	USSR State Bank
Izvestia (*News*)	Daily	Presidium of the USSR Supreme Soviet
Kazakhstanaskaya Pravda (*Kazakhstan Truth*)	Daily	Kazakh Party Central Committee
Kommunist (*Communist*)	18 times a year	CPSU Central Committee
Kommunist Tadzhikistana (*Tadzhikistan Communist*)	Daily	Tadzhik Party Central Committee, Stalinbad *Obkom*, and Supreme Soviet
Komsomolskaya Pravda (*Young Communist League Truth*)	Daily	Komsomol Central Committee
Krasnaya Zvezda (*Red Star*)	Daily	USSR Ministry of Defense
Literaturnaya Gazeta (*Literary Gazette*)	Triweekly	Soviet Writers' Union
Molodoi Kommunist (*Young Communist*)	Monthly	Komsomol Central Committee
Novy Mir (*New World*)	Monthly	Soviet Writers' Union
Ogonyok (*Flame*)	Weekly	CPSU Central Committee
Oktyabr (*October*)	Monthly	Soviet Writers' Union
Palestinski Sbornik (*Palestine Journal*)	Monthly	
Partiynaya Zhizn (*Party Life*)	Semimonthly	CPSU Central Committee
Planovoye Khozyaystvo (*Planned Economy*)	Bimonthly	State Planning Committee
Pochvovedenie (*Pedology*)		
Pravda (*Truth*)	Daily	CPSU Central Committee
Sovetskaya Kultura (*Soviet Culture*)	Triweekly	USSR Ministry of Culture
Sovetskaya Moldavia (*Soviet Moldavia*)	Daily	Moldavian Party Central Committee and Supreme Soviet

Sovetskaya Muzyka (*Soviet Music*)	Monthly	Union of Composers and Committee on the Affairs of the Arts
Sovetskoye Gosudarstvo i Pravo (*Soviet State and Law*)	Eight times a year	Academy of Sciences' Law Institute and the Institute of Judicial Science of the Ministry of Justice
Sovetskoye Vostokovedenie (*Soviet Orientalogy*)	Monthly	
Sovetsky Flot (*Soviet Fleet*)	Daily	USSR Ministry of Defense
Teatr (*Theater*)	Monthly	Soviet Writers' Union
Trud (*Labor*)	Daily	Central Council of Trade Unions
Voennaya Mysl (*Military Thought*)	Monthly	General Staff of the USSR Ministry of Defense (Circulation limited to general officers.)
Voprosy Filosofii (*Problems of Philosophy*)	Monthly	Academy of Sciences' Philosophy Institute
Voprosy Istorii (*Problems of History*)	Monthly	Academy of Sciences' History Institute
Zarya Vostoka (*Dawn of the East*)	Daily	Georgian Party Central and Tiflis Committees and Supreme Soviet
Znamya (*Banner*)	Monthly	Soviet Writers' Union
Zvezda (*Star*)	Monthly	Soviet Writers' Union (Leningrad)

2. Books

Bolshaya Sovetskaya Entsiklopediya (*The Large Soviet Encyclopedia*)
Entsklopedicheskii Slovar (*The Encyclopedic Dictionary*)
Istochniki Voennogo Moguchestva Sovetskogo Soiuza (*Sources of the Military Might of the Soviet Union*)
J. V. Stalin o Stroitelstve Kommunizma v SSSR (*J. V. Stalin on the Building of Communism in the USSR*)
Marksizm-Leninizm o Voine i Armii (*Marxism-Leninism on War and the Army*)
Ocherki Istorii Izucheniye Islama v SSSR (*An Outline History of Islamic Study in the USSR*)
O Sovetskoi Voennoi Nauke (*On Soviet Military Science*)
Politicheskaya Ekonomiia--Uchebnik (*Textbook on Political Economy*)
V Pomoshch' Slushateliam Politshkol, Uchebnoe Posobie (*Aid to Students of Political Schools*)
XX S'ezd Kommunisticheskoi Partii Sovetskogo Soiuza, Stenograficheskii Otchet (*XX Congress of the CPSU, Stenographic Report*)

Poland, East Germany, Hungary, and Yugoslavia

Borba (*Fight*)	Daily	Yugoslav League of Communists Central Committee
Szabad Nép (*People's Freedom*)	Daily	Hungarian Communist Party Central Committee
Die Tägliche Rundschau (*The Daily Review*)	Daily	German Democratic Republic
Volksstime (*People's Voice*)		Yiddish language newspaper (Warsaw)

Typical Soviet Wages and Prices in Moscow and Nine Other Soviet Cities:
September–October 1955

Occupation	Monthly Wage Rate (in rubles)
1. Sweeper in a factory	450
2. Taxi driver	500–600
3. School teacher	550
4. Bookbinder	600
5. Beginning doctor	650
6. Semi-skilled factory hand	700–800
7. Beginning engineer	800
8. English interpreter	900–1,200
9. Factory foreman	1,200
10. Experienced engineer	2,000–3,000 *
11. Chief factory engineer	3,500 *
12. Director of large factory	4,000–5,000 *

* (Higher managerial and technical personnel usually get bonuses if a factory overfulfills its plan. These can increase income sharply.)

Commodities	Prices (in rubles)
1. Cheapest rye bread	1.24
2. Cheapest wheat bread	1.70
3. Pork	17.40–24.40
4. Sausage	16.70–40.50
5. Bacon	29.20
6. Butter	26.80–29.40
7. Margarine	15.20
8. Sugar	18.80
9. Oranges	16.50
10. Apples	5.50

(All of the above prices are for one kilogram.)

11. Ten eggs	7
12. Man's shirt	78–245
13. Man's suit	1,000–1,800
14. Man's felt hat	69
15. Man's cap	27–95
16. Man's shoes	550–775
17. Women's fur-trimmed coat	650–2,800
18. Silk dresses	400–725
19. Evening gowns	525–1,645
20. Women's shoes	550–775
21. Four tube radio	181
22. Eleven tube all-wave radio	1,900

23.	Seven inch television set	1,400–1,700
24.	Ten inch television set	2,700
25.	Leica-type camera.	2,000
26.	Small baby carriage	330
27.	Small electric sewing machine.	1,500
28.	Vacuum cleaners	405–650
29.	Automatic washing machine.	2,250
30.	Small washing machine with hand wringer	750
31.	Small child's bicycle	151

(Source: *New York Times*, Nov. 8, 1955, p. 3, Harry Schwartz.)

BIBLIOGRAPHY

BOOKS

BOORMAN, HOWARD L., ECKSTEIN, ALEXANDER, MOSELY, PHILIP, and SCHWARTZ, BENJAMIN, *Moscow-Peking Axis*, New York: Harper & Brothers, 1957.

BRZEZINSKI, ZBIGNIEW, *The Permanent Purge*, Cambridge, Mass: Harvard University Press, 1956.

Central Statistical Administration, *National Economy of the USSR: 1956 Statistical Year Book*, Moscow, 1956.

CRANKSHAW, EDWARD, *Russia without Stalin – The Emerging Pattern*, Michael Joseph, 1956.

Departments of the Army and the Navy, *Handbook of Aggressor Forces (U) FM 30–120/JLFM–3*, Washington: 1955.

DEUTSCHER, ISAAC, *Russia after Stalin*, London: Hamish Hamilton, 1953.

FAINSOD, MERLE, *How Russia IS Ruled*, Cambridge, Mass: Harvard University Press, 1954.

FISCHER, LOUIS, *Life and Death of Stalin*, London: Jonathan Cape, 1953.

GARTHOFF, RAYMOND, L., *Soviet Strategy in the Nuclear Age*, New York: Frederick A. Praeger, Inc., 1958.

GRULIOW, LEO (Ed.), *Current Soviet Policies*, (I), New York: Frederick A. Praeger, Inc., 1953.

——, *Current Soviet Policies*, II, New York: Frederick A. Praeger, Inc., 1956.

GURIAN, WALDEMAR, *The Soviet Union: Background, Ideology, and Reality*, Notre Dame, Ind.: University of Notre Dame Press, 1951.

International Commission of Jurists, *Justice Enslaved*, The Hague: 1955.

Institute for the Study of the USSR, *Genocide in the USSR*, (Series I–No. 40), Munich: 1958.

KEETON, GEORGE, W. and SCHWARZENBERGER, GEORGE (Eds.), *The Year Book of World Affairs – 1956*, London: Stevens and Sons Limited, 1956.

KIRKPATRICK, EVRON M. (Ed.), *Target: The World – Communist Propaganda Activities in 1955*, New York: Macmillian & Co., 1956.

MEISSNER, BORIS, *The Communist Party of the Soviet Union*. Translated by Fred Holling. Edited and with a chapter on the Twentieth Party Congress by John S. Reshetar, Jr. London: Atlantic Press, 1957.

PENNAR, JAAN (Ed.), *Report on the Soviet Union in 1956 – A Symposium of the Institute for the Study of the USSR*, Munich: Institute for the Study of the USSR, 1956.

ROBERT, HENRY L., *Russia and America – Dangers and Prospects*, New York: Harper & Brothers, 1956.

ROSTOW, W. W., *The Dynamics of Soviet Society*, New York: The New American Library (Mentor Series) Mentor Edition, 1954.

——, *The Prospects for Communist China*, New York: The Technology Press of the Massachusetts Institute of Technology and John Wiley & Sons, Inc., 1954.

RUSH, MYRON, *The Rise of Khrushchev*, Washington: Public Affairs Press, 1958.

Russian Institute, Columbia University (Ed.), *The Anti-Stalin Campaign and International Communism*, New York: Columbia University Press, (Revised Edition), 1956.

SALISBURY, HARRISON, *Stalin's Russia and After*, London: Macmillian & Co., Ltd., 1955.

SPECTOR, IVAR, *The Soviet Union and the Muslim World: 1917–1956*, Distributed by University of Washington Press, 1956. (Mimeographed.)

St. Antony's Papers – No. 1: Soviet Affairs, London: Chatto and Windus, 1956.

SULZBERGER, C. L., *The Big Thaw*, New York: Harper & Brothers, 1956.

UNITED NATIONS, Bureau of Social Affairs, United Nations Secretariat, *Report on the World Social Situation* (E/CN .5/324 Rev. 1/ST/SOA/33), New York: April 1957.

——, Department of Economic Affairs, Research and Planning Division, Economic Commission for Europe, *Economic Survey of Europe in 1953* (E/ECE/174, Feb. 1954), Geneva: 1954.

——, Department of Economic Affairs, Research and Planning Division, Economic Commission for Europe, *Economic Survey of Europe in 1954* (E/ECE/194, Feb. 1955), Geneva: 1955.

——, Department of Economic Affairs, Research and Planning Division, Economic Commission for Europe, *Economic Survey of Europe in 1955* (E/ECE/235, Feb. 1956), Geneva: 1956.

——, Department of Economic Affairs, Research and Planning Division, Economic Commission for Europe, *Economic Survey of Europe in 1957* (E/ECE/317, Feb. 1958), Geneva: 1958.

——, Department of Economic Affairs, Research and Planning Division, Economic Commission for Europe, *Economic Survey of Europe since the War* (E/ECE/157, Feb. 1953), Geneva: 1953.

——, Economic and Social Council, International Labor Office, *Report of the* Ad Hoc *Committee on Forced Labor* (E/2431), Geneva: 1953.

VOLIN, LAZAR, *A Survey of Soviet Russian Agriculture*, Washington: US Department of Agriculture, [1951].

WOLFE, BERTRAM D., *Khrushchev and Stalin's Ghost*, New York: Frederick A. Praeger, Inc., 1956.

——, *Six Keys to the Soviet System*, Boston: The Beacon Press, 1956.

WOLFF, ROBERT LEE, *The Balkans in Our Time*, Cambridge, Mass.: Harvard University Press, 1956.

WOLIN, SIMON and SLUSSER, ROBERT M., *The Soviet Secret Police*, London: Methuen & Co., 1957.

YOUNG, GORDON, *Stalin's Heirs*, London: Derek Verschoyle, Ltd. 1953.

PERIODICALS

ACHMINOW, HERMANN, "The Changes in Soviet Policy," *Bulletin of the Institute for the Study of the USSR*, II, 7, pp. 135–144.
"Air Incidents Near the Border of the Iron Curtain," *Bulletin of the In stitute for the Study of the USSR*, II, 2, pp. 27–29.
ALEXANDROVA, VERA, "Soviet Literature since Stalin," *Problems of Communism*, III, 4, pp. 11–14.
"Anatomy of Tyranny: Mr. Khrushchev's Attack on Stalin," *Problems of Communism*, V, 4, pp. 1–6.
ARCINIEGAS, GERMAN, "Latin America," *Journal of International Affairs*, VIII, 1, pp. 86–94.
ARON, RAYMOND, "Permanence and Flexibility in Soviet Foreign Policy," *Problems of Communism*, IV, 3, pp. 8–13.
"Austria and the Berlin Conference," *World Today*, X, 4, pp. 149–158.
AVTORKHANOV, A., "The Political Outlook after the 20th Party Congress," *Bulletin of the Institute for the Study of the USSR*, III, 5, pp. 3–19.
BALDWIN, HANSON, "The Soviet Navy," *Foreign Affairs*, XXXIII, 4, pp. 587–604.
BARGHOORN, FREDERICK, "The New Cultural Diplomacy," *Problems of Communism*, VII, 4, pp. 39–46.
——, "The Partial Reopening of Russia," *The American Slavic and East European Review*, XVI, 2, pp. 146–159.
——, "Soviet Cultural Diplomacy Since Stalin," *The Russian Review*, XVII, 1, pp. 41–55.
BARTH, JOACHIM, "Wieviel Menschen kann Russisch-Asien ernähren?", *Osteuropa*, VI, 2, pp. 95–103.
BAUER, ERNEST, "Tito und die Sowjetunion," *Osteuropa*, IV, 2, pp. 94–101.
BAUER, RAYMOND, "The Pseudo-Charismatic Leader in Soviet Society," *Problems of Communism*, pp. 11–14.
BEN-SHLOMO, Z., "The Jew in Soviet Literature (1948–1957)," *Soviet Survey*, 18, pp. 13–20.
BERGSON, ABRAM, "The Russian Economy since Stalin," *Foreign Affairs*, XXXIV, 2, pp. 212–226.
BERMAN, HAROLD, "Law Reform in the Soviet Union," *The American Slavic and East European Review*, XV, 2, pp. 179–189.
——, "Soviet Law Reform – Dateline Moscow 1957," *Yale Law Journal*, LXVI, 8, pp. 1191–1215.
BIALER, SEWERYN, "I Chose Truth," *News from Behind the Iron Curtain*, V, 10, pp. 3–15.
——, "Moscow vs. Belgrade: A Key to Soviet Policy," *Problems of Communism*, VII, 4, pp. 1–8.
BOCK, ERNEST, "Soviet Economic Expansionism," *Problems of Communism*, VII, 4, pp. 31–39.
BOETTCHER, ERIK, "Hintergründe der neuen Wirtschaftspolitik Moskaus," *Osteuropa*, IV, 1, pp. 18–24.
BOORMAN, H. L., "Chronology of Sino-Soviet Relations," *Problems of Communism*, III, 3, pp. 14–21.
BORKENAU, FRANZ, "The Peking-Moscow Axis and the Western Alliance," *Commentary*, XVIII, 6, pp. 513–521.

BRYNER, CYRIL, "Russia and the Slavs," *Current History*, XXVIII, 162, pp. 74–79.

BRZEZINSKI, ZBIGNIEW, "Ideology and Power: Crisis in the Soviet Bloc," *Problems of Communism*, VI, 1, pp. 12–17.

Bulletin of the International Peasant Union (New York), 1953–1956.

BYRNES, ROBERT, "Soviet Policy toward Western Europe since Stalin," *The Annals of the American Academy of Political and Social Science*, CCCIII, pp. 166–178.

CAROE, Sir OLAF, "Soviet Colonialism in Central Asia," *Foreign Affairs*, XXXII, 1, pp. 135–144.

Central Asian Review (Oxford), 1954–1956.

CHANG, LI, "The Soviet Grip on Sinkiang," *Foreign Affairs*, XXXII, 3, pp. 491–502.

CHEN, THEODORE HSI-EN, "Russia's Far Eastern Policy," *Current History*, XXVIII, 162, pp. 95–102.

"Chronicle of Events – October 1955," *Bulletin of the Institute for the Study of the USSR*, II, 10, pp. 47–48.

"Chronik 2.–5. März 1953," *Osteuropa*, III, 2, pp. 139–152.

"Chronology for 1953," *News from Behind the Iron Curtain*, II, 12, p. 13.

"Collective Leadership," *News from Behind the Iron Curtain*, III, 7, pp. 22–28.

Commentator, "The National Liberation Movement," *International Affairs* (Moscow), 4, 1955, pp. 14–21.

"Continuing Settlement in the Far East," *Bulletin of the Institute for the Study of the USSR*, III, 3, pp. 22–24.

CONTIUS, WOLF GÜNTHER, "Der 17. Juni in der Sowjetpresse," *Osteuropa*, III, 4, pp. 269–277.

Current Digest of the Soviet Press (New York), 1952–1956.

DALLIN, DAVID, "Soviet Policy in the Middle East," *Middle Eastern Affairs*, VI, 11, pp. 337–344.

DEUTSCHER, ISSAC, "The Beria Affair," *International Journal*, VIII, 4, pp. 227–239.

——, "The Nineteenth Congress of the Communist Party of the Soviet Union," *International Affairs* (London), XXIX, 2, pp. 149–155.

"The Dilemma of the Polish Economy – Part I," *World Today*, X, 3, pp. 122–135.

"The Dilemma of the Polish Economy – Part II," *World Today*, X, 4, pp. 172–183.

"The Dilemma of the Polish Economy – Part III," *World Today*, X, 5, pp. 218–228.

"The Dilemma of Soviet Writers – Inspiration or Conformity," *World Today*, XI, 4, pp. 151–163.

"Disarmament: Proposals and Negotiations, 1946–1955," *World Today*, XI, 8, pp. 334–348.

"Eastern Germany since the Risings of June 1953," *World Today*, X, 2, pp. 58–69.

"East-West Trade," *World Today*, X, 1, pp. 19–31.

EBON, MARTIN, "Malenkov's Power Balance," *Problems of Communism*, II, 3–4, pp. 7–10.

Economic Bulletin for Europe (Geneva), 1953–1956.

"The Economic Setting: Soviet Economic Penetration in Asia," *Soviet Survey*, 16–17, pp. 7–12.

The Economist (London), 1952–1956.

Economist, "Changes in the Kremlin," *Problems of Communism*, II, 3–4, pp. 5–6.

——, "Ruble Diplomacy," *Problems of Communism*, II, 6, pp. 22–23.

EINAUDI, MARIO, "Europe after Stalin," *Yale Review*, 43, pp. 24–36.

Facts on File (New York), 1953–1956.

FAINSOD, MERLE, "The Communist Party since Stalin," *The Annals of the American Academy of Political and Social Science*, CCCIII, pp. 23–36.

——, "The CPSU Takes Stock of Itself," *Problems of Communism*, V, 3, pp. 3–9.

——, "The Party in the Post-Stalin Era," *Problems of Communism*, VII, 1, pp. 7–13.

——, "The Soviet Union since Stalin," *Problems of Communism*, III, 2, pp. 1–10.

"The Fall of Beria and the Nationalities Question in the USSR," *World Today*, IX, 11, pp. 481–497.

FAY, SIDNEY B., "Russia's Relations with the West," *Current History*, XXVIII, 162, pp. 89–94.

FEDYSHYN, OLEH S., "Soviet Retreat in Sinkiang? Sino-Soviet Rivalry and Cooperation, 1950–1955," *The American Slavic and East European Review*, XVI, 2, pp. 127–145.

"The First Steps of the New Regime," *Problems of Communism*, II, 3–4, pp. 1–4.

FISHER, HAROLD, "New Lines and an Old Gospel," *Current History*, XXXII, 186, pp. 65–76.

——, "Soviet Policy in Asia since Stalin," *The Annals of the American Academy of Political and Social Science*, CCCIII, pp. 179–191.

FLORINSKY, MICHAEL, "Russia and the United States," *Current History*, XXVIII, 162, pp. 108–113.

——, "Soviet Industry and the New Look," *Current History*, XXX, 173, pp. 8–12.

——, "United States – Soviet Relations: 1954," *Current History*, XXVIII, pp. 161, pp. 15–20.

——, "The USSR and Western Europe," *Current History*, XXXVI, 186, pp. 77–82.

"The Four Powers and Germany – The Reunification Issue," *World Today*, XI, 11, pp. 471–482.

FRANK, VICTOR, "Molotov's Apology," *Bulletin of the Institute for the Study of the USSR*, II, 11, pp. 18–20.

——, "New Changes in the Soviet Leadership," *Bulletin of the Institute for the Study of the USSR*, II, 3, pp. 3–6.

——, "The Unsolved Crisis," *Bulletin of the Institute for the Study of the USSR*, II, 2, pp. 3–9.

GALAI, N., "The New Marshals," *Bulletin of the Institute for the Study of the USSR*, II, 3, pp. 7–12.

——, "Soviet Foreign Policy and the Recent Government Changes," *Bulletin of the Institute for the Study of the USSR*, II, 2, pp. 10–14.

GARTHOFF, RAYMOND, "The Military in Soviet Politics," *Problems of Communism*, VI, 6, pp. 45–48.

——, "The Role of the Military in Recent Soviet Politics," *The Russian Review*, XVI, 2, pp. 15–24.

GELBE-HAUSSEN, EBERHARD, "Die Aussenministerkonferenz von Genf," *Osteuropa*, VI, 1, pp. 61–68.

"German Opinion and the Berlin Conference – An Interim Summary," *World Today*, X, 3, pp. 105–113.

GILBOA, Y., "Jewish Literature in the Soviet Union," *Soviet Survey*, 18, pp. 5–13.

GLOVINSKY, E. A., "Soviet-Chinese Economic Relations," *Bulletin of the Institute for the Study of the USSR*, II, 5, pp. 33–36.

GOODALL, MERRILL, "India," *Journal of International Affairs*, VIII, 1, pp. 42–51.

"Government Measures at the Time of the Congress," *Soviet Studies*, VIII, 1, pp. 106–111.

GROSSMAN, GREGORY, "Economic Rationalism and Political 'Thaw'," *Problems of Communism*, VI, 2, pp. 22–26.

——, "Soviet Agriculture since Stalin," *The Annals of the American Academy of Political and Social Science*, CCCIII, pp. 62–74.

GSOVSKI, VLADIMIR, "New Trends in Soviet Justice?", *Problems of Communism*, V, 1, pp. 25–30.

——, "Russia Five Years after Stalin – No. 6: Law and Justice," *The New Leader*, XLI, 18, pp. 16–20.

——, "The Soviet Amnesty," *Problems of Communism*, II, 6, pp. 9–14.

GSOVSKI, V. and GRZYBOWSKI, K., "Judicial Procedure in the Soviet Union and in Eastern Europe," *Journal of the International Commission of Jurists*, I, 2, pp. 271–318.

GUINS, GEORGE, "Russian Communism and the Dilemma of Power," *International Journal*, VIII, 2, 1953.

HAFFNER, SEBASTIAN, "The Meaning of Malenkov," *Twentieth Century*, CLIII, pp. 326–334.

"The Hard Road to an Austrian Treaty," *World Today*, XI, 5, pp. 190–202.

HARRIS, CHAUNCY, "Growing Food by Decree in Soviet Russia," *Foreign Affairs*, XXXIII, 2, pp. 268–281.

HARTMANN, FREDERICK, "Soviet Russia and the German Problem," *Yale Review*, 43, pp. 511–524.

HAVEN, ANDREW, "The Time Factor in Soviet Foreign Policy," *Problems of Communism*, V, 1, pp. 1–8.

HAYWARD, MAX, "Controls in Literature – Part I: 1946–1954," *Soviet Survey*, 21–22, pp. 26–32.

HAZARD, JOHN, "A Political Testament for Stalin's Heirs," *International Journal*, VIII, 2, pp. 75–82.

——, "Government Developments in the USSR since Stalin," *The Annals of the American Academy of Political and Social Science*, CCCIII, pp. 11–22.

HEALEY, DENIS, "Arms and Doctrine," *Problems of Communism*, VII, 5, pp. 44–46.

——, " 'When Shrimps Learn to Whistle' – Thoughts After Geneva," *International Affairs* (London), XXXII, 1, pp. 1–10.

HENDERSON, WILLIAM, "Southeast Asia," *Journal of International Affairs*, VIII, 1, pp. 32–42.

HENI, FELIX, "Ärztliche Stellungnahme zur Krankheit und zum Tode Stalins," *Osteuropa*, III, 2, pp. 137–138.

HERMAN, LEON, "Soviet Economic Policy since Stalin," *Problems of Communism*, V, 1, pp. 8–14.
——, "The New Soviet Posture in World Trade," *Problems of Communism* III, 6, pp. 9–16.
HOEFFDING, OLEG, "Recent Trends in Soviet Foreign Policy," *The Annals of the American Academy of Political and Social Science*, CCCIII, pp. 75–88.
HOLDSWORTH, MARY, "Africa Enters the Soviet Field of Vision," *Soviet Survey*, 16–17, pp. 26–30.
HOPTNER, J. B., "Eastern Europe," *Journal of International Affairs*, VIII, 1, pp. 95–106.
HUDSON, G. F., "Balance Sheet on Bandung," *Commentary*, IXX, 6, pp. 562–567.
——, "Soviet Policy in Asia," *Soviet Survey*, 16–17, pp. 1–7.
——, "The Communist Terms for Peaceful Co-existence," *Commentary*, XIX, 2, pp. 101–107.
ICFTU Spotlight (Brussels), 1953–1956.
International Commission of Jurists, "The 'Rule of Law' and 'Socialist Legality' in the USSR," *Bulletin of the International Commission of Jurists*, 6, pp. 10–37.
Inter-Parliamentary Bulletin (Geneva), 1953–1956.
ITO, NOBUBUMI, "The Cultural Front in Japan," *Soviet Survey*, 16–17, pp. 30–35.
JASNY, NAUM, "More Soviet Grain Statistics," *International Affairs* (London), XXXII, 4, pp. 464–65.
——, "Some Thoughts on Soviet Statistics," *International Affairs* (London), XXXV, 1, pp. 53–60.
——, "The New Economic Course in the USSR," *Problems of Communism*, III, 1, pp. 1–7.
KAFKA, GUSTAV, "Die Sowjetunion und Österreich (I)," *Osteuropa*, III, 3, pp. 171–177.
——, "Die Sowjetunion und Österreich (II)," *Osteuropa*, III, 4, pp. 257–263.
"Der Kanzler in Moskau," *Osteuropa*, V, 6, pp. 448–454.
KAUTSKY, JOHN, "From Marx to Mao," *Soviet Survey*, 16–17, pp. 35–40.
——, "The New Strategy of International Communism," *The American Political Science Review*, ILIX, 2, pp. 478–486.
KEEP, J. L. H., "Soviet Ideologies on the Treadmill," *Problems of Communism*, VII, 2, pp. 30–35.
KERSHAW, JOSEPH, "Recent Trends in the Soviet Economy," *The Annals of the American Academy of Political and Social Science*, CCCIII, pp. 37–49.
KOLARZ, WALTER, "Government and People in the Soviet Union Today," *International Affairs* (London), XXXI, 4, pp. 435–446.
——, "Recent Soviet Attitudes towards Religion," *Soviet Survey*, 13, pp. 10–20.
——, "The Nationalities under Khrushchev," *Soviet Survey*, 24, pp. 57–65.
KOVALENKO, E. E., "The Second Conference of Soviet Writers," *Bulletin of the Institute for the Study of the USSR*, II, 1, pp. 3–7.
LABER, JERI, "The Soviet Writer's Search for New Values," *Problems of Communism*, V, 1, pp. 14–20.

LAIRD, ROY, "Decontrols or New Controls? The 'Reform' of Soviet Agricultural Administration," *Problems of Communism*, VI, 4, pp. 26–32.

LANGER, PAUL F., "Japan," *Journal of International Affairs*, VIII, 1, pp. 21–31.

LAQUERUR, WALTER Z., "Soviet Prospects in the Middle East," *Problems of Communism*, VI, 4, pp. 20–25.

——, "The Shifting Line in Soviet Orientalogy," *Problems of Communism*, V, 2, pp. 20–26.

——, "The 'Thaw' and After," *Problems of Communism*, V, 1, pp. 20–25.

LAUCKHUFF, PERRY, "Germany," *Journal of International Affairs*, VIII, 1, pp. 62–72.

LAUFER, LEO, "Communist Party Strategy and Tactics in the Arab World," *Problems of Communism*, III, 1, pp. 40–45.

LEITES, NATHAN, "Stalin as an Intellectual," *World Politics*, VI, 1, pp. 45–66.

LENCZOWSKI, GEORGE, "Middle East," *Journal of International Affairs*, VIII, 1, pp. 52–61.

LEONHARD, WOLFGANG, "Party Training after Stalin," *Soviet Survey*, 20, pp. 10–16.

——, Terror in the Soviet System: Trends and Portents," *Problems of Communism*, VII, 6, pp. 1–7.

LESNY, L., "Der Slansky-Prozess," *Osteuropa*, III, 1, pp. 1–12.

LIAS, GODFREY, "Satellite States in the Post-Stalin Era," *International Affairs* (London), XXX, 1, pp. 40–49.

LICHTHEIN, GEORGE, "Soviet Expansion into the Middle East," *Commentary*, XX, 5, pp. 435–439.

LIPSON, LEON, "The New Face of 'Socialist Legality'," *Problems of Communism*, VII, 4, pp. 22–30.

LISZCZYNSKYJ, G., "Malenkov's Resignation," *Bulletin of the Institute for the Study of the USSR*, II, 2, pp. 15–18.

LOEBER, DIETRICH, "The Soviet Procuracy and the Rights of the Individual against the State," *Journal of the International Commission of Jurists*, I, 1, pp. 59–105.

LÖWENTHAL, RICHARD, "Crisis in Moscow," *Problems of Communism*, IV, 3, pp. 1–9.

——, "New Phase in Moscow-Belgrade Relations," *Problems of Communism*, IV, 6, pp. 1–10.

——, "Party vs. State," *Problems of Communism*, VI, 5, pp. 1–7.

——, "Stalinism without Stalin?", *Twentieth Century*, CLVII, pp. 218–227.

——, "Why Was Slansky Hanged?", *Twentieth Century*, CLIII, pp. 18–23.

LONDON, ISAAC, "Evolution of the USSR's Policy in the Middle East," *Middle Eastern Affairs*, VII, 5, pp. 169–178.

"Malenkov's Resignation: the Abandonment of the New Course," *World Today*, XI, 3, pp. 97–105.

MALNICK, B., "Current Problems of Soviet Literature," *Soviet Studies*, VII, 1, pp. 1–13.

The Manchester Guardian, 1953–1956.

MARIN, YU., "From the July Plenary Session of the Central Committee to the Twentieth Party Congress," *Bulletin of the Institute for the Study of the USSR*, II, 9, pp. 28–33.

MAURACH, REINHART, "Das Sowjetische Amnestiegestz," *Osteuropa*, III, 3, pp. 161–170.
MEISSNER, BORIS, "Der Auswärtige Dienst der UdSSR," *Osteuropa*, III, 1, pp. 49–54.
——, "Der Auswärtige Dienst der UdSSR," *Osteuropa*, IV, 2, pp. 112–118.
——, "Der Auswärtige Dienst der UdSSR," *Osteuropa*, V, 1, pp. 24–44.
——, "Der Nachfolger – Georgij M. Malenkov," *Osteuropa*, III, 2, pp. 84–95.
——, "Der Ministerrat der UdSSR," *Osteuropa*, III, 2, pp. 116–123.
——, "Die Administrative-Territoriale Gliederung," *Osteuropa*, IV, 4, pp. 292–294.
——, "Die Neue Parteiführung," *Osteuropa*, III, 2, pp. 108–116.
——, "Neuwahl des Obersten 'Sowjetparlaments' und Parteisäuberungen," *Osteuropa*, IV, 3, pp. 209–225.
——, "Partei und Personelles," *Osteuropa*, VI, 3, pp. 171–190.
——, "RSFSR, Moldau, Weissrussland," *Osteuropa*, IV, 5, pp. 383–388.
——, "Sowjetmarschälle – die Macht im Hintergrund," *Osteuropa*, V, 2, pp. 93–99.
——, "Tagung des Obersten Sowjet," *Osteuropa*, III, 5, pp. 361–366.
——, "Ukraine," *Osteuropa*, IV, 4, pp. 295–301.
——, Verwaltungsumbau," *Osteuropa*, IV, 4, pp. 284–301.
——, "Zweite Verwaltungsreform nach Stalin," *Osteuropa*, III, 6, pp. 454–466.
MEHNERT, KLAUS, "Der XX. Kongress der KPdSU," *Osteuropa*, VI, 3, pp. 161–170.
——, "Deutschlandpolitik der Sowjets," *Osteuropa*, III, 5, pp. 351–355.
——, "Deutschlandpolitik der Sowjets," *Osteuropa*, III, 6, pp. 434–442.
——, "Die Indochina-Konferenz in Genf," *Osteuropa*, IV, 5, pp. 368–379.
——, "Die Korea-Konferenz in Genf," *Osteuropa*, IV, 4, pp. 277–284.
——, "Die Sowjets in Asien," *Osteuropa*, III, 1, pp. 36–48.
——, "Die Sowjets in Asien," *Osteuropa*, III, 6, pp. 446–454.
——, "Die Viererkonferenz von Berlin," *Osteuropa*, IV, 2, pp. 104–111.
——, "Moskaus neuer Dreijahrplan des Konsums," *Osteuropa*, IV, 1, pp. 1–10.
——, "Peking und Moskau," *Osteuropa*, V, 1, pp. 17–20.
——, "Um die deutsche Frage," *Osteuropa*, IV, 1, pp. 27–32.
MEYER, ALFRED, "Russia after Stalin," *Current History*, XXX, 179, pp. 1–7.
——, "The Foreign Policy of Russian Communism," XXVIII, 162, pp. 114–121.
MEYER, PETER, "Has Soviet Anti-Semitism Halted?", *Commentary*, XVIII, 1, pp. 1–9.
"The Middle East: Background to the Russian Intervention," *World Today*, XI, 11, pp. 463–471.
"A Minority under Pressure," *Soviet Survey*, 18, pp. 1–5.
MOOR, JR., BARRINTON, "The Outlook," *The Annals of the American Academy of Political and Social Science*, XXXIII, pp. 1–10.
MORRIS, BERNARD, "Recent Shifts in Communist Strategy: India and Southeast Asia," *Soviet Survey*, 16–17, pp. 40–46.
"Moscow's New Course," *Twentieth Century*, CLV, pp. 208–217.
MOSELY, PHILIP, "Economic Aspects of the Nineteenth Party Congress," *Problems of Communism*, II, 2, pp. 8–10.

——, "How 'New' is the Kremlin's New Line?", *Foreign Affairs*, XXXIII, 3, pp. 376–386.

——, "Soviet Foreign Policy: New Goals or New Manners?", *Foreign Affairs*, XXXIV, 4, pp. 541–553.

——, "Soviet Policy: Some Prospects," *Journal of International Affairs*, VIII, 1, pp. 107–113.

——, "The Kremlin's Foreign Policy since Stalin," *Foreign Affairs*, XXXII, 1, pp. 20–33.

——, "The Nineteenth Party Congress," *Foreign Affairs*, XXXI, 2, pp. 238–256.

——, "The Soviet Union and the United States: Problems and Prospects," *The Annals of the American Academy of Political and Social Science*, CCCIII, pp. 192–198.

NEMZER, LOUIS, "The Kremlin's Professional Staff: The 'Apparatus' of the Central Committee, Communist Party of the Soviet Union," *American Political Science Review*, XLIV, 1, pp. 64–85.

"Neues Licht auf den Fall Wosnessenskij," *Osteuropa*, III, 2, pp. 96–98.

"The 'New Line' in Bulgaria," *World Today*, X, 1, pp. 31–39.

"The 'New Line' in Hungary – Politics and Economics Under the Nagy Government," *World Today*, XI, 1, pp. 27–40.

"The New Soviet Government," *World Today*, IX, 4, pp. 139–142.

New York Herald Tribune (European Edition), 1953–1958.

New York Times (City and International Editions), 1952–1958.

News (Moscow), 1953–1956.

"The Nineteenth Party Congress and Soviet Foreign Policy," *Problems of Communism*, II, 1, pp. 14–18.

NOVE, ALEXANDER, "Problems of Economic De-Stalinisation," *Problems of Communism*, VI, 2, pp. 15–21.

——, "The USSR after the Death of Stalin," *Soviet Studies*, VI, 1, pp. 41–52.

The Observer (London), 1952–1956.

PARRY, ALBERT, "The Twentieth Congress: Stalin's 'Second Funeral', " *The American Slavic and East European Review*, XV, 4, pp. 463–476.

PIERRE, ANDRÉ, "Religion in the Soviet Land," *Problems of Communism*, IV, 3, pp. 19–28.

"Politics and Economics in Czechoslovakia: the Tenth Congress of the Czechoslovakian Communist Party," *World Today*, X, 8, pp. 356–366.

POSSELT, ALFRED, "Das Schicksal des Ostprotestantismus," *Osteuropa*, VI, 1, pp. 45–55.

"Post-Stalin Soviet Domestic Policy," *Bulletin of the Institute for the Study of the USSR*, II, 1, pp. 32–33.

"A Revival of Religious Feeling in the USSR," *World Today*, X, 10, pp. 439–447.

RIEBER, ALFRED, "France," *Journal of International Affairs*, VIII, 1, pp. 73–85.

RIGBY, T. H., "Soviet Government Changes since Stalin," *The Australian Outlook*, IX, 3, pp. 165–171.

RONIMOIS, H. E., "Soviet Economic Planning and the Balance of Power," *International Journal*, VIII, 1, pp. 32–40.

RUBINSTEIN, ALVIN, "Russia, Southeast Asia, and Point Four," *Current History*, XXVIII, 162, pp. 103–108.

——, "Soviet Policy in South Asia," *Current History*, XXXII, 186, pp. 97–104.

"The Russo-Yugoslav *Détente*," *World Today*, XI, 1, pp. 10–19.

SCHILLER, OTTO, "Die Agrarfrage in Stalins neuer Schrift," *Osteuropa*, III, 1, pp. 13–19.

SCHLESINGER, RUDOLF, "From the XIX to the XX Party Congress," *Soviet Studies*, VIII, 1, pp. 1–26.

SCHOLMER, JOSEPH, "The Uprising at Vorkuta," *The Lithuanian Situation*, XI, 3, pp. 29–35.

SCHUMAN, FREDERICK, "The Russian Riddle," *Current History*, XXVIII, 162, pp. 65–69.

SCHWARTZ, SOLOMON, "The Communist Party and the Soviet State," *Problems of Communism*, II, 1, pp. 8–13.

——, "New Light on the Communist Party of the Soviet Union," *Problems of Communism*, II, 2, pp. 11–13.

SETON-WATSON, HUGH, "Eastern Europe since Stalin," *Problems of Communism*, III, 2, pp. 10–17.

SHERMAN, A. V., "Intellectual Ferment in the Middle East," *Soviet Survey*, 16–17, pp. 22–26.

SHEVLYAGIN, D., "For Closer All-Round Friendship between the Soviet Union and Yugoslavia," *International Affairs* (Moscow), 8, 1955, pp. 15–25.

SIMMONS, ERNEST, "Soviet Literature: 1950–1955," *The Annals of the American Academy of Political and Social Science*, CCCIII, pp. 89–103.

SLUSSER, ROBERT, "Soviet Music since the Death of Stalin," *The Annals of the American Academy of Political and Social Science*, CCCIII, pp. 116–125.

"Some Aspects of Soviet-Satellite Economic Relations," *World Today*, XI, 10, pp. 431–438.

"Some Data about Religious Communities," *Soviet Studies*, VII, 4, pp. 471–472.

SOSNOVY, TIMOTHY, "Housing in the Worker's State," *Problems of Communism*, V, 6, pp. 31–39.

"Soviet and Chinese Cooperation in the Far East," *Bulletin of the Institute for the Study of the USSR*, II, 2, pp. 21–23.

"Soviet Cultural Collaboration – The Role of the Friendship Societies in the Satellite States," *World Today*, X, 5, pp. 197–209.

"The Soviet General Staff Takes Stock," *World Today*, XI, 11, pp. 492–502.

"Soviet Interest in Africa," *World Today*, XII, 9, pp. 355–361.

"Soviet-Japanese Peace Treaty Talks – The Negotiations as Seen from Tokyo," *World Today*, XI, 8, pp. 357–364.

Soviet Literature (Moscow), 1953–1956.

"Soviet Political Strategy in Asia," *World Today*, XII, 5, pp. 192–201.

"Soviet Policy in the Middle East," *World Today*, XI, 12, pp. 518–529.

"Soviet Trade Agreements with the Free World in 1954," *Bulletin of the Institute for the Study of the USSR*, II, 2, pp. 50–55.

"Soviet-Yugoslav Economic Relations," *World Today*, XII, 1, pp. 38–46.

Soviet Weekly (London), 1953–1956.

SPECTOR, IVAR, "Russia in the Middle East," *Current History*, XXXII, 186, pp. 83–88.

———, "Soviet Cultural Propaganda in the Near and Middle East," *Soviet Survey*, 16–17, pp. 16–22.

———, "Soviet Influence on Islamic Peoples," *Current History*, XXXII, 190, pp. 350–356.

"Staat und Revolution," *Osteuropa*, III, 4, p. 306.

"Stalin's New Work – A Brilliant Contribution to Marxism-Leninism," *New Times*, 41, 1952, pp. 5–9.

"Stalinism in the Post-Stalin Regime: 'the Ministry of Truth' without 'Big Brother'," *World Today*, X, 7, pp. 300–309.

STARITZKY, N., "The Soviet-Yugoslav Talks," *Bulletin of the Institute for Study of the USSR*, II, 6, pp. 3–10.

STRANG, LORD, "Germany between East and West," *Foreign Affairs*, XXXIII, 3, pp. 387–401.

STRUVE, GLEB, "The Second Congress of Soviet Writers," *Problems of Communism*, IV, 2, pp. 3–11.

"Summary of the XX Party Congress – I," *Soviet Studies*, VIII, 1, pp. 82–106.

"Summary of the XX Party Congress – II," *Soviet Studies*, VIII, 2, pp. 185–203.

"The Summit Talks at Geneva, and After," *World Today*, XI, 9, pp. 365–369.

SWEARINGEN, RODGER, "A Decade of Soviet Policy in Asia, 1945–1956," *Current History*, XXXII, 186, pp. 89–96.

TAURER, BERNARD, "Stalin's Last Thesis," *Foreign Affairs*, XXXI, 3, pp. 367–381.

"Ten Years of East-West Relations in Europe," *World Today*, XI, 6, pp. 246–254.

TEPFERS, V., "The Soviet Political Police Today," *East and West*, 1, 1954, pp. 44–46.

TIMASHEFF, N. S., "The Anti-Religious Campaign in the Soviet Union," *Review of Politics*, XVII, 3, pp. 329–344.

The Times (London), 1952–1956.

TIMOSHENKO, VLADIMIR, "Agriculture in the Soviet Spotlight," *Foreign Affairs*, XXXII, 2, pp. 244–258.

———, "New Soviet Economic Plan: Its Agricultural Aspect," *The Journal of Political Economy*, LXI, 6, pp. 489–508.

TOWSTER, JULIAN, "The Soviet Union after Stalin: Leaders and Policies," *The American Slavic and East European Review*, XIII, 4, pp. 471–499.

"Trade between China and the Soviet Bloc," *World Today*, XI, 5, pp. 202–210.

TUCKER, ROBERT, "Stalinism and the World Conflict," *Journal of International Affairs*, VIII, 1, pp. 7–20.

———, "The Metamorphosis of the Stalin Myth," *World Politics*, VII, 1, pp. 38–62.

———, "The Psychology of Soviet Foreign Policy," *Problems of Communism*, VI, 3, pp. 1–9.

Twentieth Century, "Soviet Farm Policy," *Problems of Communism*, III, 1, pp. 8–14.

"Two Anniversaries," *Bulletin of the Institute for the Study of the USSR*, II, 1, pp. 29–32.

TYSON, GEOFFREY, "India and the Russian Visitors," *International Affairs* (London), XXXII, 2, pp. 173–180.

VOLIN, LAZAR, "Khrushchev's Economic Neo-Stalinism," *The American Slavic and East European Review*, XIV, 4, pp. 445–464.
——, "Soviet Agriculture and the New Look," *Current History*, XXX, 173, pp. 13–19.
——, "The Malenkov-Khrushchev New Economic Policy," *The Journal of Political Economy*, LXII, 3, pp. 187–209.
——, "The New Battle for Grain in Soviet Russia," *Foreign Agriculture* XVIII, 11, pp. 194–199.
VOROBYOV, YEVGENI, "People, Be Vigilant," *New Times*, 49, 1952, pp. 22–26.
VUCINICH, WAYNE, "Russia and the Near and Middle East," *Current History*, XXVIII, 162, pp. 80–88.
——, "The Russians Look Eastward," *Current History*, XXX, 173, pp. 13–19.
VVEDENSKY, G. A., "Soviet Industry on the Eve of the Sixth Five Year Plan," *Bulletin of the Institute for the Study of the USSR*, II, 9, pp. 3–9.
WALKER, RICHARD, "Pattern of Sino-Soviet Relations," *Problems of Communism*, III, 3, pp. 5–13.
WERNER, GEORG, "Aussenhandelspolitik der UdSSR nach Stalin," *Osteuropa*, IV, 1, pp. 11–17.
WHEELER, G. E., "Recent Soviet Attitudes toward Islam," *Soviet Survey*, 16–17, pp. 12–16.
——, "Soviet Policy in Central Asia," *International Affairs* (London), XXXI, 3, pp. 317–326.
WIRSING, GISELHER, "Die Konferenz von Bandung," *Osteuropa*, V, 5, pp. 330–335.
WOLFE, BERTRAM, "A New Look at the Soviet 'New Look'," *Foreign Affairs*, XXXIII, 2, pp. 184–198.
——, "Stalin's Ghost at the Party Congress," *Foreign Affairs*, XXXIV, 4, pp. 554–568.
——, "The New Gospel of Stalinism," *Problems of Communism*, II, 1, pp. 1–7.
——, "The Struggle for Soviet Succession," *Foreign Affairs*, XXXI, 4, pp. 548–565.
World Youth (Budapest).
WUORINEN, JOHN, "Russia, Scandinavia, and the Baltic States," *Curren History*, XXVIII, 162, pp. 70–74.
"Yugoslavia between Independence and Orthodoxy – Reflections on the Soviet Visit to Belgrade," *World Today*, XI, 8, pp. 322–334.
ZHUKOV, E., "The Bandung Conference of African and Asian Countries and Its Historic Significants," *International Affairs* (Moscow), 5, 1955, pp. 18–32.
ZHUKOV, Y., "In Bandung," *International Affairs* (Moscow), 7, 1957, pp. 75–81.
ZINNER, PAUL, "Soviet Policies in Eastern Europe," *The Annals of the Academy of Political and Social Science*, CCCIII, pp. 152–165.

OTHER SOURCES

"Analysis of Policy Trends inside the USSR as Revealed by the Soviet Press." [New York] (Mimeographed.)

"The Army in the New Soviet 'Parliament', " Background Notes 312, Central Research Unit, [British Broadcasting Corporation] March 23, 1954. (Mimeographed.)

"Background Information," Office of Political Information, Radio Free Europe, [Munich] Feb. 7, 1957. (Mimeographed.)

Background Notes 502, Central Research Unit, [British Broadcasting Corporation] April 28, 1955. (Mimeographed.)

"Bloc Performance on Its Loans and Aid to Free World Underdeveloped Countries: [July] 1955 through December 1957," [Press Release] International Cooperation Administration, [Washington] Jan. 9, 1958. (Mimeographed.)

British Broadcasting Corporation Monitoring Reports, 1953–1956. (Mimeographed.)

"Catholics in the Soviet Union," Walter Kolarz, European Service, [British Broadcasting Corporation] Sept. 14, 1955. (Mimeographed.)

Central Research Unit, [British Broadcasting Corporation] Jan. 23, 1958. (Mimeographed.)

"Changes of Soviet Prime Ministers," Hugh Lunghi, European Service, [British Broadcasting Corporation] Jan. 25, 1956. (Mimeographed.)

"The Chinese Angle of the Soviet Government Crisis," Central Research Unit (edited by Hugh Lunghi) European Service. [British Broadcasting System, Feb. 1955.]

"Church Leaders at Soviet Receptions," Walter Kolarz, European Service, [British Broadcasting Corporation] Sept. 22, 1955. (Mimeographed.)

"The Communication Network in the USSR," Notes – Soviet Affairs, 175, June 28, 1955.

"Communist Marshals," Walter Kolarz, European Service, [British Broadcasting Corporation] March 14, 1955. (Mimeographed.)

The Crisis in the Soviet Leadership, Aug. 1957. (Printed pamphlet.)

"The Current Status of the Soviet Press, TV, and Radio," Notes – Soviet Affairs, 194, July 24, 1956.

"The Dilemma of the Soviet Theater," Notes – Soviet Affairs, 184, Feb. 27, 1956.

DINERSTEIN, HERBERT S., The Soviet Purge: 1953 Version, The Rand Corporation, Santa Monica, California, Feb. 11, 1953.

DUDIN, L. V., "General Ideological Direction in the Policy of Collective Leadership." (Mimeographed.) [1956.]

Free Europe Press, "Analytic Survey of Major Trends in the Soviet Sphere (July 1953–July 1954)," R.R.–8, Aug. 11, 1954. (Mimeographed.) [Munich.]

Free Europe Press, "Second Analytic Survey of Major Trends in the Soviet Sphere, (July 1954–June 1955)," R.R.–39, July 26, 1955. [Munich.] (Mimeographed.)

Free Europe Press, "The New 'General Line' in the Soviet Sphere: A Chronology of Major Events, Nov. 16, 1954–March 19, 1955," R.R.–31, April 1, 1955. [Munich.] (Mimeographed.)

Fiftieth Anniversary of the Communist Party of the Soviet Union: 1903–1953, Moscow, 1953.

Forty Years: 1917–1957 – Theses of the Propaganda Department of the Communist Party of the Soviet Union and the Marxist-Leninist Institute on the Fortieth Anniversary of the Great October Revolution, Soviet News Booklet 16, London, Nov. 1957.

"The Full Circle of Freedom of Expression in Literature and Arts in the USSR," Soviet Affairs Analysis 28, Analysis of Current Developments in the Soviet Union, Institute for the Study of the USSR, Munich, Oct. 22, 1957. (Mimeographed.)

General News Service Talk, European Service, [British Broadcasting Corporation] March 24, 1954. (Mimeographed.)

"The Georgian Purge – A Final Balance Sheet," Central Research Unit, [British Broadcasting Corporation] May 16, 1954.

"Grain Yields," Alfred Zauberman, European Service, [British Broadcasting Corporation] Jan. 13, 1958.

"The 'Great Friendship' of Russia and China," Hugh Lunghi, European Service, [British Broadcasting Corporation] Feb. 18, 1955.

GSOVSKI, VLADIMIR, *The Essence of a Totalitarian State*, The International Commission of Jurists, the Hague, June 1955.

"Housing – A Failure of the Soviet System," *Notes – Soviet Affairs*, 203, Jan. 16, 1957.

"In Eastern Europe–258," European Service, [British Broadcasting Corporation] April 29, 1954. (Mimeographed.)

Intelligence Report No. 6922, US Department of State, May 11, 1955. (Mimeographed.)

JEDRYCHOWSKI, STEFAN, *The Fundamental Principles of Economic Policy in Industry*, Warsaw, 1957.

"Kazakhstan," *Notes – Soviet Affairs*, 183, Dec. 20, 1955.

KHRUSHCHEV, N. S., *"Measures for the Further Development of Agriculture in the USSR–Report Delivered at the Plenary Meeting of the CC CPSU, September 3, 1953,"* Moscow, 1954.

"Khrushchev's 'All-Around' Development," *Notes – Soviet Affairs*, 188, April 19, 1956.

"Komsomol Congress," Central Research Unit (edited by Walter Kolarz), [British Broadcasting Corporation] March 24, 1954. (Mimeographed.)

"The Kremlin's Forgotton Asian Empire," *Notes – Soviet Affairs*, 168.

LANGE, OSCAR, *Some Problems Relating to the Polish Road to Socialism*, Warsaw, 1957.

LEITES, NATHAN, "The Stalinist Heritage in Soviet Foreign Policy," US Air Force Rand Project Research Memorandum, RM–1003, May 18, 1953. (Mimeographed.)

"Local Soviet Congresses," European Service, [British Broadcasting Corporation] Feb. 24, 1954. (Mimeographed.)

"March 5–9, 1956: Bloody Demonstrations in Tiflis," Memorandum from the Research Unit, Munich Radio Center to the Russian Unit K-Program, Feb. 19, 1957. (Typewritten.)

MARCHENKO, V., "Problems of the Soviet Economy under the Sixth Five Year Plan," [Institute for the Study of the USSR, Munich, 1956.] (Mimeographed.)

"Materials for Exploitation of Soviet Sensitivities Revealed by the

30, June 1956 CPSU Resolution and Other Statements," [US Information Agency, Washington] July 1956. (Mimeographed.)

Measures for the Further Development of Agriculture in the USSR–Decision Adopted September 7, 1953, on the Report of N. S. Khrushchev, Moscow, 1954.

"Moscow Takes a New Doctrinal Look at Asia," IRI Intelligence Summary IS–95–55, US Information Service, [Washington] Nov. 25, 1955. (Mimeographed.)

"The New Soviet Line: 'Learn From the West', " Background Notes 542, Central Research Unit, [British Broadcasting Corporation] Aug. 25 1955. (Mimeographed.)

"The New Soviet Statistical Handbook," *Notes – Soviet Affairs*, 193, July 23, 1956.

"New Trends in the Soviet Union since the 20th Party Congress," Hugh Lunghi, European Service, [British Broadcasting Corporation] Sept. 12, 1956. (Mimeographed.)

"Notes From the Soviet Provincial Press," Office of Research and Intelligence, US Information Agency, [Washington]. (Mimeographed.)

Notes – Soviet Affairs, 191, June 20, 1956.

N. S. Khrushchev Report of the Central Committee – 20th Party Congress of the Soviet Union, February 14, 1956, Soviet News Booklet 4, London, Feb. 1956.

Office of Political Adviser, Radio Free Europe, [Munich] April 30, 1957. (Mimeographed.)

"Party Man to Yugoslavia as Ambassador," Background Paper 545, Central Research Unit, [British Broadcasting Corporation] August 26, 1955. (Mimeographed.)

"Party Men Replace Soviet Diplomats," Munich Radio Center 10, Jan. 2, 1956. (Typewritten.)

PIPES, RICHARD, *Moslems of Soviet Central Asia: Trends and Prospects*, Communist Bloc Program, China Project E/54–10, Center for International Studies, Massachusetts Institute of Technology, Cambridge, Massachusetts, October 29, 1954.

"Preliminary Report on XX Party Congress, CPSU," IRI Intelligence Memorandum IM–9–56, US Information Agency, [Washington] March 9, 1956. (Mimeographed.)

"Quarterly Review of Communist Propaganda, Activities (January-March 1956)," IRI Intelligence Summary IS–45–56, US Information Agency, [Washington] June 15, 1956. (Mimeographed.)

"Religion in the Soviet Union," *Notes – Soviet Affairs*, 186, March 28, 1955.

"Religion – The Janus Face of Communism," *Notes – Soviet Affairs*, 164, Aug. 23, 1954.

"Repatriation – The Pied Piper of the Soviet Bloc," *Notes – Soviet Affairs*, 199, Nov. 20, 1956.

"The Revolt of the Intellectuals in Eastern Europe," *Notes – Soviet Affairs*, 198, Oct. 30, 1958.

"Rewriting Military History in the Soviet Union," *Notes – Soviet Affairs*, 178.

"The Rise to Power of N. S. Khrushchev," *Notes – Soviet Affairs*, 167.

Royal Institute of International Affairs, "Current Soviet Policies: An Appraisal of the 20th Congress of the Communist Party of the Soviet Union," London, May 1956. (Mimeographed.)

RUDIN, V. N. (Ed.), International Research Institute on Communist Techniques, "Behind the Communist Line," Feb. 19, 1956. [New York] (Mimeographed.)

"Russia's Agricultural Bureaucracy," Background Notes 419, Central Research Unit, [British Broadcasting Corporation] Nov. 3, 1954.

"The Same Old 'Road to Socialism'?", Background Notes 757, Central Research Unit, [British Broadcasting Corporation] Sept. 28, 1956.

SCHNITZER, E. W., "German Studies: Soviet Policy on the Reunification of Germany, 1945–1952," RM–1119, July 15, 1953.

"Selected Past Eulogies of Stalin," [US Information Agency, Washington, 1956]. (Mimeographed.)

"Some Preliminary Notes on the Proclamation of the Soviet Communist Party Central Committee on the State of Soviet Agriculture Published on September 13, 1953." (Mimeographed.)

Soviet Affairs Analyst Service, Analysis of Current Developments in the Soviet Union, 19, Institute for the Study of the USSR, Munich, July 16, 1957.

"Soviet Agricultural Crisis," Hugh Lunghi, European Service, [British Broadcasting Corporation] Feb. 9, 1955.

Soviet Bloc Economic Activities in the Free World – Sixth Report to Congress – Second Half of 1954, Foreign Operations Administration, Washington, June 30, 1955.

"The Soviet Bloc Economic Offensive in Less Developed Areas," Press Release, US Department of State, Jan. 3, 1958.

"The Soviet Boarding Schools," Notes – Soviet Affairs, 196, Sept. 26, 1956.

"Soviet Diplomatic Appointments: June 1953 to Feb. 1954," Background Notes 291, Central Research Unit, [British Broadcasting Corporation] Feb. 19, 1954. (Mimeographed.)

'The Soviet Economic Challenge to US Policy," Address by Mr. Willis C. Amstrong, Director, Office of International Resources, US Department of State at St. Louis, Missouri, Jan. 17, 1958. (Mimeographed.)

"The Soviet Food Supply," Background Notes 676, Central Intelligence Unit, [British Broadcasting Corporation] May 25, 1956. (Mimeographed.)

"Soviet Foreign Trade Propaganda: A Change of Emphasis," Background Notes 288, Central Research Unit, [British Broadcasting Corporation] Feb. 15, 1954. (Mimeographed.)

"The Soviet Hierarchy Abandons Order of Precedence," Background Notes 362, Central Research Unit, [British Broadcasting Corporation] July 7, 1954. (Mimeographed.)

"Soviet Literature Maintains Its Stalinist Outlook," Intelligence Report 6636, US Department of State, July 13, 1954. (Mimeographed.)

"The Soviet Party Congress and a Possible 'Evolutionary' Trend in Asian Communism," IRI Intelligence Memorandum IM–7–56, US Information Agency, [Washington] Feb. 21, 1956. (Mimeographed.)

"Soviet Police System," Notes – Soviet Affairs, 172, May 13, 1955.

"Soviet Policies on Labor Productivity and Trade Unions," Office of Research and Intelligence Report, P–79–57, US Information Agency, [Washington] Aug. 22, 1957.

"Soviet Presidium Changes," Central Research Unit (edited by Walter Kolarz), European Service, [British Broadcasting Corporation] July 13, 1955.

"Soviet Propaganda Exploitation of Foreign Visitors," *Notes – Soviet Affairs*, 200, Nov. 28, 1956.

"Soviet 'Socialism' in Poland," *Notes – Soviet Affairs*, 201, Dec. 12, 1956.

The Soviet Union as Reported by Former Soviet Citizens, Interview Report 14, External Research Staff, Office of Intelligence Research, US Department of State, Washington, Aug. 1955.

——, Interview Report 18, External Research Staff, Office of Intelligence Research, US Department of State, Washington, Aug. 1957.

"The Soviet View," The Third Program, British Broadcasting Corporation, Feb. 6, 1957.

Soviet News (London), 1953–1956.

"Soviet Youth Problems," *Notes – Soviet Affairs*, 173.

"Stalin's Ideas of March," Walter Kolarz, European Service, [British Broadcasting Corporation] Feb. 20, 1956. (Mimeographed.)

Target Figures for the Economic Development of the Soviet Union 1959–1965. Report to the Special 21st Congress of the Communist Party of the Soviet Union and the Reply to Discussion by N. S. Khrushchev, Soviet Booklet 47, London, Feb. 1959.

"Tiflis University," Hugh Lunghi, European Service, [British Broadcasting Corporation] March 27, 1956. (Mimeographed.)

"The Three Asia's," Background Notes 552, Central Research Unit, [British Broadcasting Corporation] Sept. 6, 1955. (Mimeographed.)

"Trends in International Broadcasting of Communist Orbit Nations during the Years 1950–1955," Intelligence Summary IS–83–55, US Information Agency, [Washington] Sept. 26, 1955. (Mimeographed.)

"Two Communist Views on Early Christians," Background Notes 380, Central Research Unit, [British Broadcasting Corporation] Aug. 30, 1954. (Mimeographed.)

"Two Faces of Soviet Moslem Policy," Background Notes 364, Central Research Unit, [British Broadcasting Corporation] July 16, 1954. (Mimeographed.)

TUCKER, ROBERT, "The Metamorphosis of the Stalin Myth," US Air Force Rand Project Research Memorandum, RM 1223, April 16, 1954, Santa Monica, California. (Mimeographed.)

"The 20th CPSU Congress and the Doctrine of the 'Inevitability of War'," Intelligence Report 7284, US Department of State, June 22, 1956. (Mimeographed.)

"The Twentieth Party Congress Announced," Intelligence Brief 1801, US Department of State, July 15, 1955. (Mimeographed.)

"The Twentieth Party Congress of the Communist Party of the Soviet Union," *Notes – Soviet Affairs*, 187, April 19, 1956.

"Unrest in the Soviet Union – Part I: Intellectuals after the 20th Congress," Research Unit, MRC [Munich Radio Center], March 25, 1957. (Typewritten.)

"Unrest in the Soviet Union – Part II: Troublesome Youth," Martin Mittelacher, Research Unit, MRC [Munich Radio Center], May 2, 1957.

US House of Representatives, *Hearing Before the Committee of Un-American Activities*, (*Testimony of Nikolai Khokhlov*), 84th Congress, 2nd Sess., April 17, 1956.

——, *The Great Pretence – A Symposium on Anti-Stalinism and 20th*

Congress of the Soviet Communist Party, Union Calender No. 815, House Report No. 2189, 84th Congress, 2nd Sess., May 19, 1956.

US Senate, Special Committee to Study the Foreign Aid Program, *A Study, Foreign Assistance Activities of the Communist Bloc and Their Implications for the United States*, 85th Cong. 1st. Sess., March 1957.

——, *Tensions within the Soviet Union*, Document No. 41, 82nd Congress, 1st Sess., May 24, 1951.

"USSR Seeks International Prestige for Supreme Soviets," Intelligence Brief 1830, US Department of State, Oct. 7, 1955. (Mimeographed.)

"Workers' Cost of Living in the Soviet Union, the US, and the Belgian Congo," *Notes – Soviet Affairs*, 202, Jan. 8, 1957.

YAKEMCHUK, ROMAN, "Soviet Foreign Policy in the Light of the Resolution of the 20th Congress of the Communist Party." [Institute for the Study of the USSR, Munich, 1956]. (Mimeographed.)

YURCHENKO, A., "Questions of Government and Administration at the Twentieth Party Congress," [Institute for the Study of the USSR, Munich, 1956]. (Mimeographed.)

INDEX